DYNAMIC ASSET ALLOCATION

Strategies for the Stock, Bond, and Money Markets

David A. Hammer, CFA

Wiley Finance Editions
John Wiley & Sons, Inc.

New York • Chichester • Brisbane • Toronto • Singapore

Library of Congress Cataloging in Publication Data

Hammer, David A., 1946–
Dynamic asset allocation : strategies for the stock, bond, and money markets / by David A. Hammer.
p. cm.—(Wiley finance editions)
Includes index.
ISBN 0-471-53028-X
1. Portfolio management. 2. Investment analysis. I. Title. II. Series.
HG4529.5.H36 1991
332.6—dc20 90-21334

Printed in the United States of America

10 9 8 7 6 5 4 3 2

This book is dedicated to Laura, David Jr., Debbie and Cindy, with the hope that, someday, one of them will feel obliged to read it.

Preface

Knowing whether to be invested in stocks, bonds, cash equivalents, or real estate and in what proportions usually accomplishes more, in terms of optimizing the investor's risk to reward ratio, than attempting to select individual securities that will outperform the market. Consider the fact that over the past 10 years, either stocks beat bonds *or* bonds beat stocks by an average of nearly *6% per calendar quarter!*

It has been perhaps my favorite and most rewarding pursuit over the past 20 years or more to develop a successful, scientific basis for forecasting the relative returns of the various classes of securities. The monetary reward for maintaining a portfolio with the optimal weighting of stocks versus bonds or cash is enormous. This becomes more apparent, in comparison, if you consider the relatively small incremental portfolio return gained from owning a stock that outperformed the market by even 50 percentage points. Such a successful stock choice might only add 1 or 2% to the total portfolio return.

The degree of efficiency in the investment marketplace, which makes superior securities selection increasingly difficult, has caused many investors to rethink the potential role of asset allocation. In fact, a whole new breed of investment advisers, known as *tactical asset allocators,* has emerged. Unfortunately, many are just the same old market-timers and "closet chartists" wearing a new disguise. But, others are truly paving the way from the "art of investing" toward an exciting new science.

This book was written for the people who own, or are entrusted with, substantial assets and who have more than a casual interest in the fundamentals of investing. It is they, not the brokers or advisers they hire, who have to make the all-important decision—that of asset allocation.

The intent of the book is to demonstrate the way securities prices behave and to familiarize the reader with the various approaches of blending stocks, bonds, futures, money-market funds, and other investment vehicles into a portfolio that continually offers the greatest possible expected return with respect to the desired level of risk.

Many of my views of what makes stock and bond prices fluctuate as well as my techniques for asset allocation will be thought-provoking. This distinctive perspective manifests itself throughout the book.

Because my investment style is, for the most part, a quantitative one, the opening chapters deal with basic numbers concepts. Unlike a statistics textbook, however, this section does not begin with theories of sets, unions, intersections, permutations, and combinations. It passes over all of that and delves right into basic random-number theory and concepts of persistence (trend) and volatility (risk). These statistical fundamentals are explained through anecdotes and parables. The math is minimal and is kept simple—no Greek symbols or complicated functions.

Chapters 4 through 6 explore what makes the investment markets "tick" (literally) and how an investor can predict and capitalize on this market behavior. This is a complete overview of ways to forecast the expected return and risk associated with the various asset classes.

Chapters 7 through 10 review many of the traditional, as well as contemporary, asset-allocation models, from the most basic to the most sophisticated. Chapter 11 culminates this section with the description of a multiasset scenario to include international securities, commodities, and real estate.

Chapter 12 outlines various methods of allocation implementation through the use of derivative products such as market baskets, puts and calls, futures, and synthetic futures. Chapter 13 describes a different type of quantitative approach to portfolio management—immunization—that is an alternative to asset allocation.

The final section of the book, Chapters 14 through 16, deals specifically with issues surrounding the choice of a professional investment adviser: why most of them underperform the market, the games they can play with their historic performance figures, and the various reasons to hire—and fire—an investment adviser.

The particular approach to asset allocation and securities-class selection I have developed and used over the years has produced consistent, and exceptionally positive, relative performance. This book can be understood, and should be read, by anyone of wealth or anyone responsible for the wealth of others, including corporate financial officers, trustees, and plan sponsors as well as portfolio managers, educators, stockbrokers, lawyers, and others who have influence on the investment-decision process.

Acknowledgments

Some of the contemporary pioneers who have had a major influence on my own investments perspective and who laid the groundwork for many of the aspects of asset allocation and market behavior addressed in this book include William F. Sharpe, William L. Fouse, Randall C. Zisler, Barr Rosenberg, Martin L. Liebowitz, H. Gifford Fong, Harry Markowitz, Fischer Black, Roger G. Ibbotson, Rex A. Sinquefield, Andrew Rudd, Burton C. Malkiel, Preston W. Estep, and Frank K. Reilly.

Of all these people, the four who cannot be given enough thanks and praise for their accomplishments are Barr Rosenberg and Marty Liebowicz in the area of fixed-income-oriented portfolios, and Bill Sharpe and Randall Zisler in the areas of risk analysis and portfolio diversification. Although their actual works are not described in this book, their efforts have provided either the foundation or corroboration for several of the models described. David L. Lodefink assisted me in enhancing some of the proprietary models described in this book.

Above all, the long personal relationships I have had with certain individuals who have encouraged and nurtured the creativity, self-esteem, and inquisitiveness necessary for acquiring the knowledge and motivation for such an undertaking as this include Morgan P. Hatch, Ronald Rosenthal, Richard Davisson (deceased), Richard P. Macklem, David Norr, Richard C. Young, Thomas M. Lewry, Jerry Schellenger, Chris A. Hynes, and Mark Billings.

For my interest in the art of writing and the science of syntax (but not to be blamed for my deficiencies), I am forever grateful to my father, Ralph E. Hammer. For the painstaking task of correcting my often creative syntax and rhetoric, I must commend Laura Cleveland. For making my hopes and intentions become a reality and for preventing this volume from becoming a technical journal, I thank my talented editor, Wendy Grau.

Contents

1

Number Series: A Wealth of Information

The most important questions in life are, for the most part, merely problems in the calculus of probability.

—*Pierre Simon de Laplace*

HEADS OR TAILS? SURPRISE!

Clyde "the Slide" Sumsion not only had an interesting name, but an interesting answer to a classic question: If a person borrowed a coin, spun or flipped it 10 times, and it came to rest heads up each time, what is the probability that the eleventh spin will also be heads up? The good professor presented this problem to the entire class on the opening day of Statistics 101. I raised my hand, intending to give the obvious answer: "The odds of another heads is still 50-50." I was motioned to lower my waving fingers, since the question was intended to be the day's homework assignment. At this point, I suspected that either the question was more difficult than I had imagined or that Stat 101 was not.

The next day, we heard some interesting answers from the class. One lad had graduated from Springfield Tech High with me, but with even higher grades, which probably meant he knew just enough about math to be dangerous. He figured that since the problem had two possible outcomes (heads or tails), the odds of spinning or flipping 11 consecutive heads was equal to one chance in two raised to the power of 11, or 1/2048. Although his statement was correct, he didn't answer the question, which addressed only the odds of *one particular* spin, not of *all* the spins.

None of the students gave an answer of "over 50%" except for Ernie "the Brick," who made some crack about the coin having two heads. Professor Sumsion reminded him that the question referred to a "borrowed" coin, which implied it had not been planted; that is, it was randomly selected.

Several students, most notably sophomore Duda (usually pronounced "doo-dah," and repeated once), made reference to the so-called law of averages, which he interpreted as meaning that the odds were well under 50%. The professor explained that if there *were* a law of averages, it would merely state that as the number of flips increased, the more the percentage of heads and tails would tend to equal 50%.

The correct answer to the coin-toss problem (according to Professor Sumsion), with which I still totally agree (some decades later), is that the probability of landing heads, after 10 preceding heads, is greater than 50%. Let's examine another phenomenon to help understand why.

WHY FLY ON SEPARATE PLANES?

Because of the possibility (albeit remote) of being killed in an airplane crash, many married couples (with children at home) and top executives from the same corporation (with egos that make them feel indispensable) will not fly together on the same flight. It might surprise these mortals to know that, if the odds of going down in an airplane are, say, one in a million, then the odds of crashing are greater than one in a million if your partner's flight crashes first. Why did the first plane take a nose dive? Was it weather conditions, pilot fatigue, controller problems, faulty instruments, bad fuel, or what? How many of these factors, if present on the first flight, will (or might) be present on the second flight? Whatever the cause of the crash, that factor could cause other similar flights to crash. Therefore, when one plane goes down, the odds of another flight (particularly on the same day, to the same destination from the same origination, and maybe even involving the same airlines) are adversely affected.

Returning to the case of the coin toss, the odds of spinning or flipping *either* heads *or* tails 10 times in a row are only one in 512. In a room of 100 people flipping coins for several minutes, it would, indeed, be *probable* for someone to come up with 10 consecutive head or tails. But this would be a very remote possibility for one person on his or her first 10 tries. Therefore, a strong possibility exists that the "tosser" consciously or unconsciously duplicated his or her motions, or that the spun coin had a worn reverse edge or that something in the design of the coin favored heads. Although such extraneous factors may not be *probable*, the fact that they are quite *possible* affects the odds.

CASE OF THE WORN ROULETTE WHEEL

For many years, prominent businessman Art Ross (who bears the same name as his grandfather, the hockey legend) had New Year's Eve parties where penny-ante gambling was the main event, ranging from blackjack ("21") to bingo. After I broke the "bank" at one such party, I was invited to the next year's party on the condition that I would operate (rather than play) the roulette table. In 1971, I had noticed that the wheel produced considerably more black than red winning numbers; in 1972, I bet accordingly; later in 1973, I was invited to work at the table rather than play at it. It was then that I discovered about half a dozen eighth-inch nicks in the ridges that divide the numbers on the roulette wheel.

What if, each time the game was played, the nicks became more pronounced as a result of the nicks being there in the first place? This would result in a trend, over time, reflecting ever-increasing odds in favor of black numbers. This trend, or persistence, would be a result of prior probabilities (more balls falling into black slots) influencing the next series of probabilities (even more balls falling into black slots). This snowballing effect might be labeled "feedback."

CONCERNING WINNING STREAKS

In the popular casino game of "21" (blackjack), the player has almost a 50% chance of winning. To attain these odds, however, the player must memorize all the probabilities relating to his or her own hand compared to the dealer's up card.

The object of "21" is to win either by asking the dealer for enough cards so that the total value of points in your hand exceeds those in the dealer's hand without going over 21, or by allowing the dealer to go over 21 ("bust"). The player sees all of his or her own cards, but only sees one of the dealer's cards. The dealer must take additional cards ("hits") as long as his total points are 16 or less. If the player and dealer have equal points, the hand is a tie ("push").

The dealer's advantage is that he draws his cards last. That means each player at the table has a chance of going bust (and immediately losing the bet) before the dealer takes his turn. So, even when the dealer goes bust, other players may have gone bust ahead of him. Therefore, it is possible for the dealer to come out ahead, even on a bust hand; but the player always loses on a bust hand. One advantage the player has is that he or she receives a bonus (above and beyond the original bet) for getting a total of 21 points on the first two cards. (Aces count as either 1 or 11, at the player's option.) But, the player's main advantage is that he or she can double the bet *after* seeing the dealer's up card (but must take one, and only one, hit) or can split the original two cards dealt (if they are a pair) and play two hands against the dealer. Knowing when to "double" or "split" is the key, and that decision depends on the dealer's up card, or the dealer's odds of going bust.

Obviously, it is to the dealer's advantage if there is an abnormally large number of low cards left in the deck, because this reduces his odds of going bust when he is forced to take a hit on 16 or less. Conversely, a lot of 10s and face cards (which also count as 10) remaining in the undealt portion of the deck are to the dealer's disadvantage. If the player knew what percentage of the remaining deck was high and low cards, he or she would have a big advantage. The player does get to see all the cards that have been played by everyone at the table. But, it is illegal to count cards. There would be no stopping someone with a photographic memory, and many players have developed simple mental systems for keeping track of the proportion of high and low cards that have been played. This is why casinos that deal the players' cards face up (where players have plenty of time to view all the cards) use a stack of several decks. If players' cards are dealt face down (giving everyone only an instant to see the other players' cards when they are turned over at the end of each turn), then the casino may use a stack of only one or two decks.

Another possible "method" is for the player to vary his or her bet, which is legal, although each table has a limit on the size of the bet. That limit is what prevents a betting "system" from succeeding. The legendary player who "broke the bank" at Monte Carlo was using a system of betting known as the "double pyramid." If the player loses a hand, he or she doubles the bet on the following hand; if the player wins, he or she returns to betting the original amount. The player ultimately cannot lose. But, if the player begins with an original bet of only $100 and loses eight hands in a row (which is entirely possible) the player would have to bet $25,600 on the ninth hand to maintain the doubling technique. If the player doesn't have the money, he or she would end the night $25,500 in the hole. Moreover, if the table has a limitation on the size of the bet, which is usually around 10 times the minimum bet, the "system" is unworkable.

Many players still use some form (often undisciplined) of pyramiding on the basis that if they increase the bet after losing a hand, the next hand not only might recoup the loss, but might also produce an additional gain. There is little sense to this "system."

Other players believe in winning and losing streaks. They do just the opposite of the pyramid bettor. They increase the bet when they are winning. This makes more sense. If the dealer all of a sudden starts going bust every two out of three hands (which is way above average) maybe this says something about the undealt portion of the deck—that it contains an above-average number of high cards, for example. Similarly, suppose the first half of the stack has been played and nobody has earned a blackjack (an automatic win by having 21 points in the first two cards). Maybe this means there are an above-average number of aces left in the remaining stack, which is to the players' advantage. Taking advantage of winning streaks has nothing to do with counting cards, only with an assumption that the odds may have changed in the same direction as they appear to be changing—just like the worn roulette wheel, the improbable coin toss, or the airplane incident.

If the long-term return of the stock market were 10% per year but the market had been up 20% for each of the past three years, what would be the probability of the market being up over 10% again next year? The odds could just as likely be over 50% as under 50%. By the time you have completed the first nine chapters of this book, you will know how to compute such probabilities accurately.

THE ODDS OF LOSING

Sometimes it is easier to calculate the odds of winning by first computing the odds of losing. If the odds of winning a lottery are 1 in 100 and you buy one ticket in each of 100 such lotteries, what are your chances of winning once—obviously your chances can't be 100%. If the odds of being dealt three of a kind in draw poker are 1 in 47 (which they are), what is the probability of being dealt three of a kind if you play 47 hands? Again, the odds (intuitively) can't be 100%. If the odds of landing in "black" in roulette are 18 in 38 (nearly 1 in 2) does that mean the ball will definitely land on black within three spins of the wheel? Of course not. In other words, we do not *add* probabilities when we repeat an event of chance. Actually, we *subtract* the probability of *not winning* from unity (100%). For example, if a coin toss has a 1-in-2 chance of landing heads up, and we want to know the odds of coming up with a "heads" in either of two flips, then we calculate the odds of not winning, that is, coming up with two "tails," which is 1/2 times 1/2, or 1/4. Therefore, the odds of one or more heads in two flips is 1 minus 1/4, or 75%. In the earlier example of betting in 100 lotteries with a 1% chance of winning each, the odds of losing are 99%

multiplied by 99%, 100 times—or 37%. Therefore, the odds of winning at least one of the lotteries is 100% minus 37%, or 63%.

It's really very simple:

Odds of winning = $P = 1 -$ the percentage chance of losing

$$P_W = 1 - P_L^n$$

where P_L = probability of losing on one try and n = number of tries

The odds of being dealt three of a kind in 47 hands of draw poker?

The answer is: $1 - (46/47)^{47} = 1 - .36 = .64 = 64\%$

When a person invests in stocks or bonds, what are the odds of *not* winning? Before you try to figure this out, you should read the next eight chapters.

WHAT DOES "AVERAGE" REALLY MEAN?

In college, first courses in statistics, psychology, sociology, or lab science teach that there are three basic types of averages: mean, mode, and median. The *mean* is usually described as the simple arithmetic average (although this is often not the case in investment analysis, as we shall see). The *mode* is that value, in a series of numbers, that occurs the most frequently. The *median* is the value that lies in the middle of the series, that is, the number above which and below which half the numbers lie. Here is a series of numbers that could represent stock prices, earnings, P/E ratios, yields, or whatever:

1 2 2 3 3 4 4 5 6 6 6 8 9 11

The mean would be 5.0, or 70 (the sum of the series) divided by 14 (the number of values in the series). The mode would be 6.0, since it is the value that occurs with the greatest frequency (three times). The median would be 4.5, since there are seven numbers above 4.5 and seven numbers below 4.5.

THE ARITHMETIC MEAN

The formula for mean is the best known. Mathematically, it normally refers to the sum of all the values (x) divided by the total number of values (n) or:

$$\text{Mean} = a = \frac{\text{Sum of } (x)}{n}$$

For a large group of numbers (such as the ages of a certain population), many in the sample may have the same value (x). Exactly how many are of each particular value are the frequencies (f). Therefore, it becomes easier to measure the mean by taking the sum of all the values after multiplying them by their frequencies, then dividing that total by the number of values in the sample (n).

$$a = \frac{\text{Sum of } (x \times f)}{n}$$

For example, Table 1–1 shows how I would figure the arithmetic average (mean) age of members of my son's Boy Scout troop. This method of computing the mean is suitable for calculating the average age of a sample, but it is not appropriate for other types of data. This simple arithmetic mean is not the correct mean for a series of percentage changes or a series of ratios, both of which are very common in investments work.

THE GEOMETRIC MEAN

Suppose that over the past three years, a securities portfolio was up 30% the first year, down 10% the next, and up 10% the last year. The average annual return is not 10%, which is the arithmetic average. If the value of the portfolio started at $100, it would be worth $130 the first year, $117 (90% of $130) the next year, and

TABLE 1–1 Mean Age of Boy Scout Troup

Age (x)	No. of Scouts Frequency (f)	Weighting $(x \times f)$
11	6	66
12	12	144
13	18	234
14	20	280
15	18	270
16	12	192
17	6	102
	$n = 92$	1288

$$\text{Mean} = a = \frac{\text{Sum of } (x \times f)}{n} = \frac{1288}{92} = 14 \text{ years}$$

$128.70 (110% of $117) in the final year. Had the average return really been 10%, the portfolio would have grown to $133.10, not $128.70.

Therefore, percentage changes should usually be averaged using the *geometric mean*. This can be found by taking the antilog of the sum of the logarithms of each value (x), then dividing it by the number of values (n). It also can be found by taking the "nth" root of the *product* obtained by multiplying the values together. If the values are decimals (including percentages), the value "1" should first be added to each decimal and also subtracted from the final product.

In the example of portfolio returns, the geometric mean would be the cube root (because there are three values) of the product of (1 + .30) times (1 − .10) times (1 + .10). Accordingly, 1.30 times .90 times 1.10 equals 1.287, the cube root of which is 1.0877. Therefore, the actual "average" performance of the portfolio was 8.77% per year. To prove this, $100 times 1.0877 times 1.0877 times 1.0877 equals $128.70.

THE HARMONIC MEAN

Let's examine the need for a third type of mean. Suppose a common stock paid a quarterly dividend at the annual rate of $1.00

per share. Assume the stock sold for an average price of 10 during the first calendar quarter, 20 during the second quarter, 30 during the third quarter, and 40 during the fourth quarter. What was the average dividend yield (dividend/price) during the entire year? Since the average stock price was 25 and the dividend was constant at the $1.00 level, one might calculate the average yield to be 4.0%. But, how can this be? The yield during the first quarter was 10%; and it was 5% then 3.3% then 2.5% during the next three quarters, respectively. Those four yields average 5.2%! That is the correct answer.

To obtain the correct answer directly, you could use the "inverse mean" of the stock prices, sometimes referred to as the *harmonic mean*. We originally calculated the average stock price to be 25 because (10 + 20 + 30 + 40) divided by 4 equals 25. Instead, we should have divided 4 by (1/10 + 1/20 + 1/30 + 1/40). This gives 19.23 as the "average" stock price. A $1.00 dividend divided by an average price of 19.23 produces an average yield of exactly 5.2%.

To summarize, when calculating the mean for a series of absolute numbers, the arithmetic mean is usually appropriate. But the geometric mean is often the correct average for a series of percentage changes, and the harmonic mean may be required for a series of ratios where the denominator of each ratio varies.

"NORMAL" DISTRIBUTION

What statisticians refer to as *normal distribution* is not influenced by feedback or persistence as the defective roulette wheel, airplane trip or coin toss may have been. Past results have no effect on future results under normal distribution, whether or not there is an underlying trend. Mathematically, normal distribution is a function of only two things: the appropriate mean of a set of values and the variance (or the square of the average difference) between each of the individual values and their mean.

The population of the aforementioned Scout troop happens to have a "normal" distribution as graphed in Figure 1–1 and compares to Figure 1–2, which is a mathematically computed normal

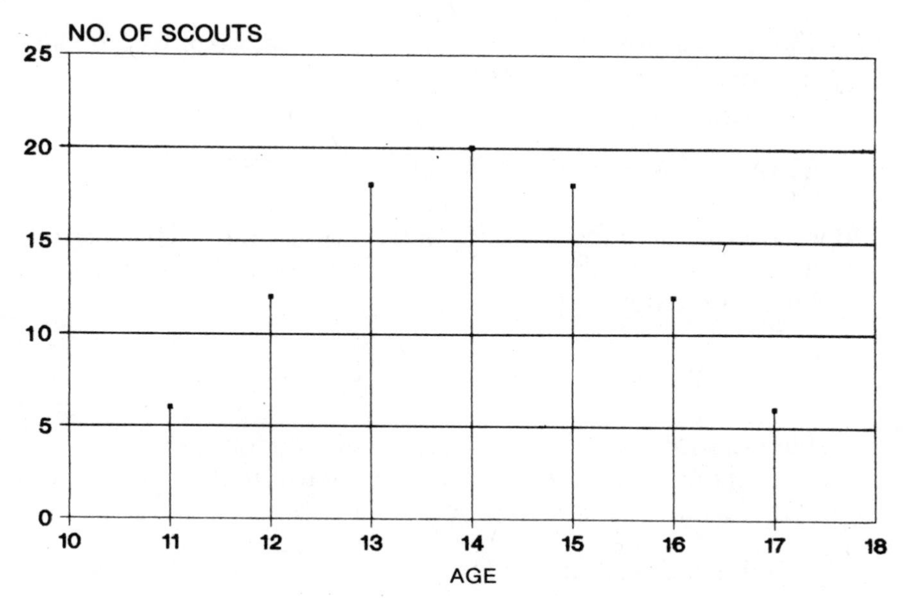

Figure 1–1. Age Distribution of the Scout Troup.

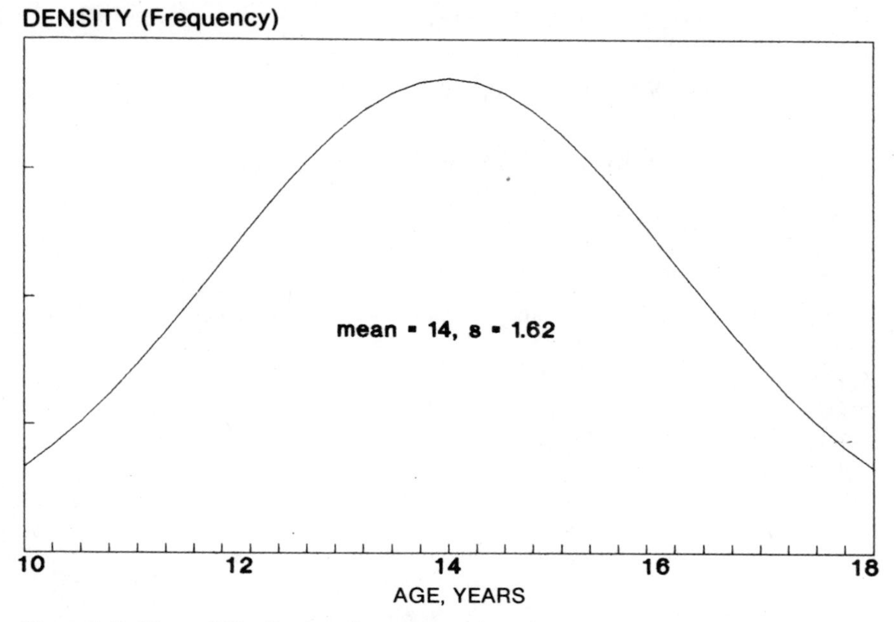

Figure 1–2. Normal Distribution of any series of numbers with a mean of 15 and a variance of 2.6.

distribution for any series of numbers with a mean of 15 and a variance of 2.6.

VARIANCE AND STANDARD DEVIATION

How did I calculate the variance in the Scout troup example to be 2.6? Since variance is the arithmetic average for all of the squares of the deviations from the mean, then:

$$\text{Variance} = v = \frac{\text{Sum of } [(x - a)^2 \times (f)]}{n}$$

Table 1–2 shows the details of the calculation for the Scout troop.

Standard deviation, which is often more useful than variance, is simply the square root of variance:

$$\text{Standard deviation} = \text{SD} = \sqrt{\text{v}} = \sqrt{2.61} = 1.62 \text{ years}$$

Here are some good rules to remember when applying *standard deviation* to a large normal distribution:

1. 68% of the values will fall within 1 standard deviation of the mean.
2. 90% of the values will fall within 1.65 standard deviations of the mean.

TABLE 1–2 Variance of the Boy Scouts' Ages

Age (x)	Frequency (f)	Mean (a)	Deviation ($x - a$)	Variance ($x - a)^2$	Weighting ($v \times f$)
11	6	14	−3	9	54
12	12	14	−2	4	48
13	18	14	−1	1	18
14	20	14	0	0	0
15	18	14	1	1	18
16	12	14	2	4	48
17	6	14	3	9	54
	$n = 92$				240

$$\text{Mean variance} = \frac{\text{Sum of weighted variances}}{n} = \frac{240}{92} = 2.61 \text{ years}$$

3. 95% will fall within 2.0 standard deviations.
4. 99% will fall within 3.0 standard deviations.

For example, if the average weight of an American adult male is 160 pounds and the standard deviation is 20 pounds, 68% of American adult males would weigh between 140 and 180 pounds, 90% would weigh between 127 and 193 pounds, and 95% would weigh between 120 and 200 pounds.

The "bell-shaped curves" in Figures 1–3 through 1–5 all represent normal distribution.

The formula used to calculate the density function (similar to frequency) for a series of normally distributed values (x) is:

$$y = \frac{e^{[-.5(x - a)^2/s^2]}}{s\sqrt{2\,\pi}}$$

where a = mean, s = standard deviation of the (x) values, and e = natural logarithm base

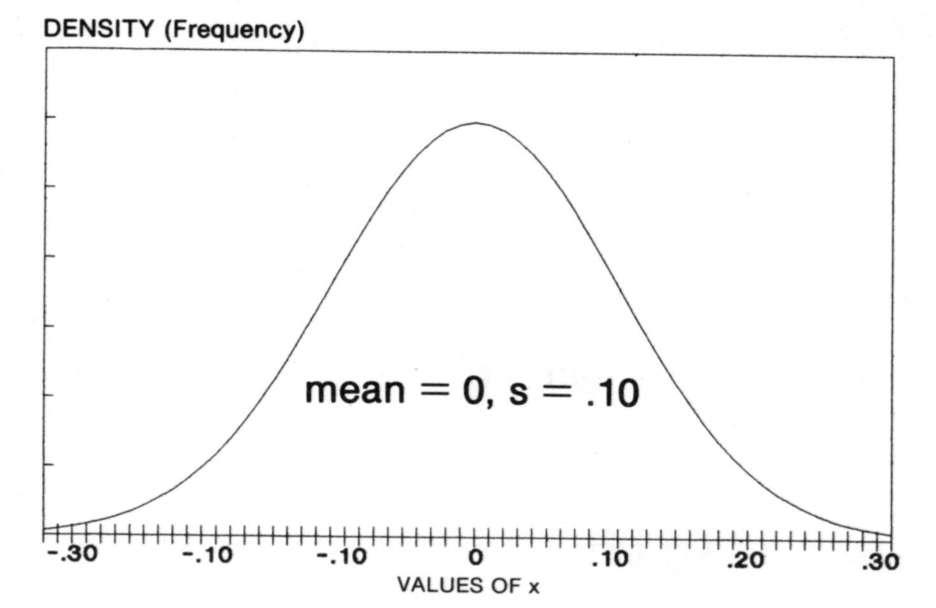

Figure 1–3. Classic Normal Distribution Curve.

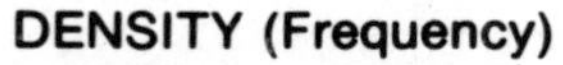

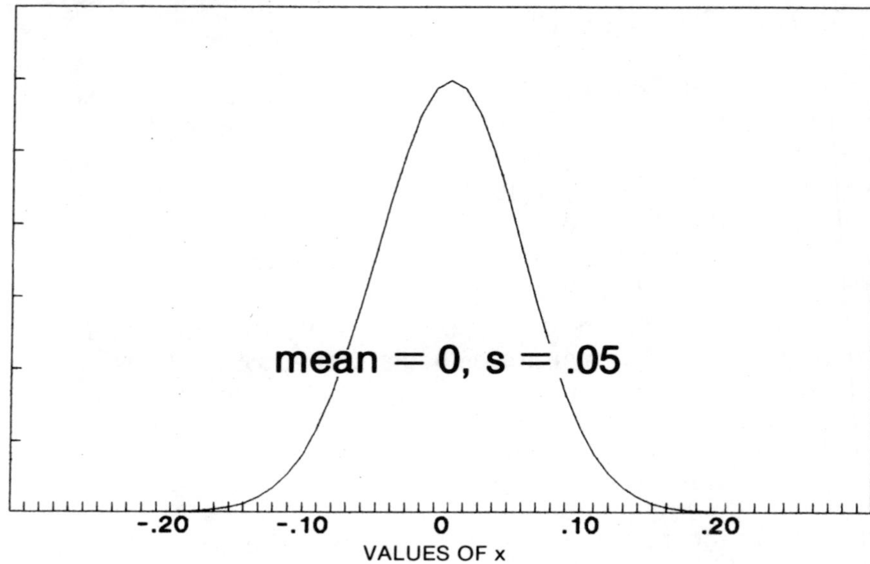

Figure 1–4. Normal Distribution with Low Standard Deviation.

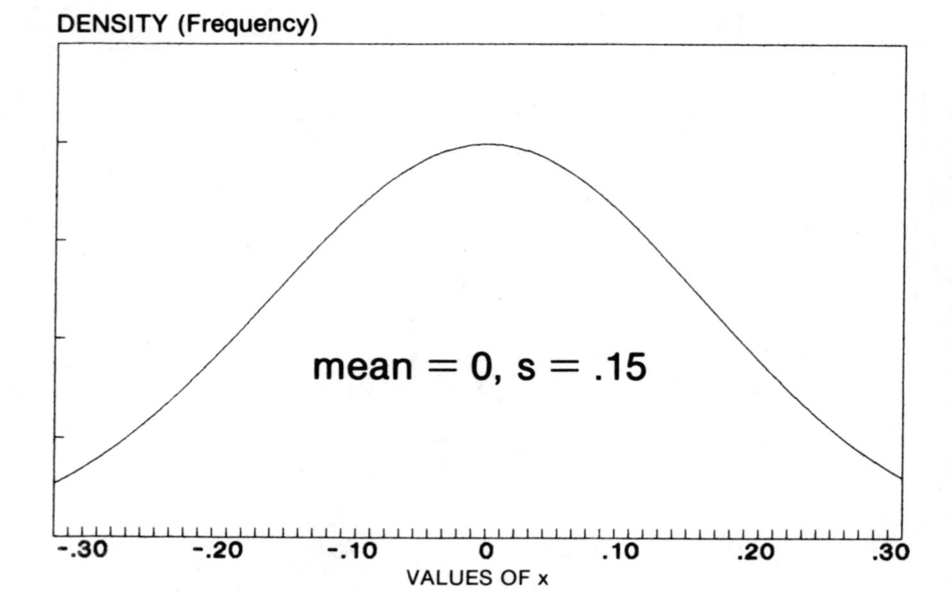

Figure 1–5. Normal Distribution with High Standard Deviation.

Normal distribution also can represent a time series, such as the returns of the stock market over the years. For example, assume over the past 50 years, the Dow Jones Industrial Average had returned an average of 10% per year (from appreciation plus dividends) and the standard deviation of that annual return had been 15%. This would mean that in 68% of the years, returns should have been between approximately 25% and −5%, (that is, 10% plus or minus 15%). Ninety percent of the time (representing 1.65 standard deviations), stock market returns should have ranged between about 35% and −15%, that is, 10% plus or minus 25% (15% × 1.65 = 25%).

FACT VERSUS PROBABILITY

Why are the curves shown in Figures 1–3 through 1–5 referred to as "normal"? The answer lies in the nature of random probability. Following are examples of statements based on fact and others based on probability:

Fact

1. The rate of a chemical reaction doubles when the temperature rises by 10° Celsius.
2. There were 365,000 phone calls made from Sundance, Wyoming, last year.
3. There are 11 possible totals of two thrown dice.
4. In five-card draw poker, there are 1,098,240 possible hands containing a pair out of 2,598,960 possible hands.
5. The rate of inflation of the Producers Price Index was 5.2% last year.
6. The stock market has risen 6% per year, on average, over the past 20 years.

Probability

1. The temperature in Boston will be 10° higher on March 1 compared to February 1.
2. There will be 1,000 phone calls made from Sundance, Wyoming, tomorrow.
3. You will roll one 7 for every six times you roll two dice. (The actual probability of a 7 in any specific six rolls is 67%.)
4. In a game of draw poker, you will be dealt a pair in one out of every 2.4 hands. (The actual probability in any 2 specific hands is 67%).
5. Due to the expected rate of inflation, 20-year government bonds will yield 9.5% next year.
6. The stock market will be up 6% next year.

The second group of statements all reflect chance. They involve different types of distribution, known in statistics as *multinomial distribution, normal distribution,* and *Poisson distribution*. What we are concerned with in investments work is mainly a variation of normal distribution called *log-normal distribution*. But first, let's examine normal distribution, which is approximated by *binomial distribution*, illustrated in the following experiment.

AN EXPERIMENT

Borrow your children's jar of pennies to use as counters and remove one penny to use as the "toss coin." Now take a piece of paper and draw nine one-inch circles in a row, about an inch apart. Place a counter on the middle circle, flip the toss coin four times, each time moving the counter one circle to the right for each heads, or one dot to the left for each tails. Now place another counter on the center circle and repeat the four tosses, moving the new counter as you did the first one. If it ends up on top of the first counter, make a pile. If you repeat this with a few dozen counters, you should get five piles that look like Figure 1–6.

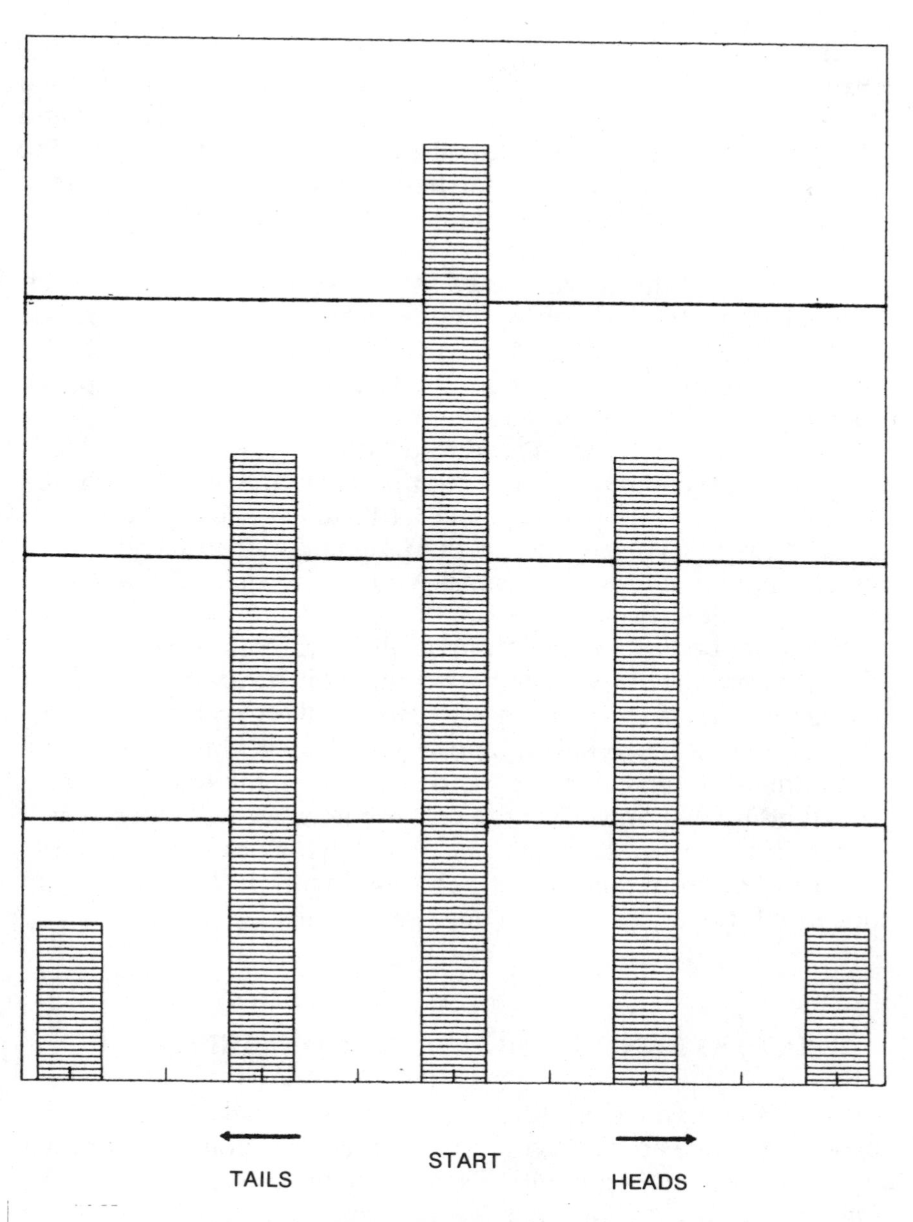

Figure 1–6. Binomial Distribution of a Coin Toss.

This shape should remind you of the age distribution of the Scout troop. In fact, if you extended your row of circles and flipped the toss coin, say 16 (versus 4) times per counter, your piles would then take on the look of a nice bell-shaped curve, if you repeat the operation enough times. This experiment demonstrates binomial distribution, which is almost identical to normal distribution when there is a large amount of data.

The shape of the curve formed by the top of the piles, in effect, characterizes the odds of flipping four heads versus three heads and a tail, versus two heads and two tails, and so on. In fact, it wouldn't matter in which order the heads and tails were flipped, just how many heads (or tails) there were.

The same curve could be produced if there were a 50-50 chance of the price of a commodity moving up or down $1.00 in each of a series of equal time periods. Just let heads equal "up" and tails equal "down." The counters would, again, end up in piles that, given enough flips per counter, would take on the shape of a "normal" bell-shaped curve.

What happens if we chain the results of the same series of coin flips that produced the bell-shaped curve? Instead of producing a curve that shows the final resting place of all the counters, we will plot a line that represents a time series. We will start at zero, and each time the coin comes up heads we will plot the next point (to the right) up one unit. Each time we flip tails, we will plot the next point down one unit. Figures 1–7 and 1–8 are examples of charts that resulted from random flips of a coin, with the line moving up one unit for heads and down one unit for tails.

WHAT DO RANDOM NUMBERS LOOK LIKE?

Now let's go to the computer and generate a similar random line, except that instead of moving each consecutive point up or down one unit, we will begin with $50 and move up or down a *random fraction* of a dollar. Figure 1–9 and Figure 1–10 are examples of "patterns" that occur. We could even imagine that each move represents changes in the price of a common stock.

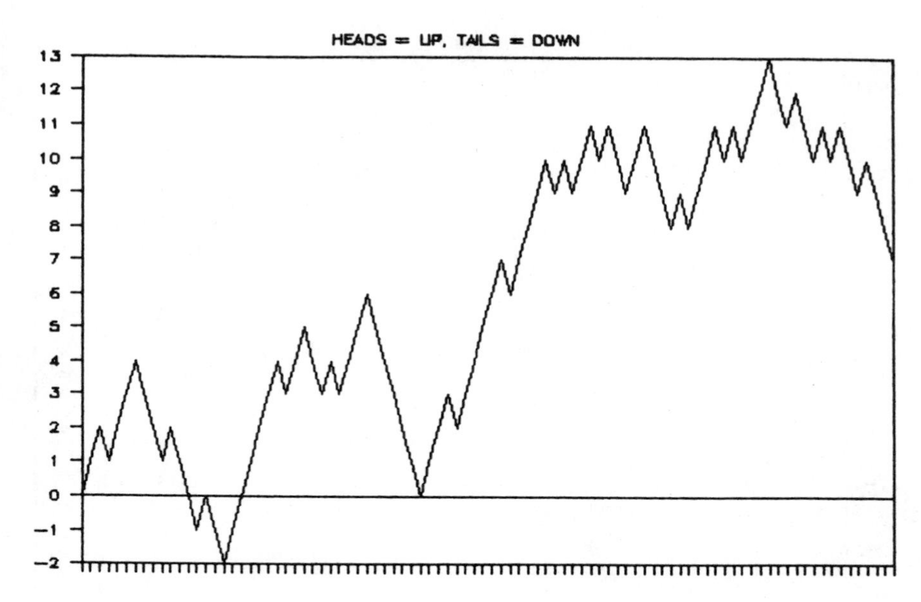

Figure 1–7. Chaining the Results of a Random Coin Toss.

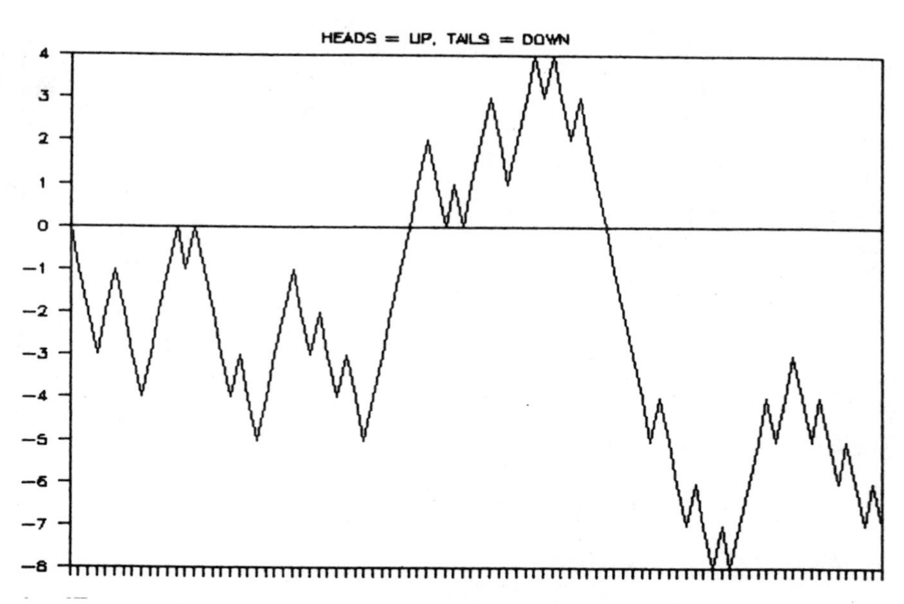

Figure 1–8. Cumulative Results of a Random Coin Toss.

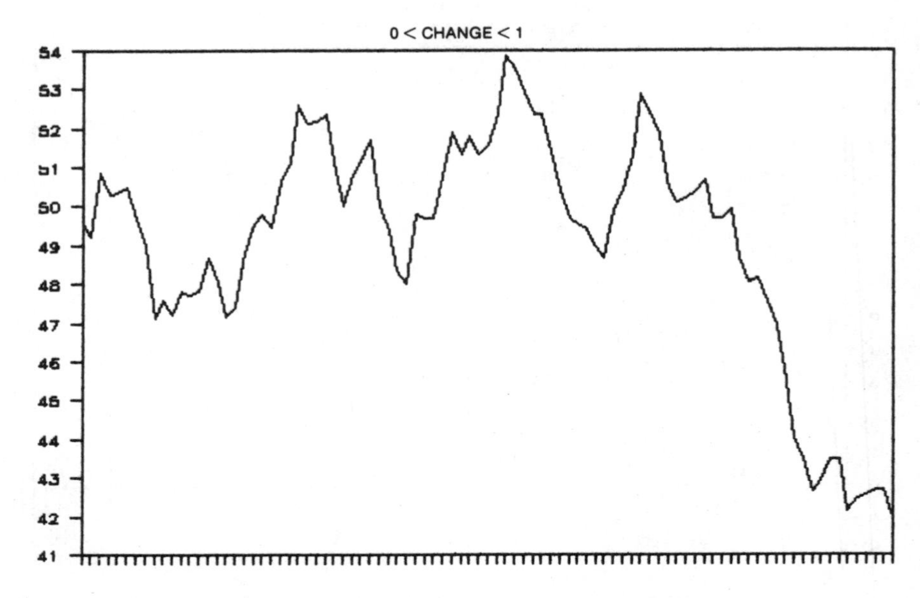

Figure 1–9. Chaining Random Amounts of Change.

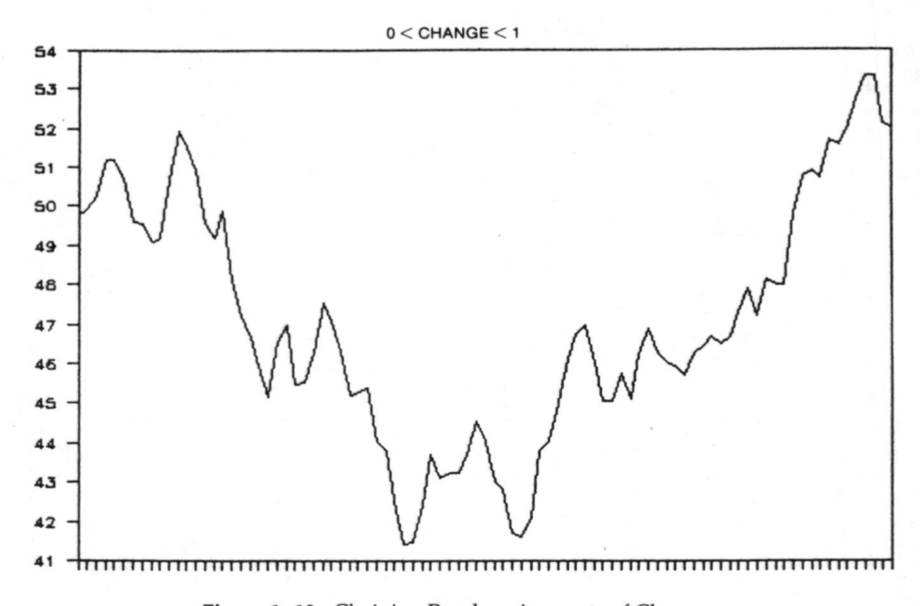

Figure 1–10. Chaining Random Amounts of Change.

Figures 1–11 and 1–12 are graphs of a random series in which the computer generated random high, low, and closing prices. These certainly look very much like the charts technical stock market analysts use to "forecast" the future! Yet, they were generated entirely from random numbers (and selected for reproduction at random). Notice in the graphs how random numbers can even produce what looks like a trend.

WHY SOME MARKET-TIMERS ARE "GOOD"

If the stock market really were a coin toss, how many market technicians could predict correctly whether the market was going to be up or down for five years in a row? The algorithm to figure this is very simple, since it is the same formula used in calculating the odds of flipping a coin and coming up with five heads in a row:

$$\text{Probability} = P = \frac{1}{A^n}$$

where A = number of possible events (outcomes)

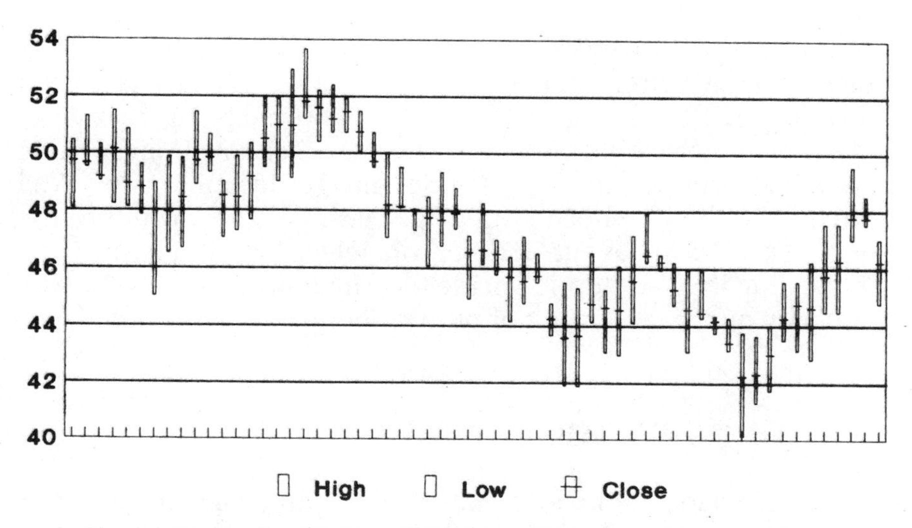

Figure 1–11. Random High/Low/Close Resembling a Stock Market Forecast.

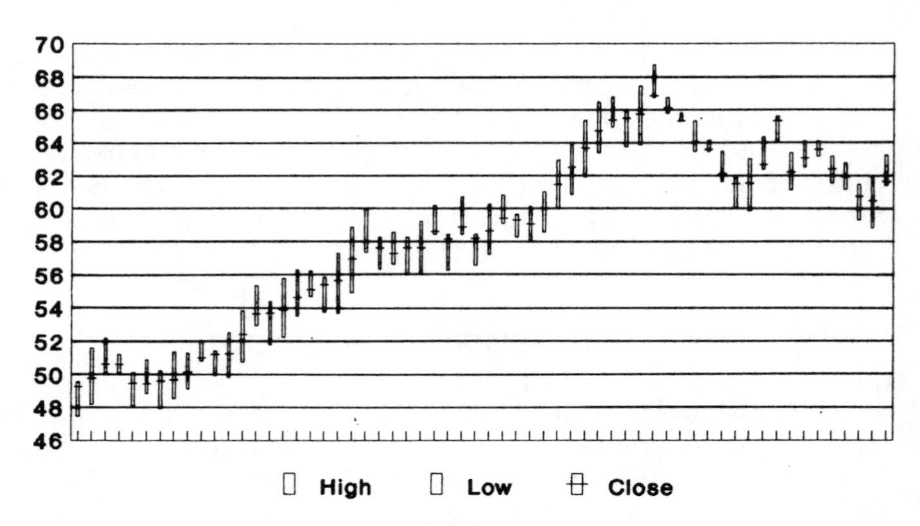

Figure 1–12. Random High/Low/Close Appearing Like a Trend.

$$P = \frac{1}{2^5} = 1/2 \times 1/2 \times 1/2 \times 1/2 \times 1/2 = 1/32$$

Accordingly, if there were, say, 3,200 professional market forecasters in the country, 100 of them would be correct five years in a row, just by chance. It also follows that 50 would be right six years in a row and 25 would be right seven years in a row. Maybe these are the 25 who are the high-salaried market technicians on Wall Street; and the 12 who are right eight years in a row could be the ones we all read about and see on television. Wouldn't it be interesting if these "top 12" made their millions and gained all the publicity merely as a result of pure randomness, or luck?

BEATING THE MARKET BY CHANCE

The performance of investment advisers and professional investors over any given period also appears to have normal distribution, just like their heights and weights do, as shown in Figure 1–13. As you can see in this hypothetical (but realistic) chart, most investors don't beat the market index. Naturally! They have transactions costs that amount to much more than just brokerage commissions. Each time a security is bought, the offering side (ask price) is paid; and when a security is sold, the bid price is received. The spread between the bid and ask generally ranges from one-eighth to three-eighths of a point and can be more on over-the-counter stocks and bonds.

You also can ascertain from Figure 1–13 that a small number of professionals beat the market by a significant percentage over the 10-year period. Are they the geniuses or is this just the manifestation of another random coin toss?

What about the stock market itself? The distribution of annual, quarterly, or monthly returns from the Standard & Poor's 500 Index or the Dow Jones Industrial Average looks almost like a bell-shaped curve, except that the two extreme ends of the curve are a little "fat"; in other words the market makes more *major*

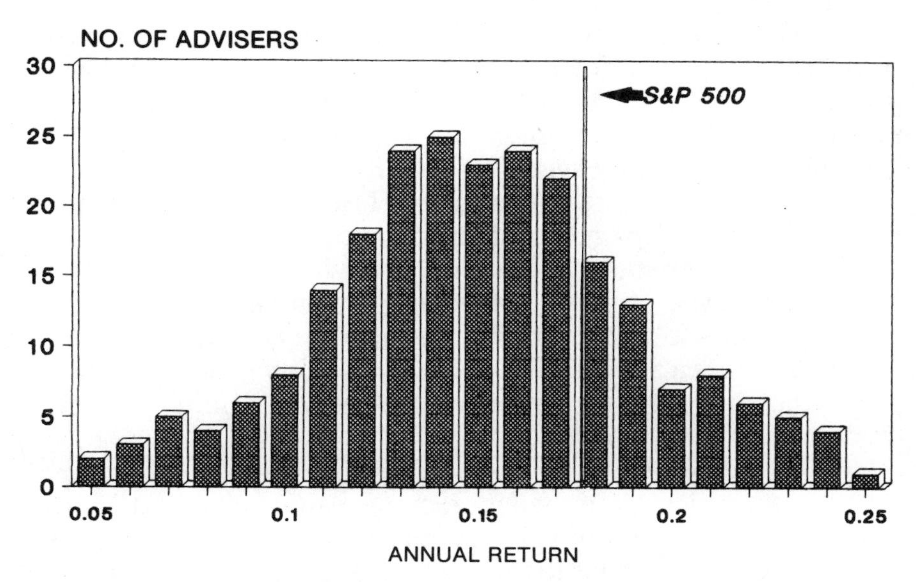

Figure 1–13. Distribution of Investment Advisers' Performance.

moves than it should under pure randomness. Another difference is that the market curve is more "log-normal," meaning that the odds of an above-average percentage return are higher than the odds of a below-average return. More about this later.

Nonetheless, much of modern stock market theory is based on this "near-randomness" of market returns. In the investments industry, as in mathematics, this is known as *random walk.*

RANDOM-WALK THEORY

The overwhelming misconception about random-walk theory is that it implies the market moves without rhyme or reason. Nothing could be further from the truth! Random-walk theory is predicated on efficient-market theory, that is, that the stock and bond markets always reflect the complete knowledge of the marketplace. In other words, securities prices might reflect all that is known about the individual investments as well as future expectations regarding factors affecting all securities prices, such as interest rates, GNP growth, taxation, and so on.

According to random-walk believers, what makes securities prices move up and down is *new* knowledge and *new* forecasts regarding the future. But, this new information is, by definition, unexpected. Therefore, it enters the marketplace *at random.*

Random-walk theory seems to be fairly accurate, at least accurate enough to have pragmatic value. However, in reality, when the market moves up one day it tends to do the same the next *day,* which is characteristic of persistence. But when the market makes a better-than-average move to the upside for one *month* or calendar *quarter,* it tends to underperform the long-term trend in the next period, which is a manifestation of reversion to the mean. Neither persistence nor mean reversion would be evident under purely random distribution.

How would you know if a series of values is random? One way would be to measure the change from one value to the next; then, clump similar changes into groups, counting the *number* of values in each group; then, plot the results on graph paper to see if the points take on the shape of a normal distribution curve. When measuring the changes, if you use percentages (versus units) such as stock and bond returns, the curve should be skewed to the right as shown in Figure 1–14.

This is known as a log-normal curve and reflects randomness of *percentage* changes. The reason it is skewed to the right, or the mean is to the right of the mode (peak), is simple. If a $100 stock moves down $20 then up $20 with equal probability, that means it moves *down 20%* ($100 to $80) with the same probability of moving *up 25%* ($80 to $100).

TESTING FOR RANDOMNESS

Several mathematical formulas test for randomness that don't necessitate plotting points on a chart. Here is the simplest test I know of:

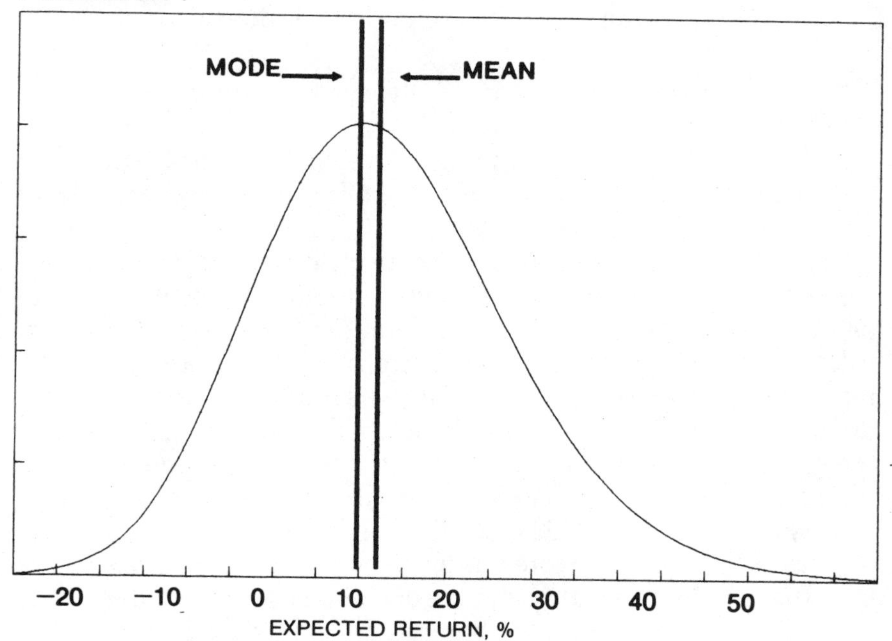

Figure 1–14. Log-Normal Distribution.

1. List the values in a column in the order in which they occurred.
2. In a second column, place a "1" next to each number in the first column that is higher than its preceding number. Put a "0" if the number is lower.
3. In a third column, put an asterisk (*) next to any "1" if the previous number (in the second column) was a "0," and also next to any "0" if the preceding number was a "1."
4. Count the number of asterisks which represent reversals in direction of the original series. Divide the number of reversals by the total number of possible reversals (total number of values in the original series minus 2).
5. If your answer is close to 1.00, then the original series went consistently back and forth in direction, showing reversion to the mean, not randomness.
6. If your answer is close to zero, then the original series moved in the same direction for long periods, indicating persistence or trend.
7. If your answer is close to .50, the series is probably random.

The longer the series, the closer the number of reversals should be to .50 (or 50%) to reflect randomness. Table 1–3 shows the results of one test for randomness.

Try substituting some daily closing prices for the Dow Jones Industrial Average over the past several months in the first column of Table 1–3 and see whether you think the stock market has been exhibiting random behavior. You could do this with weekly or monthly closing prices over several years. But, to make an accurate determination of randomness, the normal expected change due to the secular trend (about .5% per month) should be deducted from the actual price change. For example, if the Dow Jones Industrial Average moved from 2500 to 2510 in a particular month, a change of +.4%, it should be treated as a *down* month because .4% is less than the expected monthly change of .5% due to the secular trend.

There are several more sophisticated tests for randomness, the results of which are frequently inconclusive regarding the behavior

TABLE 1–3 Testing for Randomness

Series	Higher? 1 = Yes	Reversal? * = Yes
50.00		
49.63	0	
49.91	1	*
50.20	1	
50.04	0	*
50.22	1	*
49.88	0	*
50.27	1	*
50.18	0	*
49.94	0	
50.41	1	*
49.91	0	*
49.68	0	
50.05	1	*
49.69	0	*
50.13	1	*
50.24	1	
49.85	0	*
49.52	0	
49.52	0	
49.18	0	
48.84	0	
48.58	0	
48.36	0	
48.65	1	*
48.78	1	
48.98	1	
49.18	1	
48.88	0	*
49.06	1	*
48.87	0	*
48.89	1	*
49.02	1	
48.55	0	*
48.23	0	
48.00	0	
47.54	0	
47.81	1	*
48.20	1	
48.33	1	

(continued)

TABLE 1–3 (*Continued*) Testing for Randomness

Series	Higher? 1 = Yes	Reversal? * = Yes
48.45	1	
48.05	0	*
48.16	1	*
48.02	0	*
48.39	1	*

No. of Reversals = 23
No. of Possible Reversals = 43
Percentage = 23/43 = 53.5%

of securities prices. Nonetheless, substantially more literature supports the random theory of securities prices than "proves" the worth of technical trend analysis.

You must be aware that a corollary to random-walk theory is that just about any "predictive" system will work *some* of the time—just by chance—whether that "system" be one of studying the movements of the planets, changes in the Federal Reserve Discount Rate, or the apparent wave motion of the market indices.

For the purposes of this book, it is only important that securities prices move in a way that *appears* to be random. This is what allows us to utilize the calculus of probability in an effective manner for forecasting the probabilities of possible future investment returns.

CHAOS THEORY*

What if securities prices appear (and test) to be entirely random, but they really are not? Is this possible? Can there be hidden logic behind apparently random behavior? Several contemporary analysts are attempting to adapt the math and physics of chaos theory to the investments environment to prove whether or not this might be so.

---

*James Gleick, *Chaos: Making a New Science* (New York: Penguin Books, 1987).

Chaos theory demonstrates how a stable, logical system (one that is capable of being mathematically defined) can be thrown into total disarray through the introduction of the tiniest variable which feeds back into the equation time and again, compounding itself in a fashion that results in the most peculiar events.

Figure 1–15 plots the simple, but nonlinear, equation:

$$y = ax(1 - x)$$

For values of (x) between zero and one, this curve takes on a smooth, trajectory-like shape. (It should, since the formula is quite similar to those used for projectile velocities.)

Now, we will use this same equation but, instead of calculating (y) for specific values of (x), we will calculate (y) over and over again, each time using the results obtained for (y) as the input for (x) in the next calculation. We will "seed" only the first calculation with a value of (x) of .10. The strange-looking line in Figure 1–16

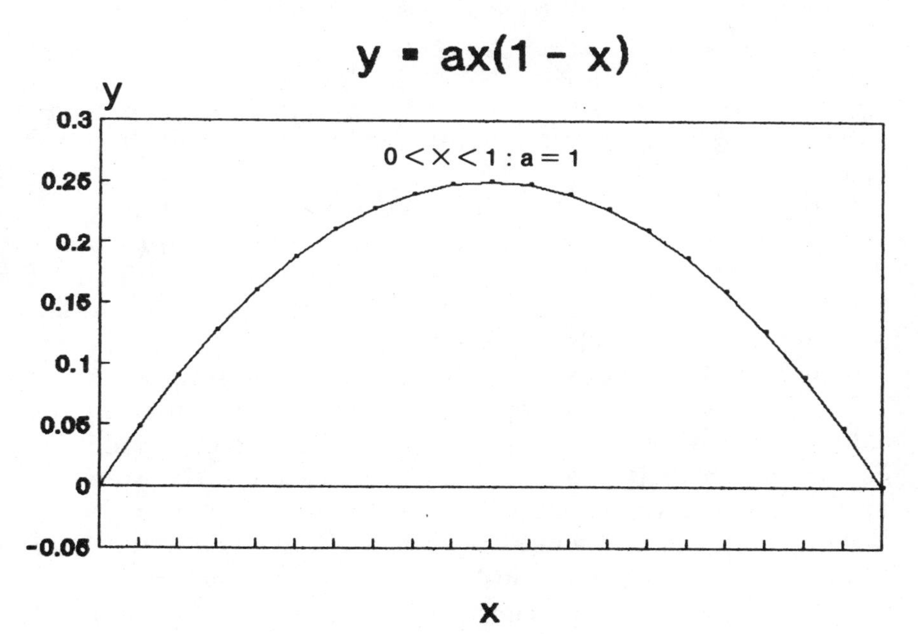

Figure 1–15. A non linear Function of (x).

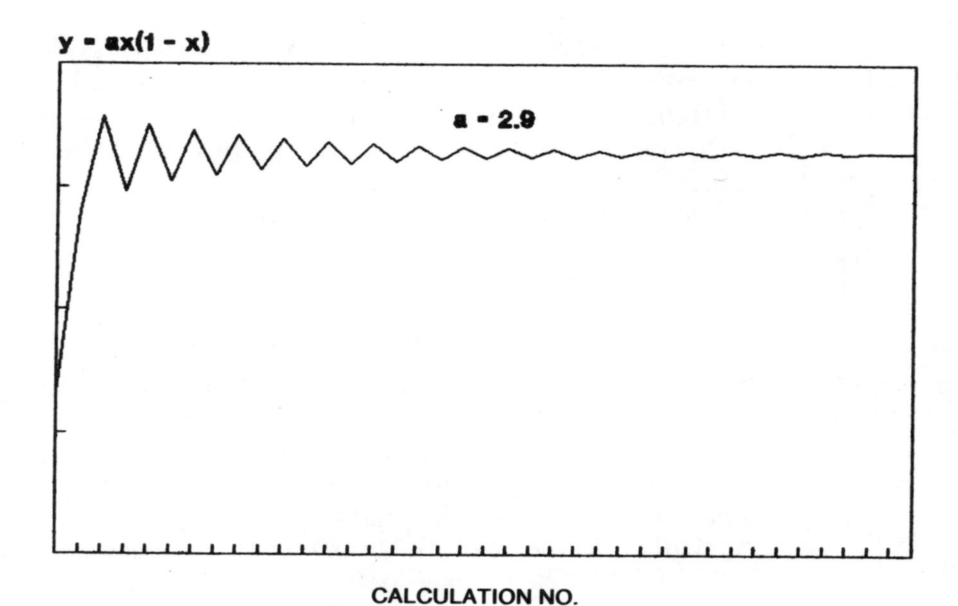

Figure 1–16. Feedback Resulting in Stability.

shows the series (from left to right) of the various results from the feedback of (*y*).

Examine Figure 1–16 in sections. If we were to see only the extreme left of right portions of the curve, we would assume definite persistence; but if we were to observe only the middle of the curve, we would assume either mean reversion or randomness, which are opposites of persistence.

Now we will repeat this process but, instead of using a value of 2.9 for (*a*) as we did in Figure 1–16, we will merely change (*a*) to a value of 3.1. The reverberating outcome is depicted in Figure 1–17. For values of (*a*) between 3.5 and 4.0 the line starts losing stability, until finally, at a value for (*a*) of precisely 4.0, the line blows apart into apparent chaos. It would be difficult, from an examination of Figure 1–18, to detect any logical system behind the volatility of the (*y*) values. Keep in mind that Figures 1–16 through 1–18 were all produced from the same equation, using the same starting value

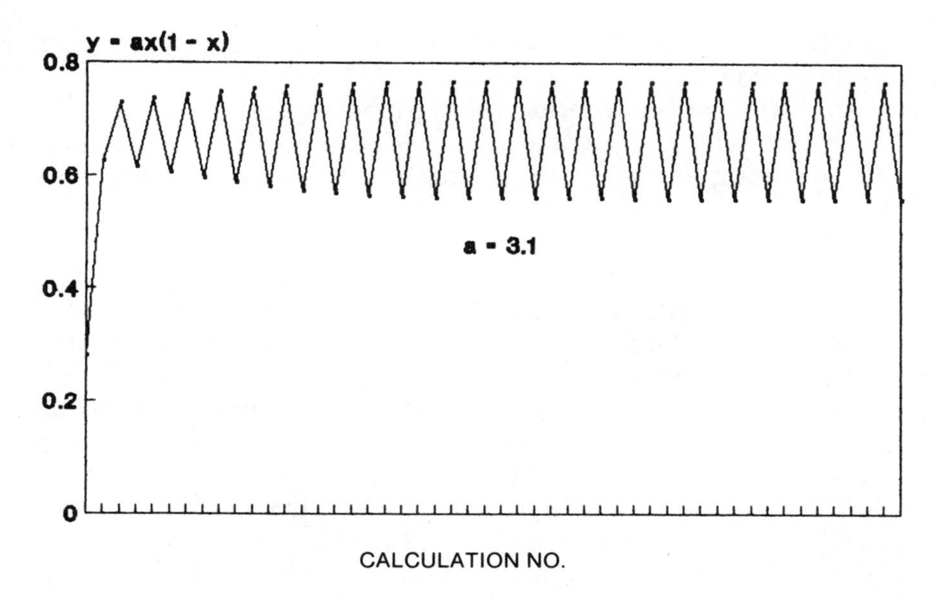

Figure 1–17. Feedback Resulting in Oscillation.

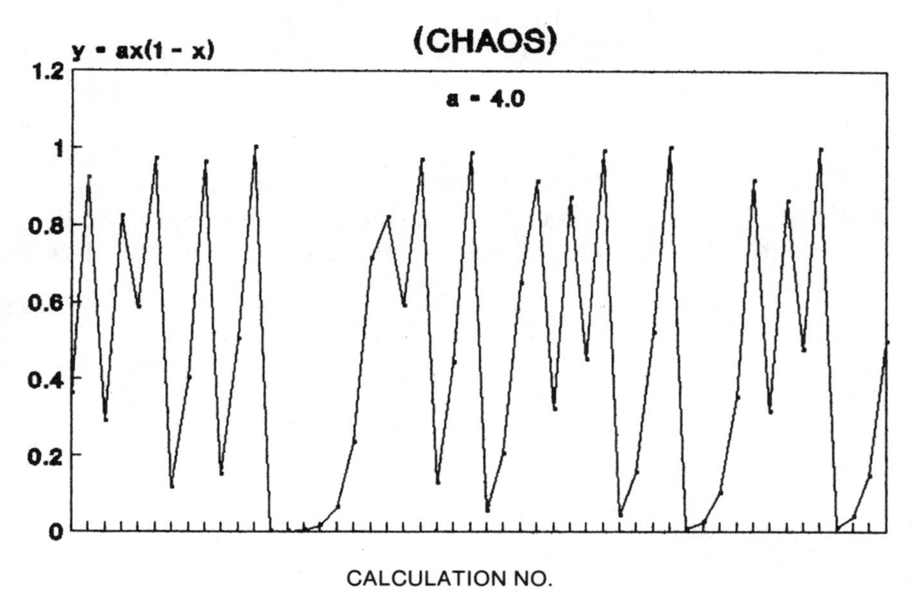

Figure 1–18. Feedback Resulting in Apparent Randomness.

(seed) for (*x*); only the constant (*a*) was varied (slightly) between these graphs.

This equation is even more intriguing when the resulting (*y*) values are plotted against a whole series of possible values of (*a*). The resulting line rises, then actually splits and oscillates, then splits and oscillates again and again. This strange behavior is known as *bifurcation*. With the aid of the computer, scientists examined these bifurcations and discovered that within the set (in this example) representing all possible values of (*y*) per value of various values of (*a*), there are subsets and subsets of subsets, and so on, that are merely miniature pictures of the original set. This would be similar to being shown an aerial photograph of an unfamiliar coastline or a close-up of a snowflake and not being able to determine from how many miles or millimeters, respectively, the picture was taken. Some of the graphics that can be produced by plotting feedback from nonlinear equations are awe-inspiring.

Most of the work done to date with chaos theory has centered around natural phenomena, such as animal population, crystal formation, weather forecasting, motion, and other aspects of science. Whether anyone will find some magic formula that, through feedback of some variable(s), will produce a simulation of stock or bond market behavior is yet to be seen. But this writer, as well as a few others, are making efforts in this area. The point is that over the past 10 or more years, chaos theory has been opening the door for the possibility that feedback of some economic variables (just like the nick in the roulette wheel) might produce apparently chaotic, but possibly predictable, securities market behavior.

2

Analyzing Risk

In Wall Street, the only thing that's hard to explain is—next week.

—Louis Rukeyser

THE LAST HEYDAY

If zest and jollity were the barometers of Wall Street, instead of the Dow Jones and Standard & Poor's averages, then the last real heyday in the stock market was the early 1970s. The stock market averages were nearing an all-time high, but wouldn't exceed that zenith for another decade. Investors and brokers were still making a lot of money. The emerging growth stocks were still in play and the big, stable companies (eventually to become the Nifty-Fifty) were gathering steam; there were still some "hot" new issues; bonds that were convertible into growth stocks were being issued for the first time; the individual "retail" investor was still heavily involved in the market; and investors weren't yet concerned about the devastating inflation that was about to emerge.

Most importantly, brokerage commission rates were still fixed at artificially high levels. A few years prior to "May Day" (when commissions would begin their prolonged slide), the brokerage business was an exhilarating enterprise to be involved with, even when a volume of 20 million shares meant a big day on the New York Stock Exchange. Having lunch or supper (when the "buy-side" and "sell-side" people got together) on Wall Street or in Boston's financial district was pure enjoyment. Salespeople and analysts literally had fun talking about the latest "go-go" stock, oil discovery, technological invention, or wonder drug. Mutual funds and giant corporate pensions didn't yet dominate the marketplace, so the professionals could still make money outsmarting the small investor. Vietnam was the main problem of that era, but President Nixon was winding that down.

Extreme market volatility was seldom considered a potential problem. Liquidity wasn't really there, but it didn't matter since stocks weren't being bought or sold in elephantine blocks. There were no minicomputers or index futures, and options were only traded over the counter; therefore, index arbitrage and program trading couldn't even be imagined.

Nevertheless, the academicians as a group *were* concerning themselves with volatility. To them, price volatility was a good definition of investment risk—and *it could be measured!* Along came *beta*. Yet, decades later, the concept of beta as a measurement of risk is still not properly understood by most investors.

THE DERIVATION OF BETA

One hot summer day in 1971, I was having lunch at Boston's famous Lockober Restaurant with Richard Davisson, the most talented investment analyst I've ever known. In Boston, he was known as the dean of the analysts. Dick was a quasi-analyst-salesman with White, Weld in "beantown," after having been an oil analyst with State Street Research in the 1950s. His principal source of income was probably not his petroleum interests in West Texas, but rather the commissions he earned from White, Weld in trading his own portfolio!

This most wonderful gentleman and I overheard an argument at another table. The heated debate was between an institutional stockbroker and his client, my good analyst friend Emo Fezman. The argument concerned whether XYZ Corp. was a risky investment. The salesman was trying to persuade the sharp analyst to buy stock in XYZ Corp., but Emo insisted that such an investment was too risky by his employer's standards, since the price of the stock was too volatile.

The broker exploded, "But the stock's beta is only 1.10!", which is about average for an industrial company's stock. Like most arguments, nobody won. Nobody should have won because beta is not a good measurement of volatility and probably was never intended to be. For the next half hour or so, Dick and I evaluated the argument at the other table.

What is beta, really? Its origin is from the *b* in the equation for a straight line: $y = a + bx$. In investments work, the straight line is produced as the "best fit" for a series of points (on a graph), each of which represent the percentage price change of a stock (for any given time period) versus the percentage move of the S&P 500 (for the same time period). Figure 2–1 provides a simple illustration:

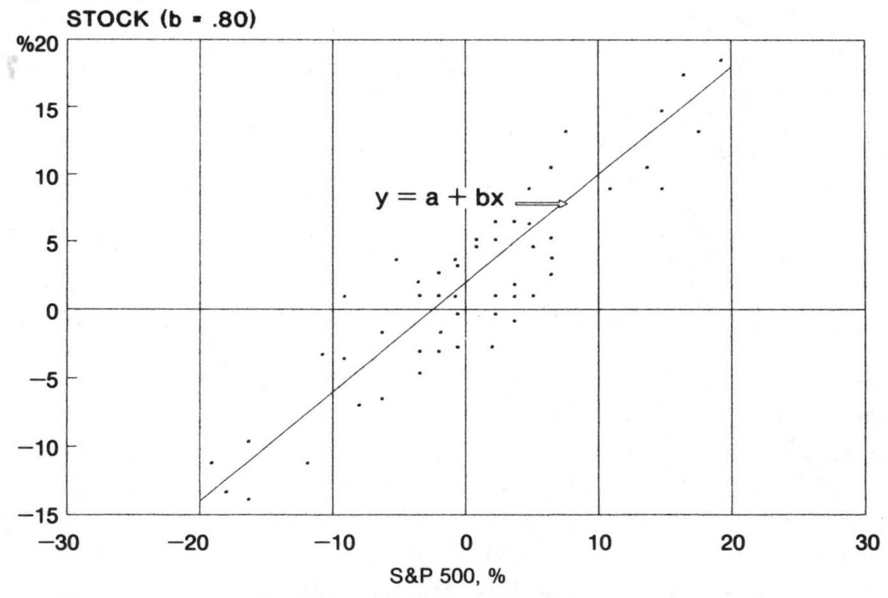

Figure 2–1. Beta Derives from Monthly Price Changes.

In the equation $y = a + bx$, (x) equals the price change of the stock market; (y) equals the price change of the individual stock; (a) equals the alpha- or y-axis intercept, which represents how much the stock is beating the market by, on average; and (b) is the beta, which equals the slope of the line, which here represents how much the stock tends to react to moves in the market.

A beta of 1.0 means the line would have a 45° slope, which implies that a 1% move in the market should result (on average) in

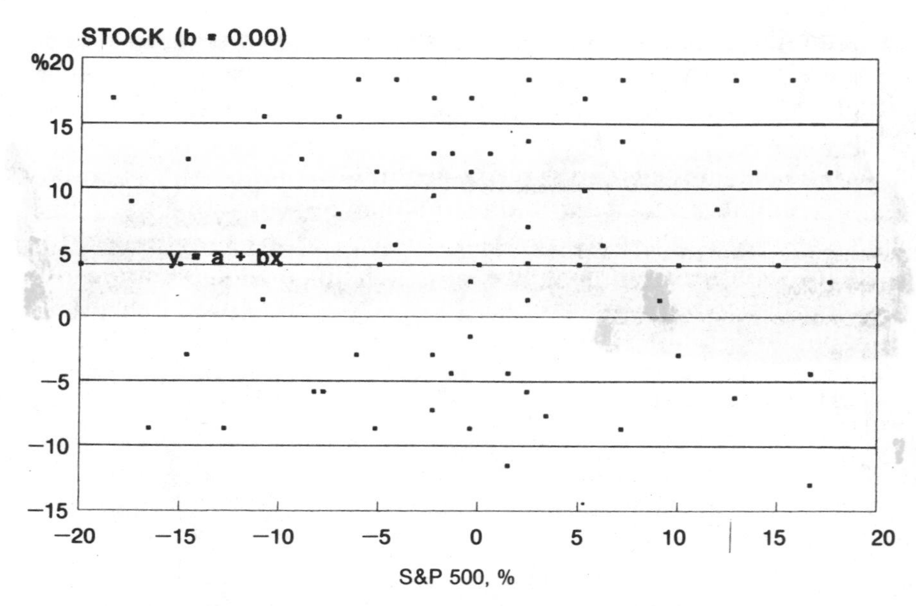

Figure 2–2. Stock with High Volatility but Low Beta.

a 1% move in the stock, in addition to the stock's own specific performance (alpha). A beta of 2.0 means the line would be very steep. For some people, this implies that the stock fluctuates much more than the market. But is that really true? Examine the scatter diagrams shown in Figures 2–2 and 2–3. One stock has a beta of 0 and the other a beta of 1.50. But, obviously, the low-beta stock is at least as volatile as the high-beta stock because the points on both charts are very scattered (in the vertical direction).

Beta does not address volatility alone, but also includes the *correlation* between changes in the stock price and changes in the overall market level. Remember that the line (linear regression) from which the beta (slope) is calculated is the line that best fits the points on the graph. Statistically, it's called a least-squares line where because it is computed by defining a line the squares of the distance between each point and the line, all totaled, are the least possible amount.

Therefore, the beta (slope) of the line reflects the tendency of a stock to move with the market, not just the magnitude of the reaction. Suppose a stock (like a gold stock, years ago) tended to move in the opposite direction to the market. The line would be sloped "down to the right" and would have a negative beta, even though the stock might be extremely volatile. So, low beta does not necessarily mean low volatility, because it might just mean low correlation between a stock and the market.

Then, what does beta accomplish? It tells us how much *market* (systematic) risk a stock has. But it does not define or explain total risk. The purpose of owning many diverse stocks in an equity portfolio is to reduce the *nonmarket* (specific) risk caused by factors that are peculiar to a particular industry or company such as a change in the price of oil, fluctuation of certain foreign currency, management changes, new legislation, a new competitor, and so on.

With the aid of a computer, we can minimize this "diversifiable risk" by owning a group of stocks whose price changes have historically shown little correlation to each other, that is, low

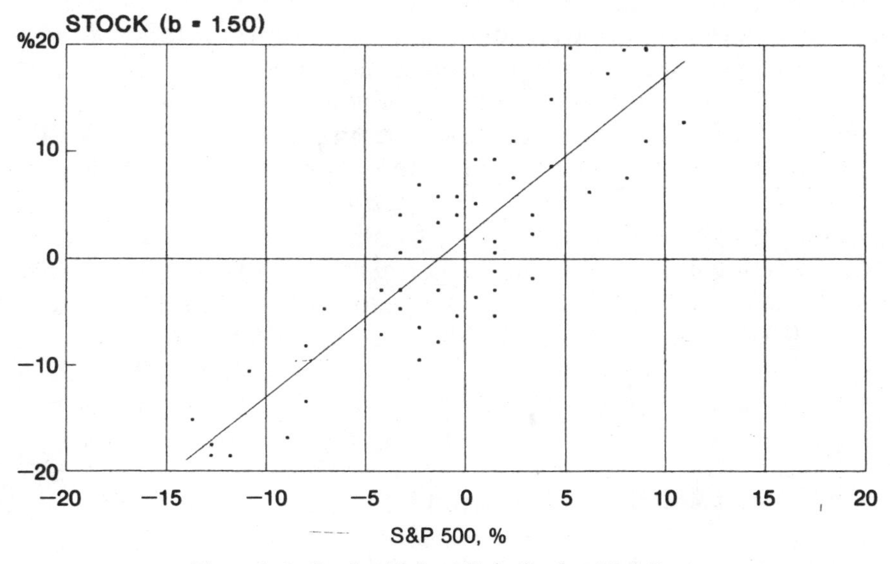

Figure 2–3. Stock with Low Volatility but High Beta.

covariance. Without a computer, we can accomplish this by owning different types of stocks (such as growth or cyclical, foreign or U.S., labor-intensive or capital-intensive, small or large capitalization) or owning stocks within different industries. But all of these stocks, no matter how heterogeneous, share some similarities, such as vulnerability to the effect of interest rates on the present value of their future dividends and their borrowing costs, or the effects of global recession or the level of investor sentiment. How do we reduce these common risk factors (market risk)? By owning a portfolio of low-beta stocks because they react less violently to factors that affect the overall market. The beta of a portfolio of stocks is simply the weighted average (mean) of all the individual stocks.

In summary, beta does not measure a stock's absolute (or even relative) volatility, but only the average effect a change in the overall market level has on a stock. Therefore, beta is both a function of volatility and correlation with the market. Obviously, some stocks such as General Electric have a high correlation to the market because they are good proxies for the overall economy. Other stocks, like Royal Dutch Petroleum, have low correlations because their stock price may depend on the price of a particular commodity or the exchange rate of a foreign currency, for example. Both stocks, however, may be equally risky (volatile).

A good way to estimate the beta of a stock (which is a proper mathematical approximation) is to multiply its own volatility, measured by standard deviation (described in Chapter 1) by its correlation (r) to the market then dividing that product by the standard deviation of the market. In other words, a stock with a standard deviation of 40% and a correlation to the market of 50% would have a beta of 1.00 if the standard deviation of the market were 20% (40% × 50% = 20%; 20% ÷ 20% = 1.00).

$$\text{Beta} = b = \frac{\text{SD of stock} \times (r)}{\text{SD of S\&P 500}}$$

UNDERSTANDING CORRELATION

Here we must mathematically define coefficient of correlation (r) because it is of utmost importance, not just in equity portfolio diversification, but also in asset allocation (which involves the cross-correlation of price between stocks, bonds, and possibly other asset classes).

Figure 2–4 shows the price changes of a typical stock relative to the price moves of the market. To measure the correlation between the two, we first calculate the coefficient of determination (r^2). To do this we must calculate the difference between each actual (y) value and the mean of all the (y) values. Then, we compute the difference between each corresponding point along the regression line and the mean. Since about half of the differences are negative, we need to square them to make them positive *variances* (v). Then, we divide the expected (regression line) variances by the actual variances:

$$r\text{-squared} = \frac{\text{Sum of } v1}{\text{Sum of } v2} = \frac{\text{Sum of } [y1 - \text{a}]^2}{\text{Sum of } [y2 - \text{a}]^2} = \frac{\text{Total \textit{expected} variances}}{\text{Total \textit{actual} variances}}$$

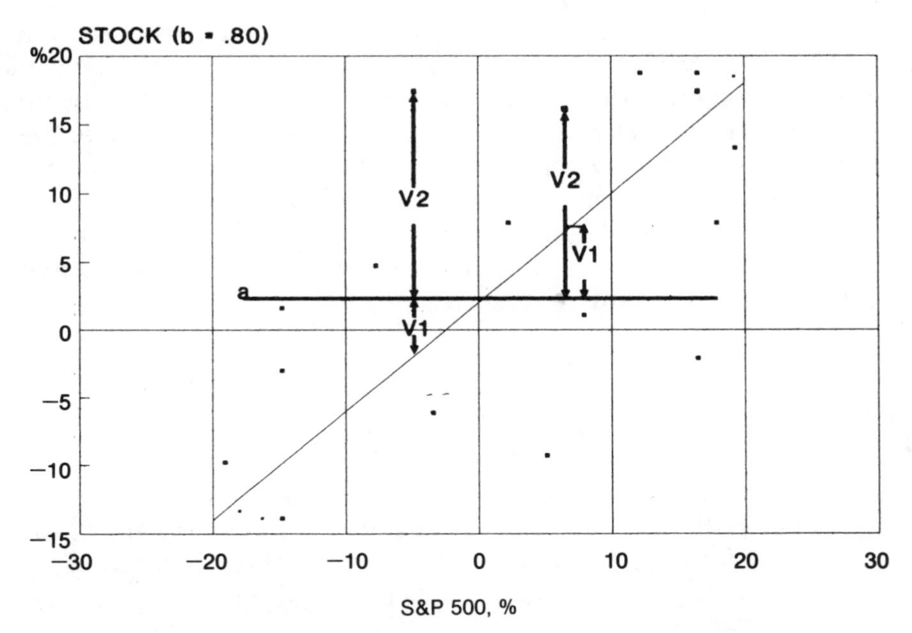

Figure 2–4. Price Changes of a Typical Stock versus Market Price Moves.

where $y2$ = the actual (y) values; $y1$ = the corresponding values along the regression line; and (a) = the mean (average) of all the (y) values.

To find the coefficient of correlation, we "unsquare" the "r-squared":

$$r = \sqrt{\frac{\text{Sum of expected variances } (v1)}{\text{Sum of actual variances } (v2)}}$$

A correlation coefficient (r) of .40 (or 40%) might mean that 40% of a stock's price volatility was explained by the volatility of the overall market or by factors that affect the market as well as the individual security.

A similar correlation can be calculated between stock and bond market returns. If the coefficient (r) were .30 (30%) that might mean that 30% of the move in the S&P 500 was due to the move in bond prices, that is, a change in long-term interest rates. If we calculated another coefficient of correlation (r) between stock market returns and Treasury bill returns and found it to be −.10, that might mean that 10% of the price change of the stock market was due to unexpected changes in short-term interest rates. In this case, the returns are negatively correlated, which means that if T-bill rates increase, stock prices have a tendency to fall.

We can also calculate the correlation between the prices of two stocks or between the returns of bonds and real estate or any two series of (x) values and (y) values.

COVARIANCE AND CORRELATION

The practical difficulty with the coefficient-of-determination (r^2) technique is the time required to compute the expected (regression line) value for each value of (y) that corresponds to an actual (x) value. Frank K. Reilly offers a simple means of calculating correlation coefficient (r), and therefore r^2, for investment purposes. Reilly arrives at the correlation number via *covariance* and standard deviation rather than via coefficient of determination.

Covariance, like standard deviation but unlike the correlation coefficient, is an absolute measurement rather than a proportion or relative value. It is simply the *average* product obtained by multiplying the difference between each (x) value and the mean of (x) by the difference between each (y) value and the mean of (y).

Keeping in mind that each (x) is paired with the (y) representing the same observation period (e.g., the price of Stock A versus Stock B, week by week), Table 2–1 and the following formula provide an illustration.

$$\text{Covariance} = \frac{\text{Sum of } [(x - \bar{x}) \times (y - \bar{y})]}{\text{N}} = (10/5) = 2.00$$

Using Reilly's methodology, we could define *correlation coefficient* as the covariance between (x) and (y) divided by the product of the standard deviation of (x) times the standard deviation of (y).

$$s(x) = \sqrt{20 / 5} = 2.00$$
$$s(y) = \sqrt{6 /5} = 1.10$$

$$\text{Correlation } (x,y) = \frac{\text{Covariance } (x,y)}{s(x) \times s(y)} = \frac{2.00}{2.00 \times 1.10} = .91$$

TABLE 2–1 Example Calculation of Covariance

Period	(x)	(y)	$(x - \bar{x})$	$(y - \bar{y})$	$(x - \bar{x}) \times (y - \bar{y})$	$(x - \bar{x})^2$	$(y - \bar{y})^2$
1	10	8	−3	−2	6	9	4
2	12	10	−1	0	0	1	0
3	13	10	0	0	0	0	0
4	14	11	1	1	1	1	1
5	16	11	3	1	3	9	1
	65	50			10	20	6

Mean = $\bar{x}$ = 13
Mean = $\bar{y}$ = 10

As shown in Figure 2–4, correlation also can be calculated by taking the square root of the result of the expected variances divided by the actual variances. Although this method is more cumbersome because the values of the regression-line equation ($y = bx + a$) have to be computed first, it shows more clearly that correlation is really just a measurement of how well the points on the graph fit the regression line. The expected-versus-actual-variance method would compute as shown in Figure 2–5 and Table 2–2 using the same data as in Table 2–1.

A coefficient of correlation can range from +1.00 to −1.00. We know if the correlation is negative because the least-squares regression line will slope *down* to the right, that is, if the beta of the line is negative. Using Reilly's technique, the covariance can be negative, which will automatically result in a negative correlation coefficient (r). An example of negative correlation might be the price change of the S&P Oil Producers Index to the price change of the S&P Airlines Index. In this instance, higher petroleum prices might have caused oil industry profits to improve and airline fuel costs to increase.

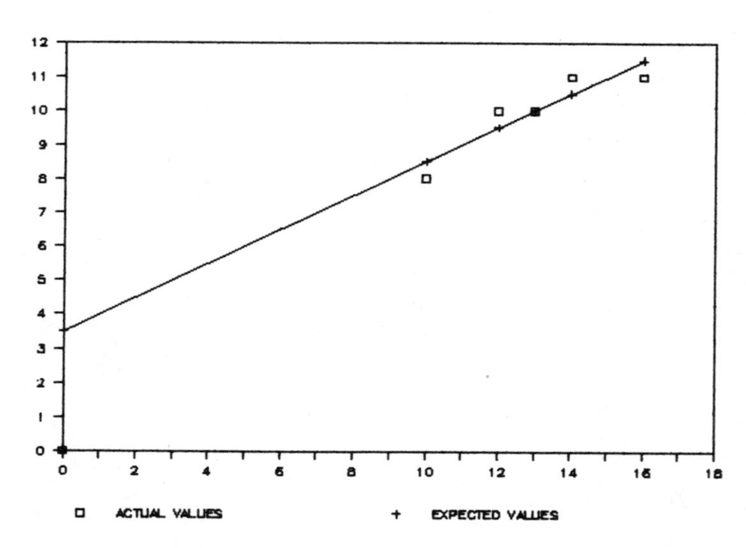

Figure 2–5. Expected-versus-Actual-Variance Method.

TABLE 2–2 Expected-versus-Actual-Variance Method

				ACTUAL VARIANCES		EXPECTED VARIANCES	
Period	(x)	Actual (y_a)	Expected (y_e)*	$(y_a - \bar{y})$	$(y_a - \bar{y})^2$	$(y_e - \bar{y})$	$(y_e - \bar{y})^2$
1	10	8	8.5	−2	4	−1.5	2.25
2	12	10	9.5	0	0	−0.5	0.25
3	13	10	10	0	0	0	0.00
4	14	11	10.5	+1	1	+0.5	0.25
5	16	11	11.5	+1	1	+1.5	2.25
		50			6		5.00

mean $= \bar{y} = 10$

Correlation $(r) = \sqrt{5/6} = .91$

*The expected (y) values are calculated by plugging the various (x) values into the equation $y + bx + a$, where b = slope of the line = .50 and a = y intercept = 3.50.

Note: As with any correlation analysis, you must be careful when implying cause and effect. A coefficient of correlation must be taken only at face value, that is, degree of correlation; whether one factor is the cause and the other the effect or both are effects of some other cause can only be surmised.

MEASURING VOLATILITY

The best way to measure total risk for a security or group of securities is to calculate the variability of return over time, using *standard deviation*. Remember that standard deviation is simply the average "unsquared" variance of a series of values from their mean. For the stock or bond markets, the standard deviation of return (if returns were distributed normally) would be the *maximum amount of variability that occurs 68% of the time*. So, if the mean annual return of stocks were 10% and the standard deviation of return were 15%, annual stock returns would range between +25% and −5%, roughly 68% of the time, as demonstrated in Chapter 1.

TABLE 2-3 Stock and Bond Returns and Volatilities

	Actual Quarterly Returns					
Date	Stocks	log (1 + R)	Bonds	log (1 + R)	Cash	log (1 + R)
79-1	7.1%	0.0686	2.6%	0.0257	2.3%	0.0224
2	2.8	0.0276	3.9	0.0383	2.3	0.0224
3	7.6	0.0733	−1.1	−0.0111	2.3	0.0231
4	0.1	0.0010	−3.0	−0.0305	2.8	0.0280
80-1	−4.1	−0.0419	−8.4	−0.0877	3.2	0.0313
2	13.3	0.1249	18.1	0.1664	2.3	0.0230
3	11.3	0.1071	−6.2	−0.0640	2.2	0.0219
4	9.5	0.0908	1.5	0.0149	3.2	0.0319
81-1	1.3	0.0129	0.7	0.0070	3.4	0.0336
2	−2.4	−0.0243	0.0	0.0000	3.5	0.0347
3	−10.3	−0.1087	−3.4	−0.0346	3.6	0.0351
4	6.8	0.0658	10.3	0.0980	2.8	0.0278
82-1	−7.3	−0.0758	3.6	0.0354	3.1	0.0301
2	−0.6	−0.0060	2.8	0.0276	3.0	0.0293
3	11.5	0.1089	13.8	0.1293	2.3	0.0223
4	18.2	0.1672	8.3	0.0797	1.9	0.0190
83-1	10.0	0.0953	3.1	0.0305	2.0	0.0195
2	11.1	0.1053	1.6	0.0159	2.0	0.0202
3	−1.1	−0.0111	1.5	0.0149	2.2	0.0219
4	0.4	0.0040	1.5	0.0149	2.1	0.0211
84-1	−2.4	−0.0243	0.5	0.0050	2.2	0.0219
2	−2.6	−0.0263	−1.7	−0.0171	2.4	0.0234
3	9.7	0.0926	8.3	0.0797	2.5	0.0246
4	1.8	0.0178	7.4	0.0714	2.1	0.0211
85-1	9.1	0.0871	2.1	0.0208	2.0	0.0197
2	7.3	0.0705	8.2	0.0788	1.8	0.0180
3	−4.1	−0.0419	2.0	0.0198	1.7	0.0172
4	17.1	0.1579	7.6	0.0733	1.7	0.0173
86-1	14.0	0.1310	7.6	0.0733	1.7	0.0167
2	5.9	0.0573	2.2	0.0218	1.5	0.0149
3	−7.0	−0.0726	2.0	0.0198	1.4	0.0134
4	5.6	0.0545	3.1	0.0305	1.3	0.0130
87-1	21.1	0.1914	1.5	0.0149	1.4	0.0135
2	4.9	0.0478	−1.9	−0.0192	1.4	0.0138
3	6.5	0.0630	−2.9	−0.0294	1.5	0.0147
4	−22.2	−0.2510	5.8	0.0564	1.4	0.0142
88-1	5.7	0.0554	3.8	0.0373	1.4	0.0139
2	6.6	0.0639	0.4	0.0040	1.5	0.0151

(continued)

TABLE 2–3 (*Continued*) Stock and Bond Returns and Volatilities

	Actual Quarterly Returns					
Date	Stocks	log (1 + R)	Bonds	log (1 + R)	Cash	log (1 + R)
3	0.3	0.0030	1.7	0.0169	1.7	0.0169
4	3.1	0.0305	1.9	0.0188	1.9	0.0186
89–1	7.1	0.0685	1.1	0.0109	2.0	0.0202
2	8.7	0.0833	8.0	0.0773	2.3	0.0229
3	10.7	0.1017	0.9	0.0090	2.2	0.0214
4	2.0	0.0202	3.8	0.0369	2.0	0.0199
Mean	4.4%	4.1%	2.8%	2.7%	2.2%	2.2%
Annualized	18.8	17.4	11.8	11.3	9.0	9.0
SD	7.9		4.8		0.6	
Annualized	15.9		9.6		1.2	

Before we examine the relationship of risk to return, let's take a look at actual stock and bond returns and their variability. Table 2–3 shows the quarterly returns for the S&P 500 and the Shearson Lehman Government/Corporate Bond Index over an 11-year period. The mean quarterly return and the standard deviation of the returns are shown at the bottom of the table.

The average returns and standard deviations are representative of an average *quarter*. In Table 2–3, the geometric mean was used since it is more meaningful for compounding or projection purposes.

How do we *annualize* quarterly data? To annualize mean returns (assuming the mean is the appropriate one), we can either take the antilog of 4 times 1 plus the log of the mean, or we can compound the quarterly mean according to the following formula:

$$\text{Average annual return} = (1 + \text{Geometric quarterly average return})^4 - 1$$

In this example, average annual return for stocks $= (1 + .041)^4 - 1 = 17.4\%$. The average annual return bonds $= 1 + .027)^4 - 1 = 11.3\%$. The average annual return for cash $= (1 + .022)^4 - 1 = 9.0\%$.

To annualize a standard deviation, however, we multiply it by the square root of the time function. In this example, we are annualizing a quarter, so instead of multiplying the average quarterly standard deviation (.079) by 4, we multiply it by the square root of 4 which is 2: $.079 \times 2 = .158 = 15.8\%$.

So risk, is a function of the *square root of time!*

This is theory, but the square-root function works fairly well in the real world. It has to do with the behavior of random numbers as discussed in Chapter 1. Remember the experiment of building piles of pennies (counters) based on moving to the right or left, depending on whether the toss coin came up heads versus tails? In that experiment, if we had *quadrupled* the number of flips per counter, *most* of the counters, *on average* would have spread out only *twice* as far. (The small end piles would be four times as far apart, but the number of counters in those piles would be relatively insignificant.)

As the number of random events increases, their standard deviation from the mean increases by a factor equivalent to the square root of the ratio representing the increase in the number of events. For example, assume baseball scores between two specific teams were actually random (which they probably are not), and the average runs per game, during a 10 game series, had been 10 and the standard deviation of the runs had been 2 runs per game. This would mean that in 68% (representing one standard deviation) of the games, the total of the runs was between 8 and 12. Then, the expected standard deviation of runs for 100 (10 times as many) games would be 2 times the square root of 10, or 2 (runs) times 3.2, or 6.4. This means that 68% of the time (or in 68 games) the total runs per game should range between roughly 16 and 4. In the other 32 of the 100 games, there would be either more than 16 or less than 4 runs.

Another example would be the roulette wheel or the blackjack table. With constant, equal betting, you *could* lose (or win) up to four times as much in four hours as in one hour, but the *odds* are that you will win or lose only twice as much. That's why the longer you play, the less significant the amount of your bet seems. In random-based games, the *average* range of scores doesn't increase in direct proportion to the number of games played (even though the extreme *possible* range does). It increases according to some root function of time—square root, if each game has two equally weighted possible outcomes.

In case it is still not clear why the volatility of return varies with the square root of time when random events are involved, here is a simple example involving a game where the player can either win $1.00 or lose $1.00 on each turn.

Imagine you are at the blackjack table and your odds of winning are close to 50%. You bet $1.00 on each hand and can either lose that dollar or win a dollar. Let's compare the distribution of possible returns after playing two hands versus four hands. The standard deviation of return for four hands should be only 1.42 (the square root of 2) times the standard deviation for two hands, even though twice as many hands are played.

The following formula shows the calculations for the standard deviation of possible returns for two hands and four hands. For two hands, there are four possible outcomes: win/win, win/lose, lose/win, and lose/lose. Since win/lose and lose/win both produce a net return of zero, the possible return of $0.00 has a frequency of 2, as shown in the first part. For four hands, there are 16 possible win-lose combinations and those probabilities are shown in the second part of the formula.

The standard deviation of return for one hand is $1.00.

(1) What is the standard deviation of return after two hands?

Frequency (f)	Win/lose	Variance (v^2)	(f) × (v)
1	$2.00	$4.00	$4.00
2	$0.00	$0.00	$0.00
1	($2.00)	$4.00	$4.00
4			$8.00

$$SD = \sqrt{\$8.00/4} = \sqrt{\$2.00} = \$1.42$$

(2) What is the standard deviation of return after four hands?

Frequency (f)	Win/lose	Variance (v^2)	(f) × (v)
1	$4.00	$16.00	$16.00
4	$2.00	$4.00	$16.00
6	$0.00	$0.00	$0.00
4	($2.00)	$4.00	$16.00
1	($4.00)	$16.00	$16.00
16			$64.00

$$SD = \sqrt{\$64/16} = \sqrt{\$4.00} = \$2.00$$

The standard deviation of possible returns for four hands is $2.00, which is exactly 1.42 times the standard deviation for two hands of $1.42.

This has a very important implication for stock and bond returns over time, if we assume a near-random (unpredictable) market. (Whether or not the market is random is, perhaps, less important than whether it behaves as though it were.)

If the standard deviation for annual bond returns were 6% and the yield on bonds were 10%, this means that in one year the returns should range between 4% and 16%, 68% of the time. In other words, if the average bond coupon were 10%, price changes would account for the possible variability of 6% up or down.

HOW PATIENCE REDUCES RISK

What would be the total compounded return and standard deviation for the bond portfolio for 10 years?

$$\text{10-year return} = (1 + .10)^{10} - 1 = 159\%$$
$$\text{10-year SD} = 6\% \times \sqrt{10} \text{ years} = 19\%$$

That's an average standard deviation of less than 2% per year!

In other words, over a total 10-year period, *bond returns don't vary any more than T-bill returns* which also vary about 2% per year (regardless of time, since they are not at all normally distributed). For stocks, over a 20-year period, the annualized standard deviation would be only about 3%.

$$20\text{-year SD} = 15\% \times \sqrt{20} = 67\%$$
$$\text{Annualized SD} = (1 + .67)^{.05} - 1 = 3\%$$

The obvious conclusion is that the longer the time period, the less risky stocks and bonds become. In fact, over 30 years, the variability of stock returns is less than that of a savings account! For example, if the expected return for stocks were 10%, after 30 years $1,000 should be worth $17,449. But even if it grew to nearly double that—$30,000 (which would reflect a return about one standard deviation above average)—the annual compounded return would be just 12%, that is, only 2% different, just as the rate on certificates of deposit might be 2% higher or lower over the next 30 years. Figure 2–6 provides a visual picture of how *annualized* volatility of return decreases over time.

WHAT MAKES SECURITIES PRICES FLUCTUATE?

Nothing in the universe moves in a straight line, at least relative to a distant observer. About the only thing that comes close to

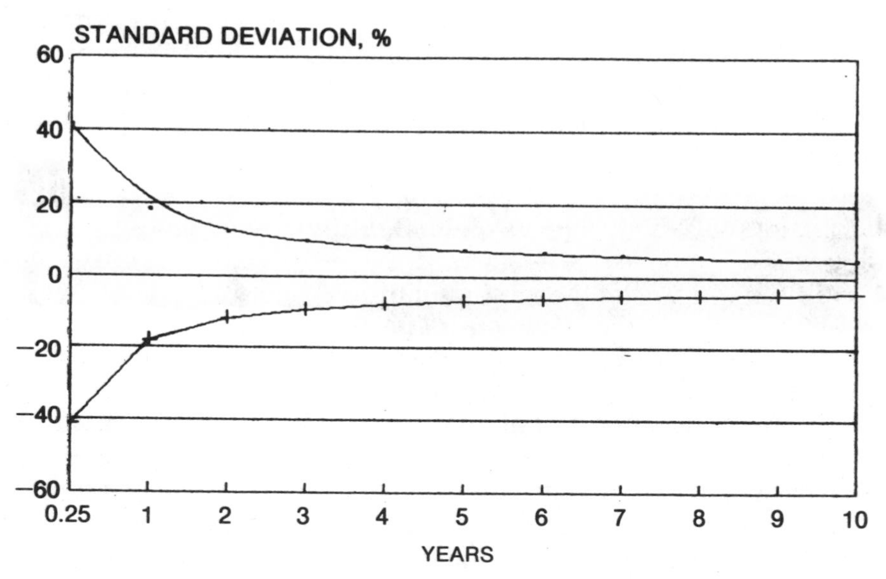

Figure 2–6. How Annualized Volatility of Return Decreases Over Time.

straight-line motion is a beam of light moving through space. But even there, the warping of the space-time manifold (which to us appears to be a gravitational force) causes light to change direction slightly as it passes by the celestial bodies. At the other extreme, we can observe Brownian motion (erratic, apparent random movement) everywhere. If everything in the universe moves with some degree of twisting, turning, or bending, why do so many investors apply a straight-edged ruler to a chart of securities prices? Most of these charts aren't even composed on semilog paper even though the chartist should be dealing with *percentage* changes; and the points are so scattered that visualizing a straight-line trend requires much imagination.

Judging by the amount of "technical" analysis that is subscribed to, you would think that securities prices moved in a precise sine-wave pattern within a perfect, straight-line secular trend. Figure 2–7 shows that nothing could be further from the truth. It is no wonder that there are as many different "wave theories" as there are possible random "waves."

How *can* we predict the future volatility of securities prices and, therefore, returns? The problem is that volatility, in the investments world, is not a constant, particularly for short-term periods. Figure 2–7 shows the range of volatilities for the S&P 500 over the past 45 years. This log-normal-looking chart shows that the standard deviation of the market has quite a high standard deviation itself!

We need to examine what makes the markets fluctuate. The basic difference between stock and bond prices is that individual stock prices have a secular upward bias, whereas the price of a bond always reverts back to its maturity value which is usually very close to its original issue price (par). For simplicity's sake (and in order to avoid the issue of possible secular trends in interest rates and dividend payout ratios) let's assume that the long-term trend for bond prices is a flat line around which prices fluctuate in the short and intermediate term and that the long-term trend for stock prices is a positively sloped, logarithmic, straight line representing an average annual appreciation of 6%. This long-term price return of 6% (excluding dividend yield) can be related to growth in the overall economy: 3 to 4% from inflation and 2 to 3% from real growth, mainly due to gains in productivity and population.

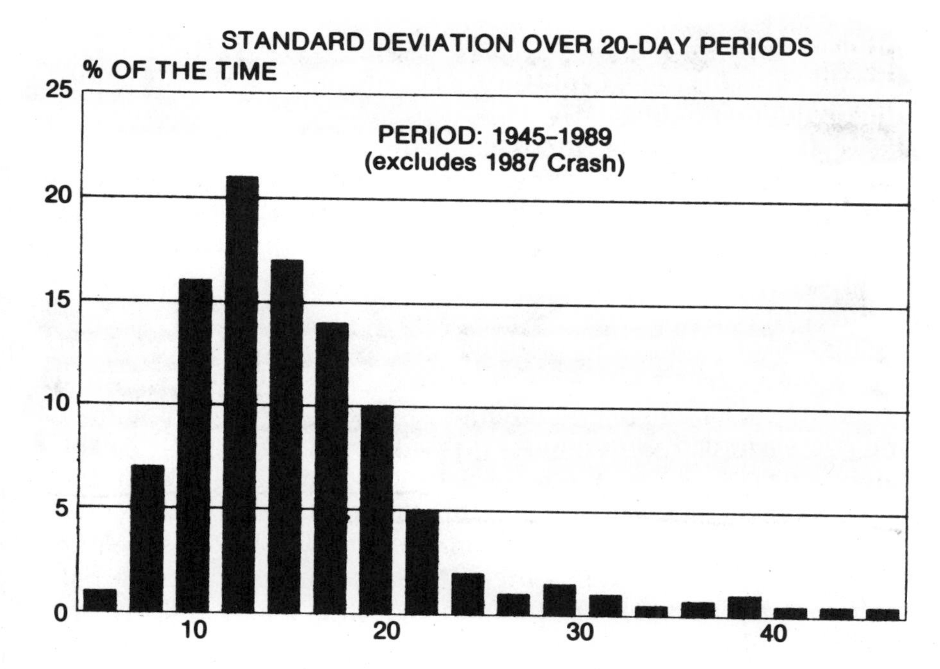

Figure 2–7. Historic Distribution of S&P 500 Volatility. Data Source: Morgan Stanley Research (11/89).

Why do prices fluctuate around these long-term, secular trends? The first of several reasons, which apply to both stocks and bonds, involves interest rates, both actual and expected. When rates rise unexpectedly, bond prices naturally fall, so that a bond's fixed coupon will provide a higher percentage return for someone buying the bond today.

If short-term rates remain unchanged, but investors' expectations suddenly change to those of higher rates in the future, bond prices will fall again. This is because the return from a bond must reflect the expected interest rates throughout its life. This will be discussed, in detail, in Chapter 5.

Stock prices also drop when current or expected future interest rates go up, all other things being equal. Unfortunately, when interest expectations change, all other things are not equal. Therefore, we can only say with certainty that when rates rise, stock prices are lower than they otherwise would have been. The principal reason higher interest rates impact stocks negatively is that the present value of the future cash flow to the company and of the dividends to the shareholder is reduced by a higher discount factor. (This will also be discussed, in detail, in Chapter 4.) In short, our original straight trend lines for stock and bond prices now have some cyclical ups and downs due to interest rates and some short-term moves due to frequent changes in the expectations of future interest rates.

But, what makes interest rates fluctuate? The answer is, mainly, changes in inflation expectations. Nominal (actual) interest rates have three main components: the real interest rate (normally around 3 to 4%), the risk element (principal risk and reinvestment-rate risk), and the inflation expectation (which is normally the largest of the three components). Short-term T-bill rates reflect only the real rate plus the going inflation rate.

Inflation expectations are the main variable that affects long-term rates. The real rate is theoretically a constant and the risk-premium is a function of duration (which is fixed) and investor confidence (which is usually less volatile than inflation expectations). All other things being equal, if inflation expectations for all foreseeable years change by 1%, interest rates for all maturities change by 1% and so does the discount factor for the stock market. Many people feel that unexpected changes in the current and expected level of inflation are the main driving forces behind the volatility of securities prices.

The role of investor confidence and sentiment is the second major factor affecting both the stock and bond markets. Keep in mind that market peaks (periods of extreme overvaluation) are mainly caused by blind greed; just as market bottoms are caused by fear. Neither are directly related to long-term growth or interest-rate expectations. Not only during market extremes, but every day, the sentiment of the investor is at work. Between greed and fear, there are all sorts of degrees of uncertainty that affect the expected returns (and therefore price levels) of stocks and bonds. Chapters 5 and 7 deal with the role of investor confidence in more detail.

The third factor, beyond interest rates and investor confidence, that affects both equity and corporate fixed-income securities prices is the outlook of corporate profits. When profits drop, credit risk increases, producing uncertainty regarding the future interest or dividend payments.

The complete list of all the factors that cause market volatility could fill a book; however, most of these factors would be subsets of the three criteria outlined here. Why try to measure or forecast all the subsets when the basic criteria themselves are measurable or able to be forecasted? Models that contain too many inputs lose effectiveness as the "noise" level increases. This becomes an important point, particularly, if we consider whether it is more important to forecast details accurately or forecast what the market is likely to expect.

In the following chapters, it will be shown that forward interest rates, investor confidence, and future profitability can be forecasted with a fair degree of accuracy. These three criteria explain most of the volatility of the market indices. There are additional fluctuations caused by technical factors such as arbitrage, program trading, and specific factors affecting individual key securities within the indices. Therefore, economic news is extremely important to the market because it affects all three of the basic criteria that affect every company.

If these three factors affect both stocks and bonds, why are stocks usually more volatile than bonds? Although there have been periods lasting several quarters or even years when bonds have been as volatile as stocks, the standard deviation of stock returns is normally more than double that of bond returns. The reason is that all three factors—rates, confidence, and profits—have a much more leveraged effect on equities.

First, as you will see in Chapter 4, the stock market is mathematically more sensitive to interest rates than are bond prices. Second, investor confidence affects stocks more than bonds because the equity risk-premium (desired return from stocks minus the risk-free rate) is much greater and can therefore vary more than the bond risk-premium (long-term rates minus short-term rates). Third, a drop in corporate profits obviously endangers dividend payments before interest payments since debt securities involve legal obligations.

Volatilities tend to remain near recent levels in the short term and revert to periodic averages in the long term. Accordingly, one of the easiest methods of estimating future volatility is to base the estimate on the past volatility that occurred over the same number of months or years being forecasted. The forecast would be improved if the more recent past is weighted more heavily than the more distant past. One simple method is to weight each period twice as heavily as the earlier period; but keep in mind that, with this method, the most recent period used (whether that be a week or 10 years) will always account for at least 50% of the total, no matter how far back one goes.

RISK CREATES RETURN

What is the mathematical relationship between risk and return? *Risk is what creates expected return* (above and beyond the risk-free T-bill rate). Obviously, the more risk the investor bears, the more return he or she expects. But how much more? In a pure academic sense, the expected return minus the risk-free (T-bill) rate should be directly proportional to the risk. For example, if T-bills yield 6% and a fairly valued security (A) has a standard deviation of return of 5% and yields 8%, then a security (B) with a standard deviation of 10% should return 10%. This relationship is shown in Figure 2–8.

A security with a reward/risk ratio shown at (C) would then be attractive (relative to portfolio A+B+T), whereas a security at (D) would not. In an efficient market, prices would then adjust accordingly. This also applies if A, B, C, and D are groups of securities or different classes of securities such as stocks, bonds, real estate, and money-market funds.

THE SUPPLY/DEMAND FALLACY

If the relative values (reward/risk ratios) are what cause securities prices to adjust, what about the independent technical forces of supply and demand? The answer is twofold. For fixed-income securities, rates are very much influenced by the new issue market,

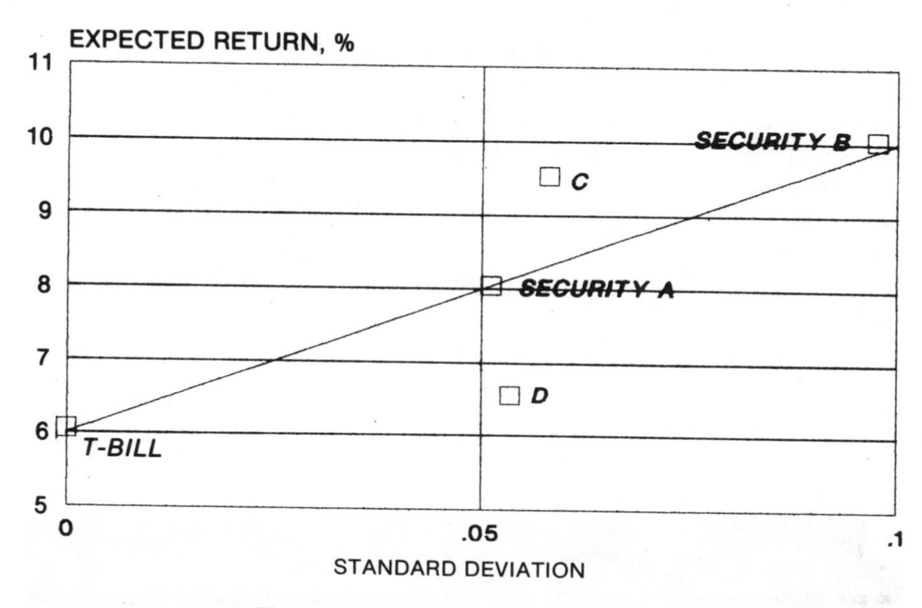

Figure 2–8. Risk versus Expected Return.

the biggest of which is the U.S. Treasury auction. There, prices are set according to supply and demand, by definition. But, stock prices are mainly *not* a function of supply and demand, other than as a reflection of interest rates.

Suppose that every company, except IBM, instantaneously went "private"; that is, assume the only stock available for investment was IBM. The supply of equities would be a tiny fraction of what it is today. Does that mean IBM would sell for millions of dollars per share? Of course not! It would eventually sell very close to where it is now. Otherwise, the return could fall below that of a risk-free investment. Both supply and demand for equities are sensitive to price, but in the long run, *stock prices are not determined by shifts in the supply or demand function* as other prices are under basic microeconomic theory.

Another fallacy related to the supply/demand assumption is the belief that only the active traders (the mutual funds brokerage firms and pension funds that account for the bulk of the day-to-day trading) influence the level of the market. The majority of all securities are still held in individual accounts. The relative value of the various securities is just as important to them as it is to the big funds. The individual investor and the inactive trader play an important role in the pricing of securities. Following the 1986 Tax Reform, for example, equity expected returns underwent a major revision, even though taxation has no consequence for the large pension funds that dominate the active marketplace.

My former business partner, Dave Lodefink, likes to pose the following thought-provoking situation. Imagine that the stock markets were to close for one year. At what levels would they reopen? The answer would have nothing whatsoever to do with the price levels on the day trading was halted. The markets would reopen at price levels that would be a function of the new current interest rates, investor confidence, and the consensus outlook for profits, dividends, and future interest rates.

The basic premise of all fundamental asset-allocation work should be that the relative expected returns and risk levels of the various classes of securities are the bases for their relative performance.

3

The Importance of Asset Allocation

Save for gold, jewels, works of art and perhaps good agricultural land, and few other things, there is no such thing as a permanent investment.

—*Bernard Baruch*

ARE YOU A RISK-TAKER?

I grew up in a middle-class, suburban neighborhood about 100 miles west of Boston. Down the street lived Larry O'Brien, Jr. of National Basketball Association fame. During my high school years, he was the campaign manager for Senator John F. Kennedy and was soon to become the chairman of the National Democratic Party. His son, Larry III, was one of my chums. On rainy days, after school, he and I would play games—card games, dice games and numbers games—all games of chance, skill, and stakes. For money we would use the make-believe stuff printed by Parker Brothers in the old brick building on the Salem-Peabody town line.

In my favorite type of match, Larry and I would take turns making up rules for a game of chance, where each player had only one turn. The object of these games was to contrive rules and criteria involving probabilities hopefully better understood by the creator than the opponent. One such game has significant investments implications concerning the purpose of asset allocation. The rules of a simplified version of this game are as follows:

1. Each player starts with $72,000, which he *must* bet, in entirety, during his or her turn.

2. Each player gets one turn, beginning with the player who was not the creator of the game.
3. Each turn consists of 12 separate rolls of one true die.
4. Prior to each roll of the die, the player whose turn it is *must* bet $6,000 on any or all numbers 1 through 6.
5. He or she may bet all $6,000 on one number, $1,000 on each number, $2,000 on each of three numbers, and so on, as long as $6,000 (no more or less) is wagered on each of the 12 rolls of the die.
6. The player is awarded a 6-to-1 payoff each time he or she bets correctly on the number that comes up on the dice rolls.

If, prior to each roll, a player bets $1,000 on each of the six possible outcomes (1 through 6), then he or she will obviously break even after each roll and still have the original $72,000 at the end of 12 rolls (his or her turn). The player's expected return is zero and so is the risk. This would be the conservative approach, but not necessarily the wrong approach, since the opponent might lose money.

The high-risk approach would be to wager all $6,000 on a single number, say 6, on each of the 12 rolls. Each time the player "guessed" correctly, he or she would win $36,000 for a profit of $30,000. Therefore, the player could win as much as 12 times that for a net profit of $360,000. However, the odds of correctly guessing the outcome of 12 consecutive rolls of a single die are less than one in two billion!

The risk-taker who puts his or her eggs in one basket by betting all on a single number has a 38% chance of losing money: an 11% chance of losing all $72,000 and a 27% chance of losing half that sum. The player has a 30% chance of breaking even and a 32% chance of winning. Even though the chances of winning are less than the chances of losing, the player can win potentially more than can be lost. But the probability of winning more than $72,000 is less than 4%.

Then there's the moderate risk-taker. This person might divide each $6,000 bet between three or four possible numbers. There would be a fair chance of making a profit and a very small chance of losing the entire kitty.

The interesting thing is that no matter how a person spreads his or her risk according to the number of possible outcomes he or she bets on, the expected (*most likely*) return is still zero. But, the distribution of *possible* returns is different for each possible method of splitting the wager.

The investment point being made here is that asset allocation (i.e. how a person divides his or her wager) is, first and foremost, a function of the investor's *risk profile, regardless of expected return.* Each of the six sides of the die could represent six types of investments, which have fairly equal probabilities of winning (outperforming) and have fairly independent outcomes (i.e., low correlations with each other). For example, the six choices to wager on, instead of being numbers 1 through 6 could be domestic stocks, domestic bonds, foreign stocks, foreign bonds, money-market funds, and real estate.

Most people, if they were to play my dice game, would probably fall into the moderate-risk-taker category, just as most investors do, since they generally own only three or four classes of securities. Choosing the number and types of asset groups in an investment portfolio is the first important step in using asset allocation to accommodate the investor's risk profile.

ASSET ALLOCATION IMPROVES EXPECTED RETURN

The second most important aspect of asset allocation relates to expected return. Suppose that, in the dice game, the die was weighted so that the number 1 had twice the probability of being rolled than the other numbers (i.e., two chances in seven rather than one in six). Even the most risk-adverse investor would then be required to wager unevenly on the six possible outcomes, otherwise he or she would lose. In my simple game, if the player still wagered $1,000 on each of the six numbers, for the 12 rolls comprising his or her turn, he or she would lose an average of nearly $10,000. In other words, there would be an expected loss.

Suppose back in 1979 that an investor who bought only U.S. stocks and bonds had a crystal ball that told on the first day of each calendar quarter whether stocks were going to outperform bonds (or vice versa) over the next 90 days. Table 3–1 shows what his or

TABLE 3–1 Allocation Returns with Perfect Knowledge

	Actual Quarterly Returns		Crystal Ball Allocation		Crystal Ball Portfolio Return	50% Stock/ 50% Bond Portfolio Return
Date	Stocks	Bonds	Stocks	Bonds		
79–1	7.1%	2.6%	100.0%	0.0%	7.1%	4.9%
2	2.8	3.9	0.0	100.0	3.9	3.4
3	7.6	−1.1	100.0	0.0	7.6	3.3
4	0.1	−3.0	100.0	0.0	0.1	−1.5
80–1	−4.1	−8.4	100.0	0.0	−4.1	−6.3
2	13.3	18.1	0.0	100.0	18.1	15.7
3	11.3	−6.2	100.0	0.0	11.3	2.6
4	9.5	1.5	100.0	0.0	9.5	5.5
81–1	1.3	0.7	100.0	0.0	1.3	1.0
2	−2.4	0.0	0.0	100.0	0.0	−1.2
3	−10.3	−3.4	0.0	100.0	−3.4	−6.9
4	6.8	10.3	0.0	100.0	10.3	8.6
82–1	−7.3	3.6	0.0	100.0	3.6	−1.9
2	−0.6	2.8	0.0	100.0	2.8	1.1
3	11.5	13.8	0.0	100.0	13.8	12.7
4	18.2	8.3	100.0	0.0	18.2	13.3
83–1	10.0	3.1	100.0	0.0	10.0	6.6
2	11.1	1.6	100.0	0.0	11.1	6.4
3	−1.1	1.5	0.0	100.0	1.5	0.2
4	0.4	1.5	0.0	100.0	1.5	1.0
84–1	−2.4	0.5	0.0	100.0	0.5	−1.0
2	−2.6	−1.7	0.0	100.0	−1.7	−2.2
3	9.7	8.3	100.0	0.0	9.7	9.0
4	1.8	7.4	0.0	100.0	7.4	4.6
85–1	9.1	2.1	100.0	0.0	9.1	5.6
2	7.3	8.2	0.0	100.0	8.2	7.8
3	−4.1	2.0	0.0	100.0	2.0	−1.1
4	17.1	7.6	100.0	0.0	17.1	12.4
86–1	14.0	7.6	100.0	0.0	14.0	10.8
2	5.9	2.2	100.0	0.0	5.9	4.1
3	−7.0	2.0	0.0	100.0	2.0	−2.5
4	5.6	3.1	100.0	0.0	5.6	4.4
87–1	21.1	1.5	100.0	0.0	21.1	11.3
2	4.9	−1.9	100.0	0.0	4.9	1.5
3	6.5	−2.9	100.0	0.0	6.5	1.8
4	−22.2	5.8	0.0	100.0	5.8	−8.2

(continued)

TABLE 3–1 (*Continued*) Allocation Returns with Perfect Knowledge

Date	Actual Quarterly Returns		Crystal Ball Allocation		Crystal Ball Portfolio Return	50% Stock/ 50% Bond Portfolio Return
	Stocks	Bonds	Stocks	Bonds		
88–1	5.7	3.8	100.0	0.0	5.7	4.8
2	6.6	0.4	100.0	0.0	6.6	3.5
3	0.3	1.7	0.0	100.0	1.7	1.0
4	3.1	1.9	100.0	0.0	3.1	2.5
89–1	7.1	1.1	100.0	0.0	7.1	4.1
2	8.7	8.0	100.0	0.0	8.7	8.4
3	10.7	0.9	100.0	0.0	10.7	5.8
4	2.0	3.8	0.0	100.0	3.8	2.9
Averages	4.4%	2.8%	56.8%	43.2%	6.6%	3.6%
SD	7.9	4.8	49.5	49.5	5.7	5.3
		Annualized average =			29.05%	15.29%
		Geometric mean =			25.73	13.95
		Annualized *SD*			11.37	10.54

her return would have been through 1989, compared to having been continually invested 50% in stocks and 50% in bonds. In both cases, we will use the S&P 500 as a proxy for stocks and the Shearson Lehman Government/Corporate Index for bonds.

When persons of wealth hire an investment adviser to manage their stocks or bonds or tax shelters, they expect the adviser to "beat the market." But since the market is now dominated by very intelligent professionals, can the investor really expect his or her stocks or bonds to outperform the other stocks or bonds? Since the market is a net-sum-zero (less transactions costs) game, the investor's hopes are probably unrealistic, particularly concerning the long term.

The real issue is whether the portfolio is structured with the appropriate blend of assets to satisfy the investor's level of risk aversion, at the same taking advantage of the differences in expected returns of each asset class.

In 1986, Brinson, Hood, and Beebower studied the investment performance of 91 large pension funds over a 10-year period. Using correlation analysis, they found a .95 *r*-squared, which is a correlation coefficient of 97%, between the asset mix of the funds and their performance. That means that *less than 5% of the funds' performance was due to things like securities selection and transactions costs*. Other, more recent studies all show that asset allocation accounts for at least 80% of the variance between the return for an individual portfolio and that of the average (typical) portfolio.

The way the Brinson, Hood, and Beebower study was performed seems statistically proper and, if anything, understates the importance of asset allocation during the period that the observations were made. For each of the 91 pension accounts that were analyzed, they created a "shadow" portfolio which was a hypothetical portfolio consisting of the popular stock, bond, and money-market averages. Each of these indices were "owned" in the same proportion as the respective actual securities held by the accounts. If the accounts all performed exactly the same as the "shadow" portfolio, that would have meant that individual securities selection accomplished nothing more than earning an excess return (over the market indices) which was enough to pay for the transactions costs.

The fact is that in each one of the 10 years, the "shadow" portfolio performed about as well as the actual portfolio. This means that if the pension funds had merely owned the equivalent of the popular averages, with no effort being made to select stocks and bonds that would outperform, the funds would have performed no better or worse than they actually did. You must understand that I am not merely saying that, on balance, securities selection was about average—that would almost always be the case, by definition. I am making a general statement that in *each* of the periods the accounts performed according to what would have been expected based *solely* on the percentages each of them held in stocks versus bonds versus cash.

The fact is that for most diversified portfolios the asset mix accounts for far more incremental return than individual securities selection. In the next several chapters, we will be examining the "expected return" aspect of asset allocation. But first, we must analyze what happens to risk (volatility of return) when we own various proportions of stocks and bonds (or any other asset combinations).

ASSET ALLOCATION REDUCES RISK

Figure 3–1 shows the actual annual returns and volatility of those returns over a recent 15-year period for various combinations of stocks and bonds. The vertical axis measures the annualized return for various stock/bond blends maintained during the period. The horizontal axis shows the volatility (standard deviation) of the individual annual returns.

Notice the "hook" shape of the curve. Observe that although stocks (alone) are more than twice as risky (volatile) as bonds, a portfolio with 60% stocks was no more risky than an all-bond portfolio! The lowest risk portfolio was one that contained 30%

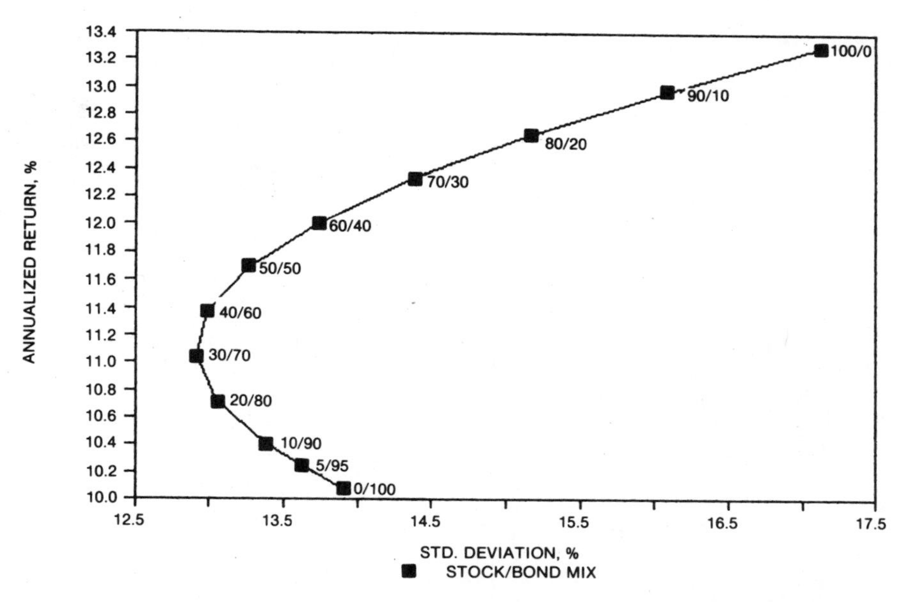

Figure 3–1. Actual Annual Returns and Return Volatility of Various Stock Bond Combinations.

stocks. This is because *stock prices and bond prices do not always move in the same direction!*

The coefficient of correlation between stock and bond returns generally ranges from 0 to 35%. The lower the correlation, the more pronounced the "hook" becomes. The higher the correlation, the more the curve tends to become a straight line, sloping up to the right.

Figure 3–2 displays the "hook curve" in times more "normal" than Figure 3–1, which depicted a period of above-average stock returns and below-average stock-bond correlation.

The fact that stocks and bonds only sometimes move in a synchronized fashion and often move independently or even in opposite directions is the basis for "strategic" allocation, that is, maintaining a long-term "fixed" blend of stocks and bonds. A primarily fixed-income portfolio holding some percentage of equities or an equity portfolio owning some percentage of bonds both have considerably less volatility of return than a single-asset-class portfolio.

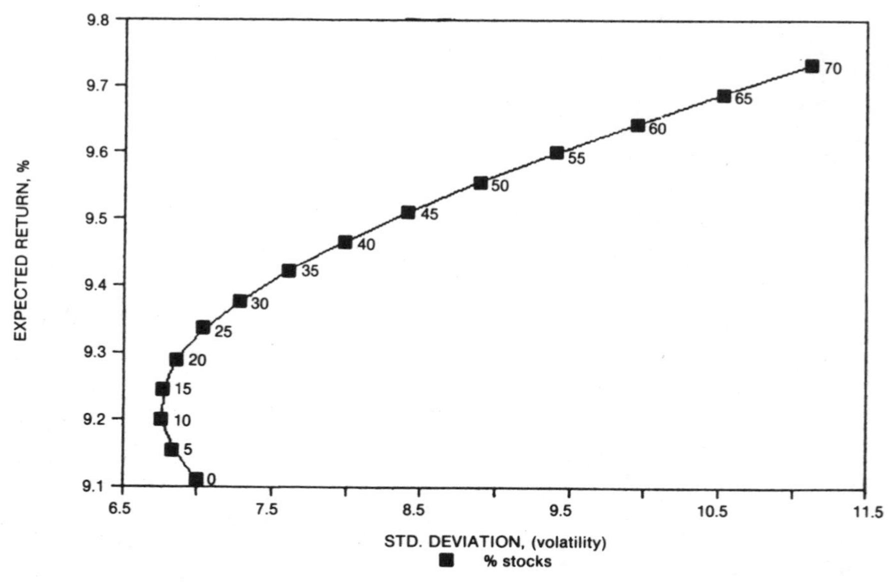

Figure 3–2. Typical Risk/Reward Ratios of a Stock Bond Portfolio.

The obvious question is, if interest rates are one of the three principal factors that determine stock prices, how can stock and bond prices move substantially in opposite directions? One instance would be when the economy suddenly slows and interest rates decline, but lower profits and future dividend expectations more than offset the lower discount factor. Another example would be when profits surge; if inflation and loan demand rise, then bond prices would fall even though stocks could be reacting positively to the improving outlook for cash flow, profits, and dividends.

The logic behind the "hook curve" also applies (but to a lesser degree) to holding a percentage of cash equivalents. Obviously, since cash returns (e.g., T-bill yields) are always positive, they are always opposite in direction to stock and bond returns when the latter are negative (i.e., in a bear market). Less apparent, but just as important, is that when bond and stock returns are positive and improving, cash returns are often declining (even though they remain positive). For example, when interest rates decline, stock and bond returns improve (*ceteris paribus*) while the yield from reinvesting (rolling over) T-bills or money-market funds declines.

THE IMPORTANCE OF LOW CROSS-CORRELATION

The concept of strategic asset allocation can be extended to other types of securities as well: foreign equities, real estate, commodity futures, limited partnerships, and so on. Even though during the 1980s, for example, we witnessed exceptional gains for those owning international equities; the main reason many portfolio managers bought these securities in the first place was because of the low correlation between U.S. stock returns and foreign stock returns. In other words, the low correlation, due both to different securities market behavior and currency translation, allows an investor to reduce portfolio risk by owning a percentage of non-U.S. securities.

In the 1970s, the same was true of oil and gas partnerships. Their value went up for one of the main reasons stock prices went down—higher oil prices.

Investing in gold is a classic example of reducing portfolio risk by owning a high-risk (very volatile) investment. Frequently, the price of gold appreciates along with rising inflation expectations, which, at the same time, cause securities prices to decline. Sometimes this hasn't been a particularly successful strategy in practice, but the theory is that since inflation expectations are the major determinant of interest rates, which are a major factor affecting securities prices, a portfolio manager would do well to invest a portion of a portfolio in an inflation-hedging vehicle such as gold.

In theory, if two very volatile investments had a negative "correlation" (beta of −1.0 relative to each other) and they both had high long-term expected returns of say 20% (because of the high risk), then a portfolio invested 50% in each would have an expected return of 20% and negligible risk (standard deviation of return).

In the real world, it would be difficult to find two investments that move, in the short term, in exact opposite directions, but still both move in a significant upward trend. However, as I have demonstrated, most commonplace investments—stocks, bonds, cash, real estate, and so on—have short-term returns that do not correlate well with each other, but have real long-term expected returns that are positive. This is the phenomenon that provides the investor with the opportunity to temper portfolio risk and simultaneously optimize expected return.

Roger Ibbotson and Rex Sinquefield,* who have probably done the most work with regard to historical relationships between the returns of the various asset classes, calculated the following cross-correlations of returns between 1926 and 1987:

Stocks versus long-term government bonds	11%
Stocks versus long-term corporate bonds	19%
Stocks versus U.S. T-bills	−7%
Long-term government bonds versus T-bills	21%
Corporate bonds versus T-bills	18%

*Roger G. Ibbotson and Rex A. Sinquefield, *Stocks, Bonds, Bills and Inflation: Historical Returns (1926–1987)*. (New York: Dow Jones-Irwin, 1989).

STRATEGY VERSUS TACTICS

The importance of asset allocation in a *strategic* (long-term) sense is that, foremost, it allows the investor to limit his or her level of risk (volatility of return). This enables the establishment of a reward/risk ratio for the portfolio.

The importance of asset allocation in a *tactical* (short-term) sense is that it allows the investor to improve the periodic return of the portfolio beyond the level of the long-term expected return. This is accomplished by dynamically readjusting the percentages invested in each asset class according to their relative levels of attractiveness as measured on some reward/risk or distribution-of-possible-returns basis.

Is it possible to simultaneously accomplish both long-term risk limitation and short-term return optimization? Sophisticated models, such as the type described in Chapter 9, offer this advantage.

The four primary sets of data (for which there are several subsets each) that are the necessary inputs for most asset-allocation models are:

1. The *volatility of returns* for the various asset classes.
2. The *cross-correlation of returns* for the asset groups.
3. The forecasted *expected returns* for each asset class.
4. The investor's *risk profile* and/or *time horizon*.

The first two sets of calculations (volatility and correlation) were described earlier in this book. The third series of projections (expected returns) are the subject matter of the next three chapters.

The fourth group of measurements, the investor's risk profile and time horizon, are often the most difficult to quantify in some respects. Yet, they are the most important aspects of asset allocation. The investor's degree of willingness to accept incremental risk in return for incremental expected return as well as the investor's time horizon (or portfolio's life expectancy) should be the foundation of any system of asset allocation.

The investor often is unable to quantify his or her own willingness to take risk. A self-questionnaire is sometimes helpful as a starting point. Following is a list of some questions the investor, trustee, consultant, or adviser could ask.

RISK-PROFILE QUESTIONNAIRE

Instructions: Circle your first choice and underline your second choice.

1. How would you categorize your investment objectives?
   a. high income
   b. moderate growth and income
   c. above-average growth
   d. aggressive growth

2. Which most closely approximates the annual long-term return you expect?
   a. 6–8%
   b. 9–11%
   c. 12–14%
   d. 15% or more

3. How long might you be willing to sustain a loss while still achieving your long-term objective?
   a. one quarter
   b. six months
   c. one year
   d. two years

4. In the short term, it is most important to outperform . . .
   a. T-bills or CDs
   b. the long-term objective
   c. market indices
   d. other investors

5. Ordinarily, which class of securities should have the heaviest weighting in your fund?
   a. money-market funds
   b. bonds
   c. blue-chip stocks
   d. growth stocks

6. The worst thing that could happen to your account in one year is that it:
   a. shows a return below the inflation rate
   b. shows a negative return
   c. underperforms the market
   d. underperforms other managed accounts
7. The period used to evaluate your return should be over what time horizon?
   a. one year
   b. two years
   c. three years
   d. five years or more
8. Portfolio turnover should not normally exceed (annually):
   a. 25%
   b. 50%
   c. 100%
   d. not sure
9. Good absolute performance depends on:
   a. discipline
   b. patience
   c. knowing when to sell
   d. playing it safe
10. The most important aspect of portfolio management is:
    a. picking the right securities
    b. asset allocation
    c. market timing
    d. diversification

Generally, what will be found is that the investor is willing to *accept* proportionally less risk as the potential risk and expected return levels increase. The investor naturally will accept only minimal risk if the expected return is equivalent to the T-bill rate. He or she will then be willing to accept some sizeable increase in risk for incremental return above the risk-free rate. But then, when the potential volatility becomes too high, the level of risk aversion increases geometrically. Figure 3–3 might describe this general case.

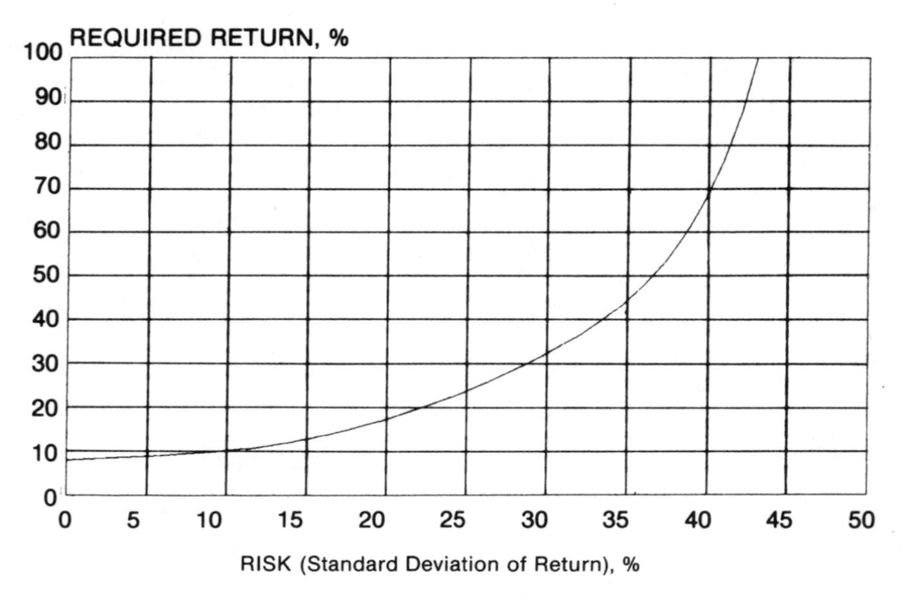

Figure 3–3. Profile of Investor Risk Aversion.

RISK AVERSION IS PECULIAR

Figure 3–3 attempts to explain that the investor readily accepts low levels of volatility; but there comes a point where the volatility becomes almost unacceptable, no matter how high the potential return might be. The point is that the *required reward/risk ratio is not a constant; it is a ratio that changes as the absolute level of risk changes.* This is not as apparent in the 5 to 10% expected return range as it is at higher levels.

It may seem peculiar, but it is true that an investor often is willing to increase his or her portfolio volatility tenfold by switching from money-market funds to common stocks in order to increase his or her expected return by 3%. But he or she may not even consider doubling the volatility above *that* level, no matter how high the expected return of the investment opportunity might be.

What *should* the investor's risk profile be if psychological deterrents were not a factor? Such a determination is always a function of ultimate purpose of the portfolio. The basic question here is, when might the portfolio be partially or entirely liquidated? If the answer is a matter of weeks or months, volatile securities (including common stocks) should be avoided. If the answer is a matter of decades, high-expected-return securities should be emphasized, with little regard for near-term volatility.

The quantification of "time horizon" and its relationship to risk and expected return will be covered in detail in Chapter 9.

SATISFACTION WITH RETURN

The counterpart to risk aversion is reward satisfaction. Just as there is a point above which volatility becomes almost totally unacceptable, there is also a point above which realized return produces little or no incremental satisfaction. This is illustrated in Figure 3–4. Notice how the investor's level of satisfaction increases (or dissatisfaction decreases) dramatically as the realized return nears the

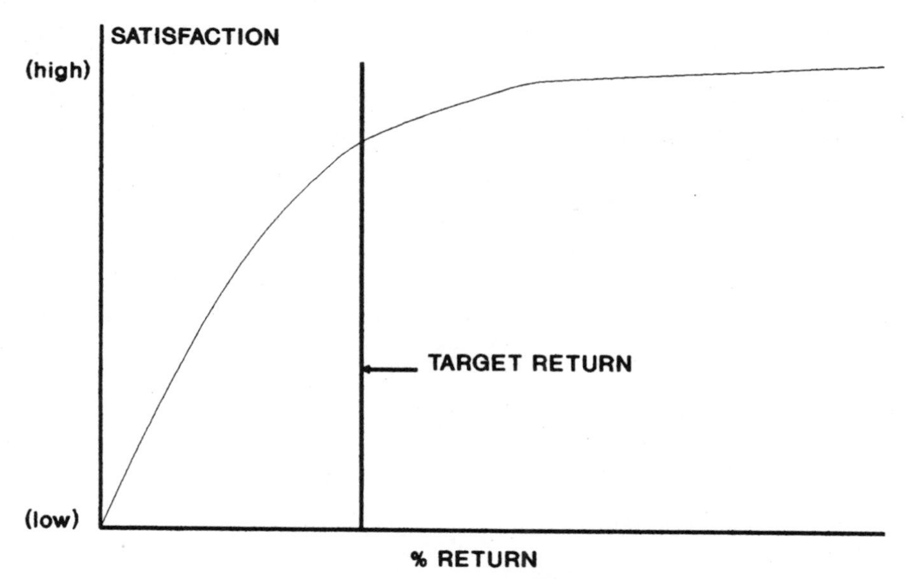

Figure 3–4. Profile of Investor Reward Satisfaction.

TABLE 3–2 Annual Total Returns (1926–1987)

Asset Class	Geometric Mean	Arithmetic Mean
Common Stocks	9.9%	12.0%
Small Company Stocks	12.1	17.7
Long-Term Corp. Bonds	4.9	5.2
Long-Term Gov't Bonds	4.3	4.6
Intermediate Gov'ts	4.8	4.9
U.S. Treasury Bills	3.5	3.5
Inflation Rates	3.0	3.2

Source: Roger G. Ibbotson and Rex A. Sinquefield, *Stocks, Bonds and Inflation: Historical Returns (1926–1987)*. (New York: Dow Jones-Irwin, 1989), p. 14.

expected return, rises somewhat less as this target return is exceeded, and then begins to flatten out. Figures 3–3 and 3–4 point out a very important lesson about investing: Excessive return can be nowhere near as rewarding as excessive risk can be devastating, both psychologically and financially.

HISTORIC RETURNS

To set the stage for the next several chapters, Table 3–2 shows the long-term average annual returns for several classes of securities.

4

Forecasting the Return from Stocks

Get yourself a portfolio of good stocks—and if they don't go up, don't buy 'em.

—*Will Rogers*

GENESIS OF A MODEL

Homer Chapin had a sort of Franklin Delano Roosevelt appearance and style. I don't know whether FDR used to grasp his No. 2 Magnolia pencil with both fists and snap it in half when he became excited, but Homer sometimes did—usually when he was disappointed with one of his subordinates' investment recommendations.

Homer was in charge of the multibillion-dollar investment operation of a major life insurer, where I began my career in the mid-1960s. One day at our morning meeting, I asked, "Mr. Chapin, did you have a chance to read my memo concerning common stock valuation?" Crack! There went the pencil—that was a bad sign. Then he rocked his chair back on its rear legs and began rubbing his forehead with both hands—that was a good sign. "Dave, I think you're on to something. . . ."

I was "on to something." These words came from one of Massachusetts' investments legends, the mailboy who became the wealthy executive vice president of one of the region's largest employers. I was excited. So was Homer, because he often had wondered if there was a quantifiable relationship between a company's dividend, growth rate, and stock price (as elementary as that may seem now). At the time, I didn't know of anyone else who had a dividend-discount model in the 1960s, but I doubted if I was the first.

In 1968, I began the rigorous five-year study program leading to my designation as a chartered financial analyst. It was then that I learned that several academic types already had been developing dividend-based valuation models. In fact, much more recently I even read a tome entitled "The Theory of Investment Value" by John B. Williams published in Cambridge in 1938 and another entitled "The Nature of Capital and Income" by Irving Fisher published in 1906, both of which propose that the value of a common stock is equal to the present value of its expected future dividends.

However, it was the works that had been put forth around 1960 that I became the most interested in. Malkiel and particularly Molodovsky both had published dividend-discount models. Malkiel's model produced a stock value that was equal to the present value of both a constantly growing dividend stream plus a terminal stock value. The latter was a function of the projected earnings and P/E ratio in some final year, with the terminal P/E being based on the expected terminal growth rate of the stock's earnings relative to those of the S&P averages. In place of a constant growth rate and a terminal value, Molodovsky utilized a three-stage dividend growth pattern: an initial growth rate for a select number of years, a linearly declining growth rate for a select number of years, and, finally, a zero growth rate for the indefinite future beyond.

Malkiel used the expected growth rate for the S&P as the discount factor, whereas Molodovsky used the investor's desired rate of return. Neither model was intended to *solve for the discount rate*. In those days prior to the desktop computer, that would have been a very time-consuming operation. The shortfall of these and other earlier models proved to be that the discount rate was usually too low and often the same discount rate was used for all stocks. Discounting the future dividend stream for all companies at the same rate would be equivalent to believing that all bonds should sell at the same yield to maturity, regardless of credit risk!

Scott Bauman came up with an interesting solution to this problem in the mid-1960s. He used a series of discount rates that varied for each stage of a company's growth pattern and generally increased as the projected dividend became more distant.

My own model was a simple one at first, using constant growth and a terminal stock value 20 years out, based on company's historic P/E ratio. Improvements were made later to allow the use of various growth patterns, future discount rates, and terminal-value computations.

The use of any dividend-discount model may not sound very profound today, but back then few other equity-valuation formulas were worth much. The most well-known was Graham and Dodd's formula, which valued a stock on the basis of its P/E ratio being a function of some constant plus a fixed multiple of its expected earnings growth rate. That was it—one variable—growth rate. Later, the formula was modified by Benjamin Graham (considered by many to be the father of modern securities analysis) to include interest rates as a second variable.

YIELD TO MATURITY OF A *STOCK?*

Actually, it was interest rates that had lured me toward a dividend-discount approach. When I graduated from college, I was shocked to find out how many professional investments people did not know the true definition of a bond's *yield to maturity*, which is the rate of interest that will discount all future cash payments of income and principal to a value equal to the bond's market price. The calculation is mathematically more complicated than it sounds, because you must solve for (i) in the following equation (which involves a trial-and-error process, even for a computer):

$$\text{Bond price} = \frac{\text{Payment 1}}{(1+i)^1} + \frac{\text{Payment 2}}{(1+i)^2} + \ldots \frac{\text{Payment } n}{(1+i)^n}$$

where each payment is either interest or principal or both.

Why not use the same formula for valuing a common stock? Can a stock have a yield to maturity? If so, could we compare the yield to maturity of one stock to another or compare that of the stock market to that of the bond market?

These were the questions I was dealing with many years ago. The breakthrough came when I figured that I could substitute some terminal stock value for the redemption value of a bond. Also I could substitute an estimated dividend stream for the bond's constant interest payment in the yield-to-maturity formula. Thus, again solving for (*i*):

$$\text{Stock price} = \frac{\text{Div. (yr. 1)}}{(1+i)^1} + \frac{\text{Div. (yr. 2)}}{(1+i)^2} + \ldots \frac{\text{Terminal Value}}{(1+i)^n}$$

If the terminal value were far enough in the future, the present value of an error in the terminal number would be minimized. The problem, which I didn't work out until a few years later, was that if I used a terminal stock price too far into the future, the growth rate of the dividend stream became very critical. Near-term growth prospects were often exaggerated because of overly optimistic assumptions on the part of the analyst.

My simple dividend-discount model, unfortunately, was not at all perfected by the time Homer Chapin retired in March 1969. For years, he had relied heavily on a company's price/cash flow ratio and earnings yield to identify value.

THE SIGNIFICANCE OF EARNINGS YIELD

The earnings-yield (or capitalization rate, as Homer called it) approach is simple, but is still considered to be superior to dividend yield for comparing stock returns to bond returns.

$$\text{Earnings yield} = \frac{\text{Earnings per share}}{\text{Stock price}} = \frac{\text{E}}{\text{P}} = \frac{1}{\text{P/E ratio}}$$

A stock's *dividend yield*, like a bond's *current yield*, represents the periodic cash returned to the investor. These two types of yield are not comparable, however. This is because the stockholder "receives" an additional periodic amount—that is, retained earnings (earnings per share less dividends per share)—that represents an increase in the book value of the business. In other words, the underlying principal value of a bond is constant, whereas with a stock, it is hoped that the underlying book value grows.

Earnings yield captures a total theoretical "return" to the shareholder—dividend yield plus increase in the net assets of the company. Over time, however, the latter usually understates the stock's price appreciation (in dollars) since most stocks sell at some multiple of book value.

LIMITS OF EXPECTED RETURN

Theoretically, earnings yield identifies the minimum expected return of a stock, and return on equity (ROE, earnings divided by book value) identifies the maximum potential return. Here is why. If a company paid out all of its earnings as dividends, earnings would not grow unless there was either a continual improvement in profitability (higher ROE due to improved margins or better asset turnover) or ongoing changes in capital structure, neither of which can go on indefinitely. In a no-growth situation, dividends would be the only source of shareholder return; that is, expected return would equal dividend yield. Since all earnings would be paid out in this example, dividends would equal earnings. Therefore, expected return would equal earnings yield. That's the no-growth, minimum-return case.

The maximum possible return would occur (but would not be indefinitely sustainable) when a company retained all of its earnings without suffering a drop in return on equity. In this case, expected return would equal earnings growth which would equal ROE.

In reality, companies may attempt to provide the shareholder with an optimal return by increasing the dividend payment (relative to earnings) when the stock price is low compared to book value or earnings or when incremental earnings cannot be reinvested at an acceptable return on assets. Accordingly, an excellent approximation of the long-term total return of a stock is the geometric mean of the minimum and maximum possible returns:

Expected return = square root of (earnings yield × return on equity).

Example: Assume *normal* earnings power is $1.00 per share and book value is $5.00 per share. If the stock's price is $10.00, the earnings yield is 10% and the return on equity is 20%; so the expected return is the square root of (.10 × .20), or 14.1%.

THE T-VALUE

A major improvement to the earnings-yield and ROE approach has been well documented by Preston (Tony) Estep. He analyzed a company's *T value*, which is similar to earnings yield (dividend yield plus growth in net asset value) but includes the additional factor of the change in a stock's price-to-net asset value ratio. Tony demonstrated that if we measured a stock's dividend yield and its earnings retention (increase in net asset value) then added these to its change in valuation (price/book ratio), we would arrive at a very close approximation to the shareholder's total return (from dividends plus appreciation) for the period being measured. The T-value has been proven to be accurate in terms of explaining past total returns for stocks; but it also provides a nice formula for projecting the future return of equities. Here is a much simplified version of the T-value formula as a means of forecasting the expected return for equities:

T-value = dividend yield + annualized change in book value + annualized change in valuation

T-value = (dividend/price) + (ending book value ÷ beginning book value)$^{(1/n)}$ − 1 + (ending price:book ratio ÷ beginning price:book ratio)$^{(1/n)}$ − 1

Obviously, the two key variables in using T-value as a tool for estimating expected return are the terminal price-to-book ratio and the terminal book value which is totally dependent on forecasted return-on-equity and payout ratio over the years. For the terminal price-to-book ratio (P/B), we might consider using one of these three alternatives:

1. The stock's historic average P/B ratio.
2. The stock market's (S&P 500) historic average P/B ratio.
3. A weighted average of #1 and #2, weighting #2 more heavily as the time horizon increases.

The same three alternatives can be used for terminal ROE and payout ratio, which can be phased in over future years to arrive at a terminal book value.

IMPLEMENTING THE DDM

Of the three basic return-type models discussed heretofore—the dividend-discount model (DDM), limits of return, and T-value—the DDM is the most versatile. This is because numerous variables can be massaged in a variety of ways. However, a DDM that begins by calculating normalized basic earnings power (return on equity) has a stronger foundation than a model based on current earnings and consensus growth expectations.

As for projecting return on equity (ROE), there are as many methods as there are pages in this book, since this is the heart of securities analysis. Any realistic method of projecting ROE should involve either "normalized" numbers and/or some sort of phasing technique, which would result in different ROEs for each of the future years being forecasted.

Since either "normalized" or actual ROEs should not be a constant in future years, the DDM provides the most versatile and manageable means of forecasting expected return. The DDM allows the user to vary the *future* growth rates, return on equity, dividend payout ratio, price-to-book ratio, and P/E ratio from period to period. Most importantly for asset-allocation purposes, the DDM gives the user the option of choosing a particular time horizon for the model.

Table 4–1 is a simplified version of a viable dividend-discount model that can be used for individual stock valuation. Notice that the model has two basic classes of outputs: projected and normalized. The projected numbers are driven by an initial growth rate assumption, which is applied to the latest earnings per share (EPS). Over the future years, that initial growth-rate assumption is phased into a terminal-growth assumption which is, in turn, a function of the company's forecasted terminal ROE. This particular model assumes that the terminal ROE (in year 20) is an average of the company's historic (past 10 years) return on equity and that of the S&P 500.

The normalized numbers are driven by a normal ROE assumption, which is either the recent five-year average or some other estimate. Over the future years, this initial normalized return on equity is phased into a terminal ROE assumption which is, in turn, an average of the company's and the market's historic ROE.

Terminal stock prices (which appear in Table 4–1 as the final dividend) are a function of a terminal price/book ratio which, in turn, is an average of the historic P/B ratio for the company and the S&P 500 average. Dividend payout ratios also are normalized and phased into a terminal payout ratio (usually the long-term average for the typical S&P 500 company—say 50%).

The particular methods used for normalizing and phasing can be a function of the company's past earnings stability. For example, substantially different methods can be used for a cyclical company versus a stable-growth company. This is usually an advisable enhancement for a good DDM since ROEs and payout ratios tend to revert to long-term *averages* in the case of cyclical stocks, but more in accordance with long-term *trends* in the case of growth stocks.

Most numbers the analyst enters into the model shown in Table 4–1 (under *Company Data* and *Market Data*) are self-explanatory. The standard deviation (*SD*) represents price volatility which, in part, determines the *Required Hurdle Rate* which must be surpassed by the *Projected Return* and/or the *Normalized Return* in order for the stock to become a "buy." The beta is used, along with the future T-bond-rate assumption, to determine the rate at which the company's dividends will be discounted at the end of each possible time horizon. All the numbers in the columns other than the *Enter* column are generated mechanically from the entered data but can be overridden manually.

Here is one final statement in favor of the dividend-discount approach to equity valuation and expected return. Measurements of earnings and earnings growth are as questionable as raw data itself, but dividends are cash on the barrelhead—you either get them or you don't—no smoke, no mirrors, no FASB opinions, no tests of materiality, no variety of acceptable methods of accounting, no intangibles, no write-offs, no potential dilution, no currency transaction adjustments, no deferred taxes or other reserves, no inflation or replacement-cost adjustment—just real dollar bills!

APPLYING THE DDM TO THE MARKET

Now let's look at a simplified version of the Hammer-Lodefink dividend-discount model for the S&P 500 (see Table 4–2). This model calculates the annualized expected return for the stock market for time horizons of 1 through 20 years. The future dividends are phased and normalized as they are on the individual company DDM. But notice that the annualized expected return for the market (S&P 500) is a *function of the level of interest rates* at the end of each possible time horizon (years 1 through 20)! How these forward rates are computed is the subject of the next chapter. Figure 4–1 shows how the DDM would work assuming a five-year time horizon.

TRADITIONAL VALUATION METHODS

The three methods of estimating equity returns—DDM, T-value, and limits of expected return—have good applicability for projecting stock market returns in an asset-allocation model. This is because these methods all involve long-term expected returns that

TABLE 4–1 **Dividend-Discount Model**

Company Data	Enter	Year	Proj. EPS	Proj. Divs.	Normal EPS	Normal Divs.
Stock Ticker Symbol	PCP	0	1.90	0.08	2.55	0.08
Type (Stable = 1; Cyclical = 2)	1	1	2.25	0.11	2.98	0.13
Stock Price	30.500	2	2.65	0.13	3.46	0.19
SD of Price	0.48	3	3.14	0.16	4.02	0.27
Beta	1.20	4	3.71	0.19	4.65	0.37
EPS (latest 12 months)	$1.90	5	4.38	0.22	5.37	0.50
Dividend (current rate)	$0.08	6	5.16	0.34	6.18	0.65
Projected 5-Yr. EPS Growth	18.2%	7	6.05	0.49	7.09	0.83
Book Value (current)	$14.00	8	7.07	0.67	8.11	1.05
ROE (past 5 years)	18.2%	9	8.22	0.91	9.25	1.31
ROE (past 10 years)	16.6%	10	9.52	1.19	10.52	1.62
Div. Payout (past 5 years)	5.0%	11	10.98	1.54	11.93	1.98
Div. Payout (past 10 years)	6.5%	12	12.61	1.96	13.48	2.40
Price/Book (last 10 years)	2.26	13	14.42	2.46	15.21	2.90
		14	16.43	3.05	17.10	3.47

Market Data	
Price of S&P 500	339.94
5-Yr. Expected Return	8.29%
Standard Deviation	15.68%
ROE (past 10 years)	14.6%
Div. Payout (past 10 years)	48.74%
Price/Book (past 10 years)	1.6
EPS Growth (secular)	6.6%
Risk-Free (T-bill) Rate	8.07%
Current 10-Yr. Note Rate	8.73%
10-Yr. Note in 5 Years	8.93%
Normal Equity Risk Premium	1.38%

Calculated Data	
Current P/E Ratio	16.1
Current Div. Yield	0.26%
Current Price/Book	2.18
Implied 5-Yr. Growth	16.1%
Terminal ROE	15.6%
Terminal Payout Ratio	27.6%
Terminal Price/Book	1.94
Terminal Growth (proj.)	11.1%

15	18.64	3.74	19.17	4.12
16	21.05	4.55	21.44	4.87
17	23.68	5.47	23.91	5.73
18	26.53	6.53	26.60	6.70
19	29.59	7.73	29.50	7.79
20	32.86	396.96	32.64	414.49
Growth =	15.3%	27.2%	13.6%	27.2%

Rates of Return	
Current Required Discount	10.52%
Future Required Discount	10.75%
Required Hurdle Rate	23.66%
Projected Return (5-year)	27.23%
Normalized Return (5-year)	29.00%
Expected Return (10-year)	12.72%
T-value (20-year)	14.16%
NPV (20 years normalized)	$67.73

TABLE 4–2 Standard & Poor's 500 DDM

Enter Market Data	Input	Years	Implied S&P 500 Return	Projected 10-Yr. Note Rates	Normal Divs.	Normal Earnings
Price of S&P 500?	339.94					
3-Month T-Bill Rate?	8.07%	0			($339.94)	$22.73
3-Month CD Rate?	7.86%	1	2.28%	8.88%	$12.10	$24.01
Confidence Index?	95.6	2	5.63%	8.94%	$12.67	$25.35
10-Year T-Note Rate?	8.73%	3	6.98%	8.96%	$13.26	$26.74
Normal Equity Risk Premium?	1.38%	4	7.78%	8.95%	$13.86	$28.20
Dividend of S&P 500?	$11.55	5	8.29%	8.93%	$14.48	$29.71
EPS (current yr. est.)?	$25.25	6	8.59%	8.93%	$15.35	$31.77
Book Value (latest quarter)?	$156.00	7	8.79%	8.94%	$16.29	$33.99
Proj. 5-Yr. EPS Growth?	5.0%	8	8.99%	8.93%	$17.28	$36.39
Normalized Return on Equity?	14.6%	9	9.16%	8.89%	$18.35	$38.97
Terminal Return on Equity?	13.5%	10	9.30%	8.85%	$19.49	$41.76
Terminal Div. Payout Ratio?	48.74%	11	9.40%	8.81%	$21.82	$44.78
Terminal Price/Book?	1.6	12	9.49%	8.74%	$23.34	$47.88
		13	9.57%	8.65%	$24.96	$51.20
		14	9.62%	8.58%	$26.69	$54.76

Calculated Data	Output
Price/Earnings Ratio	13.5
Dividend Yield	3.40%
Proj. Book Value (6 mos.)	$162.85
Proj. ROE (actual in 6 mos.)	15.8%
Initial Growth (normalized)	7.2%
Normalized EPS (current)	$22.73
Payout Ratio (actual)	45.7%
Payout Ratio (normalized)	50.8%
Annual Change in Projected ROE	−0.09%
Annual Change in Normalized ROE	−0.21%
Annual Change in Projected Payout	0.30%
Annual Change in Normalized Payout	−0.42%

15	9.66%	8.49%	$28.54	$58.55
16	9.70%	8.35%	$30.52	$62.61
17	9.69%	8.35%	$32.63	$66.96
18	9.68%	8.35%	$34.90	$71.60
19	9.67%	8.35%	$37.32	$76.57
20	9.65%	8.35%	$39.91	$81.88
Inf.	9.26%		$1,255.75	
		Growth =	6.5%	6.6%

Rates of Return and Fair Values			
T-Value (normalized)	8.72%	Normal Equity Risk Premium	1.38%
Yield + 20-Yr. Div. Growth	9.88%	Current Theoretical Premium	0.82%
Expected Return (implied)	9.66%	Actual Equity Risk Premium	0.57%
Interest Rate Sensitivity	15.66%		
Implied Change in LT Rates	−0.17%		
NPV of Dividends (normal confidence)	$322.54	Percentage Under (Over) Valued	−5.12%
NPV of Dividends (current confidence)	$349.18	Percentage Under (Over) Valued	2.72%

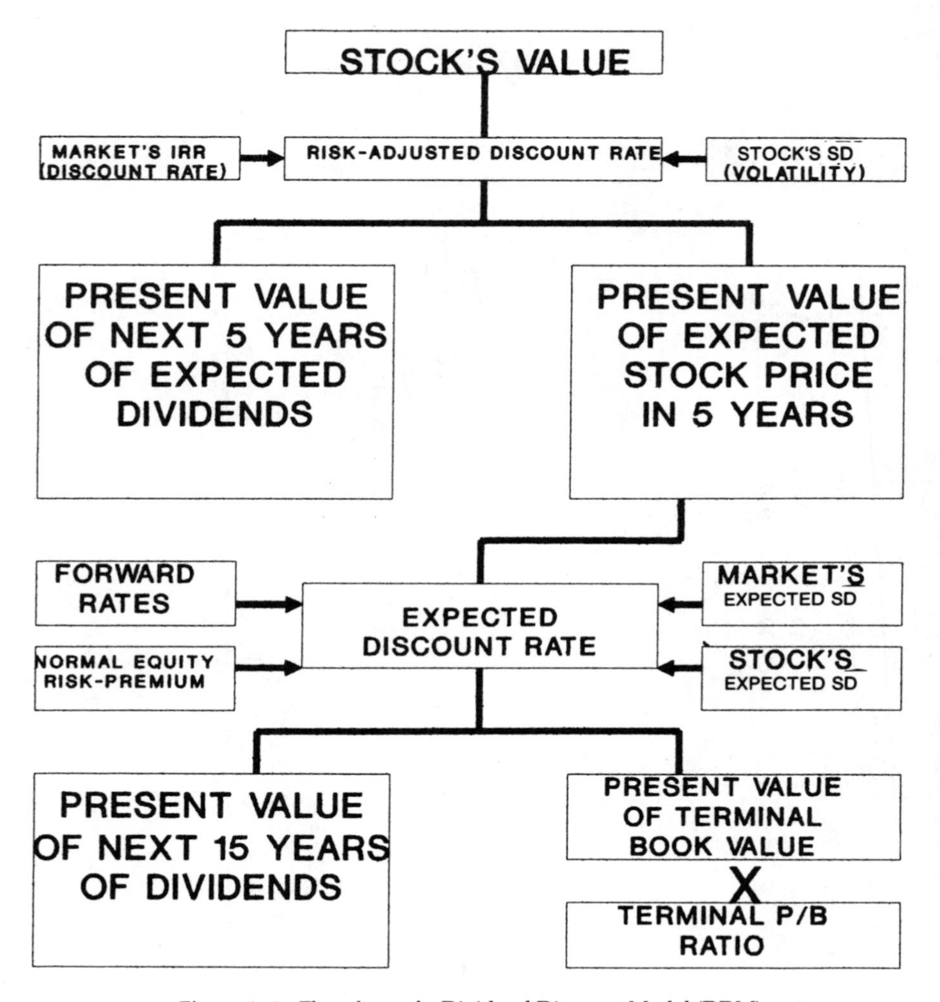

Figure 4–1. Flowchart of a Dividend Discount Model (DDM).

are expressed as an annual percentage and can be compared to bond, money-market, and real estate expected returns.

How much better these quantitative methods are than the valuation techniques of the past! Not so many years ago, most people estimated the return of a common stock by projecting earnings one year into the future then multiplying that estimate by some historic price/earnings ratio to arrive at an expected stock price one year out. The margin for error was enormous, particularly since P/E ratios are not a constant; in fact, future P/E should be one of the solutions to a valuation algorithm, not an input! Price/earnings techniques are of little value in asset-allocation work, not only because of their crudeness, but also because of the lack of comparability to bond and money-market returns.

OTHER METHODS THAT DON'T WORK

Just a few decades ago, quality growth stocks, even of large, established corporations sold as high as 40 to 80 times earnings. A popular, primitive form of the dividend-discount model was partly to blame, because institutional analysts became more "quantitative" before they really understood the mathematics.

Here is what happened. Someone who knew just enough about math to be dangerous knew that the present value of a $1.00 initial payment, growing at constant rate, was equal to $1.00 divided by $(r - g)$, where (r) is the discount rate (or expected return) and (g) is the expected growth rate.

Assume a company's dividend was growing at 6% annually and the stock's intrinsic value was assumed to be the present value of its future dividend stream. Then, if the investor's desired return (or market discount rate) were 10%, the stock would be worth the current dividend divided by (.10 − .06). If the current dividend were $1.00, then the stock would, theoretically, be worth $25 ($1.00 ÷ .04).

But, what if the expected growth rate were 9%. This shortcut, present-value formula would say that the stock was worth $1.00 divided by (.10 − .09), or $100. If the growth rate were 9.5%, the stock would be worth $200. Imagine a $100 increase in valuation due to a half-percent change in expected growth rate! This seems ridiculous, and it is.

The error is not in the math, *per se*, but in the logic. No company can grow indefinitely at a rate exceeding the expected return for the entire market. The stock market represents the value of the bulk of the U.S. (private-sector) economy. If a giant company accounted for, say, 1% of today's economy and grew at 10% per year while the rest of the economy grew at 5%, then after 100 years, this company would account for over 50% of the entire economy! Not only that, but the overall economy would be growing at nearly 8% per year, which implies an unreasonable secular increase in population, productivity, or prices.

Above-average growth rates are not indefinitely sustainable. That is why a modern dividend-discount model normalizes and phases in various stages of profitability for each company and for the popular market averages.

Another simple formula that is still used frequently and could be considered a primitive T-value states that expected return equals dividend yield plus growth. If a company's earning are growing at 10% and the stock's yield is 4%, some would say the expected return is 14%.

Not only is the growth rate questionable over a long time horizon, but if a shorter time horizon is assumed, no consideration is given to the potential change in valuation. The price/earnings or price/book ratios and yield are not constants. If they were, admittedly, the formula would work. But, in the future, these ratios will be a function of growth prospects at the end of the time horizon. Those future prospects will undoubtedly be different than they are today (as will interest rates and equity risk-premiums).

ASSET-VALUE METHODS

A few words should be said about asset values. Although they are of limited usefulness for asset-allocation work, which involves the expected return for a whole basket of stocks, asset values based on *appraised worth* provide excellent means of evaluating the intrinsic worth of *individual* common stocks and, therefore, may be useful in estimating the expected return of a specific, limited portfolio. The theory behind asset valuation is that the value of plant and equipment is not a function of the assets' book values (cost less accumulated depreciation) but rather the present value of the future cash flow they will generate. After all, if you were going to buy someone's business, what would it matter what *he* or *she* paid for it? Your concern is how much cash it will produce for *you*.

In its simplest form, the appraised worth of a company is as follows:

1. Working capital.

Plus: 2. Present value of future cash flow (from *existing* fixed assets).

Less: 3. Present value of future debt service and preferred stock payments.

For example, assume someone owned a small oil company that consisted of negative working capital of $100,000, long-term debt that could be paid off today for $200,000, and one oil well that produced 100 barrels per day. Lifting costs, royalties, and taxes are $5.00 per barrel and reserves are 300,000 barrels, which are declining (along with production) by 12% per year. If you wanted to buy this business for a 15% return on your investment, the only other significant piece of information you would need in order to make a reasonable offer would be the future estimated price of crude oil.

Big corporations can be valued the same way. Throw away the balance sheet and look at the cash being generated and consumed instead. But, what about future growth prospects? That sort of determination would require analysis of either the *cash flow return on inflation-adjusted investment* or cash flow as a percentage of the replacement value of the assets.

CASH FLOW RETURN ON INVESTMENT

This calculation gives the investor an accurate estimate of the incremental return on a dollar of retained earnings being reinvested in the business today. It is an excellent indicator of future growth prospects.

This is a worthwhile exercise for an experienced financial analyst and offers an excellent means of comparing *real* returns of common stocks to inflation-adjusted bond returns. HOLT Value Associates in Chicago has probably done the most work and back-testing for this approach.

Here is the basic formula for the market-derived discount rate or expected return (r):

$$\text{Price} = \text{sum of } \frac{\text{Future net cash flows}}{(1 + r)^n}$$

The investor faces the challenge of forecasting the future cash flows. HOLT solves this problem by using historic averages for cash flow as a percentage of investment (debt plus equity) as well as asset growth. Since 1950, the cash-flow return on investment for the S&P Industrials has been remarkably constant at 6.2% (before inflation). The growth in assets also has been quite constant at 1.8% per year (before inflation). Using these numbers and knowing the percentage of capital represented by debt and equity (and their respective costs), it is possible to estimate the constant-dollar future cash flows and thereby solve for a market-derived discount rate. This discount rate can be added to the expected inflation rate (derived from interest-rate analysis) to arrive at a nominal expected return for stocks which can be compared to that of bonds and cash equivalents.

It is my intent to describe only the technique, on a conceptual basis, for the overall stock market. The actual process is quite complex for individual companies, since it involves creating algorithms for calculating the age and expected life of the assets in order to estimate their replacement cost. A detailed analysis of distortions inherent in accounting statements also must be performed. But, the basic goal is to compute a company's cash flow and asset growth based on the level and trend of returns on today's replacement cost of its assets. These future values can then be compared to the stock's market price to arrive at an implied discount rate (expected return).

FORECASTING THE S&P 500

For asset-allocation purposes, we need to compute the expected return for a portfolio of diversified stocks, preferably over the specific time horizon that reflects the investor's risk profile. Using either the S&P 500 or S&P 400 (whichever is more appropriate) as a proxy for a typical stock portfolio is generally accepted.

In this chapter I have outlined five methods for calculating equity returns:

1. Dividend-discount model
2. T-value
3. Limits-of-return formula
4. Cash-flow return on investment
5. Asset value

The first four are appropriate for forecasting the returns of the S&P indices, with the DDM being the preferred method. There is enough historical data available for these indices to allow them to be analyzed as if they were a single stock. Yet, forecasting will be more accurate for an index than for an individual equity since the data is more stable and, therefore, more easily normalized.

A word of caution! Historical data for the market indices cannot be taken at face value in computing past growth rates. Historic average yields, average P/Es, and average price/book ratios are valid, but because the composition and weightings of the indices change continually, one period cannot be compared to another.

For example, there have been long stretches of time when the dividends and book value of the Dow Jones Industrial Average did not grow. The dividends and book values of the individual companies did grow, however. The catch is that when a stock splits or a new company is substituted in the index, the DJIA "divisor" changes, along with the earnings, dividends, and book value. Past numbers are not restated.

As for the Standard & Poor's Averages, each component company is weighted according to the market value of its outstanding common stock. So the index is never the same from one period to the next.

One viable solution to these distortions is to create a custom index that approximates the popular averages, then average the historic data of the individual companies. In the case of the DJIA, we can use the financial data of the same 30 companies that already comprise the average. It will be discovered that there is a good reason for the price/book ratio of the DJIA to be higher in the 1990s than in the 1970s. In the earlier period, there were no high return-on-equity companies in the average. We will also find that the dividends of the constituent companies have been growing faster than the average.

Also, it is good practice to normalize all the data once it is properly assembled. Even a simple smoothing technique, such as averaging each year's data with that of the year before and year after, is helpful. The stock market looks through the peaks and troughs—and so should you.

Many investment professionals forecast several possible expected returns, each based on different economic scenarios. These possible returns are then assigned probabilities in order to arrive at a weighted mean expected return. The problem with this technique, aside from too many variables, is that the resulting weighted "mean" return is often not the most probable return.

It is recommended that the investor forecast only the most probable return. This "best guess" then becomes the geometric mean and mode (most frequent) expected return around which a series of less probable returns are developed, based on the market's expected volatility (standard deviation). This methodology avoids the necessity of forecasting a multitude of economic variables and estimating each of their probabilities of occurrence. Instead, the most likely return, based on normalized profitability, should remain in the forefront while the economic uncertainties are allowed to be reflected in the estimated volatility of future market returns.

Distribution of possible future returns analysis is detailed in Chapters 8 and 9. There, it will be shown how a little mathematics can be more effective than a lot of economics.

5

Forecasting the Return from Bonds

There is nothing so disastrous as a rational investment in an irrational world.

—*John Maynard Keynes*

AN AFTERNOON AT THE RAT

Richard C. was a stockbroker with a unique skill. Using his senses of sight, smell, and taste, he could distinguish between (and identify) a couple dozen brands of beer in unmarked glasses. My lawyer buddy J.J. Hoare found this hard to believe. So one afternoon, I invited both of them out to the "Rat," the local watering hole which undoubtedly was nicknamed for the quality of its food.

J.J. and I arrived first. As was the custom, I asked the bartender to pour a glass of beer and place it in front of the empty seat where Richard would soon perch. But, this time we threw a curve. J.J. wanted the glass to be filled with draft beer rather than the bottled stuff Richard must have been practicing on at home.

Richard strolled through the doorway with his cowboy boots outside his trousers—sort of different for a Rhode Islander. He assumed his position, held the glass of beer up toward the light, and calmly whispered, "Budweiser." We waited. Then he took one sip, stared at J.J., and said, "Draft."

Legend has it that one of the bartenders at Boston's Parker House finally stumped our boy Richard. He had been saving a decade-old (probably rancid) bottle of imported beer for someone like Richard. When the usual challenge was made, the bartender secretly poured some of the ancient, foul stuff in a shot glass and handed it to Richard who, after taking a sip, screamed, "This tastes like vomit!" The bartender yelled back, "Yeh . . . BUT WHOSE?"

Bonds, like beer, are relatively homogeneous. They are all similar in composition, and it's difficult to ascertain which ones offer the best value. Basically, bonds are all legal instruments whereby the debtor owes the creditor fixed amounts on very specific dates. Accordingly, they all undergo periodic price adjustments in much the same fashion. This is to be distinguished from stocks which move relatively independently from each other because of their uniqueness.

Sometimes, high-quality bonds significantly outperform low-quality bonds and vice versa. Once in a while, a particular corporate or municipal bond moves strictly on its own. But, for the most part, the biggest variations occur because of the particular maturity, or more precisely, *duration* of a bond.

Bonds with long lives are more volatile than notes that mature in a few years. We know that the bond market, overall, has a standard deviation less than half that of common stocks; but, some bonds barely fluctuate at all, while others are as volatile as some stocks.

LIMITATIONS OF MATURITY

To measure the potential volatility of a bond, we must understand the concept of duration, as opposed to maturity. We know that a bond's maturity is the number of years it takes for the investor to receive the full principal amount of the bond (plus interest). But what meaning does this really have? Consider that the principal amount of the bond has little to do with how much the investor paid for it and, most importantly, that the interest (including reinvestment) provides the bulk of the cash flow for most bonds. The main concern involving maturity is credit risk, not systematic market risk. It is the latter (interest-rate risk) that accounts for the majority of the movement in bond prices.

The fact of the matter is, a low-coupon bond maturing in 10 years can be more volatile than a high-coupon bond maturing in 15 years. To calculate a bond's susceptibility to unexpected changes in interest rates, we need to know something about how long it takes for the investor to recover the cash he or she spent for the bond, not just when the final principal payment is made.

ADVANTAGES OF DURATION

Duration is the *average* amount of time (years) it takes for the investor to recover his or her original investment. Consider that the original investment is, in effect, the bond's market price which, by definition, is equal to the present value of all future payments of interest and principal discounted at a rate equal to the bond's yield to maturity. Remember that the present value of any future payment is explained as follows: $PV = FV/(1 + i)^n$, where (i) equals the (annual) discount rate and (n) represents when (in years) the future payment will be received.

To compute duration, all we need to do is weight each future payment (interest on principal) according to the year in which it will be received (multiply by 1, 2, or 3 . . . etc.); take the present value of each weighted future payment and divide the sum of these weighted present values by the bond's market price. Here is one formula:

Duration =

$$\frac{PMT \times 1}{(1+i)^1} + \frac{PMT \times 2}{(1+i)^2} + \ldots \frac{PMT \times n}{(1+i)^n}$$

all divided by Price

where PMT = annual interest and/or principal payments, (i) = the bond's yield to maturity, and (n) = years to maturity.

Note: There are several formulas for duration. This version is Frederick Macaulay's duration.

To give you some perspective, the following table shows the durations of various 8% (semi-annual) coupon bonds selling at par:

Years to Maturity	Duration
5	4.2
10	7.1
15	9.0
20	10.3
25	11.2
30	11.8

A zero-coupon bond has a duration equal to its maturity since there is only one payment. Obviously, the duration of a 20-year zero-coupon bond would be 20 years since:

$$\frac{\text{PMT}}{(1 + i)^{20}} \times 20 = \text{Price} \times 20$$

Figure 5–1 will give you a better "feel" for the way duration is affected by the bond's particular coupon, that is, whether the bond is selling at a premium or a discount to par.

The magical feature of *duration* is that it not only equals the average number of years it takes for the discounted cash payments to equal the market price, but also equals the *percentage change in price that will occur with a 1% change in interest rates*. For example, a bond with a five-year duration will appreciate 5% when its yield to maturity drops 1%.

Note: To calculate this relationship most accurately, divide Macaulay's duration by $(1 + Y/f)$, where (Y) equals the bond's yield to maturity and (f) equals the number of times per year that interest is paid.

SHIFTS IN THE YIELD CURVE

The first problem in forecasting individual bond returns is whether the yield to maturity will change by the same amount that interest rates (in general) change. That will depend on the nature of future yield-curve shifts.

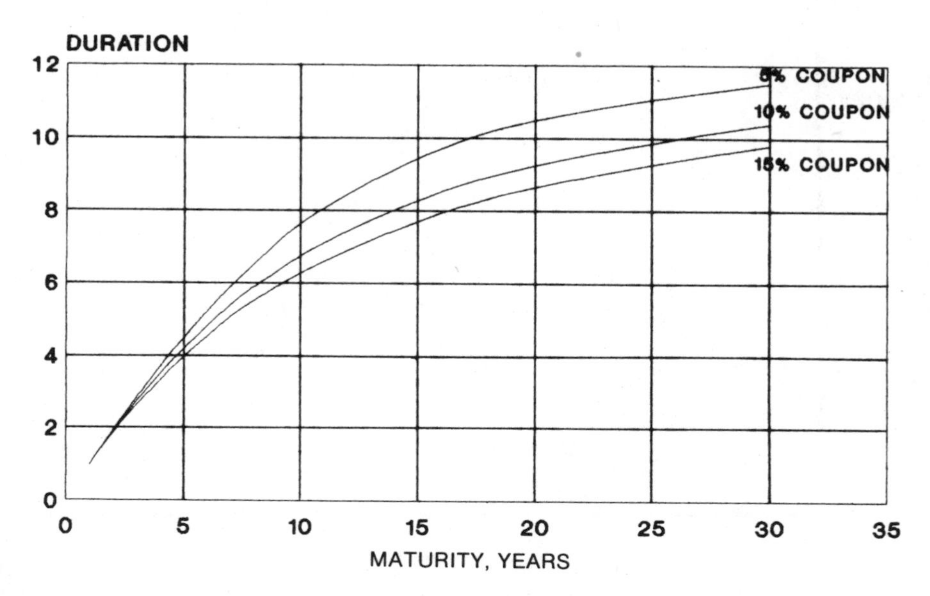

Figure 5–1. Duration of Various Bonds Yielding 10%.

Figure 5–2 shows a "normal" yield curve depicting the various yields of similar quality bonds of various maturities, at a "normal" point in time, that is, when the consensus expectation is for long-term rates to be stable.

When investors believe rates will remain unchanged or believe there is a 50-50 probability of rates moving up versus down, the yield curve slopes up to the right as shown in Figure 5–2. This mainly is due to the greater principal risk and reinvestment-rate risk of longer duration bonds and to "liquidity preference." Investors will accept a lower interest return for shorter maturities in order to be liquid (and come out whole). Similarly, investors demand a higher return for longer maturities since there is greater risk of near-term loss should rates move up unexpectedly. The degree of slope to the normal yield curve is also a function investors' confidence in their interest expectation. Normally, the difference in yield between a 1-year Treasury bill and a 20-year Treasury-bond is 1½ to 2½% (150 to 250 basis points). But, if

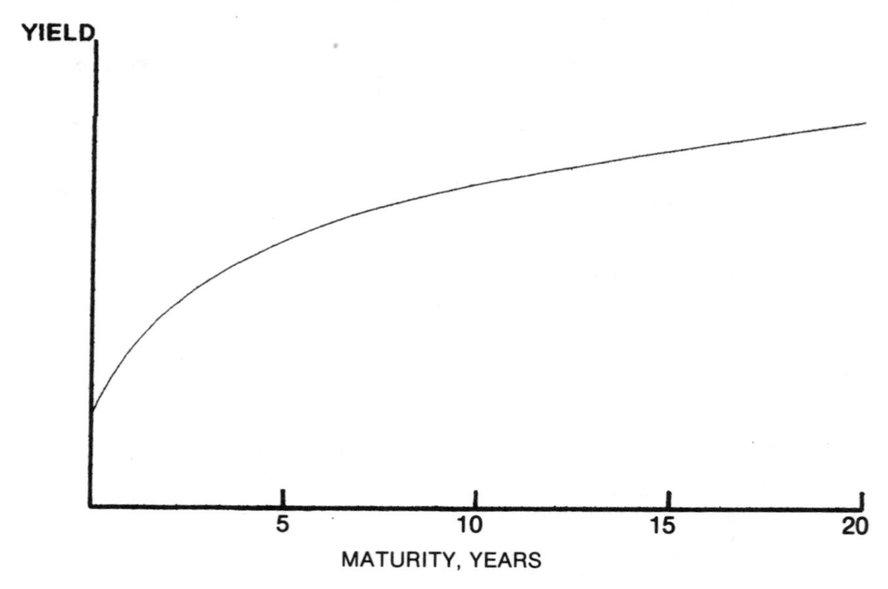

Figure 5–2. Duration versus Yield to Maturity.

interest rate *expectations* change, the *shape* of the yield curve will change.

Notice that the yield of Bond A does not change in Figures 5–3 and 5–4, but the yield of bond B moved dramatically. Thus, changes in the *shape* of the yield curve, which are the result of changes in *expected* rates, affect bond yields very differently, depending on the life of the bond.

Changes in *actual* rates affect the *position*, or level, of the yield curve. Figure 5–5 portrays a "parallel shift" in interest rates. More often than not, shifts in the shape and the position of the yield curve occur simultaneously. This is the first phenomenon that must be dealt with in forecasting bond returns, since individual bond prices do not move in tandem.

IMPORTANCE OF REINVESTMENT

The next issue is that of the *reinvestment rate*. A bond's yield to maturity assumes that the coupon will be reinvested at a rate equal to the original yield to maturity. That's quite an assumption!

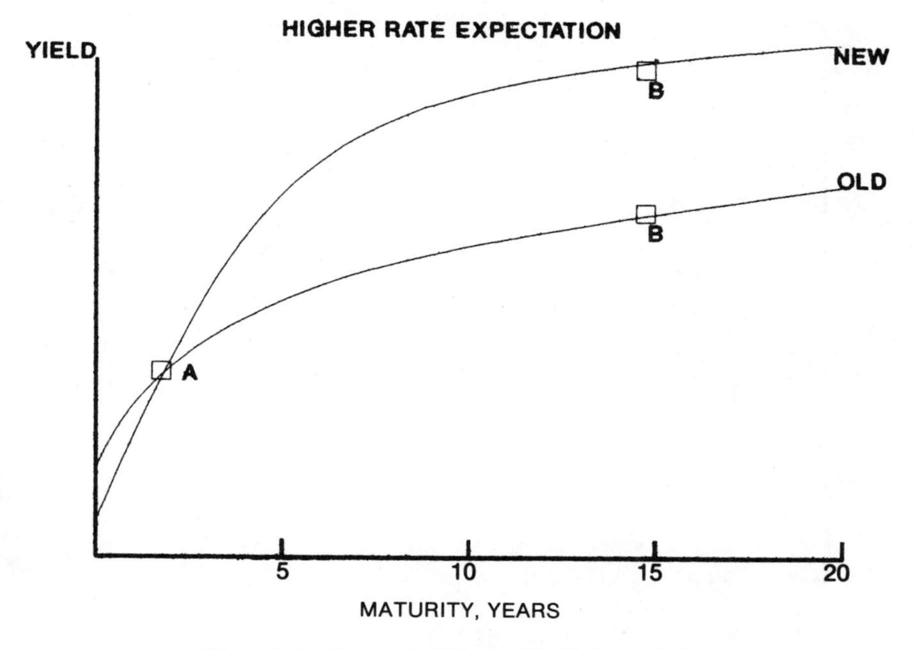

Figure 5–3. Nonparallel Upward Yield-Curve Shift.

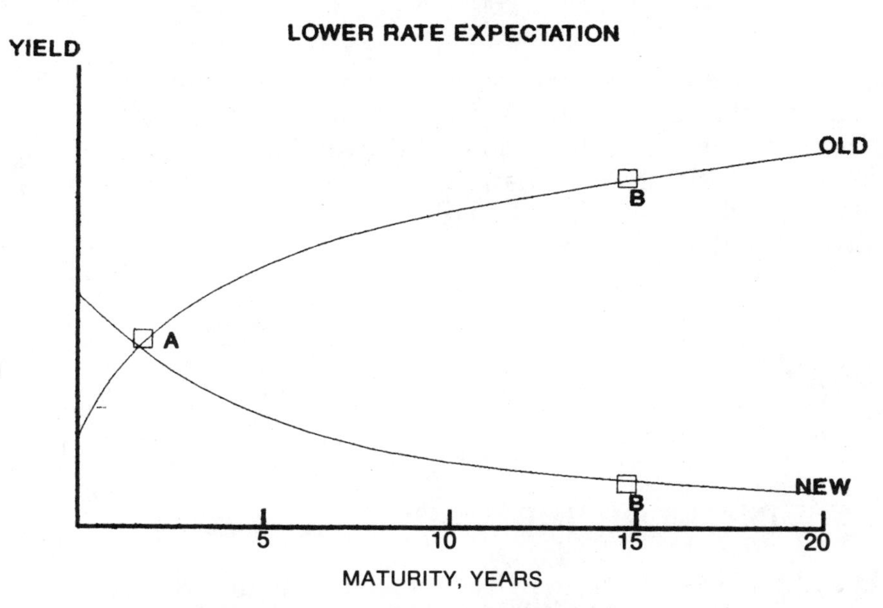

Figure 5–4. Nonparallel Downward Yield-Curve Shift.

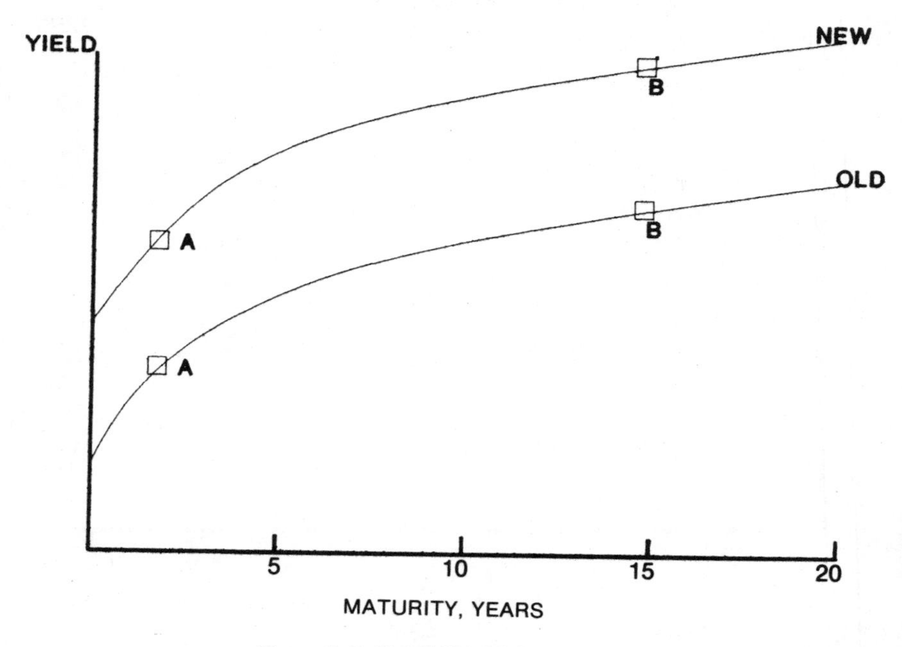

Figure 5–5. Parallel Yield-Curve Shift.

When we buy a 20-year bond at par with an 8% coupon, the yield to maturity is supposedly 8%. But, how can we know that we will be able to reinvest each coupon at 8% over the next 20 years? The following table shows what will happen to that same bond's realized yield should the actual reinvestment rate be 2% higher or lower than the original 8%:

Reinvestment Rate	Effective yield
6%	7.1%
8%	8.0%
10%	9.0%

THE IMPACT OF TIME

In addition to shifts in the yield curve and the uncertainty of the reinvestment rate, a third variable occurs without any changes in rates: the effect of time on a bond's maturity. Assume we have a normal yield curve that never changes shape or position during the life of a bond. The bond might appreciate as its yield drops with each passing year until nearing maturity. Even a bond selling at a premium over redemption value might hold its price for several years. When we buy a 20-year bond, remember that next year it will be a 19-year bond and in two years it will be an 18-year bond, and so on. The bond will "ride the yield curve" or "roll down the yield curve" as shown in Figure 5–6.

CREDIT RISK

The fourth variable in future bond pricing involves the financial position of the issue. Since this book is not intended to be a treatise on securities analysis, let it suffice to say that all non-U.S. government bonds pose some degree of credit risk that affects volatility and expected return.

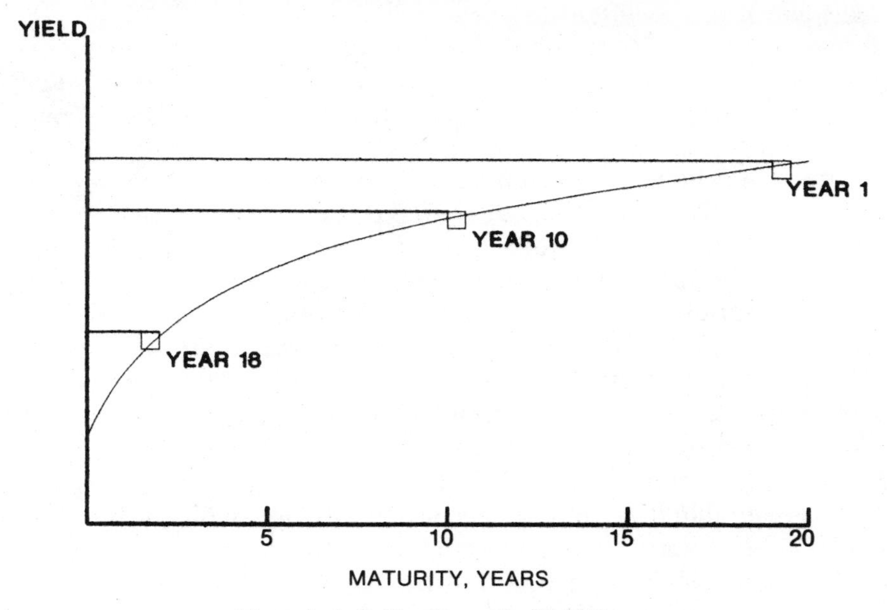

Figure 5–6. Rolling Down the Yield Curve.

Credit risk accounts for most of the specific (viz. systematic) risk of a bond. In a deteriorating economy, high-quality bonds can significantly outperform low-quality issues. History has proven that the potential reward for owning government bonds when entering a recession far outweighs the advantage of the higher coupon associated with corporate debt. This opposite is true when corporate credit improves.

For the remainder of this chapter, we will deal solely with U.S. government bonds, for it is from this credit-risk-free market that we can obtain the information needed to forecast future interest rates that influence returns for all asset classes.

THE TREASURY YIELD CURVE

There is a wealth of information in the shape of the U.S. Treasury yield curve. Since government bonds are credit-risk-free, the shape of the curve primarily reflects the consensus expectation for future U.S. Treasury rates. *Whether the consensus is right or wrong may not be as important to proper asset allocation as just knowing exactly what that consensus expectation is.* Although there is other information (relating to interest-rate risk) in the Treasury yield curve, let us assume for a moment that the curve is merely a reflection of rate expectations.

This hypothetical yield curve would be flat if the consensus expectation was for stable (unchanged) rates for the foreseeable future. It would not matter which maturity was bought, because the return would be the same over the next 30 years. Whether one bought a series of 30 1-year bonds or 6 5-year notes or 3 10-year bonds, the return would be equal under the stable-rate scenario.

What if the consensus called for higher rates? The yield curve would have a positive slope, that is, long-term bonds would yield more than short-term maturities that could be rolled into higher yielding notes more frequently without loss of principal. The curve would resemble the "new" curve shown in Figure 5–3. When the expectation is for lower rates, most investors want to own long-term bonds to lock in the high returns before they disappear. This causes the price of short-term bonds to fall and their yields to rise above the long-term rate. This creates what is known as an *inverted yield curve* (shown as the "new" curve in Figure 5–4).

THE RISK ELEMENT

In reality, a normal Treasury yield curve is not flat; it slopes up to the right, with a lessening slope as the maturity lengthens. Let's examine why.

It is tradition that the existing yield curve represents the available ability to increase return by extending maturity. This implies a direct reward/risk relationship between yield and maturity. This is such an incomplete equation that it is almost inaccurate.

If we were to exclude the rate-expectation element from the yield curve, the resulting residual curve always would be positively sloped, as in Figure 5–2, for four principal reasons:

1. Longer maturities generally have longer durations; therefore, they have prices that are more volatile. Investors must be compensated for *principal risk* over time horizons that may be nearer than the maturity date of the bond.
2. As described earlier in the section on "Importance of Reinvestment," the longer the life of the bond, the greater the *reinvestment-rate risk*. The higher the bond's coupon and the longer the maturity, the more it is affected by available reinvestment rates. As maturity lengthens, the absolute standard deviation of future interest rates widens, which affects the potential interest that will be earned on the future coupon payments.
3. All other things being equal, investors still prefer liquidity. Although Treasury issues are extremely marketable, there are both transaction costs and a psychological aversion to having to sell a bill or note rather than having it mature. *Liquidity preference* primarily affects the very short end of the yield curve (T-bills) and explains why the left end of the yield curve has a steeper slope than it mathematically should (based solely on interest-rate risk). For example, when an individual

goes to the bank to buy a CD or T-bill, he or she intends to hold it to maturity; therefore, if the rates were the same for all maturities, most investors would buy the shorter instruments. All other things being equal, people would rather have their investments converted into cash sooner than later.

4. Investor confidence plays a major role in determining the steepness of the yield curve. Here we are not referring to investor sentiment, but rather to the collective confidence of those comprising the consensus—confidence that their rate expectations are accurate. The consensus future-rate expectation, like all other consensus expectations, is a weighted average around which there are varying degrees of deviation. When the public is not sure of the future, the distribution of rate expectations widens, causing an increase in the *perceived variance* (risk) associated with future rates.

Factors 1 and 2 are very quantifiable using elementary mathematics. Factors 3 and 4 also can be determined, but with a great deal of effort. Liquidity preference and confidence measurement (and projection) are at the heart of the Hammer-Lodefink asset-allocation model described in Chapter 9.

THE FORWARD RATE ELEMENT

In the previous section, we excluded the rate-expectation element from the yield curve in order to discuss the risk-related elements. Now let's reverse this and assume we can mathematically back out the risk factors, leaving us with a residual curve that portrays only the consensus expectation for future interest rates.

Mathematically, such a yield curve would comprise a series of points where the value of each point would represent the compounding of all the expected T-bill rates up to and including that point.

For example, the point representing the present yield for the 20-year bond would be equal to the compounding of all expected 1-year T-bill rates from now through year 20. Similarly, the yield for the 20-year bond would represent the present 10-year bond yield compounded with the expected yield of the 10-year bond, 10 years from now. Likewise, the 20-year bond yield might portray today's 5-year bond yield compounded with the expected yield of a 15-year bond to be issued in 5 years. The list of possible calculations goes on and on.

Here is a simple example. Suppose that the two-year Treasury note presently yields 8% and the one-year Treasury bill yields 7%. Applying forward-rate theory to our hypothetical risk-free residual curve, the market *must* expect that one-year rates will be slightly over 9% next year. Otherwise, why would people be buying (and selling) the two-year note on an 8% basis if they could get more (or less) return by buying the one-year bill and rolling it to a new one-year bill 12 months from now? By knowing the yield on any two existing T-bonds having different maturities, we can compute the expected yield for a hypothetical bond—one to be issued when the first bond matures and to mature at the same time that the second bond matures.

For example, if we wanted to know the market's expected return for a 4-year bond six years from now, all we need to know (to get started) is the present yield to maturity of the 6-year bond and the 10-year bond as follows:

$$(1 + x_a) = \frac{(1 + i_b)^b}{(1 + i_{b-a})^{(b-a)}}$$

where (a) = the life of the future bond in question, whose yield is (x); (b) = the number of years from now it will mature; therefore, $(b - a)$ = the number of years from now it will be issued or bought.

So, in this example, if the 6-year bond now yields 8% and the 10-year bond yields 9%, then the expected yield of a 4-year bond 6 years from now is:

$$(1 + x)^4 = \frac{1.09^{10}}{1.08^6}$$

$$x = \sqrt[4]{(1.09)^{10} \div (1.08)^6} - 1$$

$$x = (2.37 \div 1.59)^{.25} - 1 = .105 = 10.5\%$$

By using this equation, it is possible to forecast interest rates for any maturity at any point in the future (albeit with the questionable accuracy of the consensus).

Table 5–1 takes an existing yield curve and extrapolates the expected rates for 1, 5, and 10 years into the future, and Figure 5–7 shows the current and projected yield curve.

Remember, this example does not take into consideration the normal positive slope of the yield curve; it hypothesizes that the "normal" yield curve is flat or that the risk factors (discussed earlier) have been backed out of the existing curve. A workable model would have to do the latter. (The Hammer-Lodefink model does this in a proprietary fashion. It also adds back the expected future risk factors for forward-yield curves.)

Once we have calculated what future yield curves are expected to look like, it should be obvious that we can then calculate the

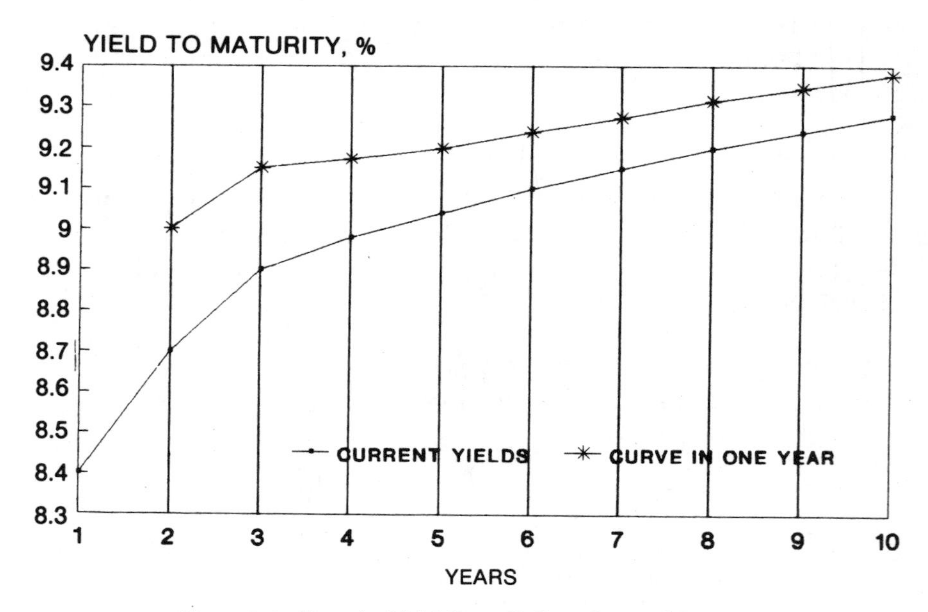

Figure 5–7. How the Yield Curve Reflects Forward Rates.

TABLE 5–1 Existing Yield Curve and Expected Future Rates

Period	Month	Year	Present Yield Curve	Implied Curve 1 Yr. Out	Implied Curve 5 Yrs. Out	One-Year Return by Maturity	Duration (Risk)	Implied Future T-Bill	Implied Future 10 Yr. Note
1	3	91	8.40%			8.40%	0.963	9.00%	9.41%
2	3	92	8.70	9.00%		8.42	1.925	9.30	9.48
3	3	93	8.90	9.15		8.46	2.783	9.22	9.52
4	3	94	8.98	9.17		8.49	3.577	9.28	9.57
5	3	95	9.04	9.20		8.52	4.312	9.40	9.61
6	3	96	9.10	9.24	9.40%	8.56	4.993	9.45	9.64
7	3	97	9.15	9.28	9.43	8.59	5.623	9.55	9.68
8	3	98	9.20	9.31	9.47	8.63	6.206	9.56	9.70
9	3	99	9.24	9.35	9.49	8.66	6.747	9.64	9.73
10	3	00	9.28	9.38	9.52	8.70	7.247	9.72	9.74
11	3	01	9.32	9.41	9.55	8.74	7.710	9.68	9.74
12	3	02	9.35	9.44	9.57	8.77	8.140	9.74	9.75
13	3	03	9.38	9.46	9.59	8.81	8.536	9.66	9.75
14	3	04	9.40	9.48	9.60	8.84	8.904	9.70	9.76
15	3	05	9.42	9.49	9.61	8.87	9.244	9.74	9.75
16	3	06	9.44	9.51	9.62	8.89	9.599	9.78	9.73
17	3	07	9.46	9.53	9.64	8.92	9.851	9.82	9.73
18	3	08	9.48	9.54	9.65	8.95	10.122	9.86	9.73
19	3	09	9.50	9.56	9.66	8.98	10.372	9.70	9.73
20	3	10	9.51	9.57	9.67	9.00	10.604	9.72	9.73

expected return (including reinvestment of interest) for any Treasury bond over any time horizon.

Recall our previous discussion of "riding" or "rolling down" the yield curve. Today's 10-year bond will be the 8-year bond in 2 years. If we know what the 8-year bond should yield in 2 years we will then know its expected price in 2 years. Thus, we can easily compute the 2-year expected price change. We know how much interest we will receive over the next 2 years, and since we know what future short-term rates are supposed to be, we can also compute the interest on interest (reinvestment rates). Accordingly, we can arrive at the *market's best guess* of what the total effective yield will be for purchasing a 10-year bond today and holding it for 2 years.

ON THE ROAD TO ASSET ALLOCATION

If we did the calculations (described in the previous paragraph) for a typical portfolio of bonds, such as an appropriate Government Bond Index, we could arrive at an expected return for the Treasury-bond market over any time horizon. Then we could compare this to the expected return for the stock market (S&P 500) for the same time horizon. Better yet, we could calculate the year by year expected return of a bond portfolio that maintains a constant (rolling) maturity or duration. We would be on the road to asset allocation!

What about all the economic variables and vagaries such as inflation, taxation, the dollar, unemployment, productivity, recession, loan demand, and so forth? The consensus estimates for all of these factors already are built into the yield curve (as we have defined it).

What if the consensus is wrong? If the consensus were not wrong, bond prices would be stable or would move in a predictable straight-line manner. But they don't. Changes in the consensus are what cause price volatility, but that volatility can be factored in to an asset-allocation model by forecasting the future range of possible returns using the arithmetic already described in Chapter 2 as part of the statistical techniques to be discussed in Chapters 9 and 10. Figure 5–8 shows a range of possible returns from bonds.

I believe that the predictability of the yield curve is greatly enhanced by assuming the curve has several layers or components: rate expectations, duration risk of principal, reinvestment-rate risk, liquidity preference, and investor confidence. I also feel that it is extremely productive, for allocation purposes, to forecast the expected return of a bond *portfolio* over the investor's particular time horizon. This technique is superior to the often-seen method of using the yield to maturity of a single Treasury bond (bearing some arbitrary maturity or even the same maturity as the investor's time horizon) as the expected return.

I acknowledge the viability of several interest-rate forecasting techniques, including the use of Treasury futures. It is the intent of this book, however, to concentrate on the methodologies that have worked the best for me over the years.

RIDING THE YIELD CURVE

If we believe that expected return is only the "best guess" around which there is an entire distribution of possible (but less probable) returns, as shown in Figure 5–8, "riding" or "rolling down" the yield curve, in and of itself, is a defensible means of determining expected return.

Under this method, no assumption is made about yield-curve shifts. The investor merely computes the expected return for each bond in the "market portfolio" by calculating what its return will be as it rolls down the yield curve over the chosen time horizon (refer back to Figure 5–6). Figure 5–9 and Table 5–2 show the computation of one-year expected returns for various maturities, based on the actual U.S. Treasury yield curve on April 2, 1990. Under the concept of "rolling yields," the one-year expected return is merely the bond's coupon plus the price change due to the one-year shortening of maturity. For simplicity, it is assumed each bond presently sells at par (100). These rolling returns become the expected (most likely) returns for the various bonds, around which

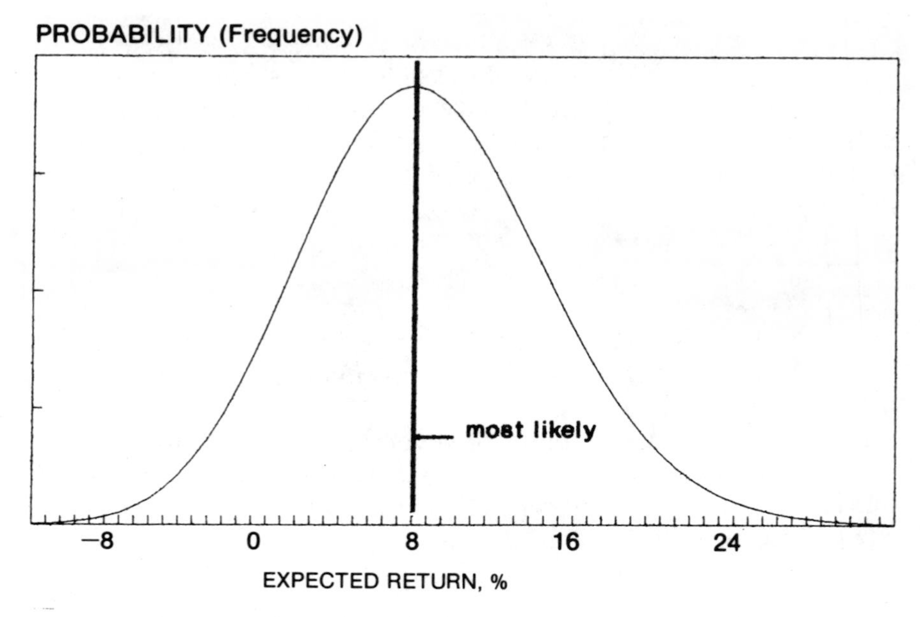

Figure 5–8. Using Probability Theory to Account for Uncertainty.

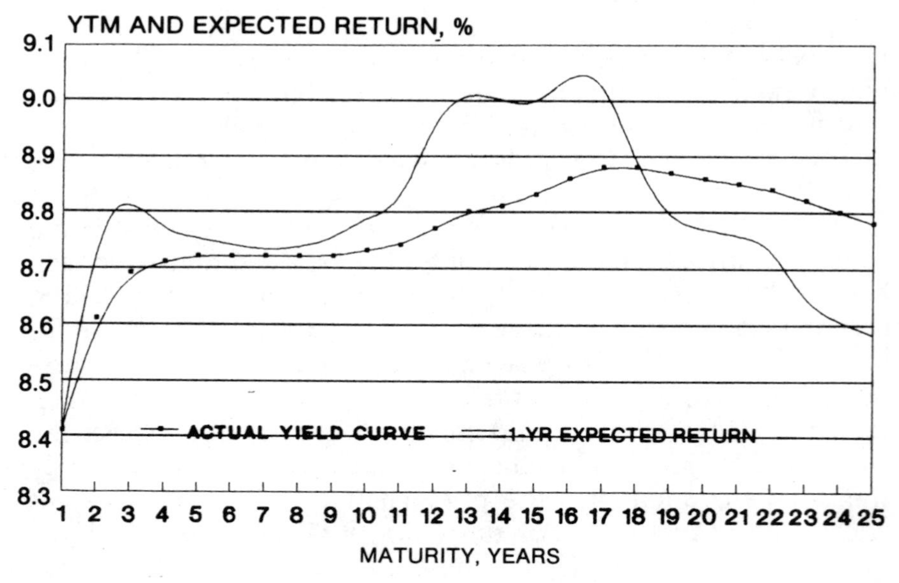

Figure 5–9. One-Year Rolling Returns.

TABLE 5–2 One-Year Expected Returns for Various Maturities

Maturity	4/2/90 Yield Curve	Next Year's Price	One-Year Return
1	8.41%	100.00	8.41%
2	8.61	100.18	8.79
3	8.69	100.14	8.83
4	8.71	100.05	8.76
5	8.72	100.03	8.75
6	8.72	100.00	8.72
7	8.72	100.00	8.72
8	8.72	100.00	8.72
9	8.72	100.00	8.72
10	8.73	100.06	8.79
11	8.74	100.06	8.80
12	8.77	100.21	8.98
13	8.80	100.22	9.02
14	8.81	100.08	8.89
15	8.83	100.16	8.99
16	8.86	100.24	9.10
17	8.88	100.17	9.05
18	8.88	100.00	8.88
19	8.87	99.91	8.78
20	8.86	99.91	8.77

there is a distribution of other possible, but less probable, returns as shown in Figure 5–8.

The use and derivation of "distribution of possible returns" will be discussed in detail in Chapter 8.

FORWARD RATE THEORY

Let us define the *normal yield curve* as the positively sloped curve that would exist at a particular point in time if the consensus expectation called for no change in rates, that is, no change in the shape or position of the yield curve. That curve would have the appearance of Figure 5–2 and would generally be positively sloped about 200 basis points (2 percentage points) between the T-bill and the 20-year bond. The slope would be higher in periods of low confidence and lower in periods of high confidence, as will be discussed in the next section.

This means that the *duration risk-premium* of a 20-year bond averages about 200 basis points. A 10-year bond would have a duration risk-premium of nearer 140 basis points since its duration is roughly 65 to 75% of that of a 20-year bond (depending on the coupon relative to the level of interest rates, as shown earlier).

If we know the duration of the various (current coupon) maturities, we can then "back out" the duration risk-premiums to obtain a residual curve with which to forecast residual rates in any future years. We then can add back the appropriate duration risk-premiums to obtain an actual forecasted yield curve (see Table 5–3).

We have taken what appears to be a roundabout way of forecasting forward rates by subtracting, then adding back, duration risk-premium. This has been done for a reason: Suppose today's "normal yield curve" is not normal—that confidence is abnormally high or low. We may want to back out *different* duration-risk premiums from the current curve compared to what we add back to future curves. *This technique is, in fact, what allows forward-rate theory to become a viable method* for forecasting future rates and returns.

FORWARD RATES IN THE REAL WORLD

As a student of investments history, I will be the first to admit that the use of pure forward-rate theory can be of questionable value. There have been sustained periods where the slope of the yield curve has not been indicative of the future direction of interest rates. In fact, during the 1980s there was actually a negative correlation between the slope of the yield curve and the one-year forward change in rates.

As a result, much can be said in favor of forecasting bond returns under the assumption of "rolling down" a motionless yield curve. This method is very acceptable for short-term forecasts. It even can be enhanced by calculating the "rolling yields" under

TABLE 5–3 Modified Forward Rate Theory

Maturity	Duration	Actual Yield Curve	Duration Risk-Premium	Residual Curve	Residual Curve 1 Yr. Out	Actual Curve F'cast	Residual Curve 5 Yrs. Out	Actual Curve F'cast
1	1.0	8.41%	0.18%	8.23%				
2	1.9	8.61	0.36	8.25	8.36%	8.54%		
3	2.8	8.69	0.52	8.17	8.32	8.68		
4	3.6	8.71	0.67	8.04	8.23	8.76		
5	4.3	8.72	0.81	7.91	8.16	8.84		
6	5.0	8.72	0.94	7.78	8.10	8.91	7.14%	7.32%
7	5.6	8.72	1.06	7.66	8.04	8.98	7.04	7.41
8	6.2	8.72	1.17	7.55	7.98	9.04	6.96	7.48
9	6.7	8.72	1.27	7.45	7.94	9.11	6.88	7.55
10	7.2	8.73	1.37	7.36	7.90	9.18	6.82	7.64
11	7.7	8.74	1.45	7.29	7.88	9.24	6.77	7.71
12	8.1	8.77	1.54	7.23	7.87	9.33	6.76	7.82
13	8.5	8.80	1.61	7.19	7.87	9.41	6.74	7.92
14	8.9	8.81	1.68	7.13	7.85	9.46	6.70	7.97
15	9.2	8.83	1.74	7.09	7.85	9.52	6.68	8.05
16	9.6	8.86	1.81	7.05	7.84	9.59	6.66	8.12
17	9.9	8.88	1.86	7.02	7.85	9.66	6.66	8.19
18	10.1	8.88	1.91	6.97	7.83	9.68	6.61	8.22
19	10.4	8.87	1.96	6.91	7.80	9.70	6.56	8.24
20	10.6	8.86	2.00	6.86	7.77	9.72	6.51	8.26

assumptions of interest rates moving 1 to 1.5% higher or lower (about one annual standard deviation) with either equal or weighted probability.

However, dynamic asset allocation (viz. tactical asset allocation) concerns itself with expected returns over time horizons longer than 6 to 12 months. With longer time horizons, forward-rate theory becomes more predictive; that is, there is a meaningful positive correlation between the slope of the yield curve and the change in interest rates two to five years out. Most importantly, we can enhance the predictability of the yield curve by making an effort to back out accurate levels (depending on the level of investor confidence) of duration risk-premium.

CONFIDENCE AS THE KEY

Earlier in this chapter, I outlined a variety of factors that entered into the shape of any yield curve. There are really only three meaningful *variables:* rate expectations, rate volatility, and investor confidence. These are what determine the risk and return over a specific time horizon.

Suppose we were in a period that might be characterized by the following:

1. Low yield spreads between T-bills and CDs.
2. Low yield spreads between T-bills and commercial paper.
3. Low spreads between high-quality and medium-quality bonds.
4. Low bond-price volatility.
5. A narrow range of the future rate expectations that make up the consensus.
6. A small equity risk-premium (based on the internal rate of return of a stock market dividend-discount model) relative to long-term government bond yields.

This would represent a period of *high confidence* and the yield curve would be less positively sloped than it would normally be otherwise. Investor concern with volatility risk is diminished!

Accordingly, the residual curve with which we had forecasted rates earlier would be determined by backing out much less than (the historic average of up to) 250 basis points of duration risk-premium. How much less? Over the years, we have developed and maintained algorithms that quantify investor confidence in the form of indices that can be used for this purpose. Also, by subtracting a lesser amount of duration risk-premium from the present curve (or adding back more to future curves) in periods of high confidence, and doing the opposite in times of low confidence, the yield curve becomes quite predictive. This is particularly true for time horizons of several years. This method even can call for higher rates in an inverted-yield-curve environment!

Have you noticed that the spreads and variances outlined in items 1 through 6 are very high when interest rates are at secular peaks? The reverse is true, also.

In Chapters 8 and 9, it also will be shown that when confidence is low (usually meaning bond volatility is high) the probability of bonds outperforming a high target return goes up dramatically.

6

Forecasting Money-Market Returns

Information about money has become almost as important as money itself.
—*Walter Wriston*

WATCH OUT!

I know a fellow (who shall go nameless for obvious reasons) whose average longevity in his series of jobs as chief investment officer of various investment organizations has been about 11.9 months. Some facetiously say that he likes to travel—even if it means bringing all of his belongings with him! It was probably never meant for him to be an investments professional, as was the case with the other mullets he associated with. Successful investors are usually imaginative, broad-minded, innovative, respectful for the opinion of the crowd, and yet are often contrarian, analytical, sometimes humble, and all the other things this character is not.

History often can repeat itself, if you allow it to. My anonymous acquaintance allows it to. For example, about one year after every major market bottom, he will inevitably say something like, "Stocks were up 20% last year. . . . that's triple the market's normal appreciation. . . . this can't continue forever."

The statement I remember the most, maybe because he said it twice (several years apart), typified his simple logic: "Stocks and bonds haven't been returning anything lately and money-market funds are yielding over 10%. . . . let's put our money where we know we can get the return."

When money markets offer a higher yield than bonds, watch out! This is an inverted yield curve and it usually means rates are to come down in the near future. The period of the early 1980s was very much an exception. Of course, that time, our chief investment officer was impressed with the high yield on long-term bonds relative to the 1960s, so he "went long" years too early.

Dynamic asset allocation avoids the pitfall of mixing apples and oranges (with a banana thrown in) that disables many tactical allocators. That pitfall is comparing the *long-term* expected return for bonds with the *going rate* on cash equivalents, or comparing the expected return of a stock market dividend-discount model (which is, by definition, long term) with the current yield of a money-market fund.

I've been in the investments business a long time and never have known anyone who could scientifically determine the *short-term* expected return of stocks or bonds. So of what use is it to factor the "going rate" on cash equivalents? What do we compare it to?

As a general statement, when money-market rates are high, either they are headed lower or the probable future returns of stocks and bonds are even higher. This may not be obvious at the time, but would become more apparent if we were to calculate bond and stock returns using forward rates and future discount factors. We also should strive to forecast money-market returns over the investor's time horizon as we do for stock and bond returns.

ARE T-BILLS REALLY RISK-FREE?

Although there is no *credit* risk with any U.S. Treasury security, none of them, including T-bills, are risk-free from the standpoint of return over time. Throughout this book, I have defined risk as being equivalent to volatility of return. Over half the time, T-bill returns vary by more than 1.5% per year!

If the benchmark 90-day T-bill presently yields 6%, that does not mean the T-bill will return 6% over the entire investment time horizon. It might yield more or less in the future. Therefore, T-bills offer significant reinvestment risk—and reinvestment opportunity.

THE SIGNIFICANCE OF TIME

When I entered this business in the mid-1960s, T-bills were yielding only 3 to 4%. Bonds had yields of 6 to 7% and stocks had been returning over 10% like clockwork. But, that was just the time everyone should have been buying T-bills! The Dow Jones Average wouldn't close over the 1,000 level again for many years, and bonds were about to enter a decade where depreciation of market value would nearly offset the coupon almost every year. Meanwhile, cash returns were (naturally) positive and were to increase annually.

The point is that the investors need to project cash-equivalent returns over the same time period they are projecting stock or bond returns. This is so they can have an idea of which class of investment offers the greatest return over that time horizon. Yield-curve analysis is at least a starting point since it contains information about what the consensus believes future T-bill rates will be.

PROJECTING SHORT-TERM RATES

Here is an example of how to calculate the market's expectation of future one-year T-bill rates. In words, to find the expected one-year bill rate one year from now, simply divide the compounded yield of the present two-year note by the yield of the present one-year bill. To find the expected T-bill rate five years from now, divide the compounded six-year rate by the compounded five-year rate, and so on. The formula is the same as the one we used in the last chapter regarding forward rates, except here we will simplify it specifically for forecasting the one-year T-bill rate (T).

$$T_n = \frac{(1 + i_{n+1})^{n+1}}{(1 + i_n)^n} - 1$$

where (n) = how many years in the future we are forecasting the rate.

So, if the six-year note presently yields 8% and the five-year note yields 7.5%, the market would be expecting the one-year bill to yield 10.5% five years from now: $(1.08^6 \div 1.075^5)$ equals 1.105. One way of looking at it is: if an investor had a six-year time horizon, he or she would be better off buying the six-year note than buying the five-year note and rolling to a one-year bill if the future one-year bill was expected to yield anything less than 10.5%. To be accurate, the investor should use the *residual* Treasury curve discussed in the previous chapter, that is, rates after duration risk-premium has been deducted. This will negate the "normal" positive slope of the yield curve which is due to duration risk rather than rate expectation.

DISTRIBUTION OF CASH RETURNS

It was shown earlier that bond, and particularly stock, returns are distributed "normally" over time. That is, they take on the look of a bell-shaped curve that is skewed slightly to the right much like a series of random changes after they are converted to percentage changes. Unfortunately, cash-equivalent returns are not normally distributed. This can be seen in Figure 6–1, which shows the distribution of T-bill returns (which were obtained from Merrill Lynch) between 1968 and 1989. Notice how steep the left side of the curve is and how "fat" the right side is, compared to normal or even log-normal distribution.

There are two important reasons why short-term rates are not normally distributed: First, they can't be negative, by definition; and second, they move in trends, as evidenced by the fact that between 1968 and 1988, they changed direction only 35% of the time. Comparable three-month equity and long-term bond returns change direction (relative to the secular trend) about 50% of the time, much like random numbers (as explained in Chapter 1).

Figure 6–2 shows the distribution of rolling 12-month returns for the Dow Jones Industrial Average. Notice that the curve approximates log-normal distribution. The tails of the curve are a little fat, which is common with stock returns; but the curve appears to

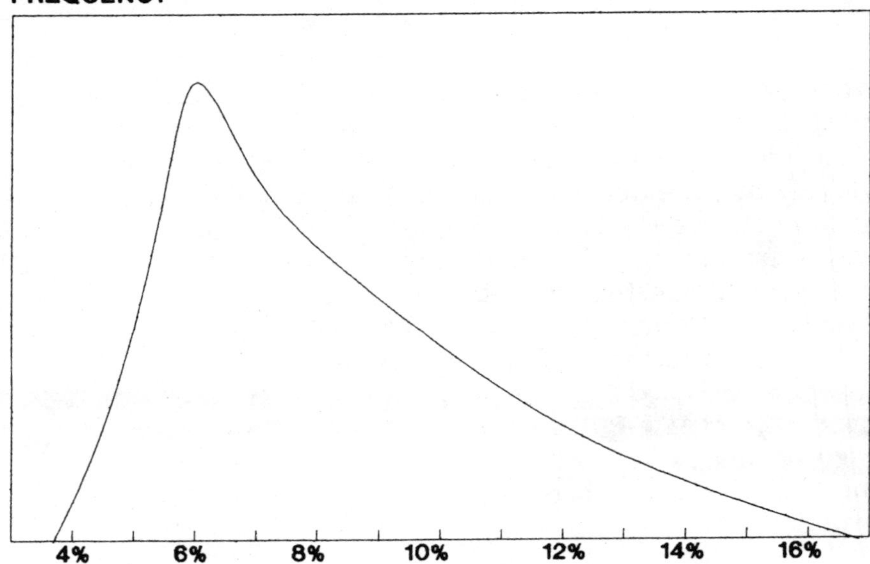

Figure 6–1. Actual Distribution of T-Bill Returns, 1968–1989.

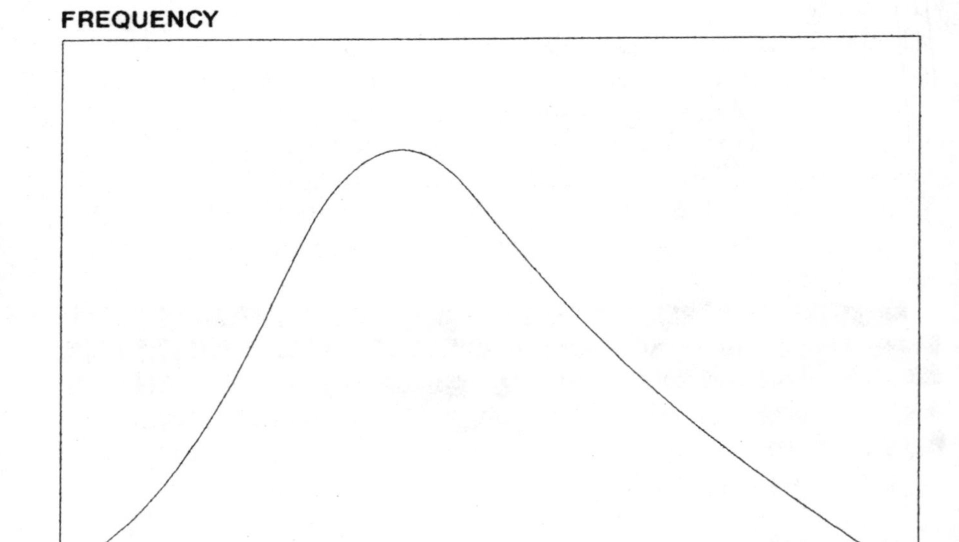

Figure 6–2. Actual Distribution of DJIA Equity Returns, 1968–1989.

come much closer to random distribution than the cash curve. Using a limited amount of data, we cannot expect any distribution to be perfect. Thousands of measurement periods would be needed for a reliable test for normality (randomness).

THE CONCEPT OF NORMAL DEVIATION

Another test for randomness involves the concept of normal deviation. A long series of random numbers would give an expected number of "strings" of various lengths. A *string* is a chain of values that moves consecutively in the same direction (up or down). The series 3, 4, 8, 15, 16 is one chain; 3, 8, 4, 15, 14, 16 is not. The series 3, 4, 8, 10, 9, 6, 8, 7, 9, 5 contains two chains (3, 4, 8, 10 and 10, 9, 6). If there are too many strings, that implies too many ups and downs and not a normal number of long strings. In that case, the normal deviation would be positive, indicating "mean reversion."

A random coin toss would have a predictable number of chains of specific lengths, such as three consecutive heads, eight consecutive tails, and so on. In other words, in 1,000 coin tosses, there would be a normal number of times that three consecutive heads or eight consecutive tails would occur. If three heads, four heads, five heads, and so forth occurred less than the expected number of times, the normal deviation would be negative, indicating trend or persistence, that is, too few short strings but several very long strings.

Cash returns have a normal deviation of between −2 and −3, which means a very low probability of randomness and a high probability of persistence (or trend).

CASH RETURNS HAVE NO VARIANCE!

The distribution pattern of cash returns poses a significant problem. Since cash returns are not normally distributed, they can have no "variance" (in a statistical sense) and therefore no standard deviation. This means that even if we have a "best guess" for future cash returns, we cannot calculate the range of *possible* cash returns and their probabilities of occurrence.

For this reason, many asset allocators do not include cash in their models. This is a mistake. Particularly for time horizons of five years or less, cash is sometimes the preferable investment.

THE REAL ROLE OF CASH EQUIVALENTS

We cannot accurately calculate what percentage of the time cash will outperform our expected return for stocks or bonds. This is because we cannot define the probabilities of cash equivalents outperforming or underperforming *any* specific target over time.

However, since stocks and bonds have fairly normal distribution-of-return patterns, we *can* calculate the probability of stocks or bonds outperforming the expected return of cash. This can be sufficient for a successful asset-allocation program that includes T-bills or money-market funds.

After all, what is the real purpose of cash in a long-term investment portfolio? *Hint:* There would be times when an investor should own some portion of cash instruments even if the expected return were zero. In fact, about half the time T-bill returns *are* negative in real (inflation-adjusted) terms. In this sense, cash is an "antistock" or an "antibond." No matter how long the time horizon, there is always *some* probability that stocks, bonds, or real estate will produce negative returns and, thus, underperform cash. If we consider cash equivalents to be the alternative to owning stocks, bonds, or real estate, then a fine-tuning of expected distribution of future returns from cash becomes unimportant.

Why do participants in a 401(k) plan, for example, often choose a money-market option? For safety, not return. Preservation of capital is the *overwhelming* consideration with money-market investing.

Since this is the case, investors and money managers waste much time trying to maximize money-market returns, particularly in a balanced portfolio. The real issue is whether an individual should be invested in money markets in the first place; and that is a function of the projected distribution of returns for stocks, bonds, real estate, and other possible investments.

TYPES OF CASH EQUIVALENTS

If cash is the "safe harbor," why use anything but T-bills and other prime paper for the cash-equivalent portion of the portfolio? A few extra basis points in return from a particular money-market fund are meaningless in comparison to the decision of what percentage of an investor's funds should be apportioned to cash equivalents in general.

We must conclude that the only worthwhile investment role for other-than-prime-quality, short-term paper is in a portfolio that continually requires maximum liquidity. This type of portfolio (such as corporate operating funds) has an exceptionally short time horizon and is not adaptable to asset allocation anyway.

We already have seen that T-bills are really not risk-free. The investor also should be aware of the potential credit risk of other types of cash equivalents. The four common money-market instruments, other than T-bills, are:

Commercial paper—originated as an IOU from a company to a supplier from which it purchased merchandise. Because of the good credit rating of the buyer, the supplier was able to sell the IOU for cash on a discounted basis. Today, commercial paper is a primary source of short-term capital for many creditworthy corporations. This paper is issued directly to investors or through dealers and is usually backed by a bank line of credit. Finance companies are the biggest issuer. Automobile credit companies, such as General Motors Acceptance Corp., issue commercial paper every day in order to finance loans to car buyers or dealers.

Banker's acceptances—originated as a means of facilitating foreign trade. An arrangement was made by a buyer in Country A to allow the seller in Country B to write a draft against the buyer's bank in Country A. The draft immediately would be honored by the seller's bank in Country B. This allowed the seller to receive immediate payment, as if the buyer were next door, while the buyer would receive credit from his or her own bank where the draft was drawn. Today, bankers acceptances are also used in domestic trade and are readily marketable on a discounted basis.

Repurchase Agreements—do not have long historic roots. Repos are issued by banks, broker-dealers, and other financial institutions. By definition, they are of high quality because they are secured by T-bills. The financial institution "sells" T-bills to the repo buyer and agrees to repurchase them at a specific date at a higher price. The difference between the sale price and the repurchase price represents the interest income to the repo buyer. The only risk involves the possibility of the issuing institution defaulting on the repurchase while the T-bills may have depreciated because of rising short-term rates.

Certificates of deposit—originated merely as evidence of a savings account at a bank. These accounts are time deposits where the bank agrees to repay the depositor on a specific date. These instruments, today, are regularly issued in large denominations and represent a major source of bank financing.

THE DIVERSE NATURE OF MONEY-MARKET FUNDS

Obviously, a money-market fund that invests strictly in T-bills and attempts to improve investor return by purchasing bills with the most attractive maturities is of much higher quality than a fund that attempts to increase returns by investing in commercial paper issued by companies with mediocre credit ratings. Some money-market funds also invest in foreign paper, which may be even more risky.

The investor should be aware of the credit risk involved with the particular fund being considered. For portfolios involved in asset allocation, incremental return from a money-market fund should not be a primary objective. Return should be managed through the stock, bond, and real estate side. This is a far more efficient use of the investor's analytical time. The real risk of money-market funds is not the potential default of one of the creditors, but rather the potential disaster that can be brought on by a credit crunch. If the public panics and commercial paper rates go to the moon within a few days, even the most sound issuer may have trouble issuing new paper to repay the old paper. This happened a couple times in the 1970s.

HOW GUARANTEED ARE GICs?

Wow! The insurance industry really came up with a good one when it marketed its debt under the name of Guaranteed Income Contracts (GICs). The word "guaranteed" conjures up the image of Uncle Sam or at least the Rock of Gibraltar. "Guarantee" normally implies that someone other than the issuer is guaranteeing its debt. It's conceivable that the insurance industry felt justified in using this terminology since GICs are not borrowings in the normal sense. That is, the insurer doesn't need the capital for its own purposes. It is just borrowing money from the public at one rate in order to lend it at a higher rate and keep the difference.

But, that's where the hitch is. Assets and liabilities are mismatched, either maturity-wise or quality-wise. What assets are behind these intermediate-term obligations? The left side of a life insurer's balance sheet is comprised of anything ranging from U.S. Treasury bonds/bills to questionable-quality real estate and buyout financings (LBOs).

There can be no magical free ride with making money. When the insurer sells a three-year GIC to the public, it must either invest the money in a longer maturity investment (if the yield curve is positively sloped) or a lower quality piece of paper, so that it can make a profit. What if the yield curve became very negatively sloped? The insurer must obviously beat the T-bill rate if it is to market new GICs (maybe to refund the old ones). So what will it invest in to be able to pay the public a competitive rate if long-term rates are well below short-term rates? Conversely, if the yield curve becomes very positively sloped, the market value of the insurance industry's assets takes a nose dive, and so might the worth of the insurer's guarantee.

The good news is that many insurers "immunize" their GIC liabilities by investing the proceeds from GIC sales in a fixed-income portfolio that has the same duration as the GIC portfolio. This way, the present value of the insurer's liabilities always will approximate the present (market) value of the underlying assets. Nonetheless, the GIC buyer is, in effect, purchasing a security backed by assets that are paying an interest rate higher than what he or she is receiving from the insurance company. In return for accepting this lower rate, the GIC buyer receives the insurer's guarantee.

How good is that guarantee? Life insurers have exceptionally diversified portfolios and, by statute, must maintain a mandatory securities valuation reserve (MSVR). Also, the real source of liquidity to an insurance company is its cash flow from insurance premiums. In general, the liability side of a life insurer's balance sheet is of significantly higher quality than that of a casualty company. A life insurance company not only knows how many of its policyholders are going to die each year, but also exactly how much each claim will be. This compares very favorably to a liability insurance company, whose reserves can only include an educated guess as to the size and number of incurred (but not reported) claims.

GICs are not money-market instruments, but they are included in this chapter since many investors treat them as though they were. But for the small investor, they lack the liquidity of a T-bill or CD; and for the large investor, they are an inefficient substitute for investing directly in the same bonds, real estate, mortgages, and private placements in which the insurance company is investing.

7

Asset Allocation: Risk-Premium Models

The stock market has a history of moving to irrational extremes because, on a short-term basis, stock prices are often more a reflection of fear, greed, or other psychological factors than of business and monetary fundamentals.

—*Joseph L. Oppenheimer*

EPISODE OF THE STORAGE COMPANY SALESMAN

One day during my tenure as the CFO of a sizeable investment operation, a strange looking dude sashayed into my office, uninvited. His name was Thaddeus. I don't remember his last name, but I can vividly recall his appearance. He was about five-and-a-half feet tall with gray, wavy hair down to his shoulders—sort of like Buffalo Bill—wearing expensive-looking moccasins, leather trousers, and a black shirt with pointed yoke and pocket flaps.

Thaddeus was representing some obscure public storage company, one of those outfits that rent garage-type storage along with physical security to people who have accumulated more personal property than they can cram into their residences. He was trying to raise some venture capital money to finance a new project. The deal he was offering was 50% of the gross rental income and 50% equity in a proposed property in Arizona in return for my company putting up all the equity capital.

He said that the expected life of the operation was 10 years, at which time the property could, and would, be sold for twice the original cost. Our share of the rental income would give us an annual cash return of 6%, and the doubling of our investment over

10 years would provide another 7.2% per year (the annual compounded rate equivalent to 100% over 10 years). So he explained how we would be earning the equivalent total return of 13.2% per year: 6% in income and 7.2% from appreciation.

"Not a bad return," he exclaimed as he opened his eyelids as far as they would go. Interest rates at the time were about 6% on government bonds and about 8% on corporates, and most real estate deals were being put together at returns of 10 to 12%. So he thought his particular offer was a bargain, particularly since Arizona was growing by leaps and bounds.

"Wait a minute," I said quietly as I whipped out my brand new HP-67 pocket computer. I knew, intuitively, that his return estimate was not right. "I don't think that 6% income plus 100% appreciation over 10 years add up to 13.2%." After pushing a few buttons on my machine, I casually mentioned that the expected return (provided his assumptions were correct) was actually 11.76%. I admitted that if one doubles one's money in 10 years, one *is* earning the equivalent of 7.2%; but income and appreciation should not be merely added together.

The reason involves the assumed reinvestment rate which must be an integral part of any investment-return calculation. The 7.2% automatically assumes a 7.2% reinvestment rate. But what's the reinvestment rate on the 6% rental income? If the return were really 13.2%, shouldn't the reinvestment rate have been 13.2% on both the income and appreciation? But that wouldn't make any sense. The only accurate way to calculate the return would entail the computation of the investment's internal rate of return, which deals with the cash flows properly.

IRR: THE MOST IMPORTANT CONCEPT OF RETURN

Internal rate of return (IRR) is the common denominator of all investment return measurements. It is identical, mathematically, to the concept of yield to maturity for a bond. If an investor purchases a 10-year bond (100 par value) at 50 and its coupon is 6%, he or she does not add the appreciation from 50 to 100 over 10 years to the 6% coupon. The investor solves for the yield to maturity.

We saw in Chapter 3 that this was a trial-and-error loop computation that solved for the rate of interest that discounts all future interest and principal payments to the cost of the bond. That's exactly what IRR is for any other investment, including the expected return for a common stock using a dividend-discount model. If (R) equals IRR, then:

$$PV = \frac{\text{PMT (yr. 1)}}{(1+R)^1} + \frac{\text{PMT (yr. 2)}}{(1+R)^2} + \frac{\text{PMT (yr. } n\text{)}}{(1+R)^n} + \frac{\text{FV}}{(1+R)^n}$$

where (PV) is the present value (cost) of the investment, (FV) is the future value of the investment, and (PMT) is the annual cash payment (net of expenses) received in years (1) through (n).

The yield to maturity of a 6% bond selling at 50 and maturing in 10 years would be 11.8%, just like the IRR of the storage project would be 11.8%.

IRR AS THE COMMON THREAD

Every type of investment, whether it be real estate, stocks, bonds, oil wells, or a piece of machinery, has an expected return that can be calculated using the formula just given. It is the common thread that ties all investment returns together. For the purposes of this book, it allows an investor to compare accurately the expected return of stocks, bonds, real estate, and cash. Yield to maturity is one form of IRR as is the discount rate that is solved for in a dividend-discount model. These are the two types of IRR that we will be dealing with in this chapter.

HISTORIC RELATIONSHIPS OF *ACTUAL* RETURNS

Over the past 50 years, common stocks have provided an average annual total return (income plus appreciation) of about 10%. Government bonds have returned about 4.5% over the same period, and corporate bonds around 5%. These figures are the average annual compounded returns of the stock and bond indices, not the returns from a buy-and-hold strategy. Thus, the bond figures reflect the returns of a hypothetical market portfolio that has a constant duration. This is different than measuring the return from buying a portfolio of bonds and holding them to maturity. In other words, each period begins with a new portfolio of securities that are of the same duration as those of the previous period.

Equity returns might have averaged 5% higher than bond returns over the past 50 years, but they aren't always 5% higher. Ibbotson and Sinquefield, who, as mentioned in Chapter 3, do exceptional work in the area of historic returns, have computed the returns for classes of securities for various five-year holding periods. They have shown that five-year stock returns have been as high as 46% per year (from 1941 to 1945) and as low as −28% per year (from 1928 to 1932). By way of comparison, bond returns during the early 1940s were about 3% and going into the Great Depression they were still positive.

Here is a look at the annual returns for stocks and bonds in more recent years:

Decade	Common Stocks	Long-Term Government Bonds	Long-Term Corporate Bonds
1960–69	7.81%	1.68%	1.45%
1970–79	5.86%	6.23%	5.52%
1978–87	15.26%	9.73%	9.47%

Source: Roger G. Ibbotson and Rex A. Sinquefield, *Stocks, Bonds and Inflation: Historical Returns (1926–1987)*. (New York: Dow Jones-Irwin, 1989), p. 83.

HISTORIC RELATIONSHIPS OF *EXPECTED* RETURNS

How do we know what the *expected* returns of stocks and bonds were in days gone by? Let's create a simple model to find out. Taking the Dow Jones Industrial Average for a recent 20-year period, let's assume that, in each of those years, the market expected the existing dividend to grow by 6% annually. Since we would have known the then-current dividend and the then-current price level of the DJIA, we could have solved for the IRR of an eternal stream of dividends growing at 6%.

For each year, the expected return (under this much simplified method) is shown in Table 7–1. The comparable yield to maturities on the 10-year Treasury note are listed, followed by the equity risk-premium (i.e., the difference between the expected long-term equity return and the simple-bond expected return).

The equity risk-premium (which is based on *expected* returns) does not vary nearly as much as the difference between *actual* annual stock and bond returns. This is substantiated by the standard deviations shown at the bottom of the table. The standard deviation of the expected equity risk-premium is under 2%, while the standard deviation of the actual excess equity return is over 13%. In fact, the correlation between the expected versus actual excess equity returns is only 21%.

CREATING A MODEL

The analysis of the previous section would not have provided a good foundation for an asset-allocation model due to the poor correlation between expected and actual returns. Had a portfolio been constructed each January 1 whereby the percentages invested in stocks versus bonds were based on the simple expected returns, the short-term performance would not have reflected a noticeable improvement over a portfolio that had been constantly invested 50% in stocks and 50% in bonds.

The bond yields in Table 7–1 were correct, and the 6% expected dividend growth for the DJIA was not unreasonable. Remember from Chapter 4 that the dividends of the Dow Jones constituent companies actually grow faster than the historic numbers indicate. Dow Jones, Inc., substituted lower yielding stocks for higher yielding stocks over the years. More importantly, when a stock splits, its weighting within the average declines, and stocks that split frequently tend to have higher dividend growth.

Two reasons this simple model does not work well also explain a couple of important shortcomings that plague many asset-allocation models:

1. Long-term expected returns cannot be presumed to correlate well with short-term actual returns, except in the most sophisticated models.

TABLE 7-1 Expected Versus Actual Returns for the DJIA, 1968–1988

			Expected			Actual		
Year	Beg. DJIA 1/1	Divs.	IRR @ 6% Div. Growth	10-Year Treasury YTM	Equity Risk Premium	DJIA 12-Mon. Return	Bonds 12-Mon. Return*	Excess Equity Return
1968	905.11	31.34	9.5%	5.5%	3.9%	7.7%	−0.26%	8.0%
1969	943.75	33.90	9.6	6.2	3.4	−11.6	−5.08	−6.5
1970	800.36	31.53	9.9	7.4	2.6	8.8	12.10	−3.3
1971	838.92	30.86	9.7	6.0	3.7	9.8	13.20	−3.4
1972	890.20	32.27	9.6	6.0	3.6	18.2	5.68	12.5
1973	1020.02	35.33	9.5	6.6	2.9	−13.1	−1.11	−12.0
1974	850.86	37.72	10.4	7.1	3.4	−23.1	4.35	−27.5
1975	616.24	37.46	12.1	7.5	4.5	44.4	9.19	35.2
1976	852.41	41.40	10.9	7.8	3.1	22.7	16.75	6.0
1977	1004.65	45.84	10.6	7.4	3.2	−12.7	−0.67	−12.0
1978	831.17	48.52	11.8	8.0	3.8	2.7	−1.16	3.9
1979	805.01	50.98	12.3	9.1	3.2	10.5	−1.22	11.7
1980	838.74	54.36	12.5	12.0	0.5	21.4	−3.95	25.4
1981	963.99	56.22	11.8	13.0	−1.1	−3.4	1.85	−5.2
1982	875.00	54.14	12.2	14.3	−2.1	25.8	40.35	−14.6
1983	1046.54	56.33	11.4	10.6	0.8	25.6	0.68	25.0
1984	1258.64	60.63	10.8	11.9	−1.1	1.1	15.43	−14.4
1985	1211.57	62.03	11.1	11.6	−0.5	32.8	30.97	1.8
1986	1546.67	67.04	10.3	8.6	1.8	26.9	24.44	2.5
1987	1895.95	71.20	9.8	7.2	2.6	6.0	−2.69	8.7
1988	1938.83	80.00	10.1	8.4	1.7			
Averages			9.0%	7.3%	1.8%	8.4%	6.6%	1.7%
Standard Deviation			4.1	3.9	1.9	16.0	11.5	13.7

**Source of Actual Bond Returns:* Roger G. Ibbotson and Rex A. Sinquefield, *Stocks, Bonds and Inflation: Historical Returns (1926–1987).* (New York: Dow Jones-Irwin, 1989), p. 55.

2. The expected return for stocks was computed for an indefinite time horizon, whereas the expected return for bonds was for a 10-year time horizon.

In other words, both the analysis and the measurement entailed comparing apples and oranges. Although there was a low correlation between the expected excess equity return and the actual excess *one-year* return, the correlation between the expected return and the actual *five-year* return, as shown in Table 7–2 improves dramatically to 66%.

IMPROVING THE MODEL

Now let's correct the problem of comparing infinite stock returns to finite (10-year) bond returns. A simple way to create a 10-year expected return for stocks would be to utilize the T-value. You may recall from Chapter 4 that a simplified version of the T-value assumes that the expected return for the stock market is equal to its dividend yield plus its expected dividend growth rate plus an annualized change in the price-to-book ratio.

In Table 7–3, we calculate a 10-year stock return by assuming that the DJIA would be selling at 1.1 times book value (the average at the time) in 10 years. The table shows what the expected return for the DJIA *would have been* on each January 1, using a 6% dividend-growth assumption and a terminal price-to-book ratio of 1.10, 10 years into the future.

Thus, the expected stock return simply becomes current yield plus 6% plus the annualized change in the price-to-book ratio. The latter is simply:

$$(1.10 \div P/B)^{.10} - 1$$

Table 7–3 reflects stock and bond expected returns with 10-year time horizons—bonds, because we used the going yield to maturity on the 10-year bond, and stocks, because we used a terminal stock value of 1.1 times book, 10 years out.

The coefficient of correlation between expected and actual *excess*

TABLE 7-2 Expected Versus Actual Returns: 5 Year Time Horizon

			Expected			Actual		
Year	Beg. DJIA 1/1	Divs.	IRR @ 6% Div. Growth	10-Year Treasury YTM	Equity Risk Premium	DJIA 5-Yr. Return	Bonds 5-Yr. Return*	Excess Equity Return
1968	905.11	31.34	9.5%	5.5%	3.9%	6.1%	−4.9%	1.2%
1969	943.75	33.90	9.6	6.2	3.4	1.6	4.7	−3.1
1970	800.36	31.53	9.9	7.4	2.6	−1.2	6.7	−7.9
1971	838.92	30.86	9.7	6.0	3.7	4.6	6.2	−1.6
1972	890.20	32.27	9.6	6.0	3.6	6.9	6.8	0.1
1973	1020.02	35.33	9.5	6.6	2.9	0.7	5.5	−4.8
1974	850.86	37.72	10.4	7.1	3.4	4.1	5.5	−1.4
1975	616.24	37.46	12.1	7.5	4.5	11.9	4.3	7.6
1976	852.41	41.40	10.9	7.8	3.1	8.1	1.7	6.4
1977	1004.65	45.84	10.6	7.4	3.2	3.0	−1.0	4.1
1978	831.17	48.52	11.8	8.0	3.8	10.9	6.0	4.8
1979	805.01	50.98	12.3	9.1	3.2	15.4	6.4	9.0
1980	838.74	54.36	12.5	12.0	0.5	13.1	9.8	3.3
1981	963.99	56.22	11.8	13.0	−1.1	8.8	16.8	−8.0
1982	875.00	54.14	12.2	14.3	−2.1	9.6	21.6	−12.0
1983	1046.54	56.33	11.4	10.6	0.8	4.7	13.0	−8.3
1984	1258.64	60.63						
1985	1211.57	62.03						
1986	1546.67	67.04						
1987	1895.95	71.20						
1988	1938.83	80.00						
Averages			8.7%	6.7%	2.0%	5.4%	5.9%	−0.5%
Standard Deviation			4.5	4.1	1.9	4.9	5.7	5.5

**Source of Actual Bond Returns:* Roger G. Ibbotson and Rex A. Sinquefield, *Stocks, Bonds and Inflation: Historical Returns (1926–1987)*. (New York: Dow Jones-Irwin, 1989), p. 81.

TABLE 7-3 Expected Versus Actual Returns Using 10-Year T-Value

					Expected			Actual		
Year	Beg. DJIA 1/1	Divs.	DJIA Book Value	P/B	10-Yr. DJIA T-Value	10-Yr. Treasury YTM	Equity Risk Premium	DJIA 5-Yr. Return	Bonds 5-Yr. Return*	Excess Equity Return
1968	905.11	31.34	476.50	1.90	4.1%	5.5%	−1.4%	6.1%	4.9%	1.2%
1969	943.75	33.90	521.08	1.81	4.7	6.2	−1.4	1.6	4.7	−3.1
1970	800.36	31.53	542.45	1.48	7.0	7.4	−0.3	−1.2	6.7	−7.9
1971	838.92	30.86	573.15	1.46	6.9	6.0	0.8	4.6	6.2	−1.6
1972	890.20	32.27	607.61	1.47	6.8	6.0	0.8	6.9	6.8	0.1
1973	1020.02	35.33	642.87	1.59	5.9	6.6	−0.7	0.7	5.5	−4.8
1974	850.86	37.72	690.23	1.23	9.3	7.1	2.2	4.1	5.5	−1.4
1975	616.24	37.46	746.95	0.83	15.0	7.5	7.5	11.9	4.3	7.6
1976	852.41	41.40	783.61	1.09	11.0	7.8	3.2	8.1	1.7	6.4
1977	1004.65	45.84	798.20	1.26	9.2	7.4	1.9	3.0	−1.0	4.1
1978	831.17	48.52	841.76	0.99	12.9	8.0	4.9	10.9	6.0	4.8
1979	805.01	50.98	890.69	0.90	14.3	9.1	5.2	15.4	6.4	9.0
1980	838.74	54.36	859.41	0.98	13.7	12.0	1.7	13.1	9.8	3.3
1981	963.99	56.22	928.50	1.04	12.4	13.0	−0.5	8.8	16.8	−8.0
1982	875.00	54.14	975.59	0.90	14.2	14.3	0.0	9.6	21.6	−12.0
1983	1046.54	56.33	881.51	1.19	10.6	10.6	0.1	4.7	13.0	−8.3
1984	1258.64	60.63	888.21							
1985	1211.57	62.03	916.70							
1986	1546.67	67.04	944.97							
1987	1895.95	71.20	986.48							
1988	1938.83	80.00	1008.95							
Averages				1.1	7.9%	6.7%	1.2%	5.4%	5.9%	−0.5%
Standard Deviation				0.5	5.1	4.1	2.3	4.9	5.7	5.5

**Source of Actual Bond Returns:* Roger G. Ibbotson and Rex A. Sinquefield, *Stocks, Bonds and Inflation: Historical Returns (1926–1987)*. (New York: Dow Jones-Irwin, 1989), p. 81.

equity returns improves significantly to 72%. The correlation between the expected and the actual five-year *absolute* equity return is 80%.

IMPROVING THE MEASUREMENT

Now, if we measure the correlation between the *10-year expected* returns and the *10-year actual* returns, we find it to be a whopping 92%! Just eyeballing Table 7–4 will give you an appreciation for how our forecasting and measurement techniques have improved over the last several pages of this chapter.

The proficient statistician undoubtedly will question the accuracy of any correlation and standard deviation where so few periods are being measured. However, thus far in the chapter, we have not been attempting to produce precise statistics. The goal is merely to show the relative improvements that can be made in a relative return model. We can make even greater improvements.

USING A TERMINAL VALUE IN A DDM

It has just been shown that a dramatic improvement can be made in the predictability of relative (shock versus bond) returns by using finite and identical time horizons for both the stock and bond expected returns. We demonstrated this by utilizing the T-value, which by design employs a terminal price-to-book ratio.

But T-value is only an approximation of internal rate of return, the latter being the preferred method. A dividend-discount model, also by design, solves for an IRR that can be compared to a bond portfolio's yield to maturity (IRR). However, to calculate the IRR of the stock market over a finite time period utilizing a DDM, a terminal value must be calculated for the end of the time horizon.

Table 7–5 shows how a simple DDM is used to calculate a five-year expected return for the S&P 500. The terminal S&P 500 value could be based on a multiple of the earnings, dividend, or book value in Year 5. Then we simply solve for the internal rate of

TABLE 7–4 10-Year Expected Versus Actual Returns

					Expected			Actual		
Year	Beg. DJIA 1/1	Divs.	DJIA Book Value	P/B	10-Yr. DJIA T-Value	10-Yr. Treasury YTM	Equity Risk Premium	DJIA 10-Yr. Return	Bonds 10-Yr. Return*	Excess Equity Return
1968	905.11	31.34	476.50	1.90	4.1%	5.5%	−1.4%	3.3%	5.2%	−1.9%
1969	943.75	33.90	521.08	1.81	4.7	6.2	−1.4	2.8	5.1	−2.3
1970	800.36	31.53	542.45	1.48	7.0	7.4	−0.3	5.2	5.5	−0.4
1971	838.92	30.86	573.15	1.46	6.9	6.0	0.8	6.3	3.9	2.4
1972	890.20	32.27	607.61	1.47	6.8	6.0	0.8	5.0	2.8	2.2
1973	1020.02	35.33	642.87	1.59	5.9	6.6	−0.7	5.6	5.8	−0.1
1974	850.86	37.72	690.23	1.23	9.3	7.1	2.2	9.6	6.0	3.6
1975	616.24	37.46	746.95	0.83	15.0	7.5	7.5	12.6	7.0	5.6
1976	852.41	41.40	783.61	1.09	11.0	7.8	3.2	11.7	9.0	2.7
1977	1004.65	45.84	798.20	1.26	9.2	7.4	1.9	12.1	9.7	2.4
1978	831.17	48.52	841.76	0.99	12.9	8.0	4.9	14.3	9.5	4.8
1979	805.01	50.98	890.69	0.90						
1980	838.74	54.36	859.41	0.98						
1981	963.99	56.22	928.50	1.04						
1982	875.00	54.14	975.59	0.90						
1983	1046.54	56.33	881.51	1.19						
1984	1258.64	60.63	888.21	1.42						
1985	1211.57	62.03	916.70	1.32						
1986	1546.67	67.04	944.97	1.64						
1987	1895.95	71.20	986.48	1.92						
1988	1938.83	80.00	1008.95	1.92						
Averages				1.2	6.2%	5.0%	1.2%	5.9%	4.6%	1.3%
Standard Deviation				0.5	4.7	3.1	2.4	4.9	3.3	2.2

**Source of Actual Bond Returns:* Roger G. Ibbotson and Rex A. Sinquefield *Stocks, Bonds and Inflation: Historical Returns (1926–1987)*. (New York: Dow Jones-Irwin, 1989), p. 83.

TABLE 7–5 Using DDM to Calculate a Five-Year Expected Return for the S&P 500

Future Years	S&P 500 Price	Projected Normalized EPS	Projected Normalized Dividends	Projected Normalized Book Value	Projected Normalized ROE	Cash Flows
Current	300.00	$27.00	$13.50	$200.00	13.5%	($300.00)
1		$28.95	$14.48	$214.48	13.5	$14.48
2		$31.05	$15.53	$230.00	13.5	$15.53
3		$33.30	$16.65	$246.65	13.5	$16.65
4		$35.71	$17.85	$264.51	13.5	$17.85
5	425.48**	$38.29	$19.15	$283.65	13.5	$444.63
IRR* = 12.06%						

*IRR equal to rate that discounts dividend stream and terminal value to current price of S&P.
**Terminal value (425.48) computed as 1.50 times book value in Year 5.

return based on a cost of $300 and future cash flows equal to the five dividends plus the terminal market value in Year 5.

What should the terminal P/B, P/E, or yield be? Price to book and yield are preferred (in that order) due to stability considerations. Long-term market averages would suffice if we were concerned with a very long-term time horizon—but not for five years or less. For instance, if the 20-year average P/B ratio for the S&P were 1.50, and the S&P were now selling at 1.00 times book value, would that make the one-year expected return over 50%?

We cannot solve this dilemma by using short-term averages, either. For example, if the S&P were selling at 1.10 times book value and the three-year average P/B were 1.00, would that mean the one-year expected return was negative?

The best solution is to assume that the terminal value is the future present value of the then-future dividend stream. In other words, the terminal value is the solution to a separate DDM run hypothetically at the end of the investor's time horizon. The five-year DDM flowchart (Figure 4–1) in Chapter 4 described the process. Unfortunately, to facilitate this process, we need to make an assumption as to the market discount rate at the end of the time horizon.

EQUITY RISK-PREMIUMS

At what rate will the market be discounting dividends in the future? To make this estimate, we must make two projections: future interest rates and future equity risk-premiums. Many professionals like to equate equity discount rates to long-term government bonds, since stocks have a duration of about 18 to 25 years. Although their preference is well founded in theory, it is impractical for projection purposes. For a variety of pragmatic reasons, I relate the stock market discount rate to the 10-year Treasury rate. Methods for projecting the 10-year-note rate were described in Chapter 5.

Assume a three-year time horizon and that we project the 10-year-note rate to be at an 8% level in three years. What will the stock market discount rate be in three years? We would need to know this if we were to use a DDM to calculate the three-year expected return for the stock market. Once we have made our interest-rate projection, we then need to estimate the equity risk-premium (relative to the 10-year note) three years from now.

How about an historic average? Well, take your pick. From 1985 until 1990, expected return for the S&P 500 averaged only 1% above the 10-year-note rate; from 1980 until 1990, it averaged 2% above, and from 1970 to 1990, it averaged 3% above. To complicate matters, the annual standard deviation of those equity risk-premiums was about 2%.

THE ROLE OF INVESTOR CONFIDENCE

Barron's, the weekly Dow Jones publication, defines *confidence* as the ratio of high-quality bond yields to medium-quality bond yields. Over the past 35 years, the ratio (*Barron's* Confidence Index) has ranged from 77 to 98% with the mean being approximately 91%.

Earlier in this book, it was shown that investor confidence could be defined by things like the yield spread between T-bills and CDs or the spread between the highest and lowest expected interest rates included in the consensus. Regardless of what specific method is used, it should be obvious that when the yield spread between government securities and other fixed-income securities is high, the spread between the expected return of government securities and common stocks should be even higher. For example, if 10-year corporate bonds normally yield 2% more than government bonds, but today they were yielding 4% more, then the expected return for stocks should also be abnormally high relative to T-bonds.

HAMMER'S CONFIDENCE CURVES

Figure 7–1 presents the theory behind equity risk-premiums in graphic form. This is the most important graph in this book!

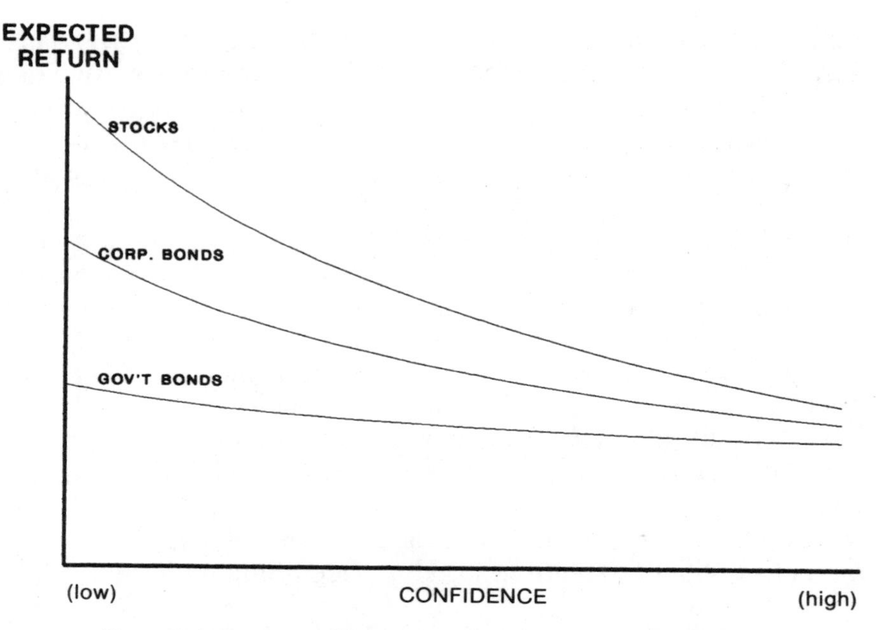

Figure 7–1. Returns and Spreads Decrease with Higher Confidence.

On a week-to-week basis, it is uncanny how often the equity risk-premium changes, along with yield spreads (confidence). The more we think about this phenomenon, the more sense it makes.

If the investor knew where interest rates were going to be in the future (an unrealistic but interesting assumption) and could predict future confidence, then the future level of the stock and bond markets could be forecasted with a high degree of accuracy.

Earnings, which produce dividends, is the variable of lesser importance. But, this is where professional investment people devote most of their effort. If they spent the same energy developing means of forecasting confidence (yield spreads) as they do forecasting earnings, the payoff would be enormous.

IMPROVING THE FORECASTS

Although it is impossible to predict future rates, yield spreads, or dividends with any significant degree of precision, it *is* possible to determine where the market thinks rates are headed, where confidence is most likely to move, and what the future dividend stream of the S&P 500 is most likely to be. The monetary reward for even coming close makes me wonder why Wall Street spends so much effort worrying about the next quarter's earnings estimates.

Let's take the easy one first—forecasting the dividend stream of the S&P 500 (or any other proxy for the overall stock market). Dividends are not based on today's earnings, *per se*, but on the basic earning power of the companies. The best measurement of basic earning power is normalized return on equity.

So the very first step in any viable stock market DDM is to calculate the normalized ROE using a good statistical method. Long-term trend analysis, including both actual historic numbers and consensus top-down forecasts of future actual ROEs, is a good method.

Next, the same statistical techniques should be applied to the market's dividend payout ratio. Thus, beginning with the current book value of the S&P, we can create a whole series of future normalized earnings, dividends, and book values.

Then, we must discount those dividends, including a distant terminal value, *beginning at the end of the investor's time horizon*. This gives us the "best guess" of what the level of the market will be at the end of the investor's time horizon. We then calculate an internal rate of return as a function of that future market level and the dividends between now and then compared to the present market level.

Discounting dividends as of some future date requires an estimate of bond yields in the future. Chapter 5 described some quantitative approaches. We also must make an estimate as to equity risk-premiums in the future, which is a function of investor confidence, just as forward rates are. If the time horizon is far enough in the future, the investor can use long-term historic averages for the equity risk-premium. Over the past 20 years, the average has been 2 to 4%, most of the time. But if we examine the next previous 20-year period, the equity risk-premium was in the range of 4 to 8%. Maybe 20 years from now the typical equity risk-premium will be negative if the double taxation of dividends is eliminated or if capital gains become only partially taxable. Sometimes an educated guess about the direction of risk-premiums works surprisingly well. A little common sense and discipline can be particularly rewarding at crucial turning points of the market.

THE CRASH OF 1987

Common sense and discipline were the key in the fall of 1987. At the time, I was managing a major regional bank's trust-investment department. Our accounts had a positive return that October, despite the worst stock market crash in history. The large pooled pension account that I personally managed produced an 11.7% return for the year, when about half the professionals in the country had to report their performance in red ink.

In August 1987, investor confidence (as measured by the yield spreads between high- and medium-quality bonds) was at an all-time high! It follows that equity risk-premiums were at an all-time low. They only could have had one way to go from there.

The yield curve was very positively sloped. That, coupled with high confidence, meant the market was expecting substantially higher discount rates in the future. In that regard, the bond market was wrong, but in the short term that often doesn't matter. *Consensus expectations are more important in and of themselves than the accuracy of the predictions.*

Government bonds were yielding 10% prior to the crash. The market thought rates were going higher, which meant stock discount rates were expected to go higher. Equity risk-premiums were actually negative, even without applying forward-rate theory.

Why would anyone have bought stocks during and after the summer of 1987? Government bonds offered a greater return than stocks even using a long-term time horizon! It was a classic case of Donald Stocking's "Greater Fool Theory" manifesting itself. Everyone knew the stock market was overvalued, but the technical factors looked good, the momentum was certainly there, and the Japanese were supposed to be feasting on American equities. As usual, greed caused the market to peak and fear caused it to crash.

Two weeks before the crash, the DDM for the S&P 500 showed a 10-year expected return 3% below that of government bonds. Two days after the crash, the stock market had a 10-year expected return 5% above that of government bonds (which had appreciated significantly during October).

CHANGING ALLOCATION TOO SOON

A number of asset allocators sidestepped the Crash of 1987. Unfortunately, though, most also had missed the big bull market earlier in the year. In late 1986, a lot of people started talking about the normalized price-earnings and price-book ratios of "The Dow" being at or above all-time highs and the dividend yield approaching an historic low.

So what? An investor cannot make an intelligent decision about owning stocks unless he or she compares the expected return for equities to that of bonds or cash equivalents! Benchmark government securities were yielding only 6 to 7% in early 1987. That made stocks cheap, in relative terms. It is true that the expected returns produced by most DDMs came in at 8 to 9% for the stock market. But that was still 2% better than bonds, when the equity risk-premium for the previous five years had been only 1%.

FINE-TUNING EXPECTED RETURNS

Another classic situation occurred in 1989. It was a poor year for most asset allocators, which was too bad since they were still revelling in the glory directed at them following the crash two years earlier. At the start of 1989, most asset-allocation models were showing an expected return for stocks, bonds, and money markets all around the 9% level. Professionals asked themselves, "Why own stocks when government paper offers the same return, and why own bonds when cash offers the same return?" As a result, most of them sat on the sidelines during one of the very best stock market years in history, with the S&P returning well over 30%.

As of January 2, 1989, the Hammer-Lodefink Model showed the five-year expected annual return of stocks as being 12% compared to 10% for bonds and 8% for cash. If you absorbed most of what was outlined in Chapters 4 through 6, you know why our expected returns were different from those of our competitors. Our clients' accounts were positioned to be 72% invested in stocks, 22% in bonds, and only 8% in cash. In fact, prior to July, when the stock market had one of its biggest rallies in history, the Hammer-Lodefink model called for a 92% equity position, even though the market was higher than it was in January.

The residual yield curve, as described in Chapter 5, had pointed to lower interest rates in each of the next five years. That meant cash returns were headed south, bonds would offer some appreciation in addition to the basic coupon, and future stock-market discount rates would likewise be lower, causing the level of the equities markets to be substantially higher.

Between 1980 and 1989, whenever the bond market reflected a new consensus interest-rate expectation, 87% of the time the stock market reacted appropriately within three months. Bond-market expectations, whether they turn out to be right or wrong, generally affect stock returns within a few weeks. This means that *changes in the long-term expected returns produce short-term results!* But the trick is to measure those changes accurately.

SETTING THE ASSET MIX

In the next two chapters, sophisticated techniques for determining the proper blend of stocks, bonds, and cash will be detailed. In this chapter, thus far, we have dealt only with the comparison of intermediate- to long-term expected returns for stocks and bonds. Once the expected returns are properly calculated, the next step is to convert those expectations into asset allocations. It would be nice if, over time, the equity risk-premium took on the normal distribution pattern of a bell-shaped curve. Then we could measure, at any point in time, how many standard deviations it was away from some historic mean.

On the one hand, it is unfortunate equity risk-premiums (the difference between stock returns and bond returns) are not normally distributed. But, on the other hand, if they were, that would imply randomness or lack of predictability. Over the long term, risk premiums exhibit "mean reversion" which allows the investor the opportunity to use historic averages. Over the short term, they exhibit persistence or trend, which opens the door for fancy algorithms to deal with projecting investor confidence.

Without having the time, inclination, or math skills needed for highly quantitative models, some investors have been very successful by applying some simple rules of thumb, such as:

1. When stocks offer a lower return than bonds over the selected time horizon, don't own any equities.
2. When stock expected returns are 2 to 3% above T-bond returns, a traditional 60:40 or 70:30 stock/bond mix is appropriate.
3. When the equity risk premium is 4% or higher, invest 80 to 90% of the investable funds in equities.
4. When stock returns are only about 1% above T-bond returns, cut back the equity exposure to 30 to 40%.

These guidelines can be enhanced significantly by allowing the equity risk-premium parameters to be a function of investor confidence. The best method is to create an algorithm that allows low-equity risk-premiums when confidence is high (yield spreads are narrow) and vice versa.

These simple rules, and all the possible interpolations in between, can work well for stocks and bonds. When cash (money markets) enter the equation, it becomes more of a task to figure the appropriate asset mix. Remember, when the current rate on money-market funds is low relative to bonds, that's usually a good time to avoid both stocks and bonds, ironically. Confidence-adjusted forward-rate theory usually deals with that issue effectively. Even if its predictive capabilities are not perfect, the investor needs some mathematical discipline to avoid being attracted to bonds at the wrong time, that is, when they appear to have relatively attractive yields.

CONCLUSIONS

The theory behind a risk-premium approach to asset allocation is that the relative returns of stocks versus bonds and cash tend to revert to some historic average relationship. Many tactical allocators use the following technique:

1. Measure the expected return of the stock market by solving for the internal rate of return of the projected long-term dividend stream of the S&P 500.
2. Compare the equities' expected return to the present yield to maturity of long-term government bonds and to the current return on T-bills or money-market funds.
3. Compare these spreads (differences in return) to the long-term historic averages.
4. Construct a portfolio initially based on some traditional stock/bond mix, such as 60:40. Overweight stocks when the equity risk-premium (stock IRR minus bond IRR) is high and vice versa; and add cash to the portfolio when short-term rates are high relative to the stock (or sometimes bond) expected returns.

This approach oversimplifies the nature of the marketplace and often produces very misleading results for the following reasons:

1. There is no way of knowing *when* the spread between the IRR of the stock market and the IRR of the bond market will return to normal.
2. Long-term expected returns do not necessarily reflect the typical investor's time horizon.
3. Returns for stocks, bonds, and cash will be substantially different, over the short and intermediate term, than even the most precise long-term forecast.
4. High-equity risk premiums may get higher and stay higher long before they decline; and the reverse also is true.
5. Comparing current returns on cash equivalents to long-term expected returns for stocks and bonds is like comparing apples to oranges.

A dynamic asset allocation approach, as opposed to a tactical approach, deals effectively with these shortcomings. Under dynamic asset allocation, we determine a strategic asset allocation mix based on the investor's time horizon and then update that mix as the risk-premiums change. Here is that technique in list form:

1. Calculate the expected return of the S&P 500 using a T-value, or preferably, a DDM over the investor's time horizon. This involves computing a terminal level of the market at the end of the investor's time horizon as discussed earlier in the chapter.
2. Calculate an expected return for a bond *portfolio* over the investor's time horizon. This involves computing and compounding the year-by-year expected return of a synthetic bond portfolio or single bond with a rolling duration that matches the investor's risk profile. You may utilize either forward-rate theory or the rolling-down-the-yield-curve approach discussed in Chapter 5.
3. Compute the expected return for cash by compounding the year-by-year expected returns, which are a function of future rate expectations.
4. Compute today's level of investor confidence by analyzing quality spreads between various classes of fixed-income investments such as CDs versus T-bills or medium-grade bonds versus high-grade bonds. Use an algorithm to determine *what the equity risk-premium should be currently*.
5. Base the asset mix on the difference between the actual risk-premium and the confidence-adjusted expected risk-premiums.

The next two chapters describe the best means of converting relative expected returns into actual percentage allocations.

8

Asset Allocation: Probability Models

The successful businessman makes money by ability and experience; but generally he makes it by mistake.

—*G.K. Chesterton*

THE EVENING BEFORE A DAY AT THE RACETRACK

Rockingham Park is situated just across the Massachusetts state line in Salem, New Hampshire. Horse racing, along with the associated legalized betting, is the principal activity there. Some years ago, it had been rumored that the racetrack was going to be shut down because of financial difficulties. So, a friend of mine asked if I would like to join him the next Saturday for an afternoon of betting, while the opportunity still existed. Rockingham never did go bankrupt, but the place did burn to the ground about a year later.

I accepted his invitation on the condition that he would first explain the betting system to me, since I had never been to a racetrack before. Once he did that, I figured I had better spend the Friday evening before the races pushing a pencil. My intent was not to come up with a winning system—after all I was just a novice—but to figure out how I might get some racetrack experience on Saturday with a minimum of risk.

I began by designing a hypothetical race, one with only three horses. I assumed a benevolent racetrack—that all monies would be paid out so the track would not retain any share of the bets. I conjectured that the betting crowd was efficient, that is, that the betting odds accurately reflected each horse's odds of winning. I concerned myself only with betting on a horse to "win" not to "show" or "place."

I pretended that I was betting on four separate races, each having the same three horses. I started with $480 and "bet" $120 on each race. Incidently, 120 is a good number to use in any probability problem because it is divisible by a lot of small numbers (1, 2, 3, 4, 5, 6, 8, 10, 12, etc.).

I imagined that there were four basic styles of betting: equal betting, where one could spread the bet amongst the horses; betting with the odds, where one would bet heavily on the favorite horse; betting against the odds, where one would wager on the "longshot"; and probability betting, where one could weight the bets according to each horse's chance of winning.

I pretended that the first horse (A) had a 50% chance of winning (and therefore paid off at 2 for 1, and that the other two horses each had a 25% chance of winning (and paid 4 for 1). Table 8–1 shows the four betting styles, along with the most probable and next most probable outcomes after four races. Notice that the most likely scenario (defined as the case where each horse performs according to the odds) is that the bettor will receive back his or her original $480 after four races. In other words, no matter what system of betting is used, the *expected return* is zero in this example.

The *volatility of return*, however, varies greatly, depending on the betting method employed. After any number of races, only the "probability bettor" is assured of getting his or her wagers back. The interesting feature of probability betting is that it doesn't matter which horse actually wins! Even if the same horse won all four races, the probability bettor still would have won back the full $480.

The moral of this true story is that a bettor can substantially reduce risk (volatility of return) without affecting expected return by spreading his or her bets in proportion to each possible outcome's odds. In Table 8–1, look at the range of possible returns for each betting method if one of the horses wins once more than expected. This is shown in the right column ("next most likely" outcome). If we were to calculate all the possible outcomes and

TABLE 8–1 Betting $120 per Race on 4 Races

Horse	A	B	C	Total Cash Back		
Chance of Winning	50%	25%	25%		After	After
Odds	1 to 1	3 to 1	3 to 1	After	4 Races	4 Races
Payoff	2 for 1	4 for 1	4 for 1	1 Race	(most likely)	(next most likely)
Equal Betting						
Wager (per race)	$40	$40	$40			$400
Cash after 4 races	$160	$160	$160	$160	$480	$480
				or $80		or 560
Betting with the Odds						
Wager (per race)	$120	$0	$0			$240
Cash after 4 races	$480	$0	$0	$240	$480	$480
				or $0		or $720
Betting Against the Odds						
Wager (per race)	$24	$48	$48			$336
Cash after 4 races	$96	$192	$192	$192	$480	$480
				or $48		or $624
Probability Betting						
Wager (per race)	$60	$30	$30			
Cash after 4 races	$240	$120	$120	$120	$480	$480

combine all the possible results, the expected return for each method is still zero. But only with the probability-weighted method is the expected return certain.

CALCULATING THE ODDS FOR SECURITIES

The investments implications of probability weighting are tremendous. An excellent method for reducing risk, without affecting the expected return by an undue amount, is to weight each asset class according to its probability of outperforming the target return or the expected return of the other classes. In the next chapter, I will return to the actual day at the racetrack to show how a variation of probability betting can even improve expected return.

How do we compute the probability of a security, or class of securities, beating a target return? It actually involves the fairly complex calculus of probability, but it can be illustrated fairly simply. Assume that the returns for, say, common stocks are distributed normally—that is, that they appear as though they occurred in a random fashion around some long-term trend.

Figure 8–1 describes the range of possible five-year annualized stock returns along with their probabilities of occurrence. This example assumes a "best guess" expected annualized return of 10% and standard deviation of return of 15%, which converts to an annualized five-year standard deviation of 6%. [Remember from Chapter 2: To determine an annualized standard deviation over time, multiply the one-year deviation by the square root of time (in this case, the square root of 5) then take the Nth root (in this case, fifth root) of that number.]

The height of the curve at any point represents the *relative probability* of the respective return, shown on the (x) axis, occurring. For example, in Figure 8–1, a return of +15% has more than twice the probability of occurring as a return of +20% or 0%. This is evidenced by the fact that the curve is more than twice as high at the 15% return level as it is at the 20% or 0% levels.

What is the probability of stocks, in this example, exceeding 6% per year, over the next five years? *The probability of a security beating a target return is equal to the area under the distribution curve to the right*

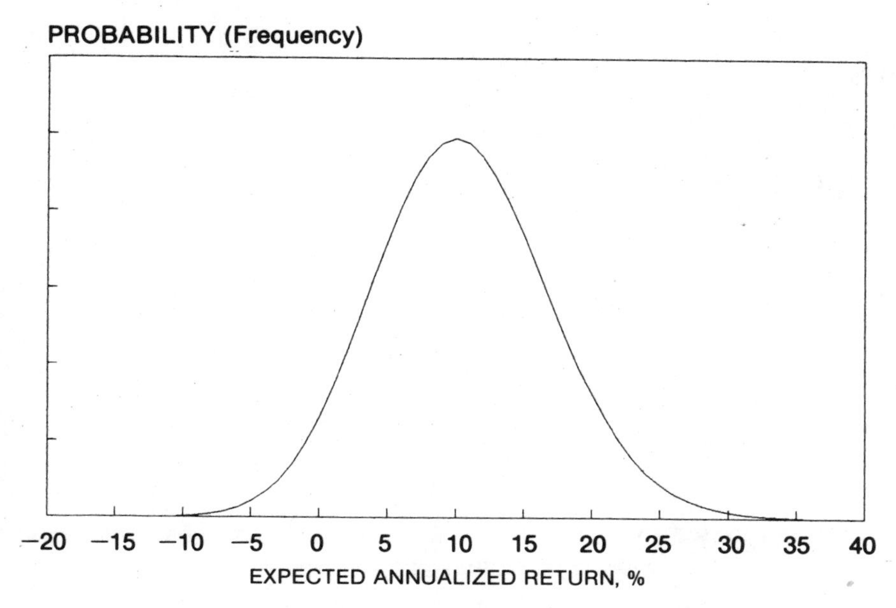

Figure 8–1. Distribution of Possible Five-Year Returns.

of the target, as a percentage of the total area under the curve. Figure 8–2 illustrates this concept. The area to the right of the 6% line in this example is 76% of the total area under the curve. Thus the probability of stock returns exceeding a 6% rate over the next five years is 76%!

WHAT IS CALCULUS?

Calculus is a major branch of mathematics that was developed over the years by physicists who needed adequate tools for measuring the rate of change as well as the change in the rate of change (acceleration). Whereas algebra deals with producing an equality between variables, calculus deals with how a change in one variable affects the other.

Differential calculus is a system whereby certain procedures are applied to an equation in order to create a new equation that defines the rate of change of (y) for any specific level of (x). That

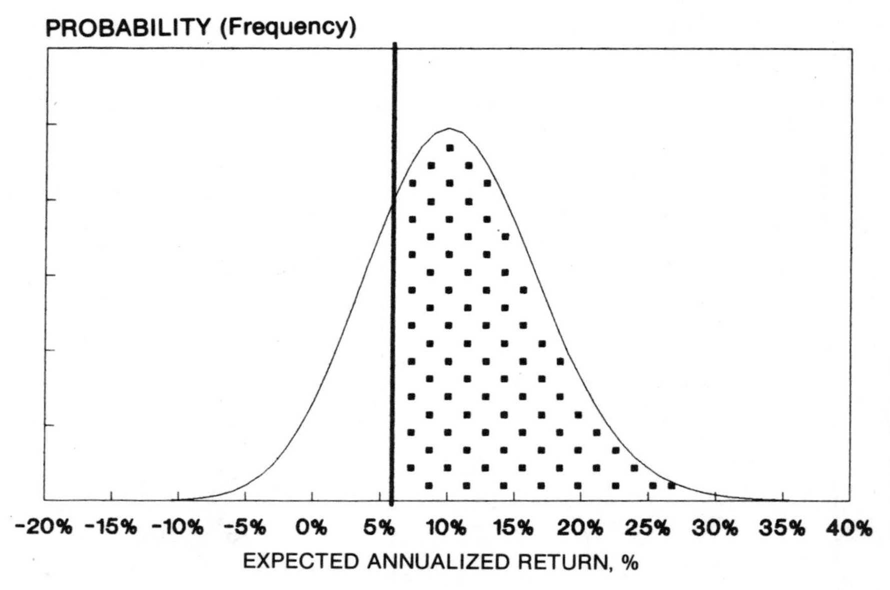

Figure 8–2. Probability of Exceeding a 6% Target Return.

transformed equation is known as the *first derivative*. That equation can, in turn, be transformed into yet another equation to determine the precise change in the rate of change of (y) at any specific level of (x). This is known as the *second derivative* of the original equation.

Whereas algebra is sufficient to determine the slope (rate of change) of a straight line, which is constant, differential calculus is needed to deal with the *instantaneous* rate of change of curvilinear functions over an *infinitesimal* interval. The business applications can be enormous since the economy, business income, and the investments markets are as dynamic as the stars and planets themselves.

The reverse of the process of differentiation (determining derivatives) is the realm of integral calculus. Integration allows the mathematician to solve for the original function when the rate of change is the known variable. By knowing the rate of change of (y) for any value of (x), we can determine the absolute value or values of (y) for any value of (x). Since the value of (y) is, in effect, the height of a curve, integral calculus allows us to calculate the area between two limits of (x) that lies under any curve defined by (y) as a function of (x).

THE CALCULUS OF PROBABILITY SIMPLIFIED

The area under (between the (x) axis and) the curve is of utmost importance in the calculus of probability. Measuring the area under a curve, for our purposes, is comparable to adding together all the heights of the curve at all possible levels of (x), or more accurately between two limits of (x), such as plus and minus three or more standard deviations. For asset-allocation purposes, the value of (x) are the range of possible returns, and the function of (x) or (y) is the relative frequency with which each return (x) is expected to occur.

It would be a very tedious task to measure the height at every possible infinitesimal value of (x) without the mathematics of integral calculus. So that we do not reach beyond the intended scope of this book, however, I will demonstrate how the area under a curve can be estimated accurately by dividing the curve into finite rectangles as shown in Figure 8–3.

If we make the width of each rectangle as small as possible, we will be able to take a sum of the areas in each of the rectangles, which will come very close to approximating the area under the curve. The more rectangles we use, the more accurate our calculation of area will be.

The width of each rectangle can be as small as we wish. For investment purposes, this could be 1%, or .1%, or preferably, .01%, in terms of expected return. We then need to calculate the height of the curve at each one of these small intervals.

The equation for calculating the height (y) of a normal distribution curve at any level of expected return (x), is a function of the mean (a) expected return and the standard deviation (s) of the returns:

$$y = \frac{e^{-[(x-a)^2/2s^2]}}{s\sqrt{2\pi}}$$

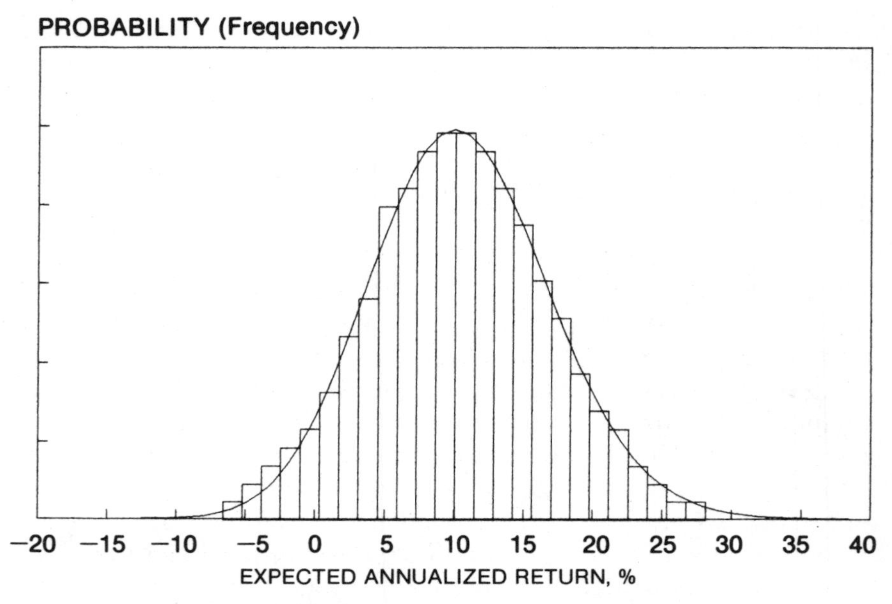

Figure 8–3. Estimating the Area Under a Log-Normal Curve.

where (e) is the natural log base. Mathematically, the height of the curve is known as the *density function*, which represents the relative frequency of occurrence of each of the (x) values.

The examples in this chapter all use *log*-normal distribution curves since they more accurately reflect the way securities prices behave. To compute the height of a *log*-normal curve, merely substitute the logarithms of $(1 + x)$, $(1 + a)$, and $(1 + s)$ in place of (x), (a) and (s).

To figure the probability of a security, or class of securities, beating a certain target return, all we have to do is add up the areas of the rectangles to the right of the target and divide that total area by the sum of the areas for all the rectangles comprising the area under the curve. Using this process, we can calculate the probability of any class of security outperforming any target return. However, the resulting probability will only be as accurate as the inputs, that is, the expected return and standard deviation.

ODDS OF STOCKS BEATING BONDS

Once we have computed an expected return for stocks and bonds, along with an estimated standard deviation of stock returns for the appropriate time horizon, it is then a piece of cake to compute the probability of stocks outperforming bonds over that time horizon. Assume that the five-year expected return is 10% for stocks and 8% for bonds and that our assumed one-year standard deviation for stocks is 15%, making the annualized five-year deviation equal to 6%. The probability of stocks beating the expected return for bonds over the next five years is 65%, as shown in Figure 8–4.

Using the same expected returns, we will now compute the probability of stocks beating bonds over a 10-year time period. The only input that needs to be changed is the *annualized* standard deviation of stocks, which drops from 6% (for a 5-year horizon) to 4% (for a 10-year horizon).

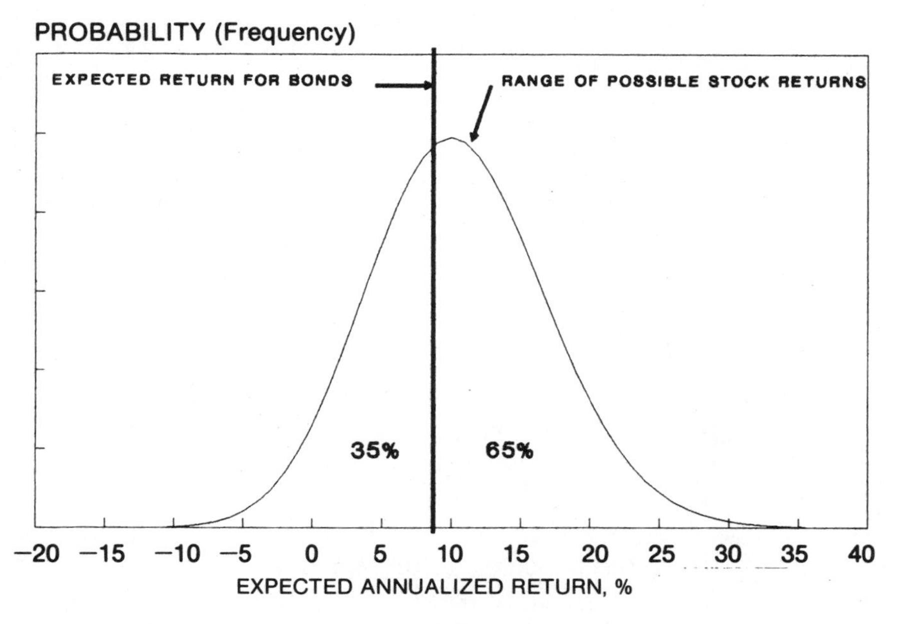

Figure 8–4. Probability of Stocks Beating Bonds over Five Years.

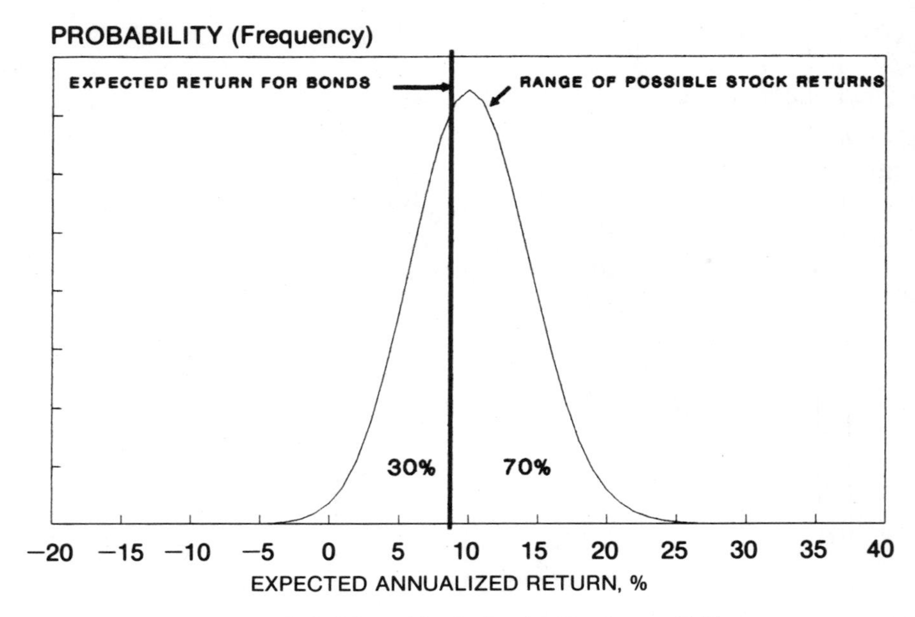

Figure 8–5. Probability of Stocks Beating Bonds over 10 Years.

Notice in Figure 8–5 how the distribution covers a much smaller range of possible returns on the (x) axis. This is because *stock returns become more predictable as the time horizon lengthens*. Figure 8-5 depicts this relationship.

ODDS OF BONDS BEATING STOCKS

I have just shown that if the expected return of stocks is 2% greater than the expected return of bonds, and the standard deviation of stock returns is 15%, then stocks have a 70% probability of outperforming the expected return for bonds over the next 10 years. This also means that stocks have a 30% probability of underperforming the expected return for bonds over the next 10 years. But, *this does not mean that bonds have only a 30% chance of beating the expected return for stocks*. This is because we are calculating the probability of one class of security beating the *expected return* of another class, not of actually outperforming the other class, *per se*.

If stocks have a 70% probability of beating bonds, then the only time bonds would have precisely a 30% probability of beating stocks is when the expected return for bonds is absolutely certain, that is, when the future bond return has no distribution of possible returns. That only would be possible when the bond for which the expected return is being computed is a zero-coupon bond that matures precisely at the end of the investment time horizon.

This is a common oversight on the part of many investors. It is much more realistic and productive to compare the expected returns of a stock *portfolio* to that of a bond *portfolio*. The point is that a bond portfolio has a distribution of expected returns, just like that of a stock portfolio. Throughout this book, I have been using the Standard & Poor's 500 as the proxy for the equity portfolio and can likewise use the Shearson Lehman Government/Corporate Bond Index (for one) as a proxy for the fixed-income portfolio.

The distribution of bond returns looks very much like that of stock returns except that it is much narrower. That is because bond returns have a standard deviation that is generally 30 to 40% of that of stocks. Figure 8–6 compares the one-year distribution of bond returns to stock returns, assuming an 8% expected return and 7% standard deviation for bonds, and a 10% expected return and 15% standard deviation for stocks.

To calculate the probability of bonds beating the expected return of stocks, we merely compute the percentage of the area under the bond curve that is to the right of the mode (expected return) of the stock curve. This is illustrated in Figure 8–7.

MEAN VERSUS MODE

In a log-normal distribution, unlike a normal distribution, the arithmetic mean and mode are not the same. For investment purposes, the mode is the expected return calculated to be the "most likely." It is our educated "best guess"—the return that has the greatest probability of occurrence. It is the peak of the curve.

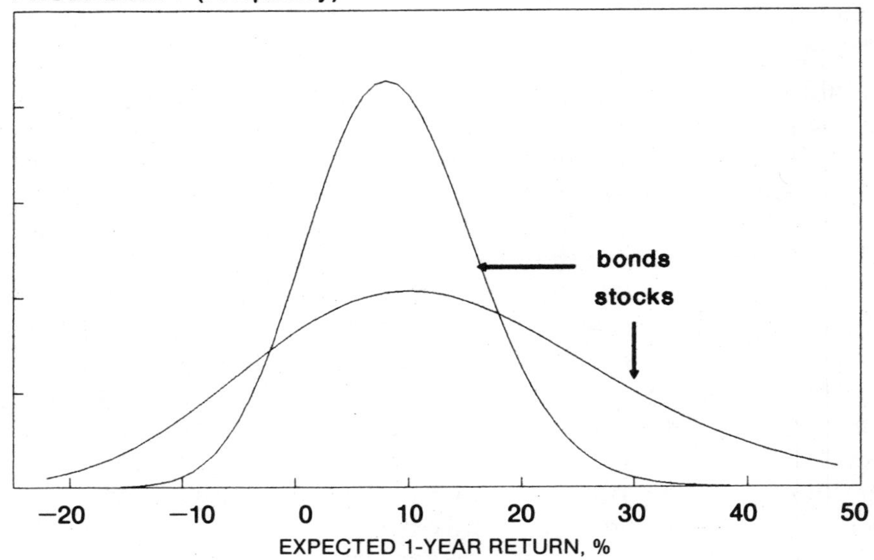

Figure 8–6. Range of One-Year Possible Returns.

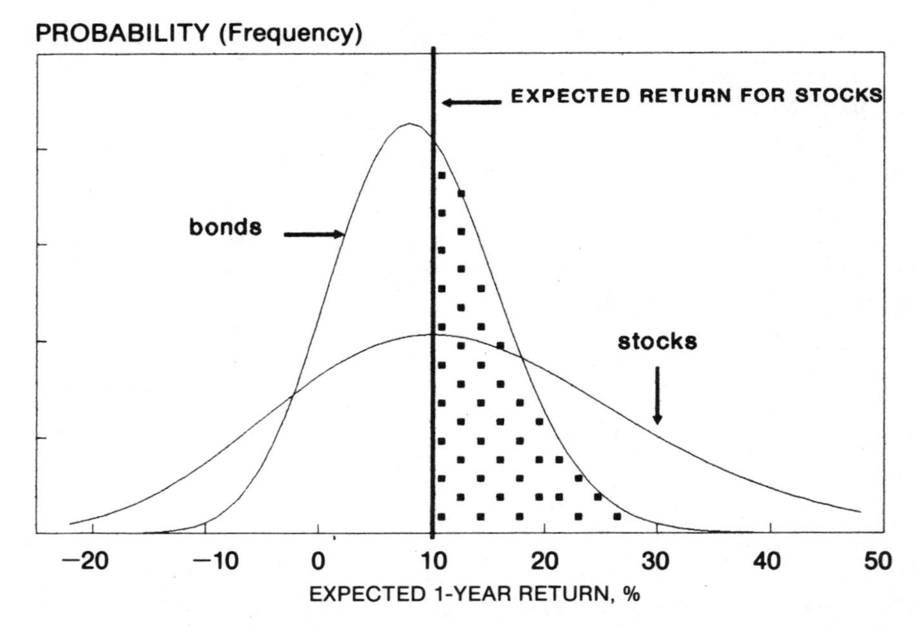

Figure 8–7. Probability of Bonds Beating the Most Likely Stock Return.

The arithmetic mean, however, is a slightly higher number. It is the weighted average of all possible returns. In other words, it is the mathematical result of multiplying each possible return by its expected frequency, all divided by the sum of all the frequencies. It is the simple arithmetic average. Because a log-normal curve is skewed to the right, the arithmetic mean is also slightly to the right of the mode.

I believe that mode, not arithmetic mean, is actually the expected return number the market analyst should compute, for three reasons:

1. The expected return is the analyst's best guess and, therefore, by definition has the greatest probability of occurrence.
2. If the expected return is to be attained, the probability of a slightly higher return has to be greater than that of a slightly lower return because of the mathematics of compounded numbers.
3. In light of item 2, as well as the discussion regarding the usage and types of means in Chapter 1, the mode of a log-normal curve is actually the *geometric mean* (viz. arithmetic mean) of the expected returns.

Looking at it in another way, if stocks return 10% on average over 20 years, then they must have returned more than 10% more often than they returned less than 10%; or they must have returned 20% more often than 0%. For example, if stocks returned 20% one year, 0% the next, and repeated this pattern for 20 years, the average annualized return would not have been 10%, it would have been only 9.5%!

This is why we prefer a log-normal distribution in the first place. With securities, there is an equal probability of prices moving up 25% versus down 20%, of moving up 50% versus down 33%, of moving up 10% versus down 9%, and so on. This has to be the case. For instance, if a $100 security kept moving up and down, say 30%, its price would eventually approach nullity. Here is a series of numbers, beginning with 100, that move up and down 30%: 100, 130, 91, 118, 83, 108, 75, 98, 69, 89, 62, 81, 57, and so forth.

ODDS OF STOCKS AND BONDS BEATING A TARGET

You have already learned how to compute the probability of stocks beating the expected return for bonds and of bonds beating the expected return for stocks. But you have not learned what to do with that information.

Let's approach this subject by first examining the case where the investor desires a specific average annual return over a specific time horizon. What should be the investor's initial stock-bond mix?

Assume the following:

1. A 10-year time horizon.
2. A target return (which could be the actuarial assumption of a pension plan) of 9%.
3. A 10-year annualized expected return of 10% and a 10-year annualized standard deviation of 4% for the stock portfolio.
4. A 10-year annualized expected return of 8% and a 10-year annualized standard deviation of 2% for the bond portfolio.

There would be two common, but unwise, approaches to this allocation problem:

1. Invest very heavily or entirely in equities, because the expected return for bonds is below the target return. This would be a terrible tactic! The risk/reward ratio would be unwarranted. In fact, the one-year portfolio standard deviation would be substantially greater than the expected return.
2. Invest 50% in stocks and 50% in bonds, since the target return is exactly halfway between the two expected returns. This is much better than the first approach, but it is still not optimal.

Remember my calculation the evening before the day at the racetrack? Risk can be minimized by wagering in proportion to the odds. Let's do the same thing with stocks and bonds. The odds of stocks and bonds each beating 9% can be considered the odds of winning. Using the density-function formula for frequency under a log-normal curve, the probabilities of stocks and bonds outperforming a 9% target, in this example, are shown in Figure 8–8.

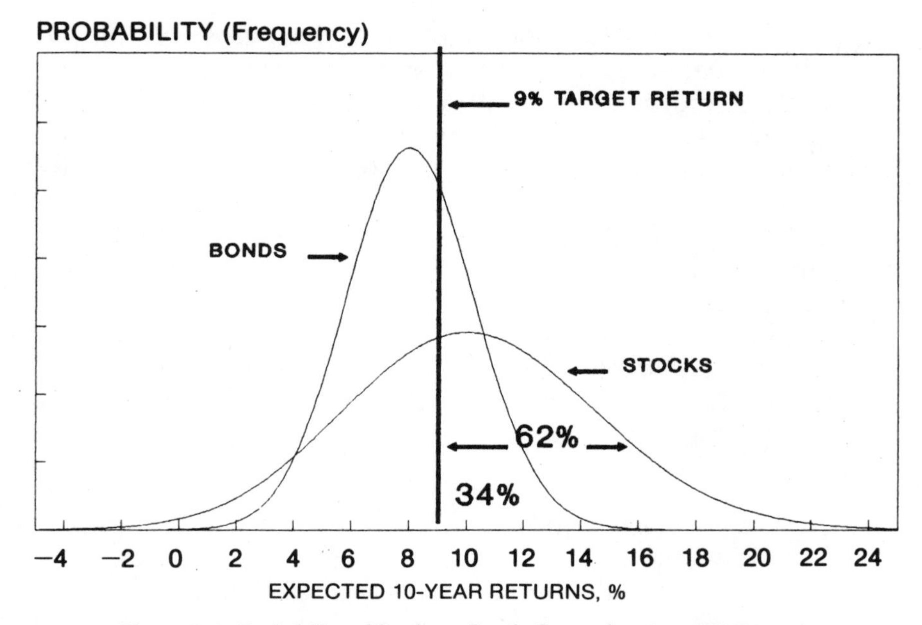

Figure 8–8. Probability of Stocks or Bonds Outperforming a 9% Target.

Here 62% of the area under the stock curve and 34% of the area under the bond curve lie to the right of the 9% target return. Thus, to allocate this hypothetical portfolio in proportion to the probabilities, the investor should allocate 65% to stocks and 35% to bonds.

ODDS OF STOCKS AND BONDS BEATING EACH OTHER

Suppose the investor has no particular target return, but wants to allocate assets between stocks and bonds in a fashion that would best reflect the selected time horizon. All we have to do is calculate the odds of stocks beating the expected return for bonds, and vice versa, over the time horizon. Assume the probability was 70% that stocks would exceed bonds' expected return, and 40% that the bond market would beat the stock market expected return.

These percentages total 110%! But don't be alarmed. They almost always total over 100%. That is because we are measuring the odds of two separate classes of securities outperforming, in effect, two separate target returns. These targets just happen to be the expected return of the other class. Remember, here we are not using the higher mathematics involved with the absolute probability of one class beating another, but rather one class beating the *expected return* of the other. We are relating the areas under two curves to two straight lines (targets). We are not comparing the areas under both curves according to their intersection. As we have seen, the process can be much simpler than that.

However, we do have to convert the percentage probabilities to proportions that add to 100%. Using the previous example, the percentage allocated to stock would be figured as a proportion using simple algebra:

$$\frac{X}{100} = \frac{70}{110} \text{ so } X = \frac{7000}{110} = 64\ (\%)$$

So, the allocation would be 64% stocks and 36% bonds.

SOME RULES OF THUMB

Often investors will claim to have a long time horizon, but when the optimal percentage they should have in equities is explained, they immediately shorten their time horizon. This is a mistake, but it is an unfortunate human tendency to be less than objective regarding personal assets.

The following table shows what the approximate *equity* allocations would have been during the 1980s as a function of the various equity risk-premiums (arithmetic differences between stock and bond expected returns), assuming a 15% standard deviation for stocks and 7% for bonds:

Equity Risk Premium	Time Horizon			
	1 year	5 years	10 years	20 years
0%	50%	50%	50%	50%
2	60	70	80	88
4	67	86	95	100

An obvious question would be, why would one have 50% invested in stocks when the expected return was no greater than that of bonds? The answer is that the equity expected return was based on a stock market value (at the end of the time horizon) that already included a future equity risk-premium. This issue will be dealt with, in detail, in Chapter 9. Also, we did not include cash, which could have reduced the equity exposure in all cases.

LET'S THROW IN SOME CASH

The models thus far in this chapter dictate allocation solely on the odds of stocks and bonds beating each other or another target. But, what if both stocks and bonds are headed south together? For instance, stocks might outperform bonds as expected, but the returns of both might be negative. This occasionally happens during periods of five years or less.

This phenomenon creates a role for cash equivalents. You may recall from Chapter 6 that cash has no true standard deviation because its returns are distributed in an odd fashion. Therefore, we cannot calculate accurately the probability of cash outperforming a target return, including the expected returns for other classes of securities.

For this reason, some well-marketed asset-allocation products do not include a cash component. I have stated already that this is a mistake. Every bear market is not like October 1987, when bonds provided a perfect alternative to owning stocks. Sometimes both stocks and bonds depreciate at the same time. As mentioned in Chapter 6, no matter what the time horizon is, there is always *some* probability that cash will outperform stocks or bonds. So, cash could be considered as an alternative for either stocks or bonds. However, it is not absolutely necessary to compute the probability of bonds and cash outperforming each other. The duration of the bond portfolio can be adjusted to create the effect of owning a percentage in cash in lieu of bonds.

Therefore, in a diversified portfolio, the investor only needs to evaluate cash as a substitute for equities. The only stock-cash calculation we can make that is statistically accurate is the probability of stocks beating our expected return for cash over the time horizon selected. We then must assume (unfortunately) no standard deviation for the cash return, and that the probability of cash outperforming stocks is merely the inverse of the probability of stocks outperforming cash. This is really okay, since the volatility of cash returns is very small. We do know that about half the time cash returns vary less than 2% year to year. So, if the probability of stocks outperforming the expected return for cash is, say, 80%, then we assume the odds of cash outperforming stocks is 20%.

There are three basic methods of blending stocks and bonds with cash, once all the probabilities are calculated. The first method is the most complex because of the need for calculating correlation of returns and does not work as well as the other two methods. But, since the first method is used most often, it should be outlined.

METHOD 1: CORRELATION ANALYSIS

The investor first computes the proper stock/bond mix according to the probabilities of stocks beating bonds and vice versa. Then the investor computes the odds of this combined stock-bond portfolio beating cash. If the stock-bond portion of the portfolio were 70% stocks and 30% bonds and, on a combined basis, had an 80% probability of beating cash, then the portfolio would be structured as follows: 56% stock (80% of 70%), 24% bonds (80% of 30%), and 20% cash.

The difficulty involves the calculation of the probability of the combined stock-bond mix beating cash. To do this, we must know the standard deviation of expected return of the stock-bond mix. This, unfortunately, is a function of the correlation between stock and bond returns. The lower the correlation, the lower the combined standard deviation. The equation for computing the combined standard deviation of stocks and bonds is rather lengthy. It is the *square root of the following:*

$$(\%\ \text{STK}^{2} \times Ss^{2}) + 2(\%\ \text{STK} \times \%\ \text{BND} \times r \times Ss \times Sb) + (\%\ \text{BND}^{2} \times Sb^{2})$$

where (Ss) is the standard deviation of stock, (Sb) is the standard deviation of bonds, and (r) is the correlation between stock and bond returns.

The reasons Method 1 is probably not as successful as the next two are that cash is almost always excessively overweighted and the future coefficient of correlation, which is part of the equation, is extremely volatile and difficult to predict. This will be discussed in detail in Chapter 10.

METHOD 2: THE STOCK-CASH MIX

The investor first computes the odds of stocks beating cash and creates a stock-cash mix accordingly. Then the probability of that stock-cash mix beating the expected return of bonds is calculated.

If stocks have an 80% probability of beating cash and the stock-cash mix has a 60% probability of beating bonds, then the allocation would be 48% stocks (60% of 80%), 40% bonds, and 12% cash (60% of 20%). Remember that the probability of the stock-cash mix beating bonds is a proportion that includes the odds of the stock-cash mix beating the expected return for bonds as well as the odds of bonds beating the expected return of the mix.

One advantage of this method is that we do not have to compute a stock-bond correlation of returns. The standard deviation of the stock-cash mix is computed as though cash had no standard deviation. Therefore, if the standard deviation for stocks were 15%, then an 80/20 stock-cash mix would have a theoretical standard deviation of 12% (not mathematically accurate, but workable).

Another advantage of Method 2 is that for short-term time horizons, cash will normally represent a significant portion of the portfolio, which seems appropriate. Conversely, for long-term time horizons, cash is normally nonexistent, since the probability of stocks beating cash over 20 years or more is nearly 100%. This also makes sense.

METHOD 3: THE HORSE RACE

The method is simple, but it has class, mathematically. It is similar to the hypothetical horse race example at the beginning of the chapter. The investor calculates the odds of each class of security beating *both* of the other two asset classes *simultaneously*. Strictly speaking, this method should involve correlation analysis, because if one security beats a second security, the odds of beating the third security are affected. For example, when the odds of stocks beating bonds is high, the odds that stocks will beat cash is higher than normal because of the positive correlation between bond and cash returns.

However, this problem is largely overcome by using the system of calculating expected returns described in Chapters 4 through 6. Also, the importance of correlation is overshadowed by the methodology itself, which is:

Probability of A beating B *and* C =
Probability of A beating B × Probability of A beating C

Again this is not totally accurate because B and C are not independent from each other. But, the method produces very workable results.

Assume the following:

	Probability
1. Stocks versus cash return	80%
2. Cash versus stock return	20
3. Stock versus bonds return	70
4. Bonds versus stock return	40
5. Bonds versus cash	70
6. Cash versus bonds	30

Remember that items 3 and 4 usually will total over 100%.

Now make the computations of each security beating the other two:

1. Stocks versus bonds and cash = 70% × 80% = 56%.
2. Bonds versus stocks and cash = 40% × 70% = 28%.
3. Cash versus stocks and bonds = 20% × 30% = 6%.

Converting these percentages to proportions that equal 100%, we get a portfolio that makes sense: 62% stocks, 31% bonds, and 7% cash.

Method 3 has produced such fine historic results that it is hard to imagine why it hasn't gained proper recognition. For long-term portfolios, cash is normally reduced drastically; and when stocks have only a slightly higher return than cash and a slightly lower return than bonds, equities can be cut to one-third (or less) of the portfolio. Also, for short-term portfolios, cash becomes an important portion, which it should.

Method 3 is simple, and it works well for all types of risk profiles in all market environments because it deals the most effectively with cash. This method reduces risk just like the horse race system did, without employing excessive cash. In the next chapter, we will explore how to weight the probabilities to improve expected return.

9

Asset Allocation: Building a Dynamic Model

Much of the best mathematical inspiration comes from experience. . . . it is hardly possible to believe in the existence of an absolute immutable concept of mathematical rigor dissociated from all human experience.

—*John Von Neumann*

EINSTEIN MIGHT HAVE HAD A TOUGH TIME

In the preface of this book, I acknowledge the works of several colleagues and contemporary pioneers of quantitative investments work. It would be an oversight, however, not to give credit to the great mathematicians who developed the tools that make quantitative investment work possible. In one sense, mathematical theory can be divided into two branches: logic and probability. A simple example of logic is: $A = B$ and $B = C$; therefore, $A = C$. Conversely, $A > C$ and $B > C$; therefore, $A > B$ involves probability since it is possible but not certain.

On the subject of probability, Pierre Simon de Laplace, Carl Friederich Gauss, and Bernhard Riemann developed methodologies for the calculus of probability and rate of change to facilitate their work in the physical sciences in the early nineteenth century. In the area of logic, we must give credit to the early twentieth-century mathematicians, particularly George Boole and John Venn, who provided the theories that allow us to better visualize and quantify even the most difficult concepts. John Von Neumann should be credited for pioneering "game theory."

It was the goal of Boole, in particular, to develop a symbolic language that ultimately could be used to express any possible thought, scenario, or concept. To the scientist, the letter C might represent electrical capacitance or the speed of light, and the letter *L*, electromagnetic inductance. But to me, in the Boolean sense, C represents the entire concept of (investor) *confidence,* which through a series of algorithms can be reduced to a single number. The letter *L* for me, does not represent the demand for money function, as it would to many financial analysts, but rather the entire logical process and the resulting numerics behind liquidity preference.

Most of us tend to forget the trailblazing efforts that were made by those early mathematicians of modern times. In my opinion, this is an unfortunate consequence of the computer technology mushroom. The computer has bridged the complexities of the classical equations allowing us to manufacture expedient solutions.

Just as I began writing this chapter, I was asked by one of my clients to figure out how much $1.00 would be worth in 100 years if it grew at a compounded rate of 6.75%. The computation took literally three seconds, including both the time needed to recall the equation and the time it took to enter the 11 keystrokes on my pocket calculator. What if Albert Einstein had been asked to make that seemingly simple calculation just 50 years ago? It might have taken him hours unless he used his slide rule, in which case 100 manipulations of the slipstick would probably have caused a slight miscalculation. For much more complex computations, the computer enables us to utilize rapid, repetitive processing as a shortcut to solving problems which, in a classical mathematical discipline, should have involved painstakingly devised equations.

I am a one of the earlier chartered financial analysts and have read, cover to cover, most bimonthly issues of the *Financial Analysts Journal*. This fine publication is loaded with mathematical formulas. But most of them, although appearing ominous, are really nothing more than classical algebra. The professional investment community, as a whole, has not even reached the mathematical awareness of the scientists of 200 years ago! Integrals, differentials, derivatives, set theory, and symbolic logic have been in place a long time. They are tools that can offer the quantitative investment professional the mean of quantifying the social behavior that has such a pervasive influence in the securities markets.

DYNAMIC ASSET ALLOCATION DEFINED

The following are my definitions:

Tactical asset allocation strives to adjust the portfolio mix through the use of any technique whatsoever, with the intent of over-weighting the class of assets that will perform the best over the short term. The stress is on short-term performance, but the intended corollary is that risk will be reduced by underweighting the asset classes that will perform relatively poorly. Tactical asset allocation attempts to manage risk through expected short-term return.

Strategic asset allocation attempts to manage return by managing risk. A long-term asset mix is maintained at a level that theoretically limits the portfolio volatility to a level commensurate with the investor's risk profile (level of risk aversion). The underlying tenet of the strategic approach is that the securities markets are totally unpredictable in the short term; therefore, a fixed blend of asset classes is the most prudent.

Dynamic asset allocation lies somewhere in between the tactical and strategic techniques. It does not attempt to forecast short-term market movement, nor does it produce an asset mix that is to be etched in stone. It computes the best long-term strategic allocation for the particular investor at a specific point in time. But then it changes that allocation as the level of the markets and the investor's risk aversion change. *Dynamic asset allocation can be considered a series of rolling strategic asset allocations*. Whereas strategic allocation looks at what will be the best asset mix, *on average*, over the years for the particular investor, dynamic allocation reflects the fact that most points in time *are not average*. Therefore, it adjusts the asset mix to reflect the *updated long-term* expected returns for the various asset classes. Dynamic allocation deals effectively with the issue confronted in this rhetorical question: If a long-term investor typically is advised to maintain a strategic asset mix that includes 65% equities, should he or she still be advised to maintain that mix if the long-term expected return of stocks were, at a given instant, less than that of government bonds?

The remainder of this chapter outlines both the reasons that make the Hammer-Lodefink dynamic asset-allocation model unique and the process involved.

A DAY AT THE RACETRACK

In the previous chapter, I used the example of the betting scheme I had devised the evening before my first experience at the horse races. This analogy was related in an attempt to illustrate the advantages of probability investing. When I actually went to the races the next day, I learned that the odds being paid frequently varied significantly from the predicted odds in the previous evening's newspaper as well as from the initial odds posted as the betting began. What should a bettor do if he or she feels the predicted odds are more accurate than the official odds? On this particular day, the earlier predictions were quite different from the actual odds offered. Therefore, the crowd really may not have been an efficient market. We could make a case that the expected return would be improved by placing probability-weighted bets based on the prediction rather than on the official "market-derived" odds.

You can observe from Table 9–1 that if I had bet according to the probabilities reflected in the posted odds (i.e., bet with the crowd), I would not have lost money, just as in the example at the beginning of the last chapter. However, if I had spread my bets according to the previously published odds (on the assumption they were more likely to be correct), I would have made a nice profit if the published odds were correct, and I would not have lost any money if the official (market-derived) odds turned out to be correct!

Strategic allocators bet with the market in order to minimize risk. They assume the market is totally efficient and that the odds of stocks beating bonds, cash, or real estate are always the same

TABLE 9–1 Predicted versus Actual Odds Paid at a Horse Race

	Horse			Total Cash after 4 Races
	A	B	C	
Probability: Earlier Prediction	50%	25%	25%	
Crowd Derived	25	50	25	
Odds	3-to-1	1-to-1	3-to-1	
Payoff	4-for-1	2-for-1	4-for-1	
Bet According to Prediction	$ 60	$ 30	$ 30	
Outcome: Prediction Correct	480	60	120	$660
Crowd Correct	240	120	120	480
Bet According to Crowd	$ 30	$ 60	$ 30	
Outcome: Prediction Correct	240	120	120	$480
Crowd Correct	120	240	120	480

because the risk-premiums are probably accurate. Dynamic and some tactical allocators bet according to their own predicted expected returns, hoping to earn a portfolio return in excess of the norm.

WEIGHTING THE PROBABILITIES

In horse racing, the horse with the greatest chance of winning pays the least amount. This is not exactly the situation in the world of asset allocation. It is true that if bonds are favored to win, but stocks win instead, equities can offer a payoff substantially greater than bonds. If stocks are favored to win, but bonds win instead, the payoff is not likely to be that great relative to the equity return. This is particularly true when cash outperforms other investments. That is, if a model states (as it usually does) that equities are supposed to outperform cash, but cash outperforms instead, the potential reward for having owned cash is usually nowhere near as great as the excess return from stocks when stocks beat cash.

It is not only important to know which class of security has what probability of outperforming, but also to know by *how much* it is expected to outperform. For example, if stocks have a 70% chance of beating a particular target, they usually will outperform that target by more than they underperform it by (the other 30% of the time). Thus, the shape of the distribution curve comes into play.

Here I will exaggerate two (unrealistic and otherwise meaningless) distribution-of-return patterns strictly to prove a point. Both investments in Figures 9–1 and 9–2 have a 50% probability of outperforming the target. That is because 50% of the frequencies (area under the "curve") is to the right of the target. But, obviously, Security B is the better of the two investments, because when it beats the target, it does so by a greater amount, on average, than Security A does.

The mean return for Security A, when it beats the target, is 15%. The mean return for Security B, when it beats the target, is 20%. Security B should be overweighted relative to Security A, even though they both have a 50% chance of outperforming the target.

Return-weighting the probabilities produces better results in portfolio management. This is because it provides an additional means of overweighting the asset class with the greatest return.

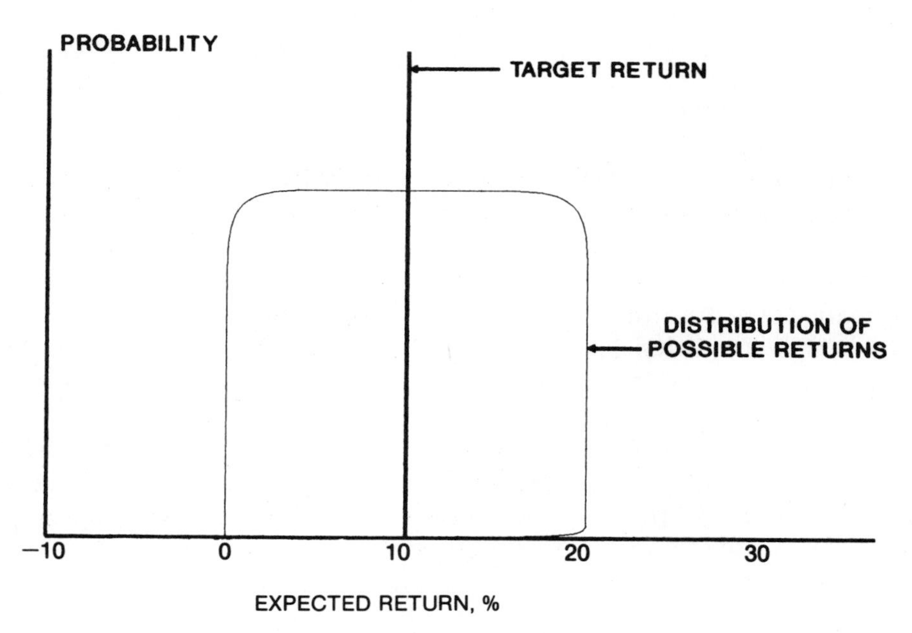

Figure 9–1. Probability of Security A Beating a 10% Target.

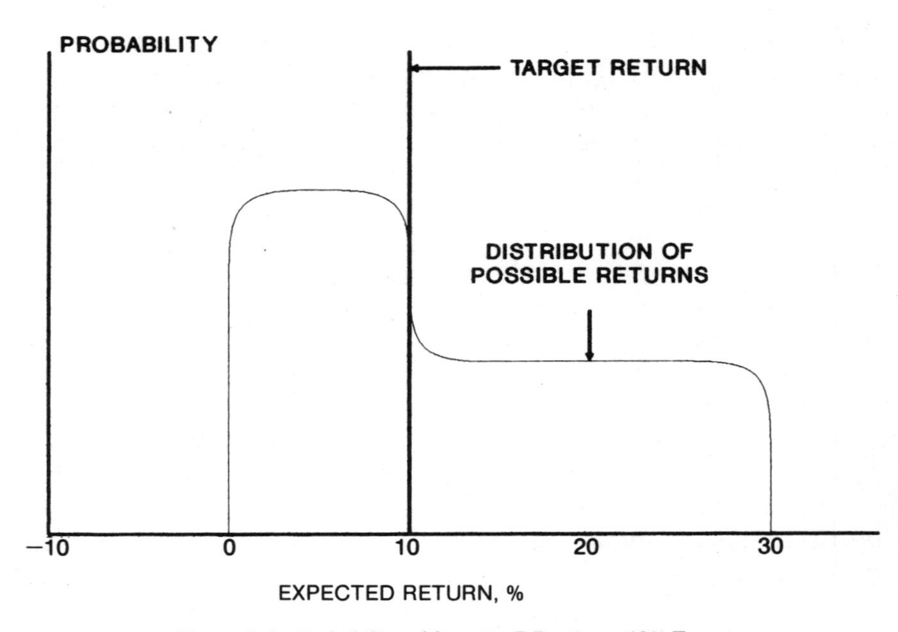

Figure 9–2. Probability of Security B Beating a 10% Target.

Sometimes this will increase portfolio volatility and sometimes it will reduce it.

Figure 9–3 shows realistically the probability of a security (with a 10% expected return and a standard deviation of 10%) beating a target return of 6%. Approximately 70% of the area under the curve is to the right of the target, which means that the security has a 70% chance of outperforming a 6% target return. However, notice that when the security does beat the target ("win"), it wins by about 11%, on average; but when it does not beat the target, it underperforms the target by only 6%.

Thus, we can conclude more than just the fact that the security has a 70% chance of beating the target. We can conclude that it has a 70% chance of beating the target by an average of 11% compared to a 30% probability of underperforming the target by 6%.

Return-weighting is one procedure that makes the Hammer-Lodefink model different from others. The most outstanding, unique feature, however, is the use of investor confidence. It is here that our asset-allocation process begins.

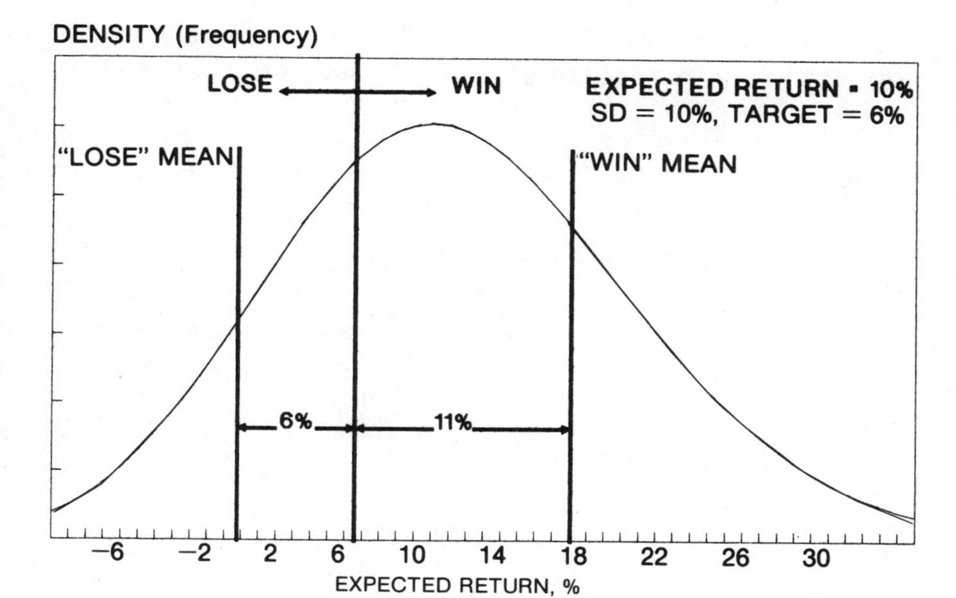

Figure 9–3. The Importance of Return-Weighted Probabilities.

STEP 1: COMPUTING INVESTOR CONFIDENCE

I have discovered, and confirmed over the years, what appears to be irrefutable evidence that *the equity risk-premium expands and contracts in direct proportion to the yield spread between medium- and high-quality fixed-income investments.* We can, therefore, create a confidence index based on the differences in yield of the following:

1. Certificates of deposit and Treasury bills.
2. Commercial paper and Treasury bills.
3. Merrill Lynch medium-grade and high-grade bond indices.
4. Aaa- and A-rated bonds.
5. The average of Wall Street's highest yield expectations for government bonds one year into the future versus the average of the lowest expectations.

An algorithm has been developed that combines all of these to produce an index number which, during the 1980s, ranged from a low of 85 (in 1980 and 1982) to a high of 98 (in 1987 and 1989). A low number indicates wide yield spreads and low confidence and vice versa. Theoretically, an index number of 100 would mean that there is no difference in yield between high- and medium-grade securities, and that the equity risk-premium could be zero.

STEP 2: FORECASTING FORWARD RATES

Based on the level of investor confidence, a hypothetical Treasury yield curve is constructed that is our best guess of what the yield curve would look like if the market believed that rates were to remain unchanged for the foreseeable future. The lower the level of confidence, the greater the slope of this hypothetical curve will be. This hypothetical curve is then compared to today's actual curve. If the actual curve is steeper than the hypothetical curve, this would be indicative of higher future rates. The reverse is also true.

Duration risk-premium and liquidity preference are a function of investor confidence. We must calculate how much the confidence factor is apt to be influencing the current shape of the yield curve. Mathematically back out this element to arrive at a residual curve to be used for forecasting purposes. For future projected yield curves assume that investor confidence will work its way toward an historical average over the long term. In the near term, confidence may in the same direction (possibly away from the secular average) since it does exhibit intermediate trends (persistence) similar to the business cycle.

On this basis, compute a series of market-derived yield curves for each of the next 20 years. We are not particularly concerned with the accuracy of these forecasts, since history has proven that the securities markets will adjust to these expectations long before they become manifest.

Using this series of forward-yield curves, an expected return for a Treasury bond *portfolio* is computed for various time horizons, 1 through 20 years. This portfolio is designed to represent a typical fixed-income portfolio with average duration of five or six years. We now have a series of expected returns for "bonds" for the next 1 to 20 years.

Note: Individual bond returns for securities-selection purposes are not derived using this methodology alone. Rolling yields, special bond features, and yield spreads are equally as important.

Confidence-adjusted yield-curve analysis also provides information regarding market expectations for future T-bill rates. Using this information, we calculate the expected return for a cash-equivalent portfolio consisting of 1-year T-bills for holding periods of 1 to 20 years. This becomes our expected return for cash for the various time horizons.

STEP 3: PROJECTING FUTURE STOCK DIVIDENDS AND BOOK VALUES

Historic growth rates for the dividends of the popular stock market averages are not useful for making projections due to the ever-changing composition of the averages, as discussed in previous chapters. There are two or more viable methods for forecasting dividends.

One is the top-down approach of making assumptions about future growth in population, productivity, inflation, and so on. But, we can use a more finely-tuned procedure to produce more accurate estimates for a specific market proxy such as the Standard & Poor's 500 Index.

We begin by computing a normalized return on equity of the index. Any number of methods may be employed. One way is to project the recent trend and average that number with a long-term historical norm. The resulting initial ROE would be a quasi-normalized number, which reflects both the secular criterion and the recent trend.

The normalized ROE is then multiplied by the current book value of the index to produce a normalized earnings per share. The actual current dividend of the index is then divided by the normalized EPS to arrive at a payout ratio. For future years, it is assumed that the payout ratio and the ROE will revert to a long-term norm. That norm could be the annual average for the past business cycle(s) providing that an equal number of peak and trough years are included. Very long-term averages are not advisable due to the changing composition of the averages, secular trends in the cost of capital, and changes in accounting practices and taxation.

Table 9–2 shows a simplified method of projecting the dividends of the S&P 500. The initial quasinormalized ROE is an average of the latest ROE and the secular average. Next to the discount rate (which will be discussed in the following section), it is the most critical factor. This is because it affects near-term dividends (which are discounted the least) and has a permanent effect on book value, which determines terminal value. A 10% (or 1½ percentage point) change in the secular ROE changes the total present value in the example by about 15%. A 10% (or 5 percentage point) change in

TABLE 9–2 S&P 500 Projected Dividends

Current Book	$150.00	Current EPS	$25.00
Current Div.	$10.00	Current ROE	16.7%
Payout Norm	48.0%	Secular ROE	13.0%
Discount	10.0%	Normal P/B	1.65

Future Year	Normalized ROE	Normalized EPS	Normalized Payout	Projected Dividend	Normalized Book
0	14.8%	$22.25	44.9%	$10.00	$162.25
1	14.5%	$23.47	45.6%	$10.69	$175.03
2	14.1%	$24.68	46.2%	$11.39	$188.32
3	13.7%	$25.86	46.8%	$12.10	$202.08
4	13.4%	$27.01	47.4%	$12.80	$216.29
5	13.0%	$28.12	48.0%	$13.50	$230.91
6	13.0%	$30.02	48.0%	$14.41	$246.52
7	13.0%	$32.05	48.0%	$15.38	$263.19
8	13.0%	$34.21	48.0%	$16.42	$280.98
9	13.0%	$36.53	48.0%	$17.53	$299.97
10	13.0%	$39.00	48.0%	$18.72	$320.25
11	13.0%	$41.63	48.0%	$19.98	$341.90
12	13.0%	$44.45	48.0%	$21.33	$365.01
13	13.0%	$47.45	48.0%	$22.78	$389.69
14	13.0%	$50.66	48.0%	$24.32	$416.03
15	13.0%	$54.08	48.0%	$25.96	$444.15
16	13.0%	$57.74	48.0%	$27.72	$474.18
17	13.0%	$61.64	48.0%	$29.59	$506.23
18	13.0%	$65.81	48.0%	$31.59	$540.45
19	13.0%	$70.26	48.0%	$33.72	$576.99
20	13.0%	$75.01	48.0%	$36.00	$615.99
			Terminal Value	$1,140.15	
PV of Future Dividends and Terminal Value =				$299.21	

the secular payout ratio or price-to-book ratio has a 5% or less effect.

When creating algorithms for the initial ROE and for the method used in phasing it into the secular norm, it is wise to select a technique that produces a realistic dividend stream such as the one shown in Figure 9–4. Notice that the dividend rises about two-thirds of the time, sometimes sharply, and plateaus about one-third of the time. This is characteristic of the actual pattern of index dividends.

STEP 4: FORECASTING FUTURE STOCK MARKET LEVELS

We begin by computing a terminal value for the S&P 500, 20 or more years into the future. This was shown in Table 9–2 as the

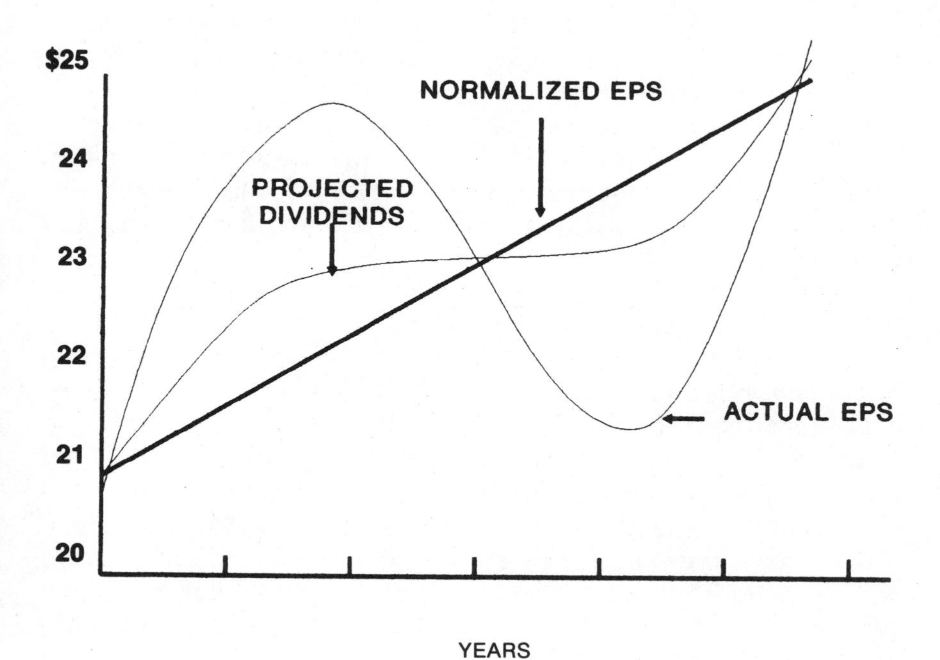

Figure 9–4. Projecting Dividends from a Normalized ROE.

$1,140 value at the bottom of the dividend column. We compute the terminal market value as a function of terminal book value and the secular price-to-book ratio. The latter should not be an exceptionally long-term average due to the changing composition of the averages and changes in what is considered to be accepted accounting. For example, during the 1980s, the quality of the book value was improved through write-offs and conservative accounting changes. This was partially responsible for the price-to-book value of the market during the latter part of the decade averaging about 30% higher than over the previous 20 years.

We now have a 20-year dividend stream plus a terminal market value, any portion of which can be discounted to a present value. To find the expected level of the market in any particular year (*N*), merely take the dividends in year *N* through year 20 along with the terminal value and discount them to a present value as of Year *N*.

The discount rate used in the example shown in Table 9–2 was 10%, which was an arbitrary choice. In practice, the discount rate used to determine the expected market level in Year N should be the T-bond rate plus the equity risk-premium (relative to the T-bond) expected in Year N.

For the interest rate, we use the forecasted rate for the future 10-year Treasury note as of Year *N*. For the equity risk-premium, we use the average equity risk-premium for (usually) the past five years, adjusted up or down for the anticipated level of investor confidence.

Computing and forecasting investor confidence is, perhaps, the most proprietary aspect of my day-to-day occupation. It should be pointed out, however, that *investor confidence can be forecasted since it moves with persistence*. Investor confidence is not a random variable—far from it. In fact, it can be said that future dividends and future equity risk-premiums are considerably more certain than the absolute level of interest rates in future years.

In summary, the future expected level of the stock market (S&P 500) is simply the expected present value *at the particular future point in time* of the then-future dividends and terminal value, all discounted at a rate equal to the expected yield on T-bonds plus the expected equity risk-premium.

STEP 5: COMPUTING THE EXPECTED RETURNS FOR EQUITIES

Figure 9–5 illustrates the process of computing the expected return for the stock market. It is very similar to the process shown in Chapter 4 (Figure 4–1) for individual stocks. The following process is repeated for 20 (minimum) time horizons, 1 through 20 years.

As Figure 9–5 shows, solving for the expected return of the stock market is simply a two-stage present-value calculation. The first stage involves computing the future present value of a terminal value and a stream of dividends that begins at the end of the investor's time horizon. The second stage involves solving for the

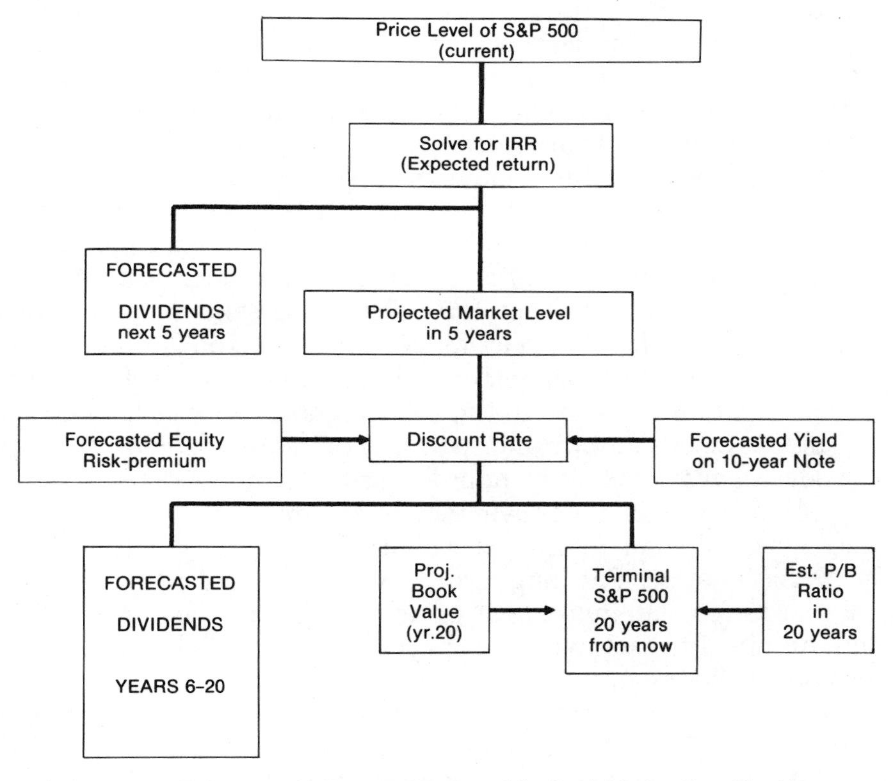

Figure 9–5. Estimating the Expected Return of the Stock Market Over Five Years.

factor (IRR) that discounts that future present value along with the dividends during the investor's time horizon to the current price level of the market.

STEP 6: CALCULATING THE PROBABILITIES

To create any normal or log-normal distribution curve, only two inputs need to be plugged into the density-function formula: an average and a standard deviation. The previous steps described how the "averages" (expected returns) are developed.

The standard deviation of those expected returns can be computed a number of ways. All methods usually involve some type of historic norm. The most common method employed is to use the average historic standard deviation over as many past years as there are years being projected. For example, the expected standard deviation for the next three years would be the same as the average for the past three years.

The Hammer-Lodefink model, however, uses a variation of this technique. For performance purposes, it is important to know what the market *thinks* volatility is likely to be. It is rudimentary human behavior to weight the most recent past more heavily than the more distant past. Therefore, we do the same in projecting future market volatility. In a one-year-time-horizon situation, we weight the past month's market volatility twice as heavily as the previous month's which, in turn, is weighted twice as heavily as the next previous month, and so forth. For time-horizon projection for several years, future standard deviations are a function of the actual markets' volatilities over the same number of past years; but, each past calendar quarter is weighted twice as heavily as the previous quarter. For long-term time horizons of five years or more, future volatility is based on actual volatility over an equivalent number of years, with each past year being weighted twice as heavily as the previous year.

Once the expected returns and expected standard deviations of returns are computed (and annualized), we use calculus to compute the following probabilities for a whole series of possible time horizons:

1. Probability of stocks outperforming the most likely bond return.
2. Probability of stocks outperforming the most likely cash-equivalent return.
3. Probability of cash outperforming stocks. Because cash returns are not distributed "normally" and therefore have no "variance" in the statistical sense, this computation is merely the inverse of item 2.
4. Probability of bonds outperforming the most likely stock return.
5. Probability of bonds outperforming the most likely return for cash equivalents.
6. Probability of cash equivalents outperforming bonds, which is the inverse of item 5.

Figure 9–6 illustrates how the inputs relate to these probabilities.

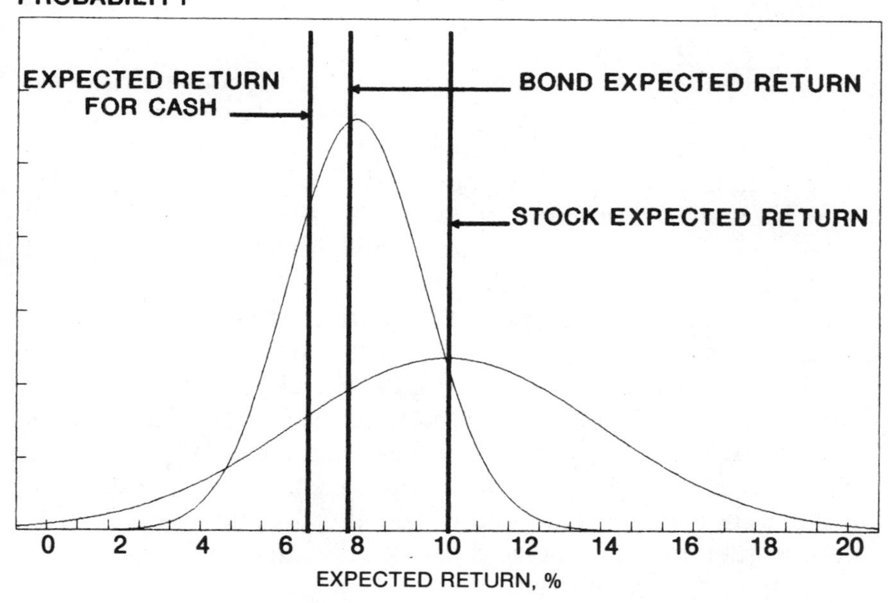

Figure 9–6. Comparing Ranges of Possible Returns.

The probabilities just referred to are computed as follows, respectively:

1. The percentage of the area under the stock curve that is to the right of the "bond expected return."
2. The percentage of the area under the stock curve that is to the right of the "expected return for cash."
3. The percentage of the area under the stock curve that is to the left of the "expected return for cash."
4. The percentage of the area under the bond curve that is to the right of the "stock expected return."
5. The percentage of the area under the bond curve that is to the right of the "expected return for cash."
6. The percentage of the bond curve that is to the left of the "expected return for cash."

STEP 7: CONVERTING PROBABILITIES TO AN ASSET MIX

There are several acceptable methods of using the probabilities just described to create an asset mix. It cannot be said that one is correct and the others are not. However, I have found that the last two of the following methods have produced the best results over the years. They are the ones incorporated into the Hammer-Lodefink model. The various methods are listed in ascending order of preference:

(A) Create a stock-cash mix in proportion to the probability of stocks outperforming cash. Create a bond-cash mix based on the probability of bonds outperforming cash. Calculate the expected return and standard deviation of both mixes. Structure the portfolio according to the probabilities of these two mixes outperforming each other. The advantage of this method is that it is the easiest to understand. The disadvantage is that the portfolio usually contains considerably too much cash. This is because cash is used as a substitute for both stocks and bonds.

(B) Create a stock-cash mix and compute its expected return and standard deviation. Structure the portfolio in proportion to the probability of the stock-cash mix outperforming the bond expected return compared to the probability of bonds outperforming the expected return of the stock-cash mix. The advantage of this method is that it treats cash only as a substitute for stocks and assumes that the bond portfolio already contains "effective cash by way of the duration. The disadvantage is that the portfolio is usually somewhat overweighted in cash.

(C) Compute the probability of each asset class outperforming *both* of the other two asset classes, that is, the odds of underperforming *neither*. Structure a portfolio in proportion to these probabilities. The advantage of this method is that the portfolio is normally light on cash, which is normally good over the long term. The disadvantage is that if we try to accurately calculate the odds of one investment beating the others, the cross-correlation of returns makes the computation difficult. A way around this is to assume that all classes of assets move independently from each other, even though often this is not true. Nonetheless, this method produces excellent results.

(D) For each asset class, calculate the "mean winning return" versus the other asset classes. This is the mean expected return of that portion of the area under the distribution curve which is to the right of the expected return of the other asset classes. Weight each "probability of outperforming" by the difference between the "winning mean return" and the expected returns of the other asset classes. This process was illustrated earlier in Figure 9–3. Blend the asset classes in proportion to these weighted probabilities using methods A, B, or C. The advantage of this method is that it takes into consideration not only the percentage of the time that each class is supposed to outperform the others, but also by how much it is supposed to outperform. The disadvantage is that it is, by far, the most time-consuming allocation process.

Table 9–3 shows an abbreviated version of the primary output of the Hammer-Lodefink dynamic asset-allocation model.

CONCLUSIONS

The principles behind the Hammer-Lodefink dynamic asset-allocation model can be summarized as follows:

TABLE 9–3 Hammer-Lodefink Portfolio Optimizer

Stock-bond Correlation	Time Horizon (years)			
34.2%	3	5	10	20
Stock Expected Return	8.77%	9.20%	9.33%	9.66%
Bond Expected Return	7.55	7.80	7.96	7.77
Cash Expected Return	6.50	6.64	5.95	5.87
Stock Std. Deviation	15.70	6.20	4.11	2.70
Bond Std. Deviation	5.21	2.23	1.54	1.05
Probabilities:				
Bonds vs. Cash	59.64%	68.70%	89.96%	95.39%
Stocks vs. Bonds	58.62	61.41	64.32	75.94
Stocks vs. Cash	61.13	67.19	79.70	90.96
Bonds vs. Stocks	43.70	30.09	21.36	4.59
Return-Weighted Prob.:				
Bonds vs. Cash	66.29%	78.95%	96.30%	98.98%
Stocks vs. Bonds	66.64	68.26	71.89	85.28
Stocks vs. Cash	70.44	77.23	89.46	97.23
Bonds vs. Stocks	40.95	19.86	11.46	1.25
Log Mean Returns:				
Stocks	11.78%	9.79%	9.60%	9.77%
Bonds	7.97	7.88	8.00	7.79
Cash	6.50	6.50	6.50	6.50
Absolute Win Prob.:				
Stocks	35.83%	41.26%	51.26%	69.07%
Bonds	24.42	13.64	10.31	1.19
Cash	15.69	10.27	2.04	0.42
Optimal Mix (Method C)				
Stocks	47.18%	63.31%	80.59%	97.72%
Bonds	32.16	20.93	16.21	1.69
Cash	20.66	15.76	3.20	0.59
Optimal Mix (Method D)				
Stocks	43.6%	59.8%	77.2%	95.8%
Bonds	38.1	22.5	13.8	1.4
Cash	18.3	17.6	9.1	2.7
Expected Return	7.9%	8.4%	8.8%	9.5%
Volatility (SD)	7.35	9.60	12.22	15.05
Equity-Only Portfolios				
Stocks	70.44%	77.23%	89.46%	97.23%
Cash	29.56%	22.77%	10.54%	2.77%

1. There is a strong positive correlation between the equity risk-premium and the yield spreads between high- and low-quality fixed-income securities.
2. Yield differences due to credit-risk differences do not fluctuate at random. They are persistent over the intermediate term and move in long cycles. Therefore, they have a significant degree of predictability over the intermediate term and revert to secular averages over the long term.
3. Therefore, equity risk-premiums can be forecasted with an acceptable degree of confidence.
4. The normalized future earnings power and dividend stream of the stock market can be accurately forecast over periods of several years or more.
5. Interest rates are the most difficult variable to predict. Yet, if we analyze the yield curve under the assumption that "time" affects its shape to a degree that is a function of the level of investor confidence, the existing yield curve becomes a much improved tool for forecasting the shape and level of future yield curves.
6. The expected returns for stocks, bonds, and cash should be estimated over the investor's particular time horizon using forward rates and risk-premiums.
7. An asset allocation should be established according to the probability-weighted spectrum of possible future returns of the individual asset classes.
8. This "strategic" allocation should be modified whenever the relative long-term expected returns of the asset classes change significantly, or whenever the investor's risk tolerance shifts.

10

Asset Allocation: The Efficient Frontier

It does not follow that just because an adept mathematician can devise an algorithm to measure something, it needs to be measured.

—*Hammer*

AN INTERESTING WAGER

Of the people to whom I am the closest, the one with the most mathematical skills is Ted Hall. He works for the school system and is presently in charge of the computer science department for the South Burlington, Vermont, school system. After he received his Ph.D., he began his career in education by teaching "gifted" students—those 10-year-old kids who "intuitively" know that the speed of light is a universal constant, whereas the speed of sound is a relative phenomenon. They can assemble tricky puzzles in a flash and know in a split second how old you are if two years ago, you were three times as old as you were eight years before you were half the age that you are now. They also have an exceptional aptitude for probability problems. Ted Hall also has become an expert at statistical probability.

Ted and I used to play backgammon a lot—more often as adults than in our younger years. Since he won more often than I did, I eventually got around to asking him to handicap me. He made an interesting offer. Since we agreed that he won about twice as often as I did, he wanted to do away with the game's doubling cube and substitute a different system of wagering. As he placed his checkbook on the table, he asked me to place 16 one-dollar bills on the table. He offered to play four games of backgammon. Each time I won, he would match whatever I had on the table. If I lost, he would take half of what I had on the table. The catch was that I had to leave my money on the table until the end of the four games, at which point I could pocket my balance.

Now, if I lost all four games, I would lose $15: $8 on the first game, $4 on the second, $2 on the third, and $1 on the last game, leaving me with $1 out of my original $16.

If I won all four games, I would make a profit of $240: $16 on the first game, $32 on the second, $64 on the third, and $128 on the fourth game. I'm sure his theatrics with the checkbook were to impress that potential upon me.

Maybe it sounds like he was offering me extremely favorable odds or even a 16-to-1 reward/risk ratio. The fact of the matter is, he was giving me about 2.4-to-1 odds if my chances of winning each game were 50%; and he was giving me exactly 1-to-1 odds, assuming his chances of winning each game were twice mine.

First, assume I did have a 50-50 chance of winning each game. He wins two games and I win two. I lose half the money on the table twice and double it twice—I make zero. Also, each of us would have a 31% chance of winning and a 38% chance of a tie. Does that make my expected return zero, however? The answer is no, because I can potentially win more than I can lose. My chance of winning $48 is exactly the same as my chance of losing $12.

If we played enough series of four games each, over time I would win an average of $23 per four-game series. Therefore, my expected return is not zero, which is my *most likely* return for four games; it is $23, which is an expected return of over 140%. Table 10–1 shows how the expected return is calculated using *return-weighted probabilities,* similar to those utilized in the Hammer-Lodefink asset-allocation model.

The investment implication relates to the fact that the distribution of possible returns in the backgammon example is a lognormal distribution, similar to that for securities returns. The expected return is $23, and I have the same probability of making about double that amount as I do of making half that amount. Securities prices behave the same way. The investor has the same probability of making 100 percentage points more than the secular

TABLE 10–1 Calculating Expected Return using Return-Weighted Probabilities

No. Games Won	Probability	Win/(Lose)	Probability Weighted
0	6.25%	($15.00)	($0.94)
1	25.00	(12.00)	(3.00)
2	37.50	0.00	0.00
3	25.00	48.00	12.00
4	6.25	240.00	15.00
	100.00%	Wtd. Exp. Return =	$23.06

(expected) return as he or she does of making 50 percentage points less than the expected return.

You might be interested to know that if the average stock has an expected return of 10% and a standard deviation of 30%, you could throw a dart at a quote page of *The Wall Street Journal* and have a 10% chance of picking a stock that will be up 50% or more within one year, compared to a 10% chance of picking a stock that will be down 18% or more. We must conclude that the "most likely return" is an incomplete concept and that the mean of the *weighted* possible returns is the most important number.

Now, let's return to the backgammon game and assume that I had only half the chance of winning each game as my opponent had. That was the assumption Ted Hall made when he offered me odds. Table 10–2 shows the probabilities of my winning four and less games, based on a 33% chance of winning (2 to 1 odds in favor of Ted).

Notice that my most likely return appears to be an average loss of $4.74 per four-game series; and I have nearly a 60% probability of

TABLE 10–2 Calculating Expected Return using 2-to-1 Odds of Losing

No. Games Won	Probability	Win/(Lose)	Probability Weighted
0	19.7%	($15.00)	($2.97)
1	39.5	(12.00)	(4.74)
2	29.6	0.00	0.00
3	9.9	48.00	4.74
4	1.2	240.00	2.97
	100.0%	Wtd. Exp. Return =	$0.00

ending up in the red, compared to only a 11% chance of making a profit. But, these statistics are practically meaningless (as are their investments counterparts). If we played enough four-game series, my expected return would not be negative, it would be zero. This is why I was willing to accept precise 2-to-1 odds because, as we both believed, Ted's playing skills gave him a 2-to-1 advantage over me. He was willing to risk losing $240 because he had a 89% chance of winning or breaking even. From my perspective, I was willing to accept nearly 60% odds of losing because the most I could lose was $15. If we played enough four-game series, my expected return would be zero, but my *potential* gain would be well in excess of my potential loss.

Over the long term, we each should have come out even; so it was a fair way of wagering. This logic should be applied to the securities markets as well. The asset allocation should be based on the long-term return-weighted probabilities, not merely the relative "most likely returns." The latter understates the potential of the classes of securities with the greater expected volatility, as demonstrated in Chapter 9. There is a good, as well as a bad, side to volatility, and it is volatility itself (the distribution of possible returns) that creates the expected return. *Asset-allocation models that deal strictly with expected (most likely) returns without weighting the probabilities of other (than most likely) possible returns are incomplete.* This is a major deficiency of the type of allocation models to be reviewed in this chapter.

HOW USEFUL IS CROSS-CORRELATION?

In addition to the unwarranted emphasis on a single expected return number, the second most important drawback of most asset-allocation models (including those described in the next several pages) is their reliance on correlation of historic returns between the various asset classes.

You might recall that only one of the asset-allocation techniques described thus far depended on the cross-correlation of stock, bond, and cash returns. So you are not misled, it should be pointed out that most traditional asset-allocation models are very dependent on correlation statistics and, therefore, their shortcomings.

The class of models I am about to describe in this chapter are very dependent on cross-correlation of returns. Before discussing these "efficient-frontier" models, you should be aware of the deficiencies of these traditional methodologies.

Stocks and bonds have moved in sympathy about one-quarter of the time over the span of my investments career. That implies that interest rates have accounted for about one-fourth of the price movement within the equity market. Does that mean that over the investors' current time horizons that stocks and bonds will continue to move together 25% of the time? According to Ibbotson and Sinquefield*, since 1925, stocks and bonds have had a cross-correlation of between only 3% and 19%, depending on the maturity and type of bonds. Our data base produces a 33% correlation during the 1980s. But, the stock-bond correlation of quarterly returns from 1980 to 1984 was 55% and was only 4% from 1985 through 1989. That's a tremendous difference!

The cross-correlation of returns for stocks, bonds, and cash very much seem to be a function of the current stage of the economic cycle. In major expansionary and contractionary periods, stocks and bonds tend to move independently or oppositely. That is because earnings and interest rates are moving in the same direction. In slow-growth periods, there tends to be a high correlation of returns, as interest rates become the main driver of stock prices. The correlation also appears to depend on the inflation rate at the time.

It appears that there are about six basic economic scenarios that affect the stock-bond correlation differently: high growth with high inflation, high growth with low inflation, slow growth with high inflation, slow growth with low inflation, negative growth with high inflation, and negative growth with low inflation. Add the possibility of deflation and there are now three more scenarios.

The point is, if we are going to use correlation of returns as an input to an asset-allocation model, how do we make a short-term or intermediate-term forecast without having a crystal ball for the

---

*Roger G. Ibbotson and Rex A. Sinquefield, *Stocks, Bonds, Bills, and Inflation: Historical Returns (1926–1987)*. Dow Jones-Irwin (New York, 1989). p. 95.

economy? In addition, correlations between long-term stock and bond returns begin to approach 1.00 over long measurement periods. This is because returns tend toward equality as the period being measured lengthens. Most importantly, the correlations are going to change substantially *during* the investor's time horizon. As we shall see, that means the investor's level of portfolio risk jumps up and down significantly over the years if a fixed allocation is maintained. What if the portfolio volatility is high at the wrong time—during periods of major contributions or withdrawals? For example, defined-benefit retirement plans which had big contributions around October 1, 1987, and large withdrawals around November 1, 1987, suffered immensely if they remained fully invested during that period.

THE EFFICIENT FRONTIER DEFINED

Comparing the reward-risk relationship of various securities or combinations of securities was a major step within the quantitative arena of the world of investments. The concept is simple, but the mathematics can be extremely time-consuming and, as we have already mentioned, can be of questionable value. Nonetheless, the efficient-frontier concept was a giant step for those attempting to introduce logic and probability into the process of portfolio diversification.

Figure 10–1 illustrates the efficient frontier. Each point on the graph can represent the reward-risk relationship either of an individual security or of a particular blend of securities.

The curve that runs across the top of the points has been called the "margin of efficiency" by some of the investment pioneers mentioned in the Acknowledgments. It represents those assets with the highest expected return relative to the various levels of risk. That is, any assets that are below the margin are inefficient because they do not offer the maximum available return for the level of risk. It generally is felt that the upper-left portion of the efficient border contains the most attractive groups of assets because of the high reward-risk ratio represented by the points in that area of the curve.

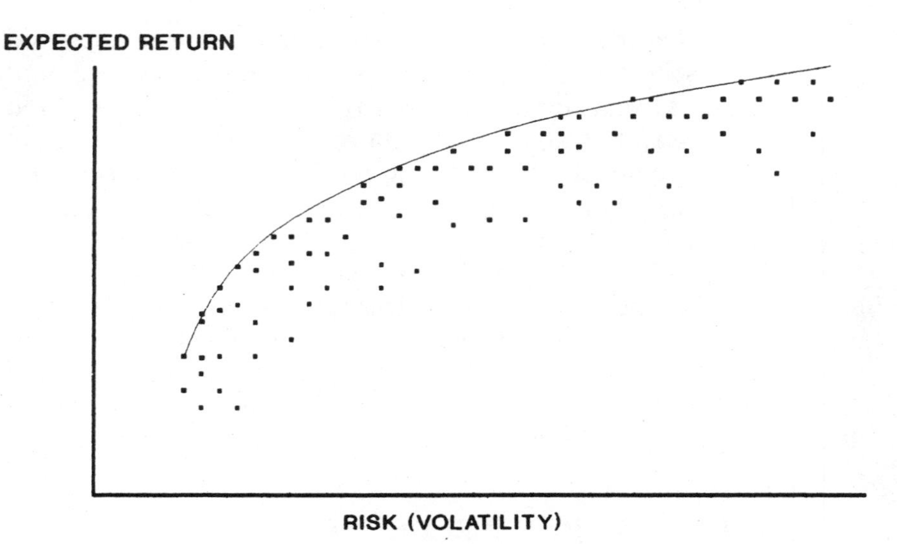

Figure 10–1. The Efficient Frontier.

MEASURING VOLATILITY OF AN ASSET MIX

We must first compute the reward-risk relationship of a blend of stocks and bonds (and possibly additional asset classes) in order to be able to determine the efficient frontier. The expected return of two or more assets is, simply, the weighted average of the expected returns of the assets. The risk (volatility) of two or more asset classes is more difficult to compute. This is because it is a function of the cross-correlation of returns between the groups.

There are several methods (none of them easy) that can be used to compute the volatility of a blend of assets. Here is an attempt to simplify the process (keeping in mind that standard deviation is the square root of variance):

1. If a group of assets has returns that are perfectly correlated (i.e., a coefficient of correlation of 1.00), then the *standard deviation* of a combination of these assets is the weighted average of their individual standard deviations.
2. If a group of assets has returns that are unrelated (i.e., a

correlation of 0.00), then the *variance* (standard deviation squared) of a combination of these assets is the weighted average of the individual variances.

3. The *variance* (V) of a group of assets with returns exhibiting some degree of correlation (the usual case) is equal to the weighted average of the individual variances (vA, vB, etc.) *plus* the "correlation factor" (R):

$$V = \text{A\%} \times v\text{A} + \text{B\%} \times v\text{B} + \ldots \text{N\%} \times v\text{N} + R$$

where the correlation factor (R) for two classes of assets (A and B) is computed as follows:

$$R = 2\,(\text{A\%} \times s\text{A} \times \text{B\%} \times \text{B}s \times r)$$

where (A%) and (B%) equal the percentage of the portfolio invested in Asset A and Asset B, (sA) and (sB) equal the standard deviations of both assets, and (r) equals the correlation between the two assets.

4. The *standard deviation*, therefore, of any two-asset-class portfolio is equal to the square root of the sum of the weighted *variance* plus the correlation factor.

There are three principal difficulties with the efficient-frontier approach:

1. The equation for variance or standard deviation (square root of variance) becomes a monster when more than two assets are involved.
2. The ability to forecast cross-correlation of returns is very questionable, except for very long measurement periods, in which case it approaches unity.
3. Even if we *could* accurately define the efficient frontier for various blends of assets (such as stocks, bonds, and cash), a process must be developed for picking the point along the efficient curve that is *the* optimal asset mix for a particular investor.

The first difficulty should be obvious after having read this section. Let's examine the other two issues.

PROJECTING CROSS-CORRELATION

As mentioned earlier, during the first half of the past decade, the correlation between quarterly stock and bond returns was only 4%, but during the last half of the decade it was 55%. Figures 10–2 and 10–3 show the differences in the reward-risk relationships under both scenarios.

In Figure 10–2, a portfolio with 15% stock has the least amount of risk. In fact, a portfolio with 25% stock has less volatility than an all-bond portfolio. In Figure 10–3, which depicts a high correlation between stock and bond returns, the all-bond portfolio is the least risky.

There are times, such as entering and leaving an economic recession, when stock and bond returns are negatively correlated.

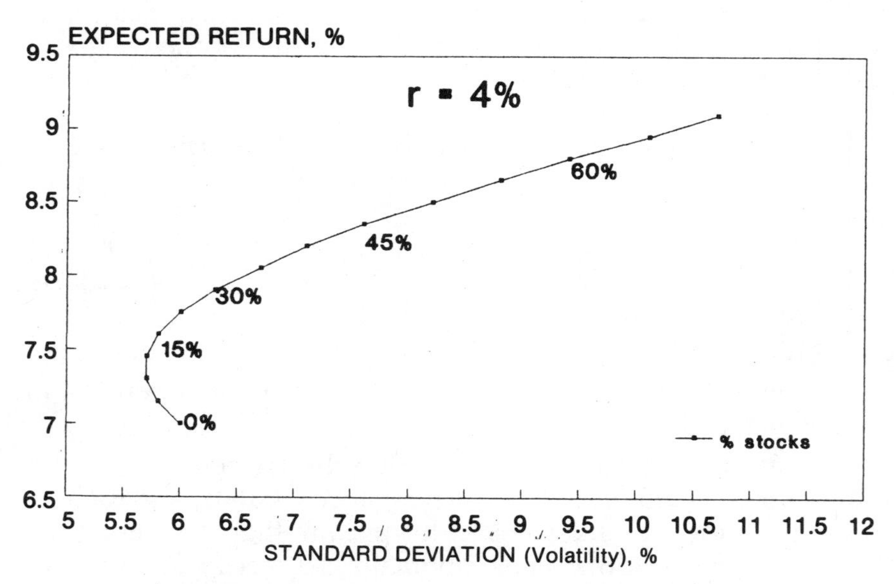

Figure 10–2. Risk-Reward with Low Stock-Bond Correlation.

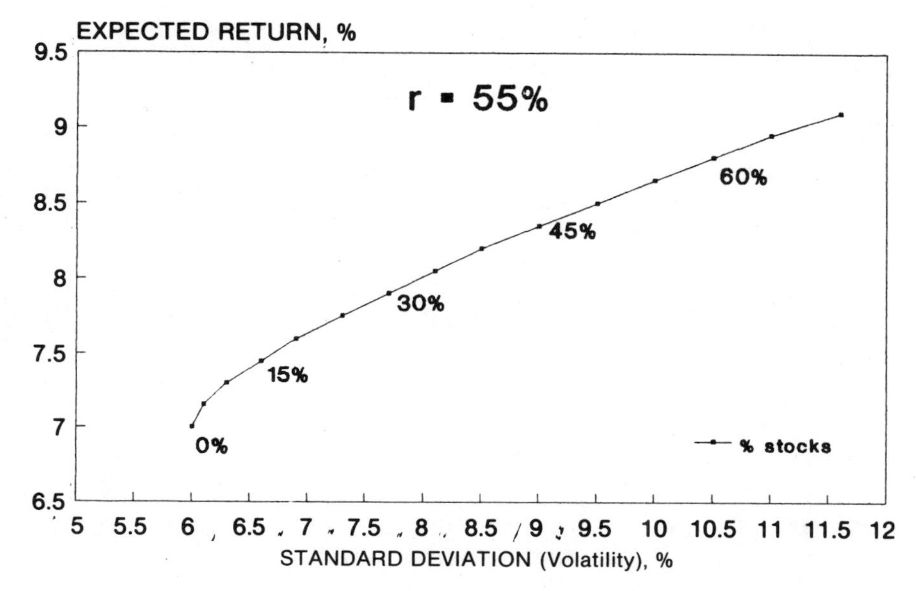

Figure 10–3. Risk-Reward with High Stock-Bond Correlation.

This occurs when stock prices and bond prices move in opposite directions. Figure 10–4 illustrates this phenomenon.

Notice that under this environment (which assumes a 10% expected return for stocks, a 7% expected return for bonds, and a negative correlation between the two) a portfolio with 50% invested in equities is barely more risky than an all-bond portfolio. This is the case even though the curve was computed on the basis of stocks having more than twice the volatility of bonds!

OPTIMIZATION AND THE RISK-FREE RATE

One method of choosing an optimal portfolio from those asset combinations that lie along the efficient frontier is to relate their reward-risk ratios to the T-bill rate. Figure 10–5 illustrates this process.

A line is drawn from the point on the (*y*) axis that represents the risk-free rate through a point that is tangential to the efficient

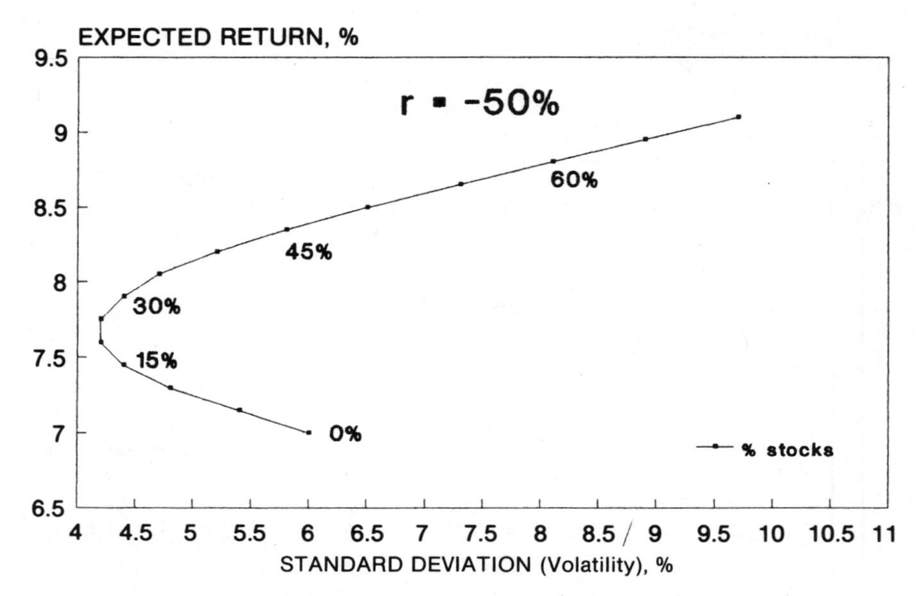

Figure 10–4. Risk-Reward with Negative Stock-Bond Correlation.

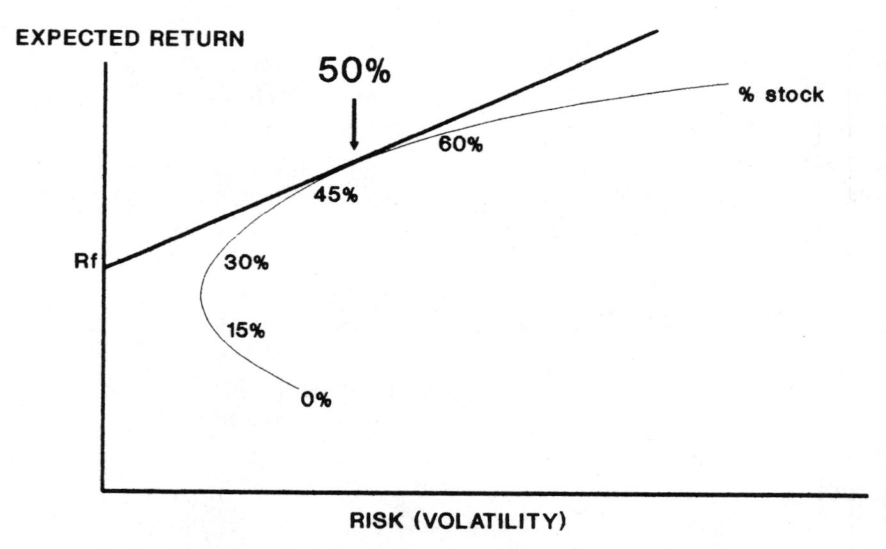

Figure 10–5. Portfolio Optimization Relative to the Risk-Free Rate.

portion of the asset-mix curve. The theory is that no point below this tangent line can offer a more attractive reward-risk ratio than any point that is on the line. Any series of points drawn from the risk-free rate offers the identical reward-risk ratio all along that line. The greater the reward-risk ratio, the greater the slope of that line. The line having the greatest slope that can be drawn within the realm of available returns is the one that is tangential to the curve. In the previous example, a portfolio that is divided equally between stocks and bonds is the most attractive at the current level of risk-free rates.

This entire concept is intriguing, in an academic sense, particularly if the investor theoretically can borrow unlimited funds at the risk-free rate. Intuitively, however, the technique appears unrealistic. It implies that when short-term rates are very high, the portfolio should be drastically overweighted in the most risky class of securities. Often this is correct; but at extreme levels of short-term rates, the level of the equity risk-premium wouldn't even matter—only whether it was positive or negative.

OPTIMIZATION AND INVESTOR RISK TOLERANCE

Another way of choosing a specific optimal blend of assets that lies along the efficient frontier would be to relate the level of risk to the investor's risk profile. Earlier in the book, it was shown how the investor's willingness to assume risk could be pictured as a curve sloping increasingly up to the right. That is, as the level of volatility increases, the desired return increases at an increasing rate.

Refer to Figure 10–6. If Curve A represents a particular investor's desired return for each level of risk, then obviously Curve C would be more attractive to the same investor. It has the same shape as Curve A, which means that desired return increases at the same rate relative to risk, but it lies outside of the realm of available returns. Curve B also could describe the same investor, but it calls for expected returns that are less than what is available at each level of volatility. Sometimes these curves are referred to as *indifference curves* since the investor is equally satisfied with being at any point along the same curve. But, the investor would be more satisfied at

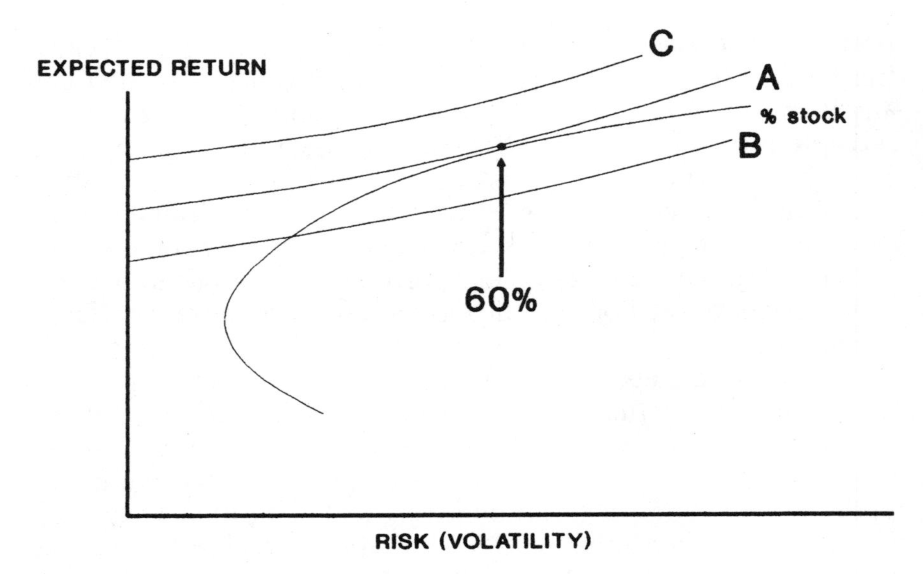

Figure 10–6. Portfolio Optimization relative to Investor Risk Profile.

any point along a higher curve than at any point along a lower curve. Therefore, it can be assumed that an investor whose risk profile can be described by an equation that produces Curves A, B, and C can find an optimal portfolio that is within the realm of available returns by selecting the asset mix represented by the point of tangency of Curve A to the asset-mix curve.

Here is an overview of a simplified (two-asset-class) model that could be developed into a portfolio optimizer. An equation first must be created to produce the investor's risk profile (such as Curves A through C). The following variation of William Sharpe's equation would do the job:

$$\text{Expected return} = M + \frac{\text{Variance}}{\text{RT}}$$

where (M) equals the minimum (or risk-adjusted) return desired at the various levels of interest rates, and RT equals risk tolerance, also distinctive to each investor, which describes how much incremental return is needed to compensate him or her for additional portfolio variance of return. Notice that we use variance here, rather than standard deviation, to represent the dispersion of returns (risk). That is because "variance" is the square of standard deviation and, therefore, produces a risk-profile curve that has the desired exponentially increasing slope.

We know the equations for determining the asset-mix curve, which includes the "monster" formula where portfolio variance is a function of the weighted individual variances plus the cross-correlations of the individual assets, and the equation where expected return is a function of the expected returns of the individual assets and their weightings within the portfolio. If we also know the equation that produces the series of risk-profile curves, where the expected return is a function of a base return plus a compensatory return for incremental risk, then we could use sophisticated algebra to solve all of these equations simultaneously for the asset mix where the two curves are tangential. The variables we would be solving for are the percentage of Asset A and the percentage of Asset B, in a two-asset model. These are used to calculate the "variance" portion of the risk-profile equation. They also occur in the equation that produces the asset-mix (hook) curve.

Since these variables occur in the equations as an arithmetic product (one multiplied by the other) and as the base of an exponential function (variance), then a linear programming solution is not appropriate. Quadratic programming is called for, which would require a very lengthy explanation and, therefore, would detract from the more important aspects of asset allocation yet to be discussed.

Despite all its drawbacks from the practical standpoint of allocation determination, the basic efficient-frontier concept offers a convenient method of depicting the purpose and effect of asset allocation. Its value, therefore, is more academic than pragmatic. But, without an efficient-frontier scenario, the extremely important concepts of the following chapter would have been all but impossible to articulate.

11

Asset Allocation: Completing the Process

I thank my Fortune for it, my ventures are not in one bottom trusted, nor to one place; nor is my whole estate upon the Fortune of the present year.

—*The Merchant of Venice* William Shakespeare

ONCE UPON A TIME AT AN INVESTMENT COMMITTEE MEETING

A normal part of the routine of working for an investment advisory firm is making periodic presentations to potential and existing clients. These talks, which are sometimes more like an Inquisition, usually are made to the investment committee of the company whose employee-benefit plan is at stake. A typical committee consists of a handful of senior executives along with someone representing the employees, such as the human resources director.

One sweltering day in Boston, I was presenting my firm and its asset-allocation skills to the investment committee of a large potential client. The chairman of the board sat at the opposite end of the table, while the president sat next to me. Placed near each end of the long, mahogany table was a shiny, metal pitcher of ice water. While we were waiting for the stragglers, the president and I were unconsciously staring at the chairman pouring himself a glass of water. Apparently he didn't get as much ice to spill into his glass as he would have liked. So, he reached into the pitcher (which was intended for everyone's use), sloshed his hand around in the water, and retrieved a handful of the tiny cubes of ice. As he was dumping them into his glass, the president, with his head tilted upward at about a 45° angle, turned to me and said, with a slow, quasi-British (probably Harvard) accent, "Kind of makes you wonder where his hands have been, doesn't it?"

Being a little nervous anyway, I burst out laughing in this otherwise solemn chamber at the Union Club. As soon as the embarrassment faded and the chairman's glare was consummated, I began wondering whether the president and Chairman were bosom buddies or arch rivals. It must have been one or the other. I was soon to find out it was the latter.

The chairman slid an enormous cigar out of his pocket, cut the tip off with a fancy, silver cigar cutter, and lit up. With a loud Southern drawl, he announced the purpose of the gathering; but then, instead of turning the meeting over to me, he began a speech of his own.

He talked about all the "evils" associated with equities (he called them all "go-go stocks"), the volatility of the bond market, and the dangers of owning bank CDs. To him, gold and real estate were the only sound investments, but he wouldn't object to seeing a few convertibles in the pension fund, as long as they were debentures (not convertible preferred stocks).

Then, finally, he asked me what I thought about real estate investment trusts, gold, and convertibles. There was no way I could give him a direct, honest answer without being prepared to run for the door. So I replied, "It depends on your time horizon. What is your time horizon?"

"Very long term. . . . long-term indeed. That's why I believe in real estate and gold. If there's one thing for certain, besides death and taxes, it's inflation. That's why I'd never be in the casualty insurance business, like your parent company."

After he finished a lengthy soliloquy about the insurance business, making it obvious to me that there were now at least two subjects about which he was illiterate, he announced that he had another pressing meeting and left as soon as he had turned the proceedings over to the president.

As soon as the door shut, there was a general sigh of relief amongst the other seven committee members. At this point, the president went on to explain how the investment committee (which was obviously dominated by you-know-who) was in charge of investment policy, which included asset allocation.

WHO SHOULD MAKE THE ALLOCATION DECISION?

It always has been disconcerting to me that so many employee-benefit funds are really more dependent, performance-wise, on the policy set by a group of noninvestment people than on the securities selection of the investment adviser. In many—too many—cases, the all-important decision of asset allocation is made by a group of businesspeople who almost always call for changes in their asset mix just at the wrong time. Of course, this is human nature, typical of most investors; but this is precisely why trustees need to take advantage of the discipline of a seasoned adviser.

Whichever class of security or investment has been performing the best recently, or whatever their peers tell them they're doing, is what the typical investment committee is most likely to act on. We know for a fact that 75 to 95% of superior or inferior pension-fund performance is usually due to asset allocation, not securities selection. Yet, it is the latter they hire the experts for and the former they perform themselves.

Admittedly, many if not most large, sophisticated companies hire separate pension consultants to assist in the asset-allocation process and in the selection of investment managers. However, this frequently results in portfolios with asset allocations that are too rigid and often do not reflect how out of balance the long-term expected returns of the various asset classes might be at any point in time.

PORTFOLIO STRUCTURE VERSUS ECONOMIC STRUCTURE

There aren't anywhere near as many investment advisers or investment committees that claim to be experts on foreign equities, financial commodities, mortgage loans, private placements, gold, and real estate as there are advisers who feel they are superb at picking domestic stocks and bonds.

From many years of scanning the *Money Market Directory of Pension Funds* and dealing directly with corporate pension plans, I can estimate that the asset allocation of a typical corporate pension or profit-sharing plan looks very similar to the pie chart in Figure 11–1.

The average individual investor doesn't pretend to know a whole lot about most aspects of investing. The typical person who comes to an investment adviser as a result of a recent inheritance or other financial windfall typically has an existing investment portfolio more akin to the one illustrated in Figure 11–2. The interesting thing about these two hypothetical, but realistic, pie charts is that both the corporate investor and the individual investor are significantly underweighted in real estate, mortgages, and to a large

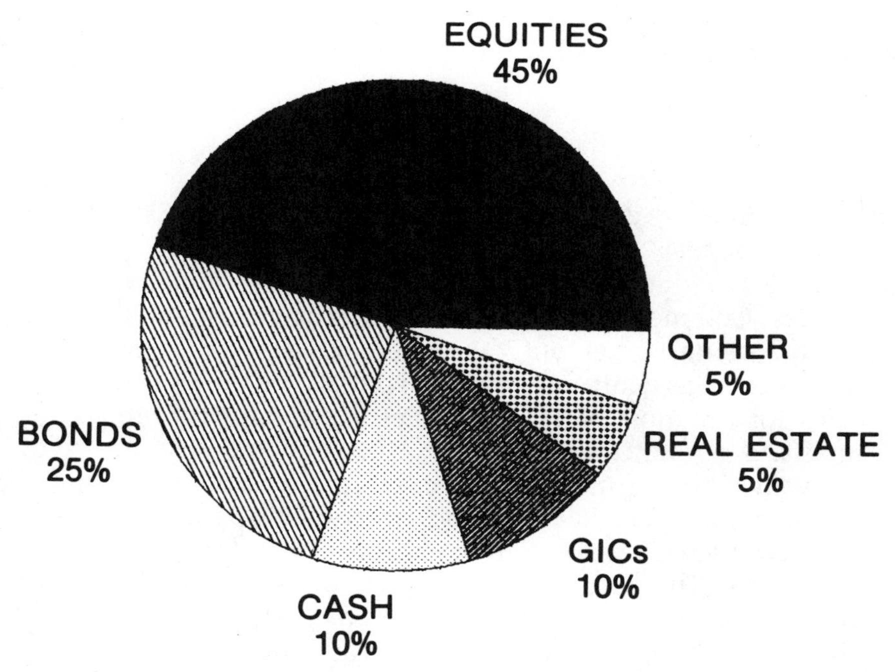

Figure 11–1. Typical Pension-Fund Asset Allocation.

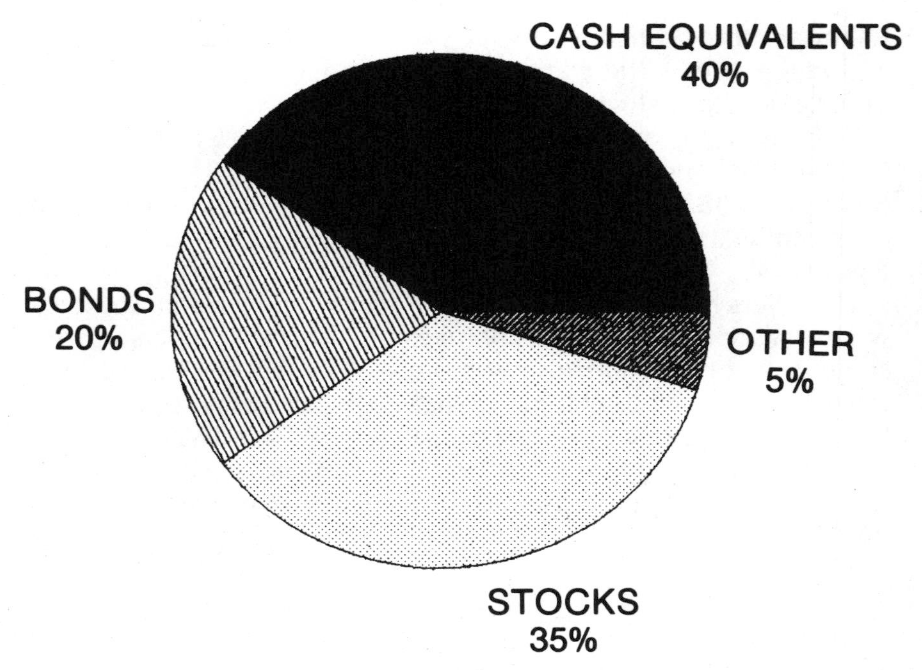

Figure 11–2. Typical Household Asset Allocation.

extent, bonds (relative to the value of what is out there, in the way of issued paper).

Figure 11–3 illustrates the breakdown of the domestic capital markets. Commercial real estate and mortgages account for well over 40% of the market. But, the owners and creditors behind these investments certainly are not individuals or employee-benefit plans, for the most part. These roles are apparently fulfilled by banks and insurance companies.

Considering the often attractive returns, why don't retirement plans own more real-estate-related investments, particularly when they have such a low correlation of short-term returns with stocks and bonds? The main answer has already been offered: Most professional investment advisers are not proficient in this area. Why not? Probably because it is not an easy task to get a handle on the risks and returns involved.

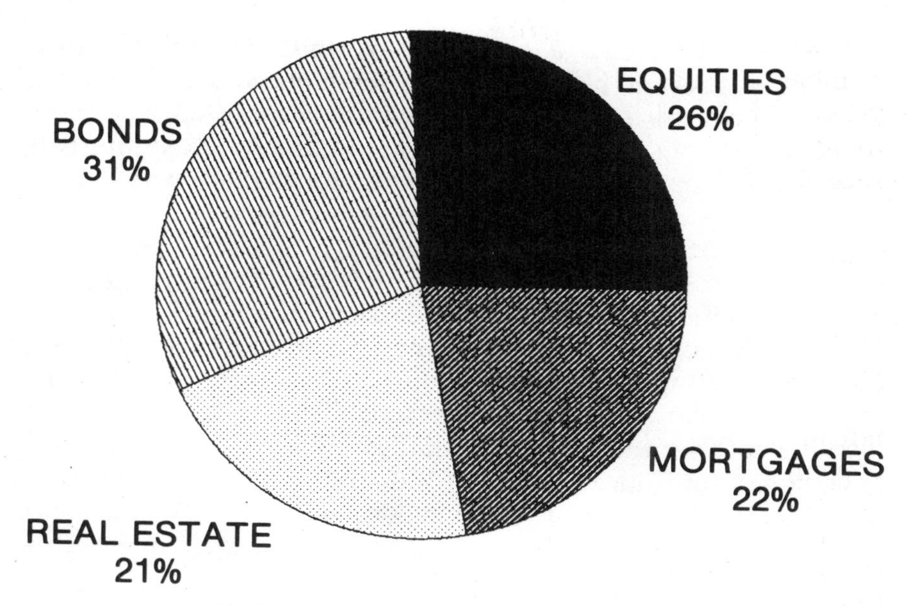

Figure 11–3. Breakdown of U.S. Captial Markets.

MEASURING REAL ESTATE RISK AND RETURN

As if forecasting returns isn't difficult enough, just getting a handle on the historic returns and their volatility is a major, if not meaningless, task when it comes to commercial real estate. The main problem is that there is no ongoing auction market for real estate that can be used to obtain current, fair valuations.

The stock and bond markets are active five days a week, producing fair market values every few minutes for hundreds of securities. The real estate market does not afford us this luxury. There are various indices, however. The one we will use in this chapter is the Frank Russell Company (FRC) Index. This is a statistic, produced quarterly since 1978, that shows the average income plus estimated appreciation return on about a thousand properties held in institutional portfolios. These involve, for the most part, equity returns that are not leveraged.

The interesting feature of the FRC Index is that it has a standard deviation of annualized total return of only 3%. This factor makes real estate sound like a fantastic investment—annual returns similar to stocks and bonds, but only about one-fourth the volatility risk! The catch is that, even though the income stream is very stable, the appraisal element probably inaccurately reflects the true volatility in property values. The values reported to Frank Russell Company are most likely based on estimated selling prices of similar properties. But, these sample properties were not traded moments ago like stocks and bonds. Chances are the appraisals reflect a significant time lag that understates the actual volatility.

To compensate for this sluggishness, Frank Russell also has a Cap-adjusted Index. Here, the values are estimated from a discounted cash-flow model. Changes in the level of income and the discount rate are the principal variables. The long-term standard deviation of this index was about 10% during the 1980s. Whereas the raw FRC Index has a negative correlation to both stock and bond returns, the Cap-adjusted series has had a slight positive correlation with stocks and bonds over the years.

Another way to measure real estate returns and their volatility is to examine the performance of the real estate investment trusts (REITs). In 1981, the value of these closed-end funds fell far more than the stock market and most were down 25 to 50% in 1988. In a good year like 1983, when the stock market was up over 20%, REITs were up over 50%.

So, depending on how we measure it, the volatility risk of investing in commercial real estate can be anywhere from nearly as low as a T-bill to as high as a common stock. But, no matter how you slice it, returns during the 1980s were somewhere in the 10 to 15% range, that is, somewhere between those for bonds and stocks. But, that's an average range of returns for commercial real estate. The problem associated with these average returns is that they depend so heavily on the specific type of property as well as the geographic location.

For example, during the 1980s, while the values of real estate in the lower Midwest and the mountain states were declining, values in the Northeast and Northwest were going to the moon. To compound the problem even further, the indices do not reflect how much leverage may have been employed on behalf of the investor.

A final caveat is the abruptness with which the values within a certain sector of the market can change. We all witnessed what suddenly happened to property values in the mid-1980s in Texas after crude oil prices tumbled. Massachusetts property is another case in point. Remember when Michael Dukakis ran for president in 1988? Part of his appeal was what his supporters referred to as the "Massachusetts Miracle." That was a phrase used to depict the fact that the Massachusetts economy was booming at a time when many parts of the country were in a recession, despite the state's record level of social spending.

Massachusetts was supposed to be living proof that a community could live high on the hog and still spend a lot of money on social reform, while much of the remainder of the country was struggling just to meet the payroll of the school teachers. But, by 1990, the situation in Massachusetts had undergone a total turnabout. The fact that Governor Dukakis had been reaping the benefits of fiscal control effected by his predecessor, Ed King, became obvious. Although Mr. Dukakis may be criticized for taking credit for the so-called "Massachusetts Miracle" during the presidential campaign, the ensuing fiscal debacle was, no doubt, inevitable. The financial service industries and Federal defense spending, upon which the state depends heavily, turned down, federal tax changes had an adverse effect on state revenues, and real estate had been bid up to speculative levels.

Nonetheless, within two years following the 1988 presidential election, Massachusetts' bond ratings fell to among the very lowest in the nation as liquidity disappeared and the budget surplus was supplanted by an awesome deficit. So sizeable was the deficit that the state, which had been sharing its surplus with the municipalities, had to withhold local aid, causing the cities and towns to lay off police and teachers—the most basic of social services!

In summary, the variables that enter into the real estate equation are far more difficult to analyze and project than the *apparent* stability of the marketplace would lead one to believe.

FORECASTING REAL ESTATE RETURNS

As was shown in the preceding section, arriving at a realistic expected return and level of risk for a real estate equity portfolio is a cumbersome task. The total lack of homogeneous characteristics within the commercial property market make any such numbers suspect as to their applicability in an asset-allocation model. It is no wonder that real estate is underweighted in institutional, professionally managed portfolios!

Let's explore the use of a valuation model by asking a seemingly simple question: If inflation increases above expectations, will real estate returns do the same, or just the opposite? At first, we might assume that real estate returns move in parallel with inflation, that is, that real estate is a good inflation hedge. In fact, the FRC Index (raw series) supports this, most of the time. According to Randall Zisler (Russell-Zisler, Inc.), there was more than a 50% correlation between the quarterly rate of inflation and the quarterly FRC series from mid-1978 to mid-1988.

But if we were to consider that the appraised worth of a commercial property could be the present value of its future rental-income stream, then obviously higher inflation (which usually goes hand in hand with higher interest rates) would likely mean a higher capitalization rate on future revenues. This would be an offset to the higher revenues that might occur as a result of higher construction costs affecting the replacement market. Indeed, the correlation between the FRC Cap-adjusted series and inflation almost disappears. In fact, Russell-Zisler's statistics show a negative correlation between inflation and REIT returns.

An approach to real estate portfolio expected return that makes the most sense is to solve for an internal rate of return similar to the dividend-discount methodology shown graphically in Chapter 4 (Figure 4–1). After all, it stands to reason to consider real estate a sort of hybrid between a stock and a bond. The rental income can be projected: Its growth and stability normally would be somewhere between the figures for stocks and bonds. The principal difference is that construction costs, specifically, are perhaps more important than general price inflation, and the type and location of the properties nullify the homogeneous advantage of the stock and bond markets. The terminal value can be a forecasted appraised value based on a long-term projection of an index such as the FRC. Figure 11–4, illustrates a five-year expected return model for a real estate portfolio.

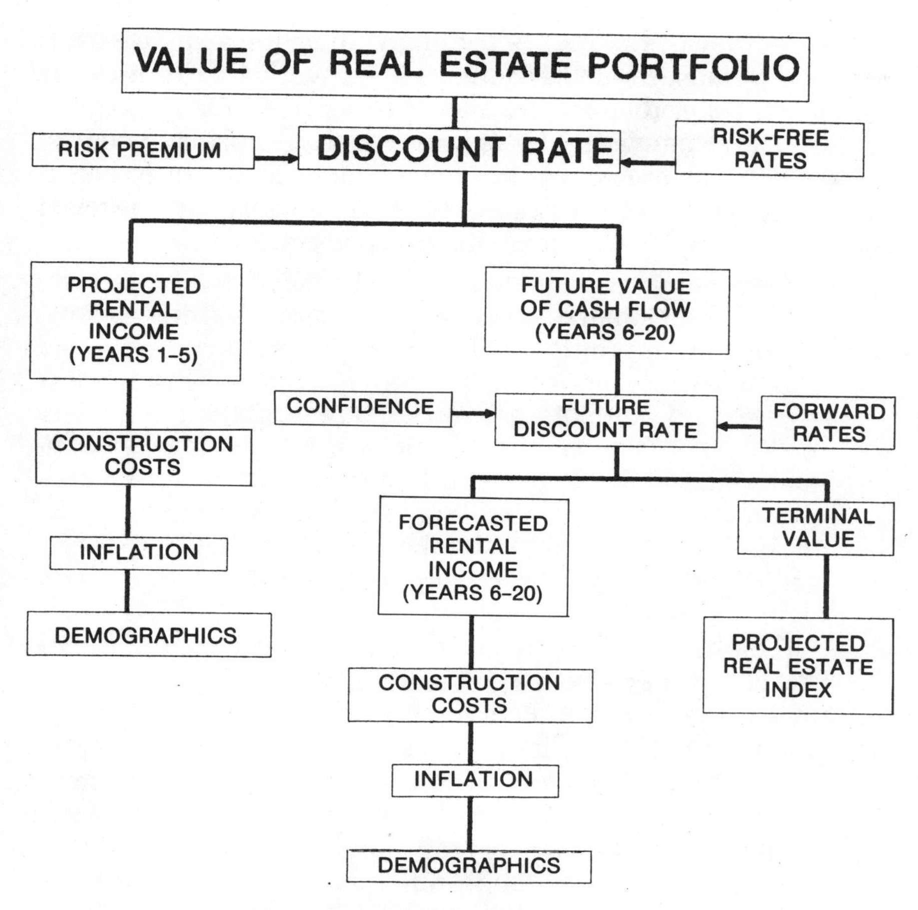

Figure 11–4. Real Estate Valuation Model.

INVESTING IN FOREIGN EQUITIES

During the decade of the 1980s, portfolios that were invested in foreign stocks performed exceptionally well relative to their all-U.S. counterparts. The two main aspects of foreign investing that offer appeal are:

1. The U.S. economy is relatively mature. Population growth is among the world's lowest, and gains in productivity are not

what they used to be. Accordingly, there are many capitalist and socialist-capitalist countries in the world that are growing much faster than we are and will continue to do so. Americans are chauvinists by nature, which is probably good for keeping us motivated; but that element within ourselves is likely responsible for the fact that Americans own far fewer nondomestic stocks than do non-Americans.

2. Foreign stock markets do not always move in tandem with the U.S. stock market. This is due, mainly, to three factors. First, overseas profits are a function of business cycles that are somewhat independent from ours (although increasingly less so). Second, different countries have different monetary objectives, which creates a variety of interest-rate environments around the world. Third, the profits of foreign companies are earned in their local currency and the dividends paid out of these profits are in local currency, not dollars. Therefore, both currency transaction and translation come into play.

   This third point is not always clear, so an illustration may be helpful. Let's examine what happens to the profits and price of Royal Dutch Petroleum stock, in dollars, when the value of the U.S. dollar declines and the value of the Dutch guilder rises. Crude oil, on the global market, is traded in dollars. Since the Dutch guilder becomes worth more dollars in this example, the cost of crude for Royal Dutch goes down. As a result, RD's refining profits increase, as measured in guilders. The company's dividend will likely be raised. To the U.S. holder of Royal Dutch, the dividend increase will be even greater because the gilder is now equal to more dollars (which have depreciated).

The effects of the first two items in the list are that investing abroad has allowed the U.S. investor to increase portfolio return (by participating in faster growing economies) and at the same time reduce risk (by owning stocks that reduce portfolio volatility through low cross-correlation, even though the individual foreign markets may be more volatile than the U.S. market). The latter can be shown mathematically by examining the correlation coefficient between a U.S. market index and a foreign market index.

Morgan-Stanley, admirably, seems to stay at the forefront of the action in the investments world. The firm has an index called the EAFE (pronounced "eefa" by those of us in the business) Index. This abbreviation stands for Europe, Australia, and Far East, and as its name implies, it is a value-weighted composite of the nonwestern world equities markets. The correlation between the returns, in dollars, of the EAFE Index and the Standard and Poor's 500 ranges from 25 to 55%. This is a low enough correlation to allow an investor to reduce risk by owning a percentage of both U.S. and non-U.S. stocks. The correlation between a U.S. stock and the S&P 500 is usually 50% or more.

Figure 11–5 shows the various reward-risk ratios of combinations of U.S. and foreign securities, ranging from 0 to 20% in foreign stocks. The curve is typical of the relationship during the 1980s.

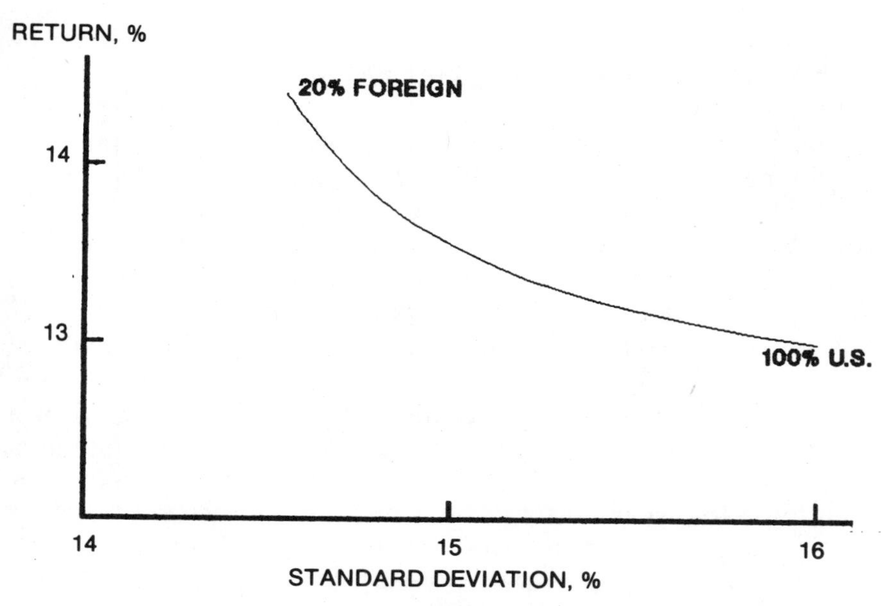

Figure 11–5. Risk-reward of Combining U.S. and Foreign Equities.

Figure 11–5 is similar (and, mathematically, almost identical) to the lower portion of the hook curve produced from various combinations of stocks and bonds, as shown in Chapter 10. It shows that having owned some portion of foreign stock (most institutional portfolios have not held over 20%) has been like having one's cake and eating it too. It has allowed the investor to increase return by participating in faster growth and reduce risk at the same time.

The main difficulty with investing overseas should be obvious: inability to forecast returns with equal success as with domestic stocks. To diversify abroad, the portfolio manager might feel obligated to forecast country-by-country interest rates and GNPs in addition to future currency-translation rates. But that's the easiest part! Consider the fact that in order to determine an optimal mix of foreign issues, the manager must make some estimate as to the correlation of returns between each of the foreign markets, if he or she utilizes an efficient-frontier type of approach. In the previous chapter, it was shown how questionable projecting past correlation is, even within the U.S. markets.

INVESTING IN PRECIOUS METALS

As far as I am concerned, there is basically one reason a portfolio might be invested in gold (and the like): to reduce portfolio volatility—and that it does. The prices of gold, silver, platinum, and diamonds have a very high correlation with the rate of inflation, particularly global inflation. Similarly, gold prices have a negative correlation with U.S. stock prices and particularly bond prices. *There is no index or value that is so highly correlated to interest rates as the price of gold.*

Here is a simple example of an appropriate use of gold in a primitive portfolio. Suppose that the expected rate of inflation is 5%, that real interest rates are 3%, and that the time premium for holding a five-year Treasury note (viz. a T-bill) is 1%. Then the expected return for a five-year note would be about 9% (5% + 3% + 1%). The expected return for gold (which normally appreciates somewhat more than prices in general, due to the perceived "natural limitations" on supply) would be about 6% or more.

Now let's also assume that the correlation between gold prices and bond prices is −40% and that gold prices are about half as volatile as bond prices. In place of owning a portfolio of all Treasury notes that has an expected return of 9% and a standard deviation of 9%, an investor could own a portfolio of 80% T-notes and 20% gold that has an expected return of nearly 8.5%, but a standard deviation of only 6%. Or, he or she could own a portfolio that had equal weightings of T-bonds and gold, providing an expected return of 7.5% and a volatility of only 3%.

In other words, by owning gold, the investor theoretically gives up a little in the way of return but gains a lot in the way of risk reduction. That's the theory, but in practice gold prices move in spurts—long periods of stability (accounting for the low standard deviation over time) followed by periods of extreme speculation.

It is not only the speculative element that gives many professionals a bias against precious metals. It is the whole concept of intrinsic value. What is the intrinsic value of gold? Fundamental investors believe that the intrinsic worth of any investment is the present value of its future cash flow, in whatever form that cash flow takes as long as it somehow accrues to the benefit of the security owner, eventually. To produce cash flow, an investment must represent an entity that does something, physically. Gold appreciates, in speculative times particularly, because people are buying it with the belief that someone else will pay more. According to pure-value investors, it does not matter if someone else will buy the investment from you for more than you paid; the investment itself is expected to provide an acceptable return. This is not the case with owning gold.

Nonetheless, an investor must not toss aside the option of investing some portion of a portfolio in precious metals, particularly gold. Gold can hedge any currency. The fact that it is a common denominator for all currencies means that gold can act as a hedge against investments that are dependent on the value of the dollar. These include foreign companies doing business in the U.S. and all U.S. securities, to the extent that their values are affected by changes in interest rates.

In summary, gold should not be bought as a speculation unless the investor intends to speculate. A gold position can be maintained as a long-term hedge against an unanticipated inflation that will erode the value of a portfolio. It also can act as a hedge against a lower dollar, which might negatively affect certain equity positions, not only because of company demographics, but also because the Federal Reserve is more likely to raise rates when the dollar is declining than when it is strong. We must keep in mind, however, that many stocks—most notably commodity and capital goods companies, including technology stocks and metal fabricators—are beneficiaries of a lower dollar. Therefore, the extent to which gold is employed as part of an asset-allocation program is a function of what the remainder of the portfolio looks like.

One must "invest" in gold with full knowledge that this normally stable "investment" is prone to periods of excessive speculation, both on the down side as well as the up side. In addition, the long-term expected return for gold may be no higher than that of T-bills much of the time. Often, it is more prudent to invest in the common stock of a gold-producing company than directly in gold, gold futures or gold coins.

BUILDING AN EFFICIENT-FRONTIER PORTFOLIO

For the next several pages, I will be making some assumptions regarding the expected returns, volatilities, and cross-correlation of returns among the various asset classes. They are based on realistic assessments of past price behavior. The assumptions are as shown in Table 11–1.

I already have addressed some of the questionable statistics in the table. For example, the standard deviation of real estate returns is certainly debatable. T-bill returns are not totally risk free over extended periods of time, because the rollover rate varies by an average of 1 to 3% per year. The expected return shown for gold is most likely too high for most periods, since the number in the table is a long-term average that may have been influenced by demonetization. Despite their deficiencies, the numbers will be employed only to demonstrate the effects of asset diversification, not to produce an ideal strategic allocation.

TABLE 11–1 Returns, Volatilities, and Cross-Correlations

	Expected Return	Standard Deviation	Cross-Correlation		
			Stocks	Bonds	T-Bills
Stocks	10%	16%	100%	30%	−20%
Bonds	8	8	30	100	0
T-Bills	6	0	−20	0	100
Comm. Real Estate	12	12	0	−10	10
Foreign Equities	14	20	50	10	−10
Gold	7	4	−20	−40	40

Refer now to Figure 11–6. Each box reflects the reward-risk ratio of the six asset classes addressed in this book, using the hypothetical statistics from Table 11–1. For example, if you look below the *Stock* box, you see that the standard deviation is 16%; looking to the left of the box, on the (*y*) axis, you observe the expected return to be about 10%.

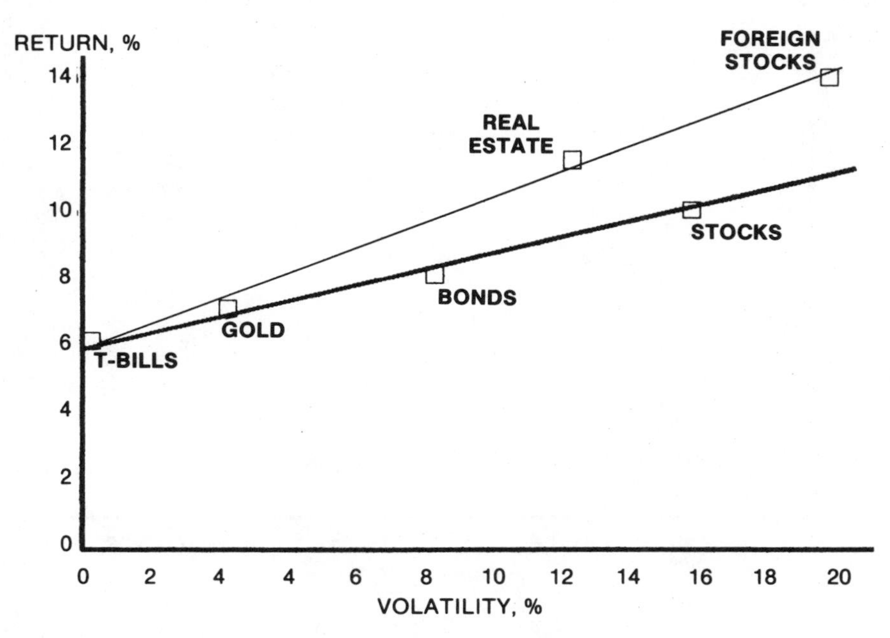

Figure 11–6. Typical Risk-Reward for Major Asset Classes.

The solid, straight line is a series of points, any one of which represents various combinations of gold, bonds, or stocks *with cash* (T-bills), *but not with each other*. For instance, it can be seen that a portfolio consisting of 50% stocks and 50% cash would have the same reward-risk ratio as an all-bond portfolio. A portfolio of 50% bonds and 50% T-bills would have a slightly higher return and volatility than an all-bond portfolio.

The fine, dotted line in Figure 11–6 represents the reward-risk relationship of various combinations of *either* real estate or foreign equities with cash. This line is more positively sloped than the solid line simply because, in this example, real estate and foreign securities have a superior reward-risk ratio to U.S. stocks and bonds.

Now, an interesting thing happens if we combine two assets other than cash. A hook curve evolves, as we saw in the previous chapter and as is shown by Curve B in Figure 11–7.

Whereas Point A (or any other point along the straight line)

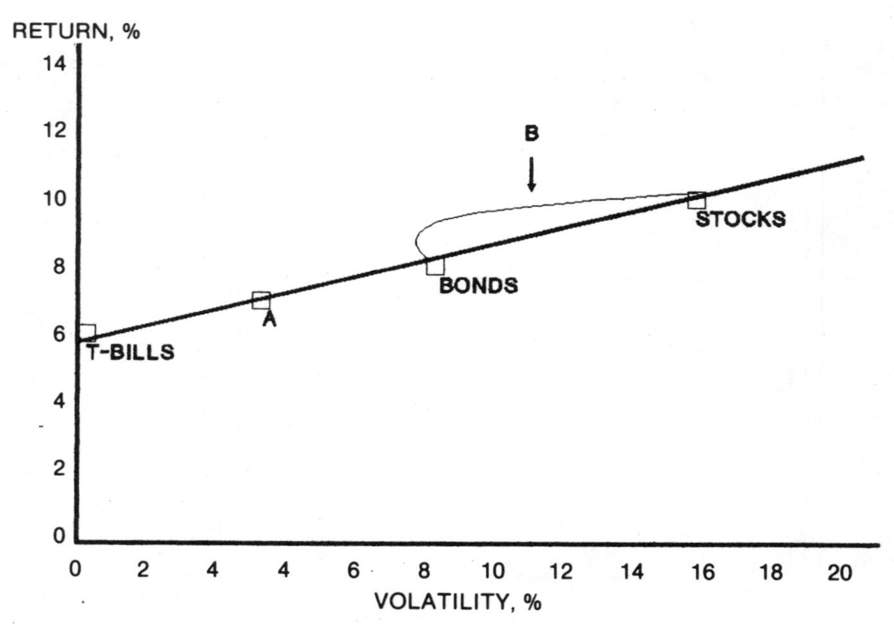

Figure 11–7. Risk-Reward for Two Assets.

represents the combination of stocks or bonds with a risk-free investment, Curve B represents the various combinations of stocks and bonds, neither of which are risk free or totally positively correlated with each other. It is the fact that stocks and bonds have a correlation of returns of less than 1.00 that causes the curve to "hook." It is this hook that gives rise to the fact that owning two assets versus one allows the investor to reduce risk by a greater amount than return. In fact, we can observe that a portfolio that is made up mainly, *but not entirely*, of bonds has not only a greater return, but also *less* risk than an all-bond portfolio.

The next step is to examine the same phenomenon for other combinations of two assets. Figure 11–8 displays three curves (A, B, and C) that represent the reward-risk relationship of a combination of bonds with gold, real estate with stocks, and foreign stocks with U.S. stocks. Notice how some curves hook to the left more than others. This favorable attribute is a function of the particular cross-correlation of returns. For example, Curve A hooks the most

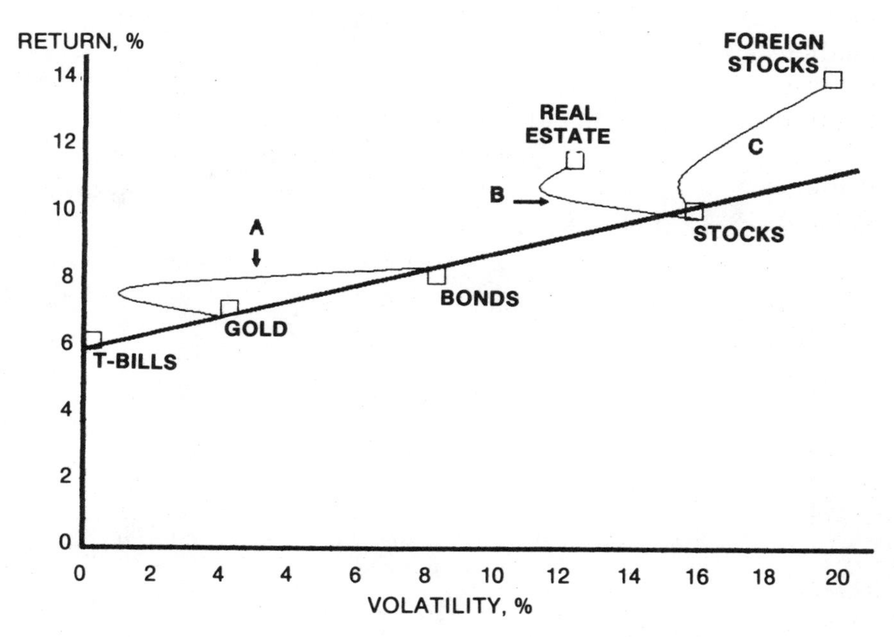

Figure 11–8. Risk-Reward for Various Two-Asset Combinations.

because bond returns and gold prices are *negatively* correlated as discussed earlier. Curve C hooks the least because U.S. stocks and foreign stocks are the most positively correlated of the combinations shown in the graph.

The greater the hook of the curve, the more advantage is to be gained from diversification. The upper-left portion of each curve, like any efficient frontier, represents the region where expected return is gaining the most, relative to volatility risk.

What happens if we combine two assets with cash? Mathematically, the benefits of imperfect correlation are dampened, and the hook becomes less pronounced. This is illustrated in Figure 11–9. Curve B represents all the combinations of stocks and bonds, whereas Curve C represents those very same proportions of stocks to bonds but with a 50% allocation of T-bills. If we increased the percentage in T-bills, the hook would become less pronounced as it moved down to the left.

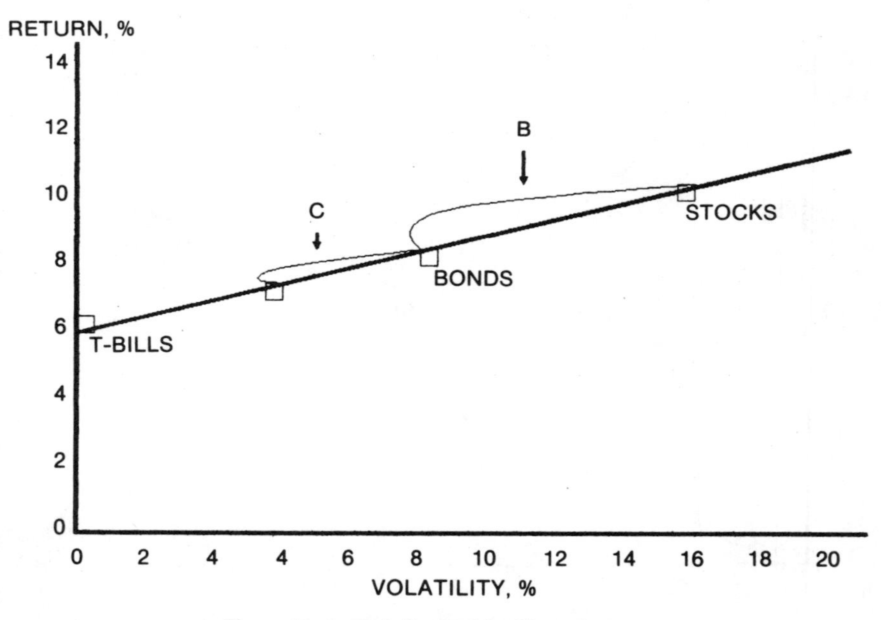

Figure 11–9. Risk-Reward for Three Assets.

FOUR OR MORE ASSET CLASSES

At this point, you should be ready to dive head first, into a situation that will require imagination. To illustrate a multiasset, efficient-frontier accurately would be a graphic stupefaction. Therefore, Figure 11–10 shows only the very beginning of the entire process.

Several possible combinations of asset classes have been connected with the appropriate hook curves. But think of all the possible combinations! That's where your imagination is needed. There not only would be a multitude of curves connecting two asset classes, but an infinite number of curves connecting the points along each of those curves! Then there would be curves connecting those curves and so forth. The net result would be a series of points, in effect, similar to those illustrated in Figure 11–11.

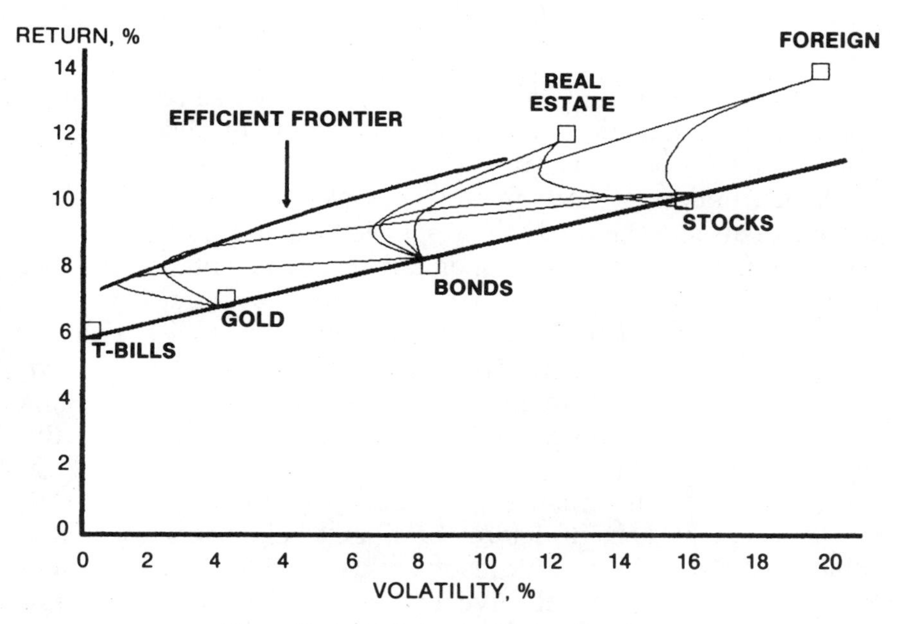

Figure 11–10. Defining the Efficient Frontier.

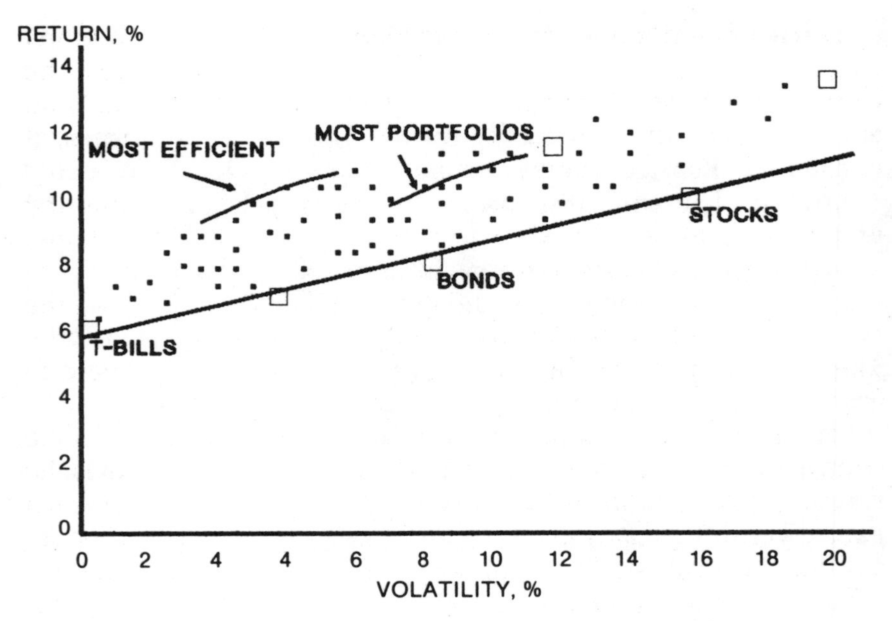

Figure 11–11. Efficient Frontier versus the Typical Portfolio.

The figure shows only a few of the points, those representing combinations of various assets in increments of 10%. But, the graph is a true one, and looks quite different than the hypothetical efficient frontiers seen in many textbooks, which often appear more like an illustration of the upper-left quadrant of the moon, partway into the lunar cycle, than a realistic presentation of asset allocation.

Throughout this and the previous chapter, the efficient-frontier has been defined as the upper-left portion of the scatter diagram. That is because it is within this area that the line of efficiency begins to lose its slope; and, if you think about it, the slope equals the ratio of return to risk.

As discussed in this chapter, most portfolios are overweighted in stocks or cash, and underweighted in foreign securities, real estate, and gold. The graphic result of this deficiency can be seen in Figure 11–11. You can observe that the typical portfolio is not efficient because there are other points (asset combinations) either to the left (less risky) or above (greater return for equal risk).

USING A PROBABILITY OPTIMIZER

The efficient frontier was described in this and the previous chapter in order to illustrate the advantages and effects of diversification. The purpose was not to demonstrate the most efficient means of calculating the optimal portfolio. The efficient frontier makes a pretty picture and provides much fodder for academia. However, not only is it a cumbersome process, but we must wonder whether the degree of accuracy obtained will be great enough to warrant the effort. This becomes a particularly acute point when reflecting upon previous discussions about the questionable predictability of historic cross-correlations.

In Chapters 8 and 9, I demonstrated how risk could automatically be reduced by dividing bets according to the probability of winning. I used racetrack betting as an illustration. But, the logic is the same for investments: Risk will automatically be minimized by dividing assets among the asset classes according to their individual probabilities of outperforming the others.

Without rehashing all of the features of the Hammer-Lodefink model, here is how that sort of approach can be easily adapted to a multiasset scenario. Be cognizant of how simple this is.

Table 11–2 outlines a series of hypothetical expected returns and realistic volatilities for the various asset classes. Then, *without any need for correlation analysis,* Table 11–3 can be produced.

Table 11–3 was derived from the calculus of probability as outlined in Chapters 8 and 9. The time it took to input the data, create the table, and perform the calculus of probabilities on

TABLE 11–2 Ten-Year Annualized Expected Returns and Volatilities

	Expected Return	Standard Deviation
U.S. Stocks	10%	16%
Bonds	9	8
T-Bills	8	2
Comm. Real Estate	9	12
Foreign Equities	10	20
Gold	7	4

TABLE 11–3 Probility of an Investment Class Outperforming the Others

	Stocks	Bonds	T-Bills	Real Estate	Foreign	Gold
Stocks	—	61%	70%	61%	50%	77%
Bonds	36%	—	68	50	36	81
T-Bills	30	32	—	36	26	76
Real Estate	41	50	64	—	41	74
Foreign Equities	50	60	74	60	—	74
Gold	1	7	24	7	1	—

home-brewed software was a matter of only minutes! Table 11–3 merely shows the percentage chance of each asset class outperforming the geometric-mean expected return of each of the others over our selected 10-year time horizon. Remember that the time horizon is the factor that represents the investor's risk profile.

The way to read Table 11–3 is as follows: An asset class in the left column has a probability of beating the expected return of an asset class along the top row equal to the percentage shown in the appropriate space on the table. The next step is to translate the probabilities into an asset mix. A number of methods were described at the end of Chapter 9. Here we will demonstrate two of those. Knowing the probabilities, all we need to do is structure the portfolio so that each asset is owned in direct proportion to its probability of being the winner (outperforming the others) over the time horizon selected.

TABLE 11–4 Converting Probabilities To an Asset Mix

	Average Probability	Portfolio Weighting	Absolute Probability	Portfolio Weighting
Stocks	63.8%	22.5%	10.0%	35.7%
Bonds	54.2	19.1	3.6	12.7
T-Bills	40.0	14.1	0.7	2.4
Real Estate	54.0	19.0	4.0	14.2
Foreign Equities	63.6	22.4	9.9	35.1
Gold	8.0	2.8	0.0	0.0
Expected Return		9.3%		9.7%
Standard Deviation		7.0		9.0

Table 11–4 shows two simple methods of converting the probabilities to a portfolio mix by taking either the average probability of each asset beating the expected return of the other assets or the absolute probability of each asset outperforming all the other assets simultaneously.

To prove that these methods (which do not utilize cross-correlations as an input) work equally as well as the time-consuming, academic efficient-frontier approach, we have employed the lengthy formula for measuring the standard deviation of a group of assets with various cross-correlations in order to show the resulting volatilities of the two portfolios. These are shown in the last row of Table 11–4.

We also have performed the necessary calculations to create an efficient frontier, using the returns and volatilities from Table 11–2 and the cross-correlations from Table 11–1. The results are shown in Figure 11–12.

Each large dot in Figure 11–12 represents the reward-risk relationship of the individual classes: T stands for T-bills, B stands for

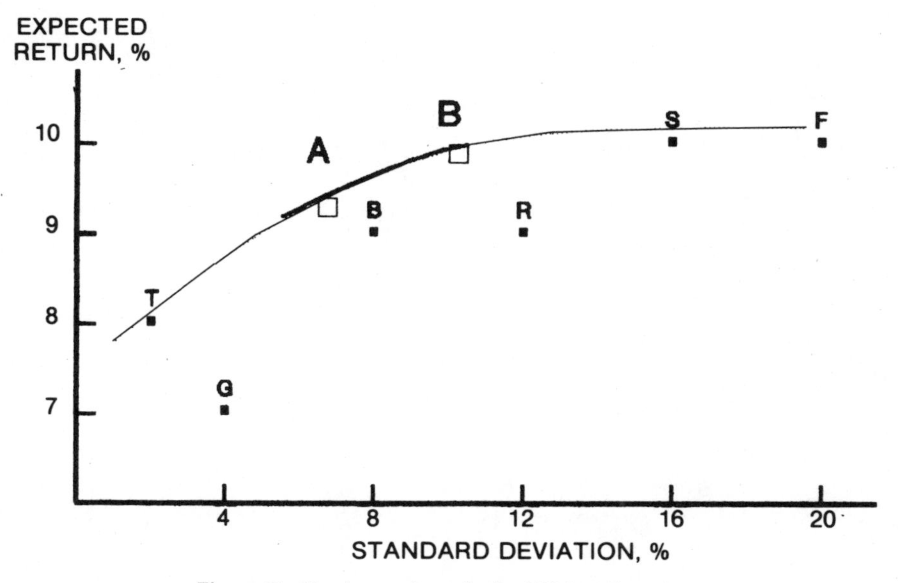

Figure 11–12. Approximately the Efficient Frontier.

bonds, R stands for real estate, and so on. The thin, dotted line is the curve representing the margin of efficiency as discussed earlier in the chapter. The bold curve is the efficient frontier, that is, the upper-left portion of the margin of efficiency.

Observe that the two portfolios from Table 11–4 (represented by Box A and Box B in Figure 11–12) fall right on and, in fact, nearly define the upper and lower limits of the efficient frontier!

There are other combinations of probabilities and a variety of methods of converting those probabilities into an asset mix. Those can be reviewed by referring back to the final pages of Chapter 9.

12

Asset Allocation: The Implementation

The pursuit of quantitative precision is as arduous as it is important.

—*Bertrand Russell*

THE WORLD-SHAKING EVENTS OF 1776

As an undergraduate at American International College, my major was economics and my postgraduate work was all in business administration. However, I used my electives to take every course in U.S. history that was offered by my college; the remaining electives were used for various courses in finance.

Over the years, I occasionally pondered the possible reasons that led me to major in economics and minor in U.S. history—particularly, since two years before graduation, I had been enrolled in the Bachelor of Science program as a mathematics major at the University of Rochester.

Little did I know that it would not be economics, but my sideline academic interests in history, finance, and mathematics that would turn out to be the most valuable with respect to the way I presently earn a living.

It was not until more recent years, after having done some part-time teaching at Boston University and two other New England colleges, that I learned enough about myself and the education process to realize why I was attracted to economics, history, and finance. It had nothing to do with any preconceptions of what

I was going to do for a career. That was later determined by the fact that an investments department of a major insurance company made me the best offer—an "accident" that I am still grateful for.

There are three separate reasons for my academic interest in economics, history, and finance, yet, really, just one principal: the charisma of three professors. Once again, this involves happenstance about which I have never had any regrets.

Dr. Michael Gural was an economics professor who might have been considered mediocre by his peers in terms of his scientific knowledge. But it would not surprise me if someone determined that Mike Gural was the most well-read person in the world. Every wall in his house was a bookcase, and as if that weren't enough, some of his rooms had library-style stacks right in the middle of the carpet. He had a most admirable, unique, historic perspective of economics and was well aware of the dividing line between theory and the real world. He was a soft-spoken, but eloquent, lecturer and aroused emotions I never knew I had. He could make a whole classroom of young people cry when he delivered his version of how the honorable intentions of the pioneers of socialism had been demoralized by the politicians and militarists who pretended to implement the theories. He could send the students home, all believing they had actually lived in Europe hundreds of years ago. He was a dreamer who used that attribute to encourage imagination and idealism within those who heard him speak. I tape recorded his, and only his, lectures—not as a source of review for upcoming exams, but as a means of arousing good feelings—feelings of omniscience, enlightenment, and optimism.

Dr. Frederick Palmer taught U.S. history in a fashion that made history seem as important to the future as to the past. He was from Oregon and instilled in me a desire to move west, which I finally fulfilled 20 years later. He spoke quietly—never a stutter or stammer, never a word misused or out of place. He knew his stuff and was a model teacher. He was the type that nice guys would like to grow up to be.

Dr. Richard Bolster, my adviser and finance professor, didn't fit the mold of the other two. As I recall, in his younger years he bummed all over the country by hopping rides aboard freight trains. He was a prisoner of war in the Pacific during World War II and wore his POW ribbon on his lapel every day at college. Eventually, after attending NYU, he became (you guessed it) a railroad analyst for the major brokerage firm of Harris, Upham (since merged into Smith-Barney).

He wore suits and long ties, not sport coats and bow ties, and had the appearance of an investment banker—except for the taps he wore on his shoes, even new shoes. He looked tough as he clicked his heels along the hallways, cigarette in hand, with his crewcut hair and massive chest (partly due to the emphysema that caused his death a few years after my graduation).

Professor Bolster's most remarkable attribute was his memory for numbers, dates, and times. One day a student approached him after class and said, "My father wants me to ask you whether he should sell the General Electric stock he bought at $22 per share 10 years ago." The professor replied, "Get your facts straight. Your father didn't buy GE 10 years ago at $22 because the last time the stock sold at that price was November 19, 16 years ago!"

His memory wasn't limited to business history. He knew the dates and times of everything ranging from the birth dates of the medieval monarchs to the time of day that the guillotine was used on anyone it had ever been used on. In a course I took on the economic history of the United States, the first question Dr. Bolster wrote on the initial exam was: Name the three most world-shaking events of 1776. Well, I could come up with two: the signing of the Declaration of Independence and the publishing of Adam Smith's *Wealth of Nations.*

The third "world-shaking" event was supposed to be "the invention of the cocktail." Apparently, during the American Revolution some soldiers stopped into a countryside tavern and ordered some liquored concoction. The barmaid embellished the drinks by putting a rooster's feather in each, as sort of a swizzle stick; accordingly, the term "cocktail" was originated.

But, it is the importance of *Wealth of Nations* that I often reflect upon when I get in a philosophical frame of mind. This (along with Adam Smith's earlier works dating back to 1859) was the first time an educated man had tried to analyze historical social behavior in an attempt to quantify the previously unquantified, so that the future could be predicted from the past.

PIONEERING THE DETERMINISM OF SOCIAL HISTORY

In the early days of economic thinking, the subject of economics was known as *social mathematics.* In a very real sense, investment analysis should be considered as a branch of social mathematics. As for the concept of the economic or financial future as history (i.e., the determinism of social mathematics), we really haven't progressed very far, considering that the *Wealth of Nations* was published over 200 years ago! Despite an inclination to consider that psychology and economics have progressed to the level of a real science, we must concede that there is no comparison between the colossal advances made by the physical sciences versus the more modest gains within the social sciences (in general) over that period.

We need more trailblazers in the social sciences—people who can train their minds to think in a different fashion. The thought process of the science pioneer is totally different from that of the stereotype accountant, lawyer, professional athlete, or physician. It is more philosophical, more mathematical, and more imaginative.

Here is an example of how the thought process begins to change for many of us. In high school we learned the 47th Proposition of Euclid, known as the Pythagorean Theorem. Pythagoras was one of those characters whose role in history lay somewhere between reality and mythology, like Confucious, his contemporary. But, no mathematical expression is more renowned than the Pythagorean Theorem: In a triangle, where one of the angles is 90°, the sum of the squares of the two shortest sides equals the square of the longest side.

Around tenth grade, we learned to "prove" this theorem. Around eleventh grade, we learned it could not be proven, except by measurement. Then in twelfth grade we discovered it wasn't true at all; it is merely an approximation, probably derived from ancient knowledge that a triangle whose sides are three, four, and five units long forms a right triangle.

A triangle laid out on your front lawn with sides of three, four, and five feet would measure to have one angle of "precisely" 90°

and a sum of the angles of 180°. Notice that the square of 3 plus the square of 4 equals the square of 5 (9 + 16 = 25).

But, if you walked from your front lawn to a point exactly 300 miles north, then turned precisely 90° and walked 400 miles east, then turned and walked straight home, you would have walked significantly more than 500 miles! Similarly, once you learn non-Euclidean geometry, you discover that a triangle can have not only 180°, but up to 360 or even 540°, and in outer space, maybe less than 180°.

By the time a student goes through college, if he or she has shown some interest in the science of mathematics, he or she realizes that the Newtonian physics our ancestors were brought up on has had such an influence over the years that 99.99% of the educated people presently on this earth are mentally deficient about even the most commonplace physical phenomenon. This is so, even though the great mathematicians, such as Gauss and Riemann, altered and improved Newtonian mathematics over a century ago, as did Einstein in the early twentieth century and many others in more recent times.

How many of us still believe, for example, that there is a "force" (gravity) between any two objects in the universe (such as the earth and the sun)? Newton stated that this gravitational force was equal to the product of the masses of the two objects divided by the square of their distance from each other. But, many years ago, scientists "discovered" that there is no such "force"—that the distribution of matter over the universe causes a warping of space-time, and it is this manifold of space-time that causes the particular motion of the stars and planets. Pioneers and potential pioneers of the physical and social sciences are intrigued by this sort of thing.

Investments pioneers must have the ability and the inclination to remain contemporary with science, mathematics, and history. They must throw away the charts and graphs of past securities prices and earnings with their straight "trend" lines. (What physical or social phenomenon moves in a straight line anyway? Are stock prices some special exception to all the laws of the universe?) It is the history of social behavior that must be quantified and then analyzed if the realm of securities analysis and portfolio management is to merge into the realm of science.

THE SELF-CORRECTING NATURE OF THE MARKETPLACE

I began the mathematical process years ago by attempting to figure out why investors sometimes demand a big premium return for owning stocks relative to Treasury bonds yet, at other significantly separate times, they demand no risk-premium whatsoever. For the purposes of this book, I first need to explain certain findings regarding the historic *depth perception* of the investing public.

If, at a particular point in time, the perceived expected returns of the stock and bond markets are both mathematically correct but are "out of sync" with each other relative to history, *when, if at all, will they move back in balance?* If the annualized, five-year expected return for stocks is 5% less than that of a government bond, will stocks underperform bonds by at least 5% per year over the next five years? (Witness the late 1970s.)

On the other hand, if the 5-year expected return for stocks is below the yield to maturity of a 5-year Treasury bond, might not the bond market appreciate relative to the stock market tomorrow? (Witness the Crash of October 19, 1987.) These types of issues are at the heart of the philosophies that separate dynamic asset allocators from either tactical or strategic allocators.

Let's pursue this issue by stating *Sociological Phenomenon 1:* the stock market *thinks* it can foresee as much as eight years into the future. This has been proved, mathematically, through an extremely complex synthesis of historic behavior. *Sociological Phenomenon 2:* Today, it takes the market about 20 days, on average, but as little as 1 and as many as 90 days to move into an equilibrium state relative to its own expectations and its level of confidence in those expectations.

What these phenomena really mean is that the market will react to changes in interest rates, taxation, earnings, and so forth, which are expected to become manifest in eight years or less. Obviously, more weight is given to expected near-term changes than to changes several years away. Changes in expectations for the very long-term, such as 10 or 20 years, have a negligible effect on securities prices. Consensus changes in expectations for the next few years, however, will measurably affect securities prices—within a matter of days or weeks following the change.

Question: Why should the investor buy or sell massive amounts of stocks, bonds, real estate, or T-bills when the system will at least think it's back in balance within a few weeks?

Example: Assume the markets are in balance to begin with. Then, the market changes its mind about the most likely level of interest rates that will prevail three years from now. Assume this causes either a steepening of the yield curve or a decline in investor confidence, or both. Imagine that on the same day this new forecast is reflected in the bond market, stocks actually go up when they should have gone down. If the investor does nothing, then he or she has an asset allocation that does not reflect the *long-term* (as well as the short-term) probabilities of stocks outperforming bonds. Also, the investor would be passing up an opportunity to capitalize on this disequilibrium. But if he or she sells stocks, this investor should repurchase them in about 20 days when the markets are in balance, which would cost commissions. Furthermore, if he or she sells stocks, the market might return to equilibrium by moving bond prices higher while stocks remain unchanged. The reverse might happen if the investor buys bonds instead of selling stocks. In either case, which stocks would the investor sell or which bonds should he or she buy?

These issues and questions deal with the essence of dynamic asset-allocation implementation. Some of the answers comprise the remainder of the chapter.

THE UNIVERSAL LAW OF LAZINESS

There is a universal law of laziness that applies to all physical and social behavior. But, the interesting thing is that this laziness is what brings about efficiency, whether it be in the factory, the office, the biological world, or in the realm of outer space. When a person walks from Point A to Point B, he or she will walk around a hill rather than over it, even though the distance traveled is longer. From the perspective of an observer in an airplane (who cannot detect the hill), the walker's path appears inefficient, even though the opposite is the case. The same is true regarding the path of the planets or of light; neither is a straight line, from the point of view of a distant observer, but rather a geodesic between two points over a specific time interval. When an airplane travels from New York City to Salt Lake City, it first travels west-northwest toward the Great Lakes to be efficient, even though Salt Lake is precisely due west of New York. The same principles apply to human behavior.

Frederic Chopin was the greatest of the great nineteenth-century composer-pianists. He was a mathematician with incomparable sensitivity and emotion. Nathan M. Rothschild was the greatest of the great financiers of the same era, also brilliant with numbers. Chopen dedicated his Waltz No. 2 opus 64 in C-Sharp Minor to Madame Nathan Rothschild.

Would Chopin's famous waltz have sounded the same in the key of D-minor, only one pitch higher? Maybe not, particularly when played by Chopin. Liszt said that each one of Chopin's fingers had a voicing all of its own. If Chopin had written Waltz No. 2 in the key of D-minor instead of C-sharp minor, it would have been easier to read because there is only one flat in the former key, compared to four sharps in the latter. But the fingering would have been different, causing subtle differences in the way the piece is played. In fact, once the notes of the waltz are memorized, it is much easier to play in the key in which it was actually written. Try playing the second theme of this piece in another key and you will undoubtedly agree that this soul dance loses something.

Music composed especially for the stringed instruments is usually written in the keys of G, D, A, and E for the same reason: It plays easier, despite all the sharps the player must contend with and, therefore, sounds better. Compositions for an orchestra are frequently written in the keys of F, B-flat, and E-flat, so that the instruments inherently tuned to the key of B-flat (such as the brass and woodwinds) can perform with equal dexterity as those tuned to the key of C. Despite the universal use of the tempered scale (which compensates for the fact that, scientifically, C-sharp and D-flat are not actually one in the same), it can certainly be argued, and usually proven, that a composition *plays easier* in one key than another (even if it can initially be read more easily in a different key). If the composition plays easier, it is more likely that it can be played as it was intended to be played.

From the movement of the fingers around the guitar frets to the movement of light around the universe, doing things the easy way or taking the path of least resistance results in ultimate efficiency. Often, the easy way is not intuitive; a learning process is called for.

SIMPLIFYING THE INVESTMENT PROCESS WITH DERIVATIVES

Over recent years, a number of investment vehicles, called *derivatives*, have been created that improve the efficiency of both the investment manager and the portfolio itself. On the surface, the use of derivatives may appear more complex—just like the walker appeared to pursue a devious course from the perspective of the passenger aboard the airplane, or just like Chopin's use of keys with many flats or sharps appears inefficient (in terms of reading the notes) until you realize that the choice of key results in playing efficiency.

The apparent complexity of derivative-investment products is probably the only reason that not everyone that can and should use them actually does. But, once investors get a "feel" for the way they work, the cost savings become obvious.

The few derivatives I will be discussing in this chapter are limited to those that are the most appropriate for asset-allocation purposes. They include:

1. *Market Baskets*. A security designed to be a hypothetical group of stocks, such as the S&P 500. It trades on the same basis as the index it was designed to represent. Its purpose is to allow the investor to purchase (or sell) the equivalent of a major

market index without having to trade all the individual stocks. More importantly, it allows the investor to *own* the equivalent of an index without having to update the holdings and their weightings within the index.

2. *Index Futures.* Legal instruments that obligate the buyer to purchase and the seller to sell the cash equivalent of an underlying stock or a bond equivalent to a Treasury-bond index on a specific date in the future. What makes equity index futures different from other commodity futures, such as those for copper or corn, is that the underlying commodity does not ultimately have to be delivered, even if the trade is not reversed. The equity index future always settles in cash—equal to the equivalent value of the underlying index less the original contract price. What makes a Treasury-bond future unique is that, even though it has a physical (viz. cash) settlement, the physical delivery is in the form of Treasury bonds whose coupon and maturity *approximate* the hypothetical bond index and are the "easiest to deliver."
3. *Index Options.* An index call gives the buyer of the call the right to purchase (from the seller) the equivalent of the underlying equity index at a predetermined price, either on a specific date or up until a specific date. An index put gives the buyer the right to sell the equivalent of the underlying equity index at a predetermined price. Index puts and calls always settle in cash rather than in the actual securities that comprise the underlying index, unlike individual stock options, which involve the delivery of securities.

Market baskets and index options are normally cash (viz. margin) transactions. The market baskets trade at a price equivalent to the full value of the underlying index. The index options trade at a price equal to the value of the put or call privilege—usually a small fraction of the value of the underlying index.

Index futures trade on margin and are subject to all the same margin rules and restrictions as their commodity-based counterparts. However, as I will demonstrate, a *synthetic future*, not subject to margin regulations, can be created through the simultaneous purchase of an index call and sale of an index put (or the reverse).

The asset-allocation function of these derivative tools is to enable an investor to make changes in his or her asset mix in a very efficient manner, that is, without having to actually alter the portfolio. This allows the investor the opportunity to increase or decrease equity or fixed-income exposure with minimal transactions costs and without having to disrupt the structure of the basic portfolio of stocks and bonds.

More importantly, derivatives present a resolution to the sociological phenomenon that the investments markets frequently move into disequilibrium with respect to relative long-term expected returns, but then return to equilibrium in the short term.

For example, suppose the investor calculated the long-term expected returns of stocks and bonds to be equal to each other (i.e., no equity risk-premium) and therefore anticipated that stocks would underperform bonds over the near term. The investor could sell stocks, but this might result in selling the wrong individual issues or creating excessive transactions costs by selling partial portions of all equity positions. It would be much more efficient to *hedge* the existing equity portfolio on a temporary basis, particularly since the market has a history of returning to equilibrium in the near term.

HEDGING WITH MARKET BASKETS

Let's assume the investor's current portfolio is valued at $10 million, and the asset mix is 50% stocks, 30% bonds, 20% cash. Suppose that the yield curve changes so that the desired asset mix is 30% stock, 30% bonds, and 40% cash. The investor does not want to sell his or her individual equities because he or she:

1. Believes they will outperform the market.
2. Does not wish to increase the level of nonsystematic risk of the equity portfolio beyond that which was originally obtained (by owning a very diverse group of stocks).

3. Does not want to incur excessive transactions costs, particularly since he or she believes the market will adjust to the new interest rates in the near term, which will cause him or her to want to be 50% or so invested in equities, again, in the near future.

But, the fact is, the investor does believe that the equities market, in general, is overvalued, at least temporarily. Therefore, he or she should consider employing a temporary hedge to the existing portfolio. One way to accomplish this would be sell (short) a market basket, such as the one for the S&P 500, which is listed on the New York Stock Exchange and has about a half-dozen specialists making a market.

The investor currently owns $5 million of common stock. He or she needs to hedge $2 million of that amount in order to effectively reduce his or her equity exposure to 30%. If the S&P 500 index were selling at 300, the bid price for the S&P market basket would be probably no less than $299 (reflecting the fact that the bid price of all the individual stocks comprising the index is normally slightly below the last traded price). Therefore, to accomplish this objective, the investor needs to sell approximately 6,667 shares of the S&P market basket to hedge $2 million of stock ($2,000,000/300 = 6,667).

The commissions would be less than those on selling individual shares, the administrative time is negligible, and, most importantly, the investor has not at all diluted the incremental effect his or her individual stocks will have on the portfolio's performance if the stocks outperform the market as expected. In other words, the investor has reduced the systematic (market) risk of the equity portfolio by 40% since he or she has effectively hedged 40% of his or her stocks, but the portfolio alpha (expected incremental return above the market return) has not been diminished.

One disadvantage of this approach is that the market basket is one of the least liquid of the derivative products. Another potential problem is that, if the portfolio is an institutional account, it may not be able to sell short, which involves margin requirements. Therefore, for certain institutional accounts, the market basket might be an appropriate tool only at times when the investor needs to *increase* equity exposure.

HEDGING WITH INDEX FUTURES

Normally, a more efficient method of temporarily changing equity exposure is to utilize financial futures. The advantages here *vis-à-vis* the market-basket approach are:

1. Dramatically improved marketability.
2. Even lower commissions.
3. The ability to hedge the bond portion as well as the stock portion of the portfolio.

Let's assume, this time, that the investor needs to reduce equity exposure by $2 million as before, but also needs to increase fixed-income exposure by $2 million. The investor should consider selling S&P 500 futures and buying Treasury note futures.

Each S&P futures contract represents the equivalent of 500 units of the S&P index. That means a single future equals $150,000 of underlying stock in this example (500 times the S&P price level of 300). Therefore, the investor needs to sell 13 contracts ($2,000,000/$150,000). The current margin requirement for the S&P 500 futures is $4,000 per contract, in this case $52,000. A daily variation margin equal to the unrealized gain or loss must also be maintained. Upon expiration of the futures contract, the variation margin account is closed out, which, in effect, represents the investor's profit or loss.

If the price of the S&P 500 is 300, in reality, a futures contract will normally sell at a premium to that price. This is because, like any futures contract, the purchaser is, in effect, buying now and paying later. Therefore, the intrinsic value of an S&P futures contract is equal to the current cash price of the index, plus the cost that would have been incurred to carry the underlying securities (which is a function of current interest rates as well as the number of days until expiration of the contract) less the dividends that would have been received on the underlying securities:

$$F = \text{S\&P} + i - d$$

Accordingly, if short-term interest rates are 8% and the dividend yield on the S&P 500 is 4%, the intrinsic value of a *three-month* S&P futures contract would be 1% above the current level of the index (8% − 4% = 4% × ¼ year = 1%). The actual price of the contract may be somewhat above or below the intrinsic value, depending on the expectations of the traders regarding the future level of the S&P. However, the contract price will not vary *much* from the intrinsic value; otherwise index arbitrage (buying the underlying stocks and shorting the future, or vice versa) would provide a risk-free investment with an above-risk-free rate of return for the brokerage firms in the arbitrage business.

Treasury futures are somewhat more complex. This is because the T-note future represents a contract for a hypothetical 8% T-note and the T-bond future represents a contract for a hypothetical 8% Treasury bond, both with constant (rolling) maturities. Therefore, the intrinsic value of the futures contract must be a function of the market price of a real T-bond equivalent of the hypothetical bond. To determine the value of Treasury futures, the price of the currently equivalent ("easiest-to-deliver") actual bond is adjusted for four factors:

1. Any difference between the equivalent bond's coupon and 8%.
2. The possibility of an interest payment on the real bond (on which the bond buyer would also have earned interest on interest).
3. The accrued interest on the real bond at the time the contract was purchased versus the accrued interest at the time of contract expiration.
4. The carrying cost (interest cost) that would have been incurred had the investor owned the equivalent bond instead of the futures contract.

A formula for the intrinsic value of a T-bond or T-note futures contract is, therefore, somewhat involved:

$$F = [B + i(B + A1) + A1 - A2 - C(1 + i)]/CV$$

where (B) is the price of an equivalent real bond, ($A1$) is its accrued interest as of now, ($A2$) is its accrued interest at the time of contract expiration, (i) is the interest (assumed carrying cost), (C) is the value of any coupon that would have been received on the real bond, and (CV) is the conversion factor that adjusts the valuation for any difference in the real bond's interest rate and 8%. The conversion factor would be above 1.00 for a real bond with a coupon in excess of 8% and below 1.00 if the real bond's yield was below 8%.

This formula may seem complicated, but it merely equates the return of the investor who owns the futures contract plus an amount in cash (equal to what would have been paid if an actual equivalent bond had been bought) to the return of the investor who owns the equivalent underlying bond.

One Treasury futures contract is equivalent to a face value of $100,000 in bonds or notes. Therefore, in the example of the investor needing to purchase the equivalent of $2 million in bonds, he or she would need to purchase 20 Treasury futures if the price of the contract were 100. If the price of the hypothetical 8% bond were 90, 22 contracts would need to be purchased [$2,000,000/($100,000 × 90/100)].

The initial margin requirement for Treasury futures is $2,000 per contract. For bond futures (as well as stock futures), a variation margin that reflects the unrealized gain or loss must be maintained on a daily basis. If the net variation margin is a debit, the investor must put up additional collateral. If the collateral is a qualified security instead of cash, only a percentage of the market value of the security is applied to the margin requirement (ranging from 90% for T-bills to 50% for stocks).

The logic of using Treasury futures in place of actual bonds is less obvious than with stock futures, because Treasury bonds are so liquid and involve negligible commissions. However, the investor may find that the portfolio often does not have enough cash to buy the actual bonds needed to meet the asset-allocation goals (as a result of owning excessive equities that have been hedged).

For example, suppose a portfolio is currently invested 50% in equities, 45% in bonds, and 5% in cash. Then assume the desired asset allocation changes to 40% equities and 55% bonds. If the investor reduces the equity component by selling S&P futures rather than selling stock, there will not be enough cash available to purchase the necessary bonds. But there will be enough cash to meet the margin requirements for purchasing the appropriate number of Treasury futures.

The financial futures markets are extremely liquid. This has become increasingly so, as the investment community has recognized the importance of asset allocation relative to individual securities selection. However, the drawback to utilizing futures is an administrative one. Although the use of futures for asset-allocation purposes is a nonspeculative, unleveraged one, futures *can* be used by speculative investors as a means to leverage available cash. Consider that $4,000 can purchase the equivalent of $150,000 of stock, if the S&P were at the 300 level. As a result, there is a fair amount of regulatory paperwork involved in opening the necessary margin account. This is designed to assure the authorities that the investor (or the investment adviser) is qualified and knowledgeable regarding the use of financial futures.

HEDGING WITH INDEX OPTIONS

Buying and selling covered (backed by cash or securities) equity index options are cash transactions and do not require the use of margin—only the pledging of assets to collateralize any *short sales.* This pledging is accomplished easily by allowing the broker to be the custodian of the underlying securities being hedged. If a bank is the custodian, it can issue an escrow receipt to the clearing firm, which simply gives assurance that the account has set aside an equivalent amount of qualified securities as collateral for the put or call that was sold against the equity index. Listed stocks usually are pledged against short calls and T-bills against short puts. The seller gets to keep the investment income from pledged securities.

Puts and calls are available on the S&P 500 and on other major market indices. The OEX index (100 largest stocks) frequently has the preferable options because it is as liquid as the underlying securities themselves. Also, OEX options may be exercised any time prior to expiration, whereas S&P options only may be exercised (presently) on the expiration date. But, neither index options series, is, in reality, exercised prior to expiration; they are sold instead.

A single index option represents the cash equivalent of 100 units of the underlying index. Accordingly, one S&P call gives the buyer the *right* (not the legal obligation as in the case of futures) to purchase the equivalent of 100 units of the S&P index at some fixed price, regardless of the level of the S&P index at the time of expiration. One S&P put gives the buyer the right to sell the cash equivalent of 100 units of the S&P 500 at a predetermined price. The predetermined price, in the case of either calls or puts, is known as the *strike price.*

Upon expiration, any open transactions are settled in cash, based on the intrinsic value of the option. The seller of the call or the buyer of the put do not deliver any actual securities, index funds, or market baskets. For example, if an S&P call was written with a strike price of 300 and the S&P index was at 330 at expiration, the seller of the call would owe the buyer $10 per share, or $1,000 per option contract.

The market price (cost) of a put or call is referred to as the *premium,* which is equal to the value of the rights involved. The value of those rights is a function of the volatility of the market, the level of interest rates (carrying costs) and dividends of the underlying securities, as well as the strike price of the option, the market price of the underlying securities, and the remaining time until expiration. The more volatile the stock market, the more expensive are the puts and calls. When interest rates rise, the value of calls rises and the value of puts falls. The higher the value of the dividends on the underlying securities, the less the call is worth (because the holder of the underlying stock is entitled to the dividend) and the more the put is worth.

Figure 12–1 shows what happens to the value of a stock portfolio (as of the option expiration date) that is partially hedged by owning one put per 100 shares, relative to the value of an unhedged portfolio. Notice that when the market declines, the hedged

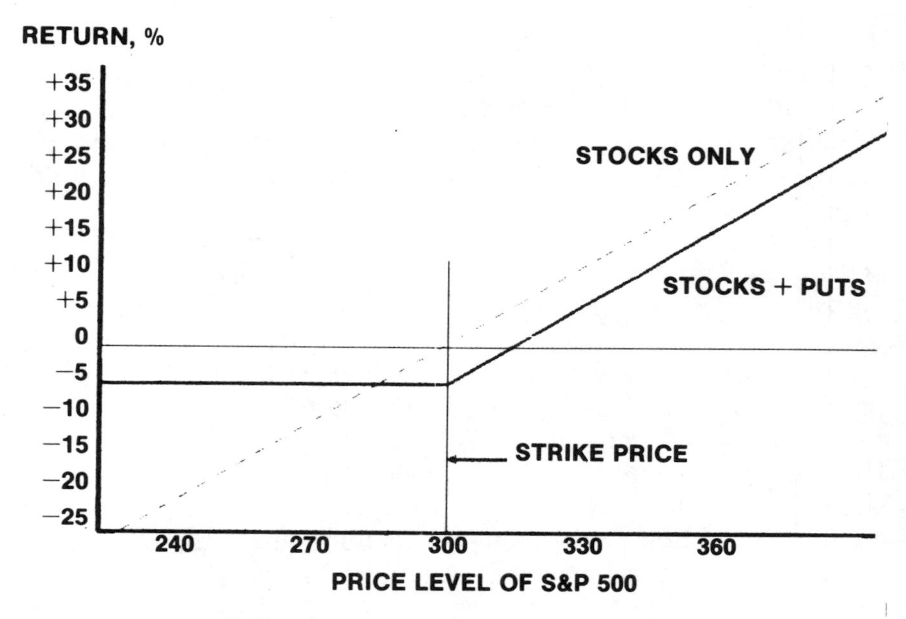

Figure 12–1. Stocks Plus Puts versus Stocks Only.

portfolio loses only the cost of the put (in this case, 5%). If the investor is wrong, however, and the stock market does not come down, the hedged portfolio participates fully on the up side, less the cost of the put. For example, if the market declines 20%, the hedged portfolio has a return of −5%; if the market goes up 20%, the hedged portfolio gains 15%.

Call options also can be used for the same purpose, even to effectively *reduce* equity positions. Figure 12–2 shows the comparative results of *selling* ("writing") one call for every equivalent amount of underlying securities held. This is known as *covered call writing*. If options premiums are high (reflecting unrealistic, high stock-price volatility) then selling options (calls) often can be preferable to buying options (puts).

In Figure 12–2, a one-for-one, covered-call hedge causes the portfolio to lose 5% less than the unhedged portfolio; but unlike the earlier example (in Figure 12–1) of buying puts on a one-for-one basis, the gain from selling an on-the-money covered call is limited to the premium received, or 5% in this case.

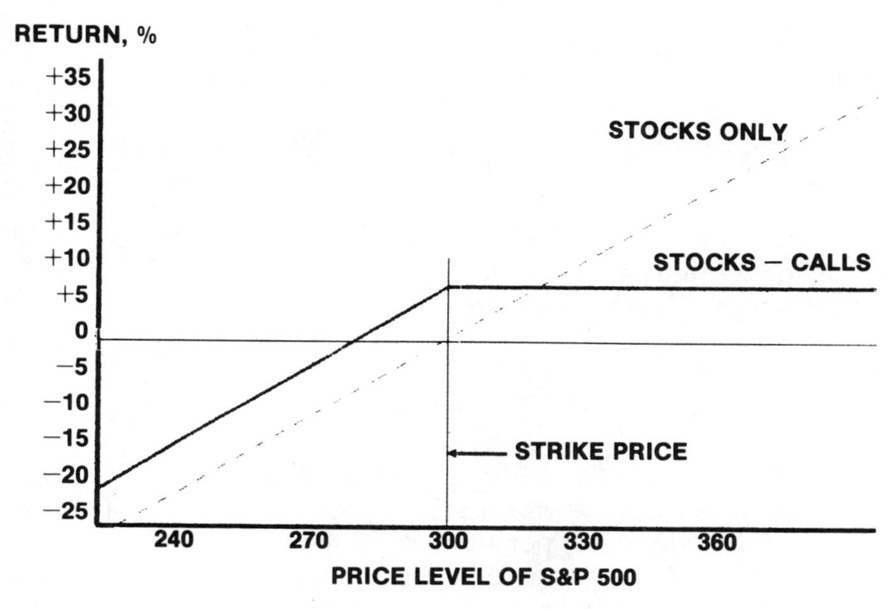

Figure 12–2. Stocks and Short Calls versus Stocks Only.

PRODUCING A NEUTRAL HEDGE

The options feature that must be fully understood is the *hedge ratio*. This is the dollar amount the option will change in price for each $1.00 (or one point) move in the price of the underlying security or index. For example, assume the S&P 500 index sells for 300 and the price of a three-month option with a 300 strike price is 10. If the hedge ratio of that option is .50, then the price of the call will move to 10.50 and the put to 9.50 if the S&P moves to 301.

Suppose a portfolio is 50% invested in common stocks in the amount of $5 million. If the desired asset allocation becomes 40% equities, then in lieu of selling $1 million of actual stocks, the investor could buy put options to hedge his or her position. The investor would purchase puts on $2,500,000 of equities if the hedge ratio of the put option was .40. If the underlying index were at 300, then the investor would purchase 83 index puts with a 300 strike price ($2,500,000/300 = 83 puts, at 100 index units per put). The cost, assuming a put price of 10, would be 100 times 10 times 83, or $83,000.

The number of options needed to produce a true hedge is as follows:

$$\text{No. of Options} = \frac{\$\text{ To Be Hedged}}{\text{Price of Index} \times 100 \times \text{Hedge Ratio}}$$

So, if the S&P or OEX index were trading at 300, the properly hedged portfolio would own *two-and-a-half puts* per $30,000 of stock if the hedge ratio on the put were .40:

$$\frac{\$30{,}000}{300 \times 100 \times .40} = 2.5$$

If the market declined, say 5%, each $300 in original market value of stock would be worth $15 less, or $285, but the put would be worth $6 ($15 × .40) per share more than was paid. Since the investor bought 2½ puts per $30,000 of stock, the profit of $15 (2.5 × $6) on the puts would equally offset the $15 loss on the underlying stock that is held.

If the on-the-money put (one where the strike price approximately equals the price of the underlying index) is expensive relative to fair value, the investor may wish to purchase a put with a strike price above (in the money) or below (out of the money) the index price. In this case, the hedge ratio might not be in the .40 to .50 range. Obviously, an out-of-the-money put is nowhere near as sensitive to the underlying index as one with a strike price above the index price. A put that is 10% out of the money might have a hedge ratio of only .10, depending on the number of days until expiration. In that case, the investor would have to purchase puts on 10 times as much stock as he or she wants to hedge. Conversely, the investor would need to buy puts on only two times (or less) the desired amount to be hedged if the put's strike price is in-the-money.

Figure 12–3 compares the range of possible portfolio returns (including dividends) of being long stock only, being long stock plus 1 put per 100 shares, and being 100% hedged by owing stock plus 2.5 puts per 100 shares. The illustration assumes that the original options positions are maintained until expiration date.

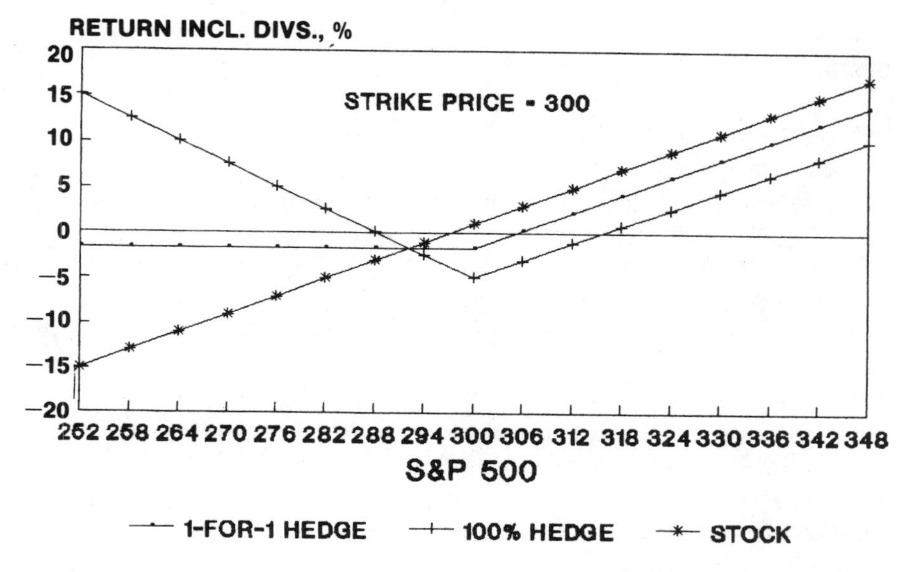

Figure 12–3. Buying Puts to Create a Neutral Hedge.

Figure 12–4 shows the range of possible portfolio returns (including a 1%-per-quarter dividend return) for an unhedged stock account compared to an account that is hedged by having sold one index call per 100 shares and to an account that has an initial 100% hedge by having sold 1.7 calls per 100 shares.

Notice in both Figure 12–3 (hedging with long puts) and Figure 12–4 (hedging with short calls) that a theoretical 100% hedge will either make or lose money if the initial hedge is held constant until expiration. In hedging with index options, an investor must be aware that the hedge ratio on any options that are held changes constantly as the level moves up or down relative to the strike price. The trick is to keep the portfolio properly hedged at all times, which means adjusting the number of options positions as the hedge ratio of the option changes. When the market goes up, the hedge ratio of a put declines, requiring that more puts be purchased or that the existing puts be "rolled" into different puts that have the appropriate hedge ratio. Also, a rising market causes the hedge ratio of a call to increase, requiring either that outstanding calls be rolled to a different series or that a portion of the short-call position be closed out by repurchasing some of the outstanding options.

If a proper hedge ratio is maintained, the total portfolio will behave (in terms of total return) as though the hedged stocks were never owned in the first place. Yet, by utilizing puts to accomplish this effect, the investor saves substantial transactions costs (unless the hedge ratio substantially changes frequently) and maintains a portfolio of his or her favorite stocks (which hopefully will outperform in either a bull or bear market). Figure 12–5 shows what happens to the hedge ratios of index puts and calls as the market moves up or down relative to the strike price.

The transactions costs and other administrative costs of adjusting equity allocation through the use of index options is minimal. Significant problems occur only when puts and/or calls are selling for unreasonable prices or when the options positions have to be changed frequently, as a result of market fluctuations that cause the hedge ratios to change.

Both of these problems can be avoided by simultaneously buying puts and selling calls as a means of reducing equity

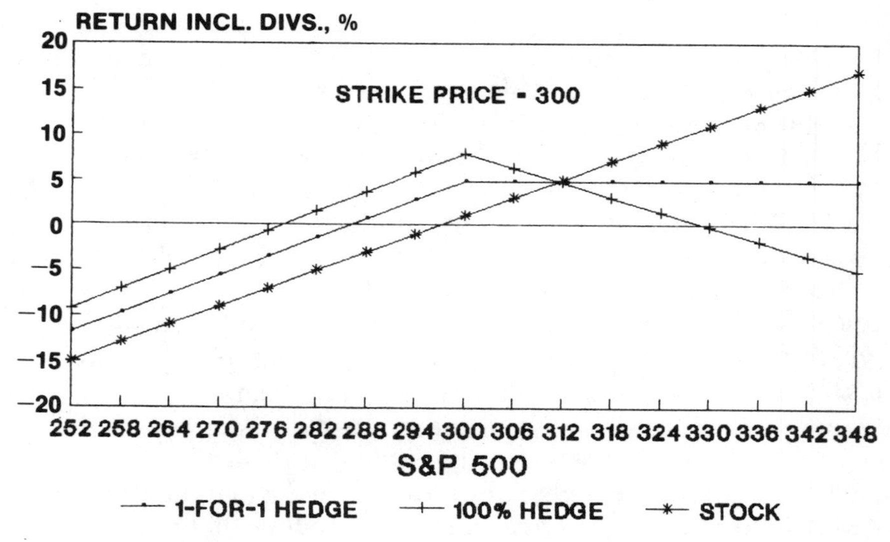

Figure 12–4. Selling Calls to Create a Neutral Hedge.

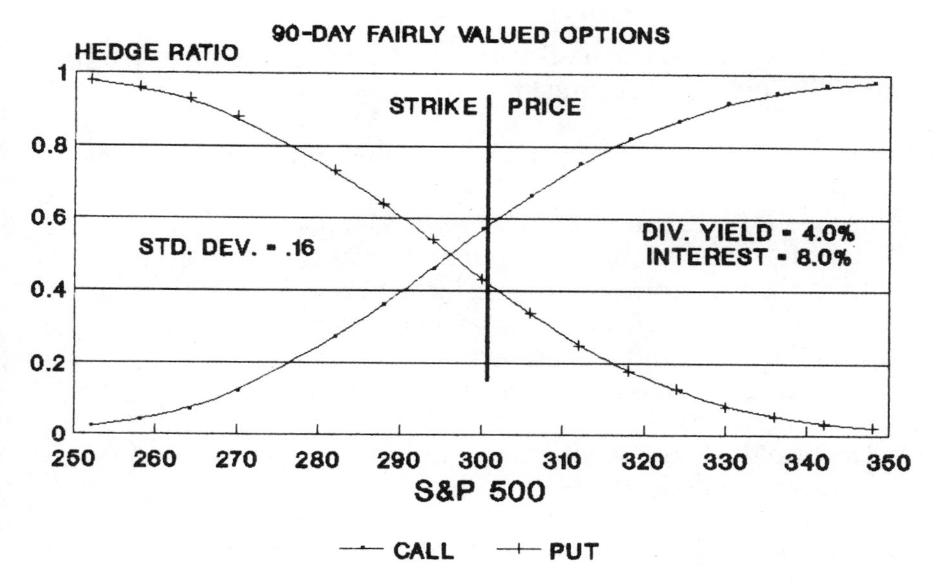

Figure 12–5. Hedge Ratios for Puts and Calls.

exposure (or simultaneously buying calls and selling puts to temporarily increase equity exposure). This leads us to what is normally the most efficient means of adjusting asset allocation over the near term: synthetic futures.

CREATING SYNTHETIC FUTURES

Consider the following basic relationship:

$$\text{Stock} + \text{Put} = \text{Cash} + \text{Call}$$

The investor with $1 million of stock and a put option on that stock will have a portfolio return identical to that of an investor with $1 million in T-bills and a call option on $1 million of the same stock, *no matter which direction the market moves*. This assumes, of course, that the options are both fairly valued—that the call premium minus the put premium equals the interest on the T-bills minus the dividends on the stock.

Since the previous equation is true, then, using simple algebra, the following equation must be true:

$$\text{Stock} = \text{Cash} + \text{Call} - \text{Put}$$

This means that an investor who owns $1 million in T-bills and has bought a call option and sold a put option on $1 million of stock will have the same return as the investor who bought $1 million of the same stock. This, again, assumes fairly valued options with the same strike price and expiration date.

We can now make two mathematical conclusions:

1. Since the second equation is true, the sum of the hedge ratio on the call plus the hedge ratio on the put must equal 1.00. It is a fact that the combined hedge ratio of a put and call with the same strike price and expiration date always will equal unity.
2. Since owning $1 million in T-bills plus a (long) futures contract on $1 million of stock is the same as owning $1 million of the stock, then:

$$\text{Cash} + \text{Futures} = \text{Cash} + \text{Call} - \text{Put}$$

Therefore:

$$\text{Futures} = \text{Call} - \text{Put}$$

The fact is, in buying a call and selling an equivalent put on the same underlying security, a synthetic futures contract has been created. Similarly, an investor can *sell* a synthetic futures contract by buying a put and selling an equivalent call.

Selling a synthetic index futures contract is normally the most efficient means by which an investor can reduce equity exposure. Here are the advantages, relative to the alternatives of selling stock, short-selling market baskets, selling call options, buying put options, or selling actual futures:

1. For each dollar equivalent of 100 shares of the equity index that needs to be hedged, exactly one index put would be

bought and one index call would be sold. This is because the combined hedge ratio of equivalent puts and calls is 1.00.

2. It does not matter whether the entire series of index options is undervalued or overvalued (relative to the computed fair value) because the investor is both buying and selling an option.
3. The initial hedge can be maintained until expiration date because the hedge ratio of a future is constant, regardless of any price changes of the underlying security or index.
4. Since the differences in fair value between a call and an equivalent put is the going rate of interest less the underlying stocks' dividends, selling a fairly-priced synthetic future against stock guarantees the investor the T-bill rate of interest, no more and no less, on the principal amount of equities that are hedged.
5. Trading costs are minimal because the sale of a call and simultaneous purchase of a put involve a principal amount, upon which the commissions are based, that is only 5 to 10% of the amount of stock that otherwise would have been sold.
6. Liquidity of many of the index options is as great as the underlying securities themselves. Also, the administrative costs are minimal because only two trades are involved, regardless of the amount of stock that is being hedged.
7. Nothing is bought or sold on margin. The puts are paid for in cash, and the short-call position is backed by actual securities. Therefore, a margin account is not necessary, and institutional accounts are qualified to invest in covered options.

Figure 12–6 shows how a futures contract (real or synthetic) sold on a one-for-one basis against a long stock position is the only means, other than selling stock and investing the proceeds in T-bills, that reduces risk to zero and guarantees a risk-free rate of return.

The figure shows the return to expiration date, including dividends of the three fully hedged strategies discussed. It assumes a 3-month holding period, using 90-day, fairly priced options that where bought or sold on the money at a current level of 300 for the

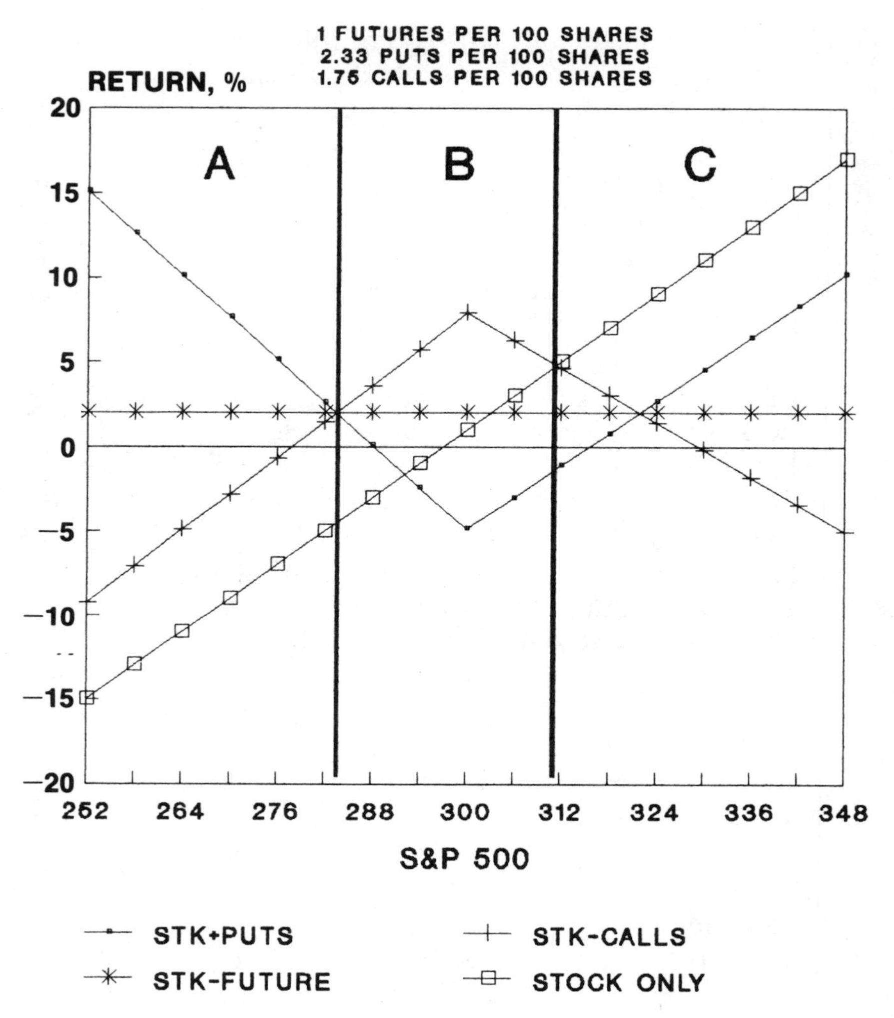

Figure 12–6. Comparison of Hedging Strategies.

S&P index. In Area A, where the stock market declines significantly, the investor would have been best off if the stocks were hedged by selling puts in an amount based on the puts initial hedge ratio. In Area B, where the stock market remained relatively stable, the investor would have been best off writing calls against stock. In Area C, where the market showed significant appreciation, the investor would have been better off not hedging at all.

However, this analysis of Areas A, B, and C assumes that the investor is speculating on the near-term direction of the market. If the investor is wrong, he or she can lose money in all three cases. This is not what the dynamic asset allocator is attempting to accomplish. The allocator is merely attempting to use options to effectively convert a portion of an account's equities to cash (T-bills); the market decision as to what percentage of the equity portfolio to hedge was made previously. Accordingly, the only foolproof means of effectively converting equities to cash without selling them is by selling a futures, or synthetic futures, contract. The synthetic future is usually preferable because it does not involve trading on margin.

Table 12–1 shows an actual example of the possible results for various moves in the market for the three basic hedging strategies. Although the stock-less-future approach is the risk-free hedge, there are times when options are significantly overpriced or underpriced; in this case, the investor may do well to capture some incremental return by either selling calls (if they are overvalued) or buying puts (if they are undervalued) and adjusting the number of options positions as the hedge ratio changes with the level of the market.

There are numerous variations of hedging strategies using derivative securities—so many that the entire subject matter could fill several volumes. For the purposes of this book, it is enough for the investor to be aware of the basic uses of index futures and options as efficient methods for adjusting asset allocation.

CONCLUSIONS

It is true that, on average, a portfolio that is invested more heavily in stocks than bonds and more heavily in bonds than cash tends to have a very favorable reward-risk ratio. Yet, the investor should not be lulled into believing that a 60/30/10 stock/bond/cash mix (for example) is always prudent. There are times when any good asset-allocation model will show that equities are less attractive

TABLE 12–1 Comparive Returns for Fully Hedged Options Strategies

Beginning Values:		
	Stock	300
	Std. Dev.	0.16
	Div. Yield	4.0%
	Interest	8.0%
	Strike Price	300
	Expiration	90 days
	Call	$10.92
	Hedge Ratio	0.57
	Calls/Share	1.75
	Put	$7.96
	Hedge Ratio	0.43
	Puts/Share	2.33
	Syn. Future	$2.96
	Hedge Ratio	1.00
	Futures/Share	1.00

Values and Total Returns At Expiration

Stock	% Change	Call	Put	Stk + Puts	Stk − Calls	Stk − Future
252	−0.16%	$0.00	$48.00	15.1%	−9.2%	2.0%
258	−0.14	0.00	42.00	12.6	−7.1	2.0
264	−0.12	0.00	36.00	10.1	−4.9	2.0
270	−0.10	0.00	30.00	7.6	−2.8	2.0
276	−0.08	0.00	24.00	5.1	−0.7	2.0
282	−0.06	0.00	18.00	2.6	1.5	2.0
288	−0.04	0.00	12.00	0.1	3.6	2.0
294	−0.02	0.00	6.00	−2.4	5.8	2.0
300	0.00	0.00	0.00	−4.9	7.9	2.0
306	0.02	6.00	0.00	−3.0	6.3	2.0
312	0.04	12.00	0.00	−1.1	4.7	2.0
318	0.06	18.00	0.00	0.8	3.1	2.0
324	0.08	24.00	0.00	2.7	1.4	2.0
330	0.10	30.00	0.00	4.5	−0.2	2.0
336	0.12	36.00	0.00	6.4	−1.8	2.0
342	0.14	42.00	0.00	8.3	−3.4	2.0
348	0.16	48.00	0.00	10.2	−5.0	2.0

than bonds or cash, even for holding periods of many years. At times when equities are relatively rich, even using a long-term time horizon, their weighting within the portfolio should be reduced.

The stock market frequently underperforms bonds or cash via a substantial near-term correction whenever the long-term expected returns are out of balance with respect to each other. The investor does not need to weather this correction. But the investor does not need to sell his or her equities only to turn around and repurchase them after the correction, either.

The equities can be hedged temporarily using derivatives of securities. This is not attempting to be a market-timer, because if the market does not correct, the investor should remain underweighted in equities until such time that they offer a competitive return. It is prudent to sell stocks when they offer a low long-term expected return and to buy stocks when they offer a high risk-adjusted rate of return. It is also prudent to minimize the associated transactions costs. The use of derivatives goes a long way toward accomplishing these objectives.

When periods like the late summer of 1987 occur—that is, when it is obvious (with or without a sophisticated asset-allocation model) that the stock market is substantially overvalued—the investor need not fret about which particular stocks to sell, what limits to put on the trades, which brokers to use, what effect massive sales will have on portfolio diversification, and so on. These concerns frequently result in no action. Investors frequently lull themselves into complacency by rationalizing that any market correction would only cause them to repurchase what already had been sold. So they think, "Why bother? Over the long term it will all come out in the wash."

This sort of thinking causes an investor to forfeit a perfect opportunity. Instead, let the universal law of laziness do its thing and take the easy way out: sell index calls, buy index puts, or both. Take *advantage* of the sociological phenomena pertaining to short-term corrections; don't use them as an excuse to do nothing. If, at this instant, the stock market were to offer the lowest *long-term* expected return of the various alternative asset classes, why remain 60% invested in equities?

If you are a long-term investor, don't use the logic that over the long term, 60% (or whatever) in stocks is appropriate, if *today* stocks offer a lower 10-year expected return than government bonds. Each week, each month, or even each quarter, the relative long-term returns of the various asset classes should be reassessed; and the portfolio should be repositioned accordingly, if significant changes have occurred. Market baskets, index options, and, particularly, synthetic futures are the most efficient tools for repositioning asset allocation, particularly since the adjustments are likely to be temporary.

13

Alternative to Allocation: Immunization

The future is a direction in which we no longer look with confidence, but with vague forebodings and a sense of unpreparedness.

—*Robert L. Heilbroner*

HOW TO LOSE MONEY ON A "RISK-FREE" INVESTMENT

Louise Quinn Nagel has been an institutional broker-trader in Boston for more years than she or I would care to remember. She has a wonderful sense of humor and enjoys telling a good story. One of her favorites is a yarn about a stockbroker traveling across Minnesota whose car broke down in front of a large farm. He asked the farmer for use of the telephone to call a tow truck. While waiting for help to come, the broker attempted to make small talk with the farmer.

"How much corn did you plant this year?"
"Didn't put any corn in. . . . figured the chances of blight were too high."

"Did you plant soybeans instead?"
"No beans. . . . figured there wouldn't be enough rain this year."

"How was your wheat crop?"
"I didn't put in any wheat. . . . probably should have . . . but the almanac said it was going to be a long winter."

"Your potatoes must be about ready to come out."
"I didn't plant any. . . . the bugs could be back any year now."

Well . . . what *did* you plant?"
"Nothing'. . . . I didn't want to take any chances!"

I can think of many true-to-life stories that relate the same message. For instance, a friend of mine has worked for the same employer all 20 years of his career and he intends to retire from the same company in another 20 years. In the mid-1970s many firms that had on-the-ball personnel departments created 401(k)-type savings plans for the employees. My friend's company was early onto the bandwagon in offering two options: a fixed-income choice and an all-equity plan. He elected the fixed-income (bonds) plan, even though he didn't expect to touch the funds for 30 or more years. As of 1988, his funds had grown to $100,000. If he had been contributing to the equity plan instead, over the same period his vested interest would have increased to over $150,000. Not only had he selected the wrong plan from the point of view of his age and realistic risk profile, but his logic for selecting the bond alternative was erroneous. He had figured that since bonds have a definite maturity, the principal was ultimately protected against loss. In reality, the fund managers (like most) didn't use a buy-and-hold-to-maturity strategy; and even if they had, contributions to and withdrawals from the plan always cause a certain percentage of realized and unrealized gains and losses—theoretically *ad infinitum*.

Another acquaintance, who had taken early retirement, decided to invest his liquid assets in securities for a period of 10 years, at which point he would liquidate his investments and build a retirement home in the hills of western Massachusetts. He would use the investment income earned during the interim for living expenses. Therefore, he wanted the maximum return over the 10 years that was consistent with complete safety of principal. Now in this case, this gentleman's assessment of his investment needs was not too far off the mark. But his friendly stockbroker talked him into a government bond fund. He was told that the fund was risk-free since the bonds in the plan posed no credit risk. Well, in 1990, it came time to build his log cabin in the Berkshire Hills. But lo and behold, his original $200,000 savings were now worth only $160,000! The broker could have recommended that he buy (and not intend to sell) $200,000 of Aaa bonds (with current coupons) that matured in 10 years, rather than a bond *fund* where the manager would continually be swapping and trading. A knowledgeable investment adviser might have come up with an even better program. But of course, the broker would have only gotten a fraction of a percent as a commission from any Treasury bond strategy, compared to the several-percentage-point gross commission on a mutual fund.

Take another situation where an investor wants complete safety of principal, but he does not need to spend the investment income. Instead he wants a guaranteed return over his particular time horizon. In this case, buying a Treasury bond with the appropriate maturity does not give him that guarantee, because the investor has no way of knowing what rate of interest he will be getting as the interest is reinvested. To be guaranteed a compounded return of 9%, for example, the original investment *as well as the interest received* must earn 9% over the life of the security.

The reinvestment rate cannot be stressed enough. For example, if a person buys (and holds) a 9% 20-year bond bought at par, *over 60% of the total return comes from interest on interest* (assuming 9% reinvestment rate)!

One way to avoid the uncertainty of the reinvestment rate is to purchase a zero-coupon bond, that is, one that pays no interest. If an investor buys $100,000 face value of T-bonds that mature in 10 years for a cost of about $42,000, that investor will, *for certain*, earn a compounded return of better than 9%. The discounted price automatically factors in the effect of compound interest without there being any actual reinvestment.

But, suppose the investor has a time horizon (representing when the funds need to be liquidated) of three, five, or seven-and-a-half years, and no low-risk, zero-coupon bonds are available with those particular maturities. If the investor wants a guaranteed return, what are the choices? Perhaps a GIC is one alternative; but as shown in Chapter 6, these contracts are not really guaranteed in the sense that a government bond is.

Let's approach the problem from a different perspective. If the investor wants to know, with absolute certainty, what the portfolio return will be over a long period of time, he or she is really demanding a portfolio that will avoid permanent depreciation and is immune to changes in interest rates, at least ultimately. The word "ultimately" is used to mean that on the day that the funds are needed, the market value of the portfolio will equal the value originally expected, regardless of what fluctuations occurred in the interim. The individual securities may be at unpredicted prices at the end of the time horizon, but the total value of the portfolio (much of which is a function of reinvestment) will provide the necessary terminal value and, therefore, expected return.

There are strategies that can *ultimately* protect the portfolio against changes in interest rates and provide a portfolio market value that *always* approximately equals the *present value* of the amount needed at some future date. This latter feature is particularly useful from an accounting standpoint.

WHAT REALLY IS BEING IMMUNIZED?

Most totally risk-averse investors are *not looking for a portfolio* of which the market value is always constant or independent from interest-rate levels. Such a portfolio might consist of a group of variable-rate securities; such a portfolio might have extremely low volatility of principal, yet the variability of investment income creates unpredictability with respect to total return. What most risk-adverse investors are looking for is *to immunize a future liability* against changes in interest rates. This is accomplished by designing a portfolio with a *special average life*, so that its market value will move up and down in exact proportion to the present value of the future liability. That future "liability" might be a log cabin in the mountains for the individual investor, a workers' compensation payment, a GIC redemption that must be met by an insurance company, or an annuity that a corporation must purchase for a retiree. To accomplish this, the investment portfolio value must *ultimately* be protected against changes in interest rates—thus the term *immunized portfolio.*

Whether the entity having the future liability is an employee pension fund, an insurance company, or an individual, the use of asset allocation as it has been described thus far in this book is not a viable alternative if the investor never wants to show a significant deficit between the present value of the liabilities and the assets. Although liabilities *theoretically* can be immunized with equities and real estate (because they have a hypothetical duration), the only investments that have truly quantifiable average lives are those involving contractual, periodic payments and/or a precisely defined terminal value. For this reason, the discussion in this chapter will be limited to bonds. Therefore, I will categorize "immunization" as an alternative to, not a type of, asset allocation.

IMMUNIZATION USING CASH FLOWS

One particular insurance company's management believes that its future claim payments (loss reserves) are immunized because its bond investments all mature in the same year and in the same amounts as the actuaries have computed with respect to its unpaid claims. This approach is way off base, because no consideration is given to the investment income that will be earned between the current period and the date when the claim is to be paid. Therefore, the "immunized" portfolio is redundant and potentially wasteful.

Another insurance company believes its liabilities are properly immunized because, not only are the bond maturities matched with the estimated timing of the future claim payments, but the face value of the bonds *combined with the interest* that will be earned over the periods approximately equal the respective, estimated claim payments. This is a step in the right direction, but the approach still does not take into account what will be done with the interest income between the time it is received and when it will be used to pay claims. In other words, there is no reinvestment assumption. This, again, results in a redundancy in the size of the portfolio.

A very efficient and proper method of using interest and principal cash flows (which is only one approach) to immunize a stream of future liabilities is to begin by working backwards from the most distant liability. An investor buys a bond that matures on the date of the *final* liability, then *applies the interest payments on the longest maturing bond to the interim liabilities*. This then reduces the necessary principal amount of the bonds needed to mature in each of the interim years. The next step is to compute how many bonds will be needed to mature in the next-to-last period, after factoring in the interest that will be received during the next-to-last period from the longest bond. Then, the interest to be received from that second (next-to-last) bond also is applied to all the interim years, thereby reducing even further the number of bonds needed to mature in these interim years.

This process of working backwards is repeated until all the liabilities are covered. The result is that the immunizing portfolio will be smaller than originally anticipated. This is particularly true when the yield curve is positively sloped, because other methods, even if they did include reinvestment income (interest on interest) would require excess assets to offset a declining reinvestment rate. Keeping the immunizing portfolio at a minimal value frees up investable funds that may be used to improve the surplus position. Using the recommended method of cash-flow matching, the cash receipts (principal and interest) never need to be reinvested; they are paid out approximately as received.

In Table 13–1, the amount to be immunized is $1 million per year for five years, and it is assumed that the bonds are all purchased at par and have coupons of 10%. This approach works exceptionally well for immunizing any sort of future liability. It is certainly more effective than buying bonds whose interest (including reinvested interest) and principal are matched with liabilities of the same maturity. The latter approach, in effect, involves buying bonds where the market values are equal to the present value of the future liabilities. As appropriate as this might seem at first, it only works if the bonds are all zero-coupon (stripped) issues. When interest-bearing bonds are used, an investor cannot assume that the interest earned will make up the difference between the present and future value of the liability.

TABLE 13–1 Cash Flow Matching

Year	1	2	3	4	5
Liability	$1,000,000	$1,000,000	$1,000,000	$1,000,000	$1,000,000
	Interest Cash Flows				
Bond Due Year 5 ($909,091)	$90,909	$90,909	$90,909	$90,909	$90,909
Bond Due Year 4 ($826,446)	82,645	82,645	82,645	82,645	
Bond Due Year 3 ($751,315)	75,132	75,132	75,132		
Bond Due Year 2 ($683,013)	68,301	68,301			
Bond Due Year 1 ($620,921)	62,092				
Interest Due	$379,079	$316,987	$248,685	$173,554	$90,909
Principal Due	$620,921	$683,013	$751,315	$826,446	$909,091
Total Due	$1,000,000	$1,000,000	$1,000,000	$1,000,000	$1,000,000

Table 13–2 compares the performance of two portfolios:

Portfolio A. Buying bonds where the expected interest and principal payments of each bond are made to equal the liability due in the same year as the bond matures (the insurance company's approach).

TABLE 13–2 Correct and Incorrect Immunization Using Current Coupon Bonds

	Year				
	1	2	3	4	5
FV of Liability	$1,000,000	$1,000,000	$1,000,000	$1,000,000	$1,000,000
PV of Liability	909,091	826,446	751,315	683,013	620,921
Portfolio A (Incorrect)	909,091	826,446	751,315	683,013	620,921
Portfolio B (Correct)	620,921	683,013	751,315	826,446	909,091

Note: Assumes 10% coupon bonds and a 10% discount factor.

Portfolio B. Buying a bond where the face value and final interest payment equal the final liability, applying the interim interest to the interim liabilities, then working backwards, repeating the process (as illustrated in Table 13–1).

Because it is assumed that both portfolios are comprised of interest-bearing bonds (viz. stripped bonds), Portfolio A does not adequately perform the immunization function, but Portfolio B does.

For example, Portfolio A gets all the cash flow it needs in Year 1 from the interest and principal of the bond maturing in Year 1. *But Portfolio A also receives interest payments in Year 1 from all the other bonds it holds*. This means the *duration* (average life) of the account is too short. Excess cash is received in the early years, and possibly not enough cash is received in the later years. Portfolio B, on the other hand, receives its principal and interest virtually when, and in the amounts, needed.

Imagine what would happen to Portfolio A if interest rates declined. For one thing, it would not earn enough interest on interest to fund the liabilities in the later years. In other words, there is a high degree of reinvestment risk. Also, the balance sheet would erode. When rates decline, the present value of the liabilities would increase more than the market value of the portfolio. Now, maybe some insurance companies don't care a lot about present value (even though they should) because of statutory accounting considerations; but a pension fund sponsor would care plenty if the plan's surplus eroded or turned into a deficit.

For a *defined-benefit plan*, the market value of the portfolio should equal or exceed the present value of the future benefits—both the prior-service costs, which may not be tied to inflation, and the liability for current employees, which escalates with wage inflation.

Immunization, as described in Table 13–1 and in Portfolio B of Table 13–2, is designed to provide the necessary protection. But, the strategy is very rigid. It does not offer the investment manager the opportunity to increase the return above the original assumption. It could be called "passive management." What is needed is a system that *mathematically approximates cash flow matching* but allows the manager some leeway with the *specific maturities* and/or has the potential of earning a return in excess of the immunized return.

IMMUNIZATION USING AVERAGE DURATION

The liabilities in Table 13–2 have a duration (average life) of over 2.8 years, not 3.0 years (which is the average of the future values rather than present values). Remember from Chapter 5 that "duration" is calculated by taking the *present value of each payment*, weighting it by the number of years until it is to be received, then dividing the sum of the weighted present values by the combined, unweighted present value of all the payments.

Table 13–3 reviews the process of computing duration for an individual security. The calculation is for a 10% coupon bond due in five years, selling at par. For the sake of simplicity, the assumption is made that interest is paid once per year beginning in one year. A more realistic assumption of semi-annual interest would produce a duration of 4.05 years rather than 4.17 years.

If the same computations were made for Portfolio A, we would find that it has an average duration of only 2.4 years, assuming semi-annual interest compared to a 2.8-year duration for the liabilities. That is why Portfolio A does not immunize the liabilities; that is, the present value (market value) of the assets will not

TABLE 13–3 Duration of a 10% Coupon, Five-Year Bond Yielding 10%

Year	Principal/ Interest	Present Value	Weighted PV
1	$ 100	$ 91	$ 91
2	100	83	165
3	100	75	225
4	100	68	273
5	1,100	683	3,415
	Totals	$1,000	$4,170

Weighted PV/Market Value = $4,170/$1,000 = 4.17 years

change by the same amount as the present value of the liabilities when interest rates change.

What would happen if we created an immunizing portfolio with a duration exactly equal to that of the liabilities, even if the timing of the cash flows was not precisely matched as in Portfolio A? The answer is, if interest rates moved up or down, within reason, the new present value of liabilities would continue to match (or remain under) the market value of the portfolio! Therefore, a drop in rates would not cause a deficiency in the portfolio.

However, the durations of the assets and liabilities change, both over time and as the general level of interest rates change. Accordingly, the trick is to maintain the duration match by periodically adjusting the duration of the bond portfolio. The bad news is that this involves transactions costs and administrative time. The good news is that it gives the investment manager some flexibility. For example, there are an infinite number of combinations of fixed-income securities that can produce an overall portfolio duration of, say, 2.81 years.

As a general management rule, however, the longest bond should have a duration slightly longer than the most distant liability so that the shortest bond can have a duration shorter than the nearest liability. The remaining bonds should have durations that come as close as possible to matching those of the individual liabilities. Although it is necessary to have only the duration of the overall bond portfolio equal the average duration of all the liabilities, there is an advantage to minimizing the individual duration variances.

ADVANTAGES OF DURATION MATCHING

Remember that under cash-flow matching there is no reinvestment risk (because all the interest is paid out as received), but there is also no chance for a return above and beyond the original assumption. Under duration matching, however, if interest rates change *instantaneously* (or even over time, as we shall see), the bond portfolio produces a return slightly in excess of the assumed (immunized) rate.

Let's examine the case of one asset immunizing one liability, to demonstrate this key advantage of duration matching. You must understand, however, that in the more typical case of immunizing an entire stream of liabilities, the portfolio duration needs to match the average *duration* of the stream of liabilities, not their average maturity. The average duration of a stream of liabilities is a time weighting of their present values, whereas average maturity is merely a time weighting of the ultimate (future) payments.

In a single-liability situation, the duration and maturity of the liability are identical because there is only one cash payment involved. The liability could be immunized by buying a zero-coupon bond, which also would have a duration equivalent to its maturity, but there would be no chance for an excess (of immunization rate) return. But, if the investor immunizes with interest-bearing bonds, there is an opportunity for excess return.

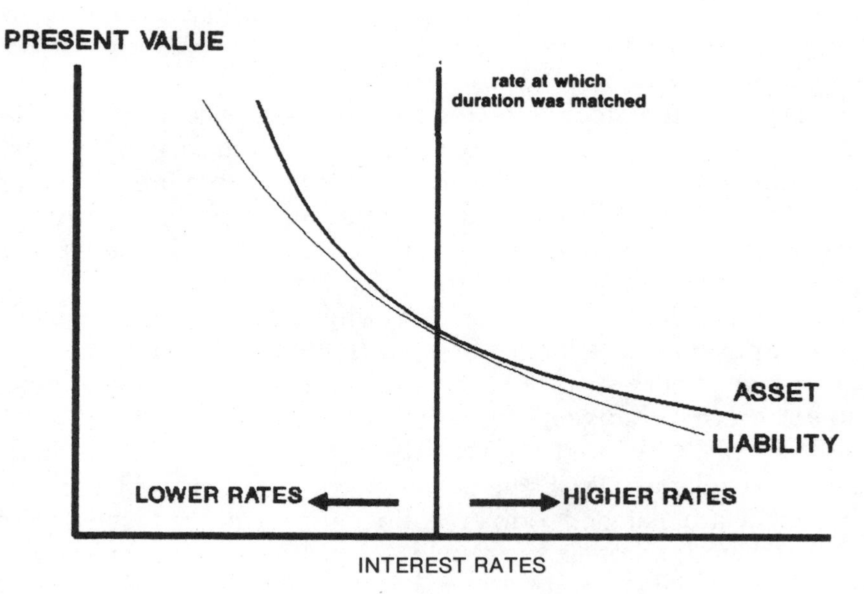

Figure 13–1. Asset-Liability Convexity.

Figure 13–1 shows what happens to the present value of a single-payment liability compared to the present value (market value) of an interest-bearing bond when interest rates change from the original immunization level. Notice that when rates fall instantaneously, the bond appreciates slightly more than the present value of the future liability. Conversely, when interest rates rise, the value of the bond falls less than the present value of the liability. This is the basis of classical immunization, which many believe was originally developed in the 1930s by Frederick Macaulay, who also is credited with being the pioneer of the duration concept.

Since Macaulay's time, we have discovered that this same excess-return principal is applicable not only to *instantaneous* changes in interest rates but also to portfolio return versus immunization rate, *over time.* In other words, when interest rates fall, the appreciation of the securities prices more than offsets the lower rate received on reinvested interest. Similarly, when interest rates rise, the higher reinvestment rate more than offsets price depreciation. Both of these statements refer to total return of the bond portfolio *relative to percentage change in the present value of the immunized liability.*

It is true that matching the duration of a single liability with the duration of a single bond, *even though they have different maturities,* produces the opportunity for excess return. Therefore, it is true that a bond *portfolio* can produce a return in excess of the original immunization-rate assumption if the durations of the individual bonds match the durations of the individual liabilities.

Figure 13–2 illustrates how a fund (whether it be a pension fund, an insurance fund, a bank's loan portfolio, or GIC liabilities) can move from a zero-surplus status to a positive-surplus status with an unexpected change in the overall level of interest rates.

This probably seems too good to be true. Well, it is true, but there are a few glitches. First, the duration of the assets and liabilities, once they are matched, don't remain matched automatically, over time. Second, whereas Figures 13–1 and 13–2 refer to changes in the "general level" of interest rates, the fact is that interest rates very often do not change by the same magnitude for all maturities or durations. Therefore, there is a risk element to duration matching.

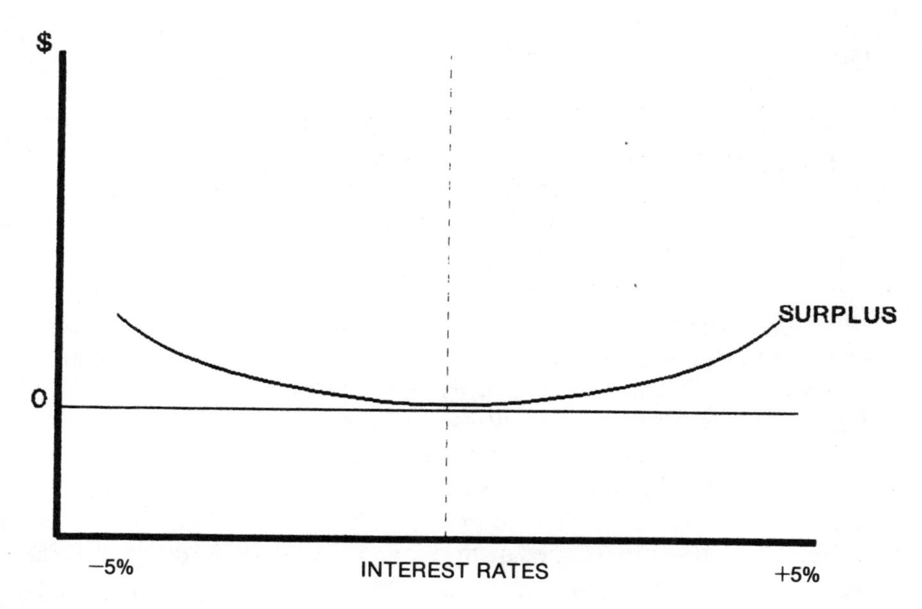

Figure 13–2. Surplus Changes Due to Parallel Yield-Curve Shifts.

DISADVANTAGES OF DURATION MATCHING

The duration of a bond or a portfolio of bonds does not decrease linearly over time. For example, a 10-year bond with a 7-year duration does not move to a 6-year duration after 1 year, even though the maturity lessens by 1 year. Conversely, a single-payment liability, such as a GIC redemption or a liability insurance payment, has a duration that declines 1 year for each year passed. A liability that involves a series of payments, such as a worker's compensation claim or a retirement benefit, may have a duration that declines at a different rate than the duration of bonds that were used to immunize the future payments. In general, it can be stated that a portfolio of assets and a portfolio of liabilities that are initially matched with the identical duration usually will not incur reductions in duration at the same rate over time.

Figure 13–3 compares the change in duration, over time, of a single-payment liability due in five years to a typical, interest-bearing bond with a duration of five years. Notice that, in the initial years, the asset duration declines more slowly than that of the liability. This means that if no changes were made in the holdings of the immunizing portfolio, as time elapsed, the liabilities would become progressively less immunized. For example, after two years the volatility of the market value of the bond portfolio (due to interest-rate changes) would be substantially greater than the volatility of the present value of the future liability payment.

As a result, if nothing else happens other than the passage of time, the composition of the immunizing portfolio must be periodically adjusted in order to maintain a proper duration balance between the assets and liabilities. If the duration variances (between the assets and liabilities) become significant, then the investor is no longer assured that the investment portfolio will have a market value that equals or exceeds the present value of the liabilities.

Therefore, the first disadvantage of duration matching is that it requires a monitoring and trading effort. However, with a stream

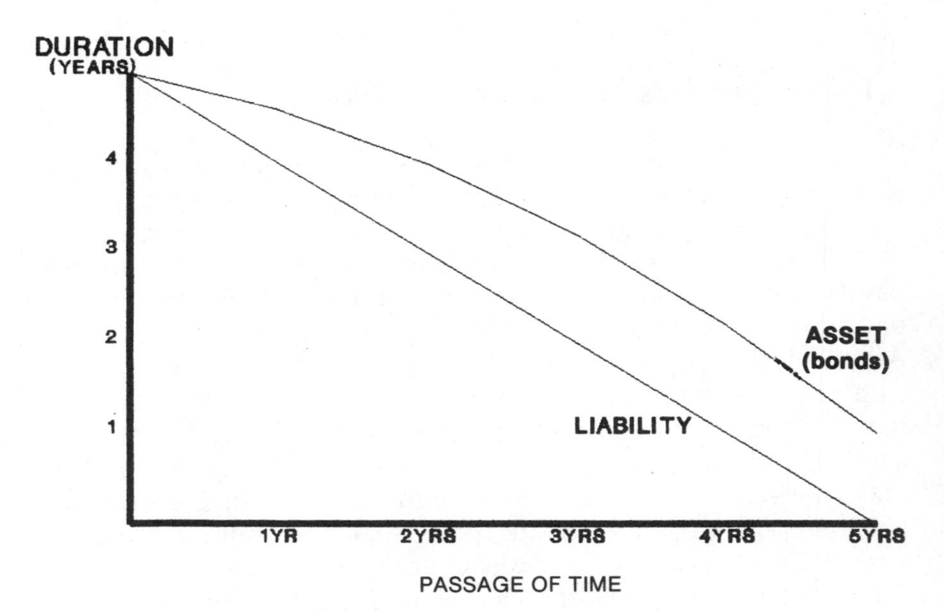

Figure 13–3. Time versus Duration.

of liabilities that are matched by a whole series of securities, much of the necessary adjustments can be made when securities need to be sold to pay the liabilities.

There are two other problems involving changes in the general level of interest rates: one caused by a parallel shift in the yield curve and another, more serious problem arising as a result of change in *shape* of the yield curve. This latter problem is the reason it is important that a portfolio (which is immunized by duration matching) be managed by an investment professional. Duration matching, unlike cash-flow matching is not a passive strategy—it could be considered "semi-active management."

Let's deal with the easier situation first: a parallel shift in the yield curve. The simple fact is that when interest rates change, the duration of a portfolio changes; therefore, some adjustments may be required, depending on what happened to the duration of the liabilities.

The longer the maturity of the bond, the more its duration will change with a rise or fall of the general level of rates. It is easy to see why. If interest rates move up, for instance, we know that all bond prices will decline and that a 30-year bond will depreciate a lot more than a 3-year bond. For illustration purposes, assume that interest rates rise so high that the price of a bond falls from 100 to 50. This means that both the interest payments and the maturity value become exactly twice as high relative to the new market price. But since the interest payments occur prior to the maturity payment, the *present value* of the interest becomes relatively more important than the present value of the maturity payment. Thus, duration decreases. Therefore, since bonds with long maturities depreciate more than bonds with short maturities, the longer the maturity, the more duration will decline with a rise in rates. Conversely, when interest rates fall, the duration of long bonds will increase more than the duration of shorter maturity bonds. Figure 13–4 illustrates the magnitude of this phenomenon. The values are based on 11% coupon bonds.

The simple conclusion is that when the general level of interest rates changes, the duration of a portfolio changes. Therefore, some adjustments of the individual holdings may be called for if a duration match is to be maintained.

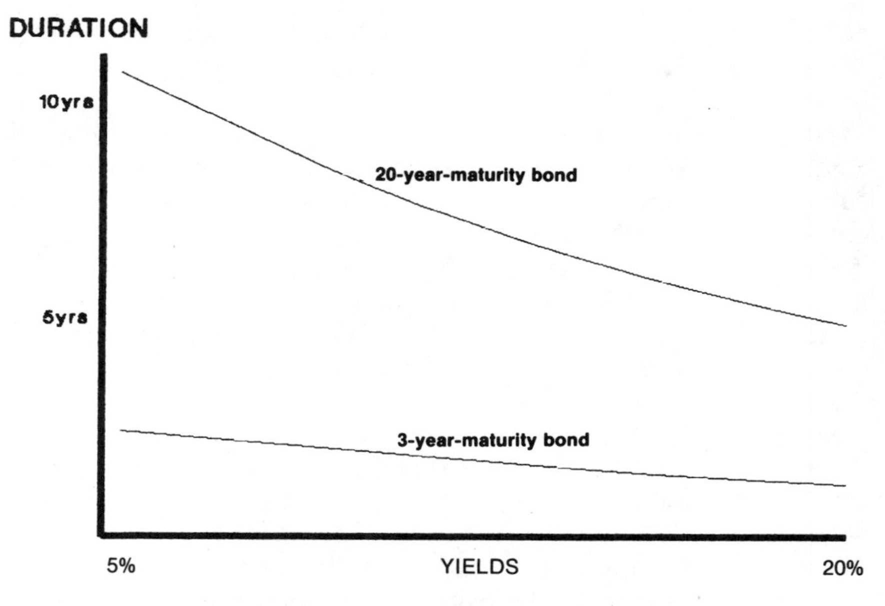

Figure 13–4. Interest Rates versus Bond Duration.

Remember from the earlier discussion, illustrated in Figures 13–1 and 13–2, that when interest rates change there is a small, but immediate, profit that accrues to surplus (the difference between the market value of the portfolio and the present value of the liabilities). In other words, the portfolio rides up either side of the curve depicted in Figure 13–2. But, if interest rates move back toward their original level, this gain to surplus will be given up. Therefore, to capture the "profit," the portfolio would have to be readjusted so that the new asset and liability durations remain matched.

However, a portfolio manager could speculate that rates were going to continue moving in the same direction, thus causing the portfolio to rise further up the curve and the surplus to increase even further. But, speculation is not an integral part of immunization. Also, even if the portfolio *is* adjusted, there still will be an additional profit (although not as significant) if rates continue to move in the same direction; *and* there will be a small profit if rates move in the opposite direction. So, the prudent move is to rebalance the portfolio whenever there is a significant change in rates.

But, how often does the *general* level of interest rates change in uniform fashion across the entire yield curve? The answer is probably never. A nonparallel shift in the yield curve (where short rates and long rates change by different amounts) causes a significant problem, because it cannot be solved simply by adjusting the portfolio.

What actually happens is that the reinvestment rate changes to a level that cannot be compensated for. Suppose, for example, that today an investor bought a 12% five-year bond (which would have a duration of four years) to immunize a liability due in four years. He or she bought the bond in the amount whereby a 12% return would provide the amount required to meet the liability payment. Assume the yield curve was flat and the computations were made on the assumption that it would remain flat. But suppose, tomorrow, the yield curve turned down on the short end, that is, it became "normal." If the yield curve were to remain normal, the investor's interest on interest would not be at a 12% rate as originally planned. Thus, the portfolio would be of insufficient value when it came time for the first rebalancing.

There is no way to compensate for this change in the shape of the yield curve, except to anticipate it. But interest-rate anticipation is not, by definition, what immunization is all about—in fact, it is the antithesis. Therefore, when all is said and done, *there is a certain degree of reinvestment risk with a duration-matching approach to immunization.*

Despite the risks just discussed, duration matching is not only a viable portfolio-management tool for highly risk-averse investors, but it gives the manager some options regarding both the maturities (or even individual durations) of securities comprising the portfolio and the moment selected for rebalancing. Therefore, there is some room for interest-rate anticipation, but with a much lower element of risk than would be the case in a nonimmunized portfolio. Thus, duration matching really can be a quite "active" (viz. "passive") strategy in comparison to cash-flow matching.

There are many nuances concerning duration matching that

easily could have been the subject matter of several additional chapters. But it is my intention merely to offer an overview of a technique that can be used *in combination* with the asset-allocation methods described in the previous chapters.

APPORTIONING A PORTFOLIO: COMBINED STRATEGIES

A common occurrence is a profit-sharing or 401(k) plan where the participants consist of two distinct types: a few key individuals with a lot of money in the plan who are near retirement and a larger group of younger employees with much smaller individual vested interests. The older employees do not want to take much, if any, risk with their funds because retirement is right around the corner. The younger employees want to maximize their return over a long time horizon. Since members of the older group usually are at the helm, the needs of the younger employees are frequently squelched. If the opposite occurs, and the older employees allow the plan to be heavily invested in equities, they would be taking an unwarranted amount of risk with their own vested interests.

The simple solution is to immunize the liabilities of the fund represented by the vested interests of those within five years or so of retirement and optimize the remainder of the portfolio. In other words, for portfolio-management purposes (no special, separate fund has to be legally created), the account manager invests a portion of the fund in a group of bonds that will provide an immunized return and invests the balance in stocks, bonds, real estate, and whatever else. Even though the funds are all commingled, this solution is a sensible compromise. A better solution would be to legally separate the funds.

A more appropriate use of a combined immunization-optimization strategy is with a defined-benefit plan that is fully funded. Why not immunize the present value of the liabilities and optimize the surplus (overfunding)? This is like having your cake and eating it too. The fund still can have performance as one of its goals (mainly through the equity portion of the surplus portion) while the liabilities are not at risk. Figure 13–5 illustrates this concept.

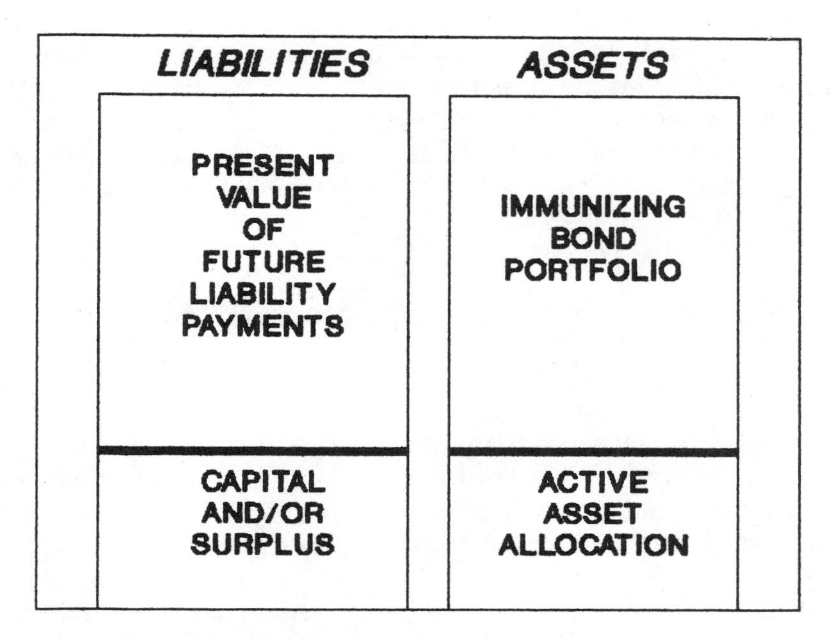

Figure 13–5. Combining Asset Allocation and Immunization.

A combined management strategy has endless applications. Suppose, for instance, an individual investor has $1 million in liquid assets and that in seven years he or she plans to retire, at which time he or she plans on investing $500,000 in a condominium in Hawaii or in a retirement annuity. If interest rates on government bonds were 10%, the person could create an immunized portfolio with a duration of seven years in the amount of approximately $250,000, which would have a nearly guaranteed terminal value of $500,000 after seven years (as long as the duration is adjusted with the passage of time). The $750,000 balance could be invested in an optimization portfolio to meet the investor's income needs, time horizon, and risk profile.

In short, a combined immunization-optimization strategy should be considered as a viable alternative in any investment situation that involves specific future payments along with a surplus (representing the available funds less the present value of the future payments). A classic situation of this sort is the balance sheet of a bank, credit union, or insurance company. Since by nature of their line of business, the assets of a bank or credit union are, for the most part, their loan portfolios rather than securities, this chapter will conclude with an insurance company illustration of combined-strategy investing. I will use the example of a casualty insurer where the assets are typically marketable securities.

INSURANCE COMPANY ASSET MANAGEMENT

A casualty insurer underwrites a variety of risks, including property damage, workers' compensation, liability, theft, business malpractice, business interruption, personal injury, and so on. The claims involved in these lines of business have "tails" of various lengths. That is to say, there is a varying, and often significant, elapse of time between the date the insurance premium is received and the date the claims are paid. In most cases, the company is insuring the *accident year*, not the policy year. That means that if a claimant is insured by ABC Company today when he discovers that his lungs are damaged, XYZ Company would be liable if it, not ABC, insured the individual five years ago when he was breathing the harmful vapors that caused his lung damage.

Accordingly, casualty insurers base their premiums on the *ultimate loss* expected on a policy written today, which includes claims that may not be reported for several years. Even claims that *are* reported in the current policy year frequently have tails. Workers' compensation is a good example: If a worker becomes disabled today, his or her indemnity (wage compensation) payments and medical payments may go on for years. The insurer must charge premiums for this.

As a result, the casualty insurer receives a lot of cash up front that won't be paid out for several years. This gives the casualty insurer a sizeable amount to invest. A life insurer also has a sizeable amount available for investment. But since the life insurance company knows exactly what its liability is (the face value of the policy) and approximately when the claim will be paid (based on mortality tables), it needs only a high degree of solvency, not liquidity. As a result, life insurers typically invest in illiquid assets such as real estate, mortgage loans, and other private placements because they offer relatively high expected returns. Casualty companies, on the other hand, need both a high degree of liquidity and solvency. A casualty insurer knows neither the timing of the claims with any degree of certainty nor the precise amount of the claim. On top of that, the casualty insurer is subject to catastrophe, such as hurricane, massive fire, earthquake, and so on. It is also subject to unexpected regulatory changes that can alter its future claims payments, such as an escalation in a particular state's workers' compensation benefits schedule. Even less predictable are the social changes that occur, such as a sudden, nationwide surge in the amounts that are awarded by a judge or jury in liability cases. For all of these reasons, a casualty insurer must remain highly liquid. Therefore, stocks, bonds, and cash equivalents are the typical haven for investable funds.

The insurance business is not (as of the time this book was being prepared) regulated by the federal government. But the various states all have laws designed to protect the consumer. One such law is designed to regulate the way the companies account for their assets and liabilities. Statutory accounting principles are a far cry from generally accepted accounting principles. In a nutshell, most states require that future claims payments be recorded as a liability at an amount fairly close to the expected future (actual) amount of the claim, even though the payment may not be made for years. On the other hand, future expected cash receipts may not be recorded as an asset (accounts receivable), with some small exceptions relating to very current receivables.

These accounting practices affect the investment portfolio: Securities are carried at the lower of cost or market value (with the exception of certain bonds that can be carried at cost), but the liabilities are carried at face value (with the exception of certain claims that can be conservatively discounted). In effect, this means that assets are booked at the present value of the future payments (which is what "market value" actually is), whereas the liabilities are booked at their future value.

This practice has caused much of the industry to consciously or unconsciously manage the present value of the assets on the basis of the future value of the liabilities. This does not have to be the case. Figure 13–6 compares a statutory-accounting-statement approach of asset management to what should be the management approach.

A casualty insurer's miscellaneous current assets, such as prepaid commissions ("agents' balances") and accounts receivable, are relatively small and generally approximate miscellaneous current liabilities (such as wages and taxes payable). Therefore, they will be ignored for the purpose of this discussion.

The casualty insurer should maintain, in the form of cash equivalents and current bond maturities, a balance at least equal to the claim it expects to pay within the next 12 months. But there is no reason that its bond portfolio needs to be as large as the future value of its expected claim payments beyond one year. An immunized bond portfolio would adequately cover these future losses and would need to be maintained only in the approximate amount of the *present* value of the future claims.

Therefore, the *real* surplus position of the company is substantially greater than what the statutory statement shows. There is

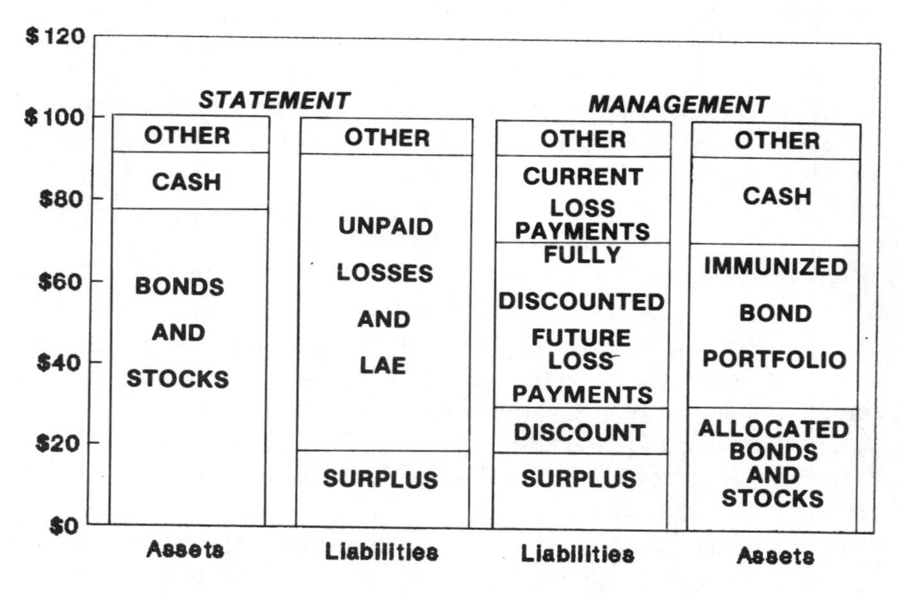

Figure 13–6. Casualty Insurance Portfolio Management.

probably no insurance regulator who would believe this at the present time because of the frequent gross understatement of loss reserves by many companies. This understatement is usually not intentional; it arises as a result of all the vagaries (with respect to the predictability of casualty losses) discussed earlier.

But if we assume the loss reserves are being carried at the proper level, then the company's surplus (which from a statutory standpoint is a cushion against inaccurate loss reserves, rather than an amount that belongs to the shareholder or policyholder) is considerably greater than what is indicated on the statutory statement. That is because the statutory statement reflects neither the present value of the losses nor the future value of the investments. Yet, from an investment management standpoint, present value should be used for both the assets and liabilities, assuming the loss reserves are not deficient. Even if they are deficient, management can make an estimate of the maximum (within reason) amount of deficiency.

The amount of assets available above and beyond the present value of the reserves (plus any estimate of deficiency or minus any estimate of redundancy) should be invested and managed on the basis of optimization. The time horizon of this "surplus" is very long; therefore, common stocks are a very appropriate investment. The portion of the investment portfolio representing the present value of the future losses should be immunized, either using cash-flow matching or duration matching. The end result will be an investment portfolio that adequately protects the policyholder and, at the same time, gives the company a performance portfolio with which it can fund future growth.

14

Why the Experts Underperform

Repeatedly in my market operations, I have sold a stock while it was rising; and that that has been one reason why I have held on to my fortune.

—*Bernard Baruch*

AN INVESTMENTS RETREAT WITH "MACKINAW MEL"

Curbstone Financial Corporation is a highly innovative investments firm located in Manchester, New Hampshire, with which my own firm is affiliated. I was a principal in the company during the mid-1980s, as was Mel Severance and the company's founder, Tom Lewry. About halfway through one summer, the three of us came to the realization that it had rained nearly every day since May in northern New England. So we made a pact that, on the first day of sunshine, we would postpone whatever we were doing and head out on a trout-fishing expedition.

It is probably true that I can "match the hatch" of mayflies on the Green River of northeastern Utah or bounce a #18 scud along the bottom of the Colorado River in Glen Canyon better than either of the other two fellows. But, there's nobody I know that can find the lunker lake trout of New England like "Mackinaw" Mel Severance. So, one day in late July, when the forecast called for fair skies, we made plans to go trout fishing on Lake Winnepesaukee, New England's largest lake, with "Mackinaw" Mel as our guide.

There wasn't a cloud in the sky on the morning we left Manchester. But, about 20 minutes after we got the boat in the water, the sky turned red and enormous thunderclouds began floating over the hills to the east. In New England, weather from the east means trouble. By the time we got our 19-foot fiberglass boat back to shore, the clouds had opened up—lightning and all. We took refuge in a cabin in the little community of Alton Bay. But by the time it became obvious that the weather was the beginning of one of the region's infamous "nor'easters," which sometimes last for days, we were fully engrossed in a heavy discussion about money management.

Curbstone Financial, which acquired its name as a result of Tom Lewry's fascination with the history of the American Stock Exchange ("the Curb"), was and still is engaged in a variety of investments-related businesses: retail brokerage, real estate tax shelters, oil and gas limited partnerships, insurance-structured settlements, actuarial consulting, group-insurance products, institutional research, stock-market-timing services, and portfolio management.

As if we hadn't already branched out into enough areas, Mel said, "I think we should start a fund where the securities we own would be shares in no-load mutual funds. Being a part of the greater-Boston investment community, we know who the best mutual fund people are. We could combine our mutual fund expertise with Lewry's market momentum work and Hammer's asset allocation work—it would be a terrific product."

My immediate reaction was, "why would the investor want to pay, in effect, two management fees—one to us and another that is embedded in the mutual fund return . . . and how would we determine which funds to buy?" While we were still in the planning stages of the "Fund of Funds," I volunteered to put together criteria I believed could identify those managers who were the most likely to outperform the market over the years. Using these criteria, along with sophisticated statistical analysis of past performance records, an investor should be able to weed out the losers and the managers who had merely been lucky. Knowing how to identify the strengths and weaknesses of professional money managers is as important to every investor or trustee as it is to the Curbstone organization.

In 1990, Curbstone Financial did create a private "fund" where clients deposited $50,000 to $500,000 with a broker (Charles

Schwab & Co., in this case) and allowed Curbstone to direct the broker as to which publicly traded mutual funds to buy and sell for their accounts. Curbstone manages these clients' accounts as if the combined funds were a single pool of money; and Schwab splits the fund shares among the individual accounts and performs the "participant accounting," which includes monthly statements to each participant.

The "Fund of Funds" was and still is very successful in terms of both new subscribers and performance. Asset allocation—knowing whether to be overweighted or underweighted in equity funds, fixed-income funds, or money-market funds at each point in time—is a major factor. The particular mutual funds purchased are selected on the basis of momentums of asset values and sophisticated statistical analysis. The "families" of mutual funds that represent the universe from which individual funds are selected are chosen on a partially subjective basis, according to certain qualities of the various fund managers. Because most of the professional fund-management companies are staffed with large, apparently well-qualified analysts and portfolio managers and often have indistinguishable performance records, it is productive to consider the various emotional pitfalls that can cause an investment advisor to stumble.

Why do so many firms (in fact, most), with their high-paid professionals, underperform the popular market averages? The reasons most frequently given are:

1. Transactions costs, which include commissions and the spread between the bid and ask price.
2. The management fees themselves.
3. It's a net-sum-zero game. Since the market is now dominated by professionals, rather than individual investors, the competition is among the "pros." If the market virtually *is* the professional investment advisers, then by definition they cannot outperform themselves, as a whole.
4. All popular market averages are stewed in some fashion and do not provide an appropriate yardstick for relative performance.

Nonetheless, there are firms that beat the market by several percentage points on a consistent basis; and there are many others who generally underperform, except for sporadic periods (when these firms engage in an all-out marketing effort) that give them enough breathing room to stay alive and recover some of their lost market share.

If Curbstone Financial, in its proposed role as a quasiconsultant (picker of money managers), could identify the pitfalls besetting the majority of investments professionals, then it would have some guidelines with which to begin narrowing the universe of potential fund managers. I felt I knew some of the answers, and most of them related to the human element. For the prior 20 years I had had top decile performance myself, as a money manager, and I believed I knew why.

THE OVERWHELMING FACTOR OF EMOTION

It is one of the unfortunate traits associated with human behavior to be overly influenced by the current scenario. When the bear in the woods crosses our path, we don't act in accordance with any logical process any more than the bear does. The same is true regarding the bear (or bull) on Wall Street.

Investors have the unfortunate tendency to make long-term projections on the basis of what has transpired in the most immediate past. This not only applies to making predictions regarding securities prices, but also to the most fundamental tasks of making sales, earnings, and dividend projections for the companies we invest in. When profitability is high, the assumed "normalized" return on equity for the typical company is 15%. When the economy is in a recession, analysts use a "normalized," typical ROE of 12%. The same skewing occurs with sales and earnings growth rates, margins, and turnover.

Interest rates, the most important factor affecting all securities prices, are almost never analyzed with a truly long-term perspective. If rates were 6% just three years ago, and today they are 10%, nobody would ever dream that rates could be back at the 6% level in another three years. Sometimes the opposite occurs under economic extremes. Take the late 1970s, for example. We had double-digit inflation and interest rates were 15 to 20%. Nobody believed it would last, so the yield curve was very negatively sloped; yet, rates remained at historically high levels for several years. Why was it that nobody believed it? Because most had never experienced it. By the time they finally did believe it, it was too late to profit. Interest rates move to extremes because there are overreactions that are the direct result of projecting the immediate past into the distant, as well as immediate, future.

Stock prices are, of course, a classic example. Market peaks are caused by greed which inevitably is rationalized by some new theory of why prices should "fundamentally" (or technically) be so high. Warren Buffet once said that the three most dangerous words in investing are "things are different." Market bottoms are caused by fear—another emotion. One prominent money manager at a major Boston-based mutual fund once stated that he was not buying bonds because of the "potential landmines that are out there." But, he couldn't name a single one; he simply cited examples of times in the past when the market had been taken by surprise. As it turned out, when he uttered these words regarding the mysterious landmines that were supposed to be lurking all about, it was within a week of one of the most significant bond-market bottoms in history.

Real estate investments are another classic example of how the "pros" can be susceptible to neglecting all of financial history when the chance to make an above-average return appears to be in the bag. In the early 1980s, it didn't matter what part of the United States you were in, it seemed as though real estate prices would go up forever. But, "forever" is a long time, and you would think that the most senior bankers, who had spent a lifetime in the business, would have some sense of history. But mortgage demand was high, the returns were good, and the collateral had been fantastic—so fantastic that these lenders couldn't resist lending mortgage money with only a 5 or 10% equity cushion. They couldn't resist the opportunity to make an extra buck, particularly since if they didn't play the game, their competition might get one leg up on them. The result was that, 10 years later, the American taxpayer and stockholder had to pay for the blind-sighted greed of financial management. It was "blind-sighted" because any common sense of history would point to the unreasonableness of an assumption that real estate values would appreciate at a double-digit rate *ad infinitum,* without a major correction.

Emotion also causes people to act in a hurry. One of the most successful managers in the investments business has a philosophy: When you get all excited about an idea, wait a week before you act. Another prosperous money manager, with whom I am indirectly affiliated, is a firm in the West that manages about a hundred employee-benefit plans; yet, the company doesn't have a quotation machine anywhere in the office. These folks believe that an investor who watches the ticker tape all day will frequently trade in sympathy with the tide of the moment which, of course, can change direction in a split second. One of the most successful portfolio managers in the country seldom reads *The Wall Street Journal,* even though he believes in its reputation as the best financial tome available. He does not want to get caught up in the news of today. Instead he lets others react to the news of the day and uses the resulting market effect as an opportunity to buy cheap or sell dear, relative to the long-term underlying values.

Effective fund managers—the ones who are the most successful—look at things with a sober prospective that encompasses a future time span of several years, not days, weeks, or months. Sure, they might miss the latest trend or fad, but they don't get caught with their pants down when the game is over.

Emotion is the most disruptive element to proper asset allocation. If the history of securities markets behavior were to be characterized by a single thing over the span of my career, it would be that people tend to buy today what was good for yesterday.

THE HERD INSTINCT

Homo sapiens may be the most insecure branch of the animal kingdom. Maybe the course of social history, which seems to show that a child is never considered to be (or allowed to be) an adult until he or she is 18 to 21 years of age, has something to do with it.

Without someone holding our hand, we feel uncertain and, as a result, are too often uncommitted.

As a result, even mature investment managers are doubtful about nearly every decision they make. So, the easy way out is to follow the crowd. They become like mullets at sea, following the group, making every turn the others make. But, just as with the mullets, there only can be a few leaders, by definition. These are perhaps the independent ones; in any case, they are the ones that see something the others don't. It is these leaders, not the herd or the mullets swimming behind, that make the money.

When the experts are all in agreement, their hopes, fears, and prognostications already have reached the financial marketplace. At an unforgettable board of directors meeting at a major regional bank, the chairman turned to the trust investments officer (guess who) and firmly argued, "There isn't a single person in this room of distinguished businessmen who believes that interest rates are headed lower."

If everyone felt that way, who would be left to sell bonds? It would be time to become a "contrarian." For those of you who have never worked in the financial districts of New York or Boston (which seems to be the most provincial), it might be hard to imagine the degree to which everyone thinks alike. In fact, a person who does work in Boston would probably need to take a sabbatical in Montana for a year, then return to the city, to be cognizant of the phenomenon. When it comes to feelings about the status of the securities markets, the plurality is usually the majority, and the majority usually approaches unanimity. Of course, once in a while the majority is correct; but ironically, at those times, it seems investors usually don't put their money where there mouths are.

Consider the great economists of Wall Street—or maybe don't consider them. They spend many of their breakfast and lunch hours giving speeches before groups of investments professionals. The implication and intent of such gatherings is that the gurus will have something to say that will either make the members of the audience feel more comfortable or will rid them of their uncertainty and get them to climb down off the fence, on one side or the other. In fact, it is the economic guru who should be in the audience and one of the investment types who should be at the podium. If you want to know what the stock market is going to do over the next six months, there could be little less meaningful information than an educated guess as to what the economy is going to do over the next six months. The securities markets already have discounted the experts' best guesses. Conversely, if you want to know what the economy is going to do over the next six months, it may be wise to pay careful attention to what the financial markets have been doing lately.

The most optimistic estimate about the consensus is that it is correct about half the time. An investor need not go out of the way to be a contrarian, but shouldn't be afraid to be one either, at least from time to time. There was an article in *Time* magazine many years ago that compared the IQ of various professionals; investment analysts came out on top. It is a shame that this gift of intelligence so often is squelched by the doubt and uncertainty that are the other side of our innate being.

MISINTERPRETING ONE'S OWN PERFORMANCE RECORD

Naturally, with so much brain matter floating around the investment community, there are bound to be some ego problems. Super-egos combined with the other two traits—historical blindness and insecurity—often gel into a dangerous manifestation, that is, interpreting one's own recent performance record to mean that everything is going according to plan. Managers have an uncanny ability to forget about or, more commonly, rationalize periods of poor investment performance and gloat over periods of exceptionally good performance.

This would be an appropriate time for you to reread Chapter 1 of this book. If that inclination is not there, then remember that randomness (luck) produces some very interesting numbers sequences. Even a monkey throwing a dart at the back section of *The Wall Street Journal* has one chance in eight of beating the Averages three times in a row.

Many money managers would be surprised to know their own *performance record probably contains so few measurement periods that, statistically, it is usually meaningless.* If a fund manager were at the helm of the same pool of money for one hundred quarters and that particular fund outperformed the popular market indices 80% of the time, that would be significant. But, if a fund manager beat the market 80% of the time solely because he or she excelled in four out of five quarters, that means very little. The chances that those results were attained by sheer luck are shockingly high.

But, when managers are on a winning streak, due to luck or otherwise, egos become inflated. Their apparent success causes them to truly believe that their own particular strategies or methodologies are what is responsible for their outperforming the competition. So, feeling smart and comfortable, they proceed as in the recent past, totally unaware that their chances of outperforming in the next period might be no better than cutting a deck of cards and producing either a club or a spade.

Everyone in the investments business will have a turn at getting lucky. Those who let it go to their heads become top heavy and eventually fall flat on their faces. Peter Lynch, the investments wizard at the helm of Fidelity's Magellan Fund during the years when it grew by $billions annually, was as humble a gentleman on the day he retired as on the day he entered the business. Many of the people who sat at the same luncheon meetings with him were not as modest, despite their inferior abilities. It was always amazing that whenever someone asked Peter Lynch what stocks he was buying, they would always find a dozen reasons why he was wrong—even though everyone knew that most of what Peter touched turned to gold.

Investment managers with a long track record of even modestly above-average results are the winners in the long run. But too many of the mullets in the business try to grab hold of the coattails of the person who is in the midst of a period of exceptionally good performance. This is often a mistake. A good investment manager is one who is satisfied with his or her performance as long as it is above average, relative to the amount of risk taken—not one who is always trying to be a hero.

SELLING STOCKS THAT AREN'T "ACTING WELL"

Benjamin Graham, considered by many to be the grandfather of modern securities analysis, repeatedly wrote that he found no logic in buying a stock one week and turning around and selling it the next, for no other reason than it had underperformed the market. His point, which seems to be valid, is that if an investor buys a stock at one price because he or she believes it is worth a significantly higher price, it should be an even better bargain at a lower price.

What happens more often than it should is that an investor, even a professional, buys a stock and then, just because it goes down, feels that he or she must have made a mistake. Where is the logic if, when the stock was purchased, the investor made no particular assumption about *when* the stock would appreciate? (Some could make a good argument that these comments do not apply to the market technician, who *does* make an assumption of when and where a security will be sold.)

The best solution is to rely on the advice and be guided by professionals who have done their homework. These are the people who know their investments inside out and will not be intimidated when the market price temporarily moves in the unexpected direction. They are the ones who are likely to buy more of a stock when it underperforms. All it takes is the knowledge and confidence that good money is not chasing bad money. That usually takes only a telephone call to an officer of the company whose securities are under consideration.

Selling a security solely because it is not acting well can be extremely costly, particularly if an investor gets whipsawed (sees the security go up, as originally expected) after it has been sold. If an investor buys a stock at $50 and sells it one month later at $45 because it went down in a flat market, then that investor has incurred a loss of 72% on a compounded, annualized basis! This sort of action had better not be part of a regular routine. It is this type of activity that often makes a "stop-loss" trading strategy become a "guaranteed-loss" strategy.

HOLDING ON TOO LONG

The biggest single problem facing investors who have a good sense of knowing which stocks to buy, and when, is not knowing when to sell. There are a surprisingly large percentage of professionals who, although they seldom admit it even to themselves, feel the most comfortable when they are buying stocks that have a "good story" to them. The story gives them a rationale for purchasing the security, above and beyond the numbers. The problem is that if an investor buys a stock for some reason other than the numbers, he or she is likely to hang on too long after the expected return numbers are no longer attractive.

The vast bulk of research that comes out of Wall Street represents "buy" ideas. There are good reasons for this, many of them political. But, nonetheless, the professional investor who sits on the "buy side of the Street" such as the investment adviser or mutual-fund manager sometimes relies heavily on Wall Street research. But, the odds are that the same brokerage firm who publishes a buy idea that works out well will not be calling the clients to tell them when it's time to sell.

Accordingly, investors or their advisors must have a "sell" discipline. This can be as simple as having a rule to sell any stock that has outperformed the market by 50% or more in less than two years, or relying on a more sophisticated valuation model that triggers a sell signal in the very same fashion that a buy signal was generated. All valuation models should have hurdle rates of return that need to be exceeded in order to warrant purchase, as well as minimum return numbers that, if they are not surpassed, require a sale. Both the minimum (sell) rate and the hurdle (buy) rate of return should somehow be reflective of the relative riskiness of the investment.

In short, managers who have an inferior track record frequently do not have an effective sell discipline. They hang on to a profitable situation too long. This is greed. Sometimes it is rationalized as an asset-allocation or market-timing decision. But, asset allocation and securities selection should be distinctly separate decisions because they involve distinctly separate economic processes.

THE FOREST AND THE TREES

Over the past decade or two, there has been an overwhelming unfurling of the technology relating to investments and information systems. There is so much data readily available and so many ways to massage it with a modern high-speed, large-memory minicomputer that investment analysts and portfolio managers continually invent more variables and factors to be plugged into more equations.

All these variables and factors can, sometimes, cloud the underlying logic of an investment. Think of some of the very simple strategies you've seen or read about that have produced above-average results for extended periods. They might include such methods as:

1. Buying stocks at a below-average price/book ratio where the replacement value of the assets is significantly above book value.
2. Buying stocks with a unique consumer franchise that would be next to impossible to replicate, where that "intangible" does not show up on the financial statements.
3. Buying stocks at four times cash flow and selling them at eight times cash flow, regardless of the near-term earnings outlook.
4. Buying the stocks in the Dow Jones Industrial Average that have the 10 lowest normalized price/earnings ratios or highest dividend yields, least leveraged balance sheets, and so on.

Securities analysis, which involves an excessive number of estimates, often is plagued by a compounding of errors. There is no correlation between the amount of numbers that are crunched and the success ratio of the analysts doing the numbers crunching. One of the most successful portfolio managers of all time didn't rely on individual company analysis at all. He believed that stock prices already reflected the relative attributes of each company within an industry. He merely would buy a whole group of stocks in an industry when he detected an otherwise unrecognized upsurge in demand for the product manufactured by that industry.

Mature analysts eventually acquire the attitude that almost every company knows how to run its business better than they do. When they visit with that company, silly questions about the company's product and markets are dispensed with. Instead, the analysts want to learn more about management style, philosophy, and goals; then they bring back the company's annual reports—management's report card—and study the footnotes and accounting policies and read the previous year's president's message to see if what he or she promised or predicted actually happened.

PREOCCUPATION WITH SHORT-TERM PERFORMANCE

It is hard to tell with certainty whether competition among the investment managers or pressure from the clients has caused the inordinate amount of importance given to short-term investment results. Whatever the cause, it is an outright shame that professional investment advisers don't have the patience with their own investments, many of which were purchased in accordance with a sound, long-term value objective.

Today, stocks are bought and sold for every imaginable reason or with any possible excuse, whereas the real motivation is often quick results. There is a tremendous reluctance to own stocks that are running out of steam and a strong urge to buy stocks that are on the move, both without due regard to value. That is not to say that value-investing always works; but, value should always be one of the prerequisites for buying a security.

Any professional investment adviser will have countless stories of clients who claimed to be long-term investors interested in value and stability; but, at a pension-review committee meeting, they rake the adviser over the coals for having results that are one percentage point under the S&P 500 in the latest quarter.

Similarly, all securities analysts will remember times their superior kept hounding them about a stock because it was lagging the market.

The results of excessive pressure concerning performance are obvious:

1. Excessive transactions costs.
2. Selling stocks just before they take off.
3. Buying into a group just when it is about to run out of steam.
4. Window dressing a portfolio so that the quarterly statement won't show all the stocks that were bought at higher prices, which forces the investor out of stocks that are even a better bargain than before and into holding on to stocks that are no longer attractively priced.

There is one large pension plan based in Salt Lake City which, when it hired its investment managers, told them all that they would be monitored quarterly, but not seriously evaluated for retention for at least three to four years. This attitude encourages the advisers to buy good securities with sound, long-term values. There should be more sponsors with this philosophy; the entire investments community and all plan participants would benefit. It makes no sense when a company hires an adviser after careful evaluation, then fires him or her after two or three quarters, unless there has been a structural change within the advisory firm. This issue of firing investment managers will be discussed, in detail, in Chapter 16.

THE PROS AND CONS OF STICKING TO ONE PHILOSOPHY

It should be self-evident that investors who frequently change their philosophy or style are losers, in general. But, it is surprising how many do. The change usually is made after a sustained period of underperformance. Of course, by then it is normally too late. The principal risk of change in style is the whipsaw—moving out of the type of stock that traditionally has been bought, just in time for those stocks to have their heyday.

One of the most well-known investment advisory firms in the

country (based in Boston) still bears the name of its founder, who was an early (1950s) believer in the quality, growth stocks. This firm had phenomenal performance until the mid-1970s. The adviser's relative performance peaked in the early 1970s with the blow-off of the "Nifty-Fifty." Those were the moderate-to-high growth companies with the large capitalizations which, for a couple years, appreciated 50% or more when the rest of the market was up less than half that amount. The theory of those who were new to the large-cap-growth company style was as follows: Because the market was rapidly becoming institutionalized, the stocks that would perform the best were the ones that were large enough to be purchased by the large mutual and pension funds that were beginning to dominate the marketplace.

As a result, these stocks were driven to exorbitant prices, and many investment advisers suddenly became "believers"—just at the wrong time. It was the wrong time because this country was just entering a period of near-devastating inflation that was partially driven by commodity shortages. The place to be during the last half of the decade of the 1970s was in the basic industries—petroleum, chemicals, metals, coal, and so on.

Sure enough, by 1980 the same people who had become "believers in the Nifty-Fifty" had now come to believe that the growth stocks of the future were the oil companies, coal producers, and railroads. Unfortunately, even the Boston adviser mentioned previously, who had been *the* bastion of the growth-stock philosophy, changed its long-standing style to include the traditionally cyclical stocks. Their timing could have been worse, but not by more than a year or two, because within two years the commodity shortages had turned into gluts and inflation was on the way down—both of which bode well for growth stocks and poorly for basic industry valuation.

Frequent, or even infrequent but dramatic, changes in investment philosophy are, of course, an offspring of the performance-game problem discussed in the previous section. It is very uncomfortable to stick to your guns quarter after quarter while the market is favoring only special types of stocks that do not fit with your investment philosophy.

One solution, which is a philosophy in and of itself, is to always own different types of stocks. One of New England's foremost individual portfolio managers has had a very successful career by approaching the portfolio-diversification problem from the perspective of treating the stock market as though it were a group of several markets, vis-à-vis a market of stocks within different industries. Accordingly, he *always* owns a group of large-cap, moderate-growth stocks; a group of cyclical stocks; a group of small, emerging growth stocks; a group of asset-value situations; a group of strong balance-sheet companies, a group of takeover candidates; a group of "story" stocks, and so forth. No matter what is in vogue, he always participates; and yet, almost every one of the individual securities represents good long-term value. The net result is his performance is never in the top decile or bottom decile, but almost always well-above average.

That brings us to the other side of investment-philosophy issue. Many managers are so acutely aware of the pitfalls of changing style that they stick to their own philosophy through thick and thin, even though it may not be a sound one. Take the example of the trust company with investment activities all over the western United States. It believes in buying stocks that offer dividend yields about twice the market average. There is another trust company in the Northeast that buys only equities selling at less than 10 times earnings. The sales pitch to potential customers of both trust departments sounds conservative and value oriented. But, what is the necessary connection between value and yield or P/E ratio? A steel company selling at 6 times earnings today could be selling at 20 times earnings next year even after the stock price has fallen by half. Conversely, a growth stock yielding only 1% today might be yielding 50% based on a project dividend several years from now.

Value means a lot of things to a lot of people, and the market is comprised of a lot of people. Before adopting an attitude to never change style, the manager should be certain that his or her philosophy is well thought out. The investor also should be certain that the particular methodology really works, in practice. Too many investors forget about the periods when their philosophy does not work, but are quick to recall the years when they beat the pants off the marketplace.

MAGIC FORMULAS AND BLACK BOXES

There is a real statistical flaw involved with back-testing of which many people are not aware. Most investment professionals, whether they be technicians or fundamentalists, who use special trend lines, magic formulas, or any sort of "black box" often arrived at their "system" through some sort of historical analysis. In other words, they looked back in time to see what would have worked. *This methodology is statistically erroneous.* But, it fools many people, because they don't have a proper understanding of statistical analysis.

Nearly any imaginable formula or charting technique would have worked *sometime* in the past, merely due to the behavior of random numbers. For example, suppose that during the 1920s the stock market always performed well during periods when Earth was nearest to Venus. If these two planets were relatively far apart in October of 1929, then the market analyst who, 60 years ago, was observing this interplanetary phenomenon would have been absolutely convinced of its relationship to the stock market, even though it occurred by chance and the relationship was never to happen again.

Take the true-to-life example of the electrical engineer who, in his spare time, spent years studying massive amounts of market data. In 1980, he was so convinced of the relationship between certain economic data in the current quarter and stock market performance in the next quarter that he quit his job at Raytheon and began selling a market-timing service using direct mail. From the day he began his new service, his "magic formula" never worked more than 50% of the time.

An article in a leading financial publication in 1971 told the story of a fellow who had discovered that, over the previous 20 years, an investor could have significantly outperformed the market by buying the 10 lowest P/E Dow Jones Industrials and short-selling the 10 highest. Now that fellow bombed out for the next several years, looked like a champ a few years later, and probably could have done as well by flipping a coin thereafter.

In fact, to visualize this issue, you might want to flip a coin every day before the market opens. Let "heads" represent a prediction that the market will be up that day and "tails" be a prediction that the market will be down. You may be surprised to discover how often a coin toss proves correct 60% or more of the time for months on end! If you are surprised when it works for you, read on before you quit your job or call your stockbroker.

Another illustration, which would take you only a few minutes, is to draw a "trend line" under the "bottoms" of a series of securities prices or series of random numbers. Notice that when the points on the chart "penetrate" down through the trend line, it almost always would have been a good time to "sell." If you think about it, you will realize why this happens. Here is a hint: Close your eyes and draw a squiggly line across a piece of paper. Now draw a line under the first series of dips if the trend of your line is initially upward, or draw it on top of the peaks if the trend of your line is initially downward. Notice that when the "random" line you drew penetrates the straight line, the rest of the "random" line will be either above or below the straight line according to the direction

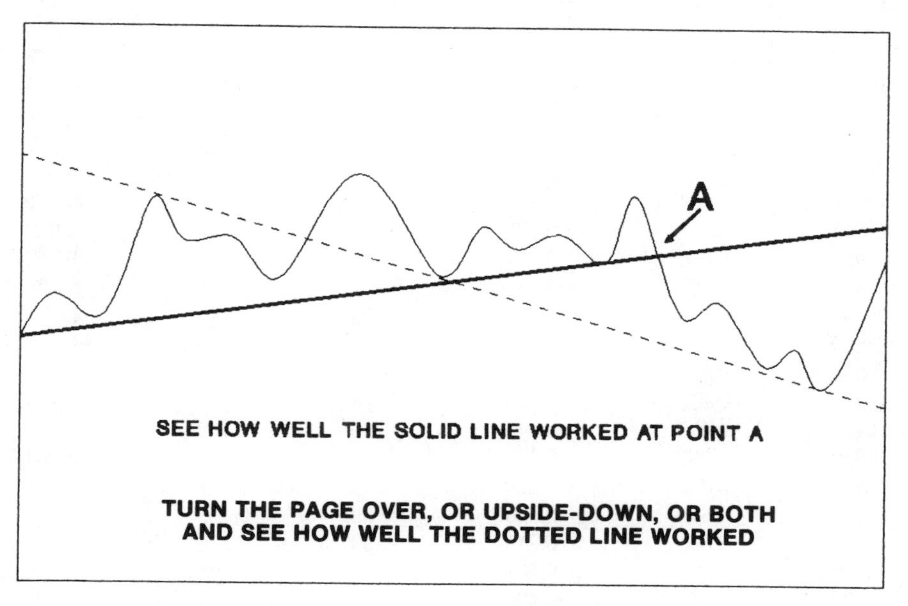

Figure 14–1. How Random Series Appear to Have "Resistance Levels."

of the penetration. Figure 14–1 was done on the computer with eyes closed.

Table 14–1 shows how random numbers can sometimes be highly correlated. Columns A and B are computer-generated random numbers, as are columns D and E. Column C is the difference between A and B; column F is the difference between D and E. Look how the numbers in columns C and F seem to move and change direction together. In fact, there is a correlation

TABLE 14–1 Computer-Generated Random Numbers

A	B	C	D	E	F
0.271	0.368	−0.097	0.137	0.969	−0.832
0.558	0.216	0.342	0.980	0.661	0.319
0.723	0.499	0.224	0.961	0.793	0.169
0.081	0.475	−0.394	0.418	0.720	−0.302
0.814	0.316	0.498	0.833	0.593	0.240
0.814	0.979	−0.165	0.798	0.578	0.220
0.214	0.474	−0.260	0.213	0.660	−0.446
0.047	0.381	−0.333	0.169	0.305	−0.137
0.142	0.546	−0.404	0.003	0.836	−0.833
0.378	0.188	0.190	0.880	0.309	0.571
0.535	0.586	−0.051	0.526	0.814	−0.288
0.427	0.005	0.422	0.798	0.402	0.396
0.443	0.008	0.435	0.357	0.086	0.272
0.267	0.451	−0.184	0.219	0.272	−0.053
0.792	0.611	0.181	0.622	0.490	0.132
0.979	0.741	0.238	0.571	0.395	0.176
0.853	0.925	−0.072	0.619	0.661	−0.042
0.981	0.610	0.371	0.493	0.136	0.357
0.340	0.828	−0.488	0.336	0.212	0.124
0.354	0.068	0.286	0.398	0.148	0.250
0.660	0.779	−0.119	0.573	0.646	−0.073
0.080	0.895	−0.815	0.362	0.688	−0.327
0.254	0.930	−0.676	0.146	0.443	−0.297
0.413	0.955	−0.542	0.430	0.968	−0.538
0.960	0.087	0.873	0.965	0.961	0.004
0.574	0.803	−0.229	0.508	0.874	−0.366
0.986	0.650	0.336	0.853	0.457	0.396
0.132	0.846	−0.715	0.263	0.276	−0.013
0.935	0.488	0.447	0.668	0.958	−0.290
0.529	0.958	−0.430	0.126	0.320	−0.194

coefficient between the two of over 50%! In reality, the figures shown in Table 14–1 are just a portion of a much larger table that was generated. These particular numbers were selected merely to show that, at times, *any* two sets of figures can appear to have some causal relationship.

The point is, if enough different types of data are examined, there always will be an *apparent* correlation between *some* sets of data and the stock market, or anything else for that matter. Similarly, there always will be what appears to be trends and repetitive cycles. That is the nature of random numbers. (Refer back to the charts at the end of Chapter 1.) The thing to remember is that any two sets of random numbers will have time intervals where the two sets of data appear to correlate very well. When devising a securities market "system," you must be sure the correlations that appear in the back-testing are not a statistical fluke.

The way around this problem is to develop a well-thought-out model *first*—one that *should* work—*then* go back and test it. Do not test data first in an attempt to find correlations, predictable cycles, or whatever. You will undoubtedly fall into a trap. "Experts" who claim to have a "system" and can "prove" it with historic data should be listened to with a great deal of skepticism.

15

Performance Measurement

If at first you don't succeed, you're running about average.

—M. H. Alderson

A PRESENTATION TO THE ALASKAN NATIVES

Bush pilot Bob Gillam has always lived in Alaska. His official occupation is that of a stockbroker in Anchorage. One summer he invited me and my associate on a fishing expedition to the region west of Anchorage where most of the red salmon (Sockeye) in the world spawn. That is the inland area between Bristol Bay and Lake Clark, which includes Lake Iliamna, the New Halen River, and the Tazimina River where, in some spots the water was so red, it seemed there was a greater volume of fish than there was water.

After we landed Bob's float plane and took his boat across Lake Clark and down the New Halen River to the mouth of the Tazimina, we realized the timing of our expedition was either a few weeks early or a few weeks late. The Sockeye had already spawned and their skins were turning red from the bacteria that engulfs their flesh as they slowly die following the spawn. In those final days of their lives, the salmon aren't the least bit interested in chomping down on a lure. So we returned to Bob's cabin, one of the very few on Lake Clark, which is surrounded almost entirely by national park and native subsistence land.

After the sun set and the beauty of the purple sky faded near midnight, we sat around the fireplace discussing how we would spend the rest of the week. Bob was familiar with several of the native villages and also knew how big the village corporation bank accounts were as a result of oil royalties. So, to make a long story short, the next day we headed out by boat and then by all-terrain vehicle into the hinterlands of Alaska in search of new investment accounts. After all, our advisory firm could certainly earn the natives a better return than they were getting on their CDs. How many investment advisers would the natives have been exposed to anyway? We doubted if many other investment firms made a practice of flying to Anchorage, finding a guide who knew the natives, taking a float plane inland, and getting hold of a boat or ATV to travel into these remote areas.

Our first presentation was to a small village with only 70 inhabitants, but with a sizeable bank account. The chief of the village corporation was a young, pleasant fellow who spoke English very well, as did a few of the others. The "others" who attended the presentation included the entire village, dogs and all. The meeting place was the grounds next to the sweat lodge.

First, I needed to gain an understanding of how the native corporations were organized. The chief gave me a vivid picture of the cultural shock that must have occurred in the years since the first Atlantic Richfield gusher on the North Slope in 1968. The villages all are organized into corporations for financial purposes. The oil royalties are divided amongst the corporations on a *per capita* basis according to a census taken several years ago whereby only natives who have attained a certain age would currently be members. The revenues to the corporation are then doled out to the villages on the same basis. But, it's more complex than all that.

The Kijic village on Lake Clark, for example, receives royalties from a molybdenum mine on its land which it must share with the other native corporations. Conversely, when the Kijic people used the gravel (a scarce commodity in muddy Alaska) on their own land to construct a small airplane runway, they had to pay a royalty to their own corporate organization.

The point is, it wasn't many years ago that the natives believed the land and the water belonged to God and were available to whomever needed to use it, no strings attached. But, its more complex than all that.

After I had a better understanding of the corporation setup and learned about the village way of life, I began my sales pitch. I had a hard time reconciling the fact that I knew how much money was potentially involved with the obvious lack of concern about the dollars of principal, never mind the investment income. The only signs that any of the royalty funds had been expended by the natives were the satellite dish antennas, the TV sets, and the snowmobiles and ATVs. In fact, the local currency was Pepsi Cola cans. Somehow I needed to convince the natives that they could get a higher return on their savings, but I wasn't sure they cared.

After all, they had it made. The subsistence land the government had set aside for their habitation and use would be valued at $billions by West Coast or East Coast standards. They worked (making dolls to be sold in Anchorage) whenever they felt like it, fished and hunted whenever the urge struck, and played games (children and adults) any time. The scenery was spectacular, and they knew and appreciated it. Why should they be concerned about making an extra $100,000 per year when they didn't seem to feel they needed the $millions they already had?

They already had been burned on some deposits with the S&L companies, so I thought I could talk about equities as the "safe" way to invest—that would be a switch! Several times during my painfully slow presentation, I was given the signal to shut my mouth so the villagers could watch the approaching caribou or enjoy the beauty of the sunset.

I was making no progress in my attempt to explain the concept of *relative* returns. The villagers believed they already were making a satisfactory return on their CDs; it was a period of high short-term rates, so they may have been right. But, I still wanted to tell them that my company could do better. I was not making any progress.

Bob Gillam came to the rescue. He asked the chief whether he would be satisfied if he went fishing and came home with 18 rainbow trout. The leader replied, "That depends on how many fish everybody else caught." Voila! They now understood the concept of relative performance.

HOW MEANINGFUL ARE PAST RESULTS?

Today, in the investments business, relative performance is the name of the game. Everyone who manages money is compared to everyone else who manages money and to the market indices, as well as to the goals that were set and the amount of risk taken.

The two overlying challenges are comparing apples to apples for the current period and being able to draw some meaningful conclusions from the results of prior periods. This chapter will deal with both issues; let's begin with the historical issue.

Over the past five years, Manager A and Manager B have performance records that show they earned a total return of 70% for the period, which is an equivalent of 11.2% per year or 2.7% per quarter. The market return for the period was 50%, which is equivalent to 8.4% per year or 2.0% per quarter. Both managers had a portfolio beta of 1.05. The excess portfolio returns of 2.8% per year appear quite acceptable for the managers having taken only slightly more than average market risk. Assuming these are satisfactory returns, the question is, which manager is the most likely to repeat this performance of a 2.8% excess return over the *next* five years?

One analytical method often used is taking the standard deviation of the returns. This way, the potential client can compare the average variance of the manager's quarterly returns to the manager's average return. The quarterly standard deviation of return could vary from 0% for a manager who earned 2.7% every single quarter to 15% for a manager who earned the entire return all in one quarter, or even higher for a manager whose quarterly results showed some major negative return periods.

There is another method, which I adapted from basic statistics, that is quite intriguing. A statistical test can be made to calculate the odds that the manager beat the market by chance. It involves a very complex series of calculations regarding combinations, permutations, and other factorials. But here is an example of the odds that a portfolio manager beat the market by chance, assuming there was a 50-50 chance of outperforming the market by luck in any one period.

Table 15–1 assumes that the managers reported their quarterly performance results for the past five years. If Manager A beat the market in 12 of the 20 quarters, there would be a 25% probability that it was accomplished by luck. If Manager B outperformed the market in 15 of the 20 quarters, there would be only a 2% chance that it happened by chance. If both managers had the same return

TABLE 15-1 Probability of Beating the Market by Chance (Based on 20 Measurement Periods)

No. Periods Outperformed	Probability by Chance
10	58.81%
11	41.19
12	25.17
13	13.16
14	5.77
15	2.07
16	0.59
17	0.13
18	0.02
19	0.00
20	0.00

for the period and there was no discernible difference in the return variances, then Manager B would be the manager of choice. That is because there is a higher probability that Manager B will repeat his or her superior performance.

It is interesting that a portfolio manager can beat the market by an average of 2% per quarter and have a very low return variance, but there still is a significant chance that the manager was just plain lucky. The greater the number of measurement periods, the more important the statistic of what percentage of the time the manager outperformed.

If a manager beats the market by 2% in three out of four quarters, there is a 31% chance that it occurred by chance, since only four measurement periods are involved. If he or she beat the market by the same amount and the same percentage (75%) of the time, but did it in 15 out of 20 periods, there would be only a 1% chance that it happened by luck. If he or she did it in 30 out of 40 periods, there would be almost no chance of luck having been involved. There would be almost complete certainty that the excess return was accomplished through the skill of the manager.

An investor must be aware that the variability of return and the consistency with which a manager outperforms are as important, and sometimes more so, than the historic total returns themselves.

THE IMPLICATIONS OF NORMAL DISTRIBUTION

There are numerous statistics that point to the difficulty involved with beating the market over a sustained period of time. The odds are less than 50-50. For those managers who do consistently outperform the markets or their competition, the odds are they did it either by taking above-average risk or through proper asset allocation. Securities selection is one of the least likely means by which a manager can outperform, assuming a properly diversified portfolio with a few dozen individual issues.

Remember from Chapter 1 that if you were to plot all of the possible results of 100 coin tosses (100 heads, 0 tails; 99 heads, 1 tails; 98 heads, 2 tails, etc.) against each of their probabilities of occurrence, a normal (bell-shaped) distribution curve would result. That is because a coin toss involves two possible outcomes (heads or tails) that have equal probability of occurrence. Therefore, this is a situation where all the possible combinations of heads and tails occur with frequencies representing binomial distribution. When enough data points are involved, binomial distribution becomes almost identical to normal (bell-shaped) distribution.

If there was a 50-50 chance of a manager beating the market (equivalent to flipping "heads"), then the distribution of returns for all money managers (specific returns plotted against the number of managers who earned those returns) should approximate a normal distribution. This is the case. That means that 68% of all managers earn returns within one standard deviation of the mean return, and 95% of all managers earn a return within two standard deviations of the mean return.

That implies that if a manager is in the top decile, performance-wise, of all money managers, his or her average return must have been about 1.65 standard deviations above the average for the group. But the important corollary is that 10% of the managers always will have a return 1.65 standard deviations above average.

That will occur simply as a matter of random probability. Therefore, if 10 money managers were selected at random, one of them should have a return 1.65 standard deviations (which might represent 15 percentage points) above average, even though all 10 might have picked their investments by throwing a dart at a quotation page from a newspaper.

The inescapable conclusion is that an investor who is selecting an investment adviser must look at much more than just the raw historical performance numbers. Consistency of return, amount of risk taken, the objectives of the clients whose performance was included in the data, and the number of periods being measured are some of the other areas that must be investigated.

GAMES PLAYED WITH PERFORMANCE NUMBERS

Many games can be played with performance numbers. The most common one is where the investment advisor picks and chooses which accounts are to be included in the performance data. Here are some examples:

1. Over the past five years, an adviser's best performing account is his or her largest account. Therefore, when a presentation is made to a large potential client, the adviser uses the performance data from the largest account on the basis that it is representative of the firm's results on accounts that are similar in size to the prospective account.
2. Over the past five years, an adviser's best performing account was that of a cement company. So when a presentation is made to another cement or any other building materials company, the adviser implies that he or she has some expertise in managing the retirement funds for building materials workers and uses the performance from his or her best account as proof.
3. In recent years, an adviser's best performing account is that of a profit-sharing account based on Omaha. So the next time a presentation is being made in Omaha, the adviser offers to

"confidentially" show the prospective client the performance figures of the company down the street.

4. An investment adviser notices that the performance record for his or her diversified portfolios is not as outstanding as the relative performance of the all-equity or all-bond accounts because a poor job has been done with *asset allocation*. Therefore, when making a presentation to a diversified (balanced) account sponsor, the adviser uses the separate performance of the equity and fixed-income accounts as a "proxy" for what sort of combined performance can be expected.
5. An investment adviser has a commingled equity fund where most of the equity clients are placed. However, the fund was heavily invested in cash at the wrong time, so the adviser shows how well the individual stocks have performed.
6. A client is interested in placing funds in the adviser's equity pool and fixed-income pool. The percentages in each pool will be left to the discretion of the adviser. The adviser proudly shows the prospective client that the equity pool has consistently beaten the S&P 500 by 2% per year and the fixed-income fund has outperformed the Shearson-Lehman Index by 1% per year. What the adviser neglects to show is that the existing clients were 80% invested in the fixed-income fund over a period when stocks significantly outperformed bonds.

The examples can go on and on. Investment advisers and pension consultants have a knack for creating all sorts of overlapping subsets of the total group of accounts under management in order to suit the particular needs of the moment.

An investment adviser always should be required to report the performance of all accounts under management, either on an individual or type-of-account basis or in total. If a total (average) is used, it should be reported on an unweighted as well as weighted (for account size) basis. Even if the average of the total accounts may not be appropriate for a specific client because of special risk-profile considerations, the overall number is still a good thing to know.

Assuming that an adviser does report the performance for all similar accounts—no picking and choosing—there is still the issue of *how* performance is being calculated.

THE CONCEPT OF TIME-WEIGHTED RETURNS

It is hard to believe in today's performance-oriented investment environment that a mere 25 years ago performance calculations were not even being made. Total-return computations were being done by actuaries back then, but there is a difference between total return and performance. The actual return to a pension fund, for example, is the dollar-weighted return which is the internal rate of return of the cash flows. Performance, on the other hand, is a time-weighted rate of return that removes the effect of the timing of the contributions and withdrawals which are not, of course, determined by the money manager.

In the mid-1960s, there were very few independent money managers, and there were almost no pension consultants. There were no 401(k)-type plans. Defined-benefit plans (basic pension accounts) represented the vast bulk of employee retirement funds. Most of this money was managed by bank trust departments and life insurance companies. A significant portion of the pension business involved pooled funds (viz. separate investment accounts) where the client's funds were commingled with the life insurer's own assets.

The insurance actuaries would make a computation each year to determine the rate of return of the fund compared to its actuarial assumption (target return). This computation was basically an internal rate of return—the rate of interest that discounts the ending portfolio value plus the cash inflows and outflows over the period to the value of the fund at the beginning of the period. All that matters in this dollar-weighted method is what the cash flows were and during which periods they occurred. It represents the fund's real return; but it is heavily influenced by the timing of the cash flows, over which the investment adviser has no control. For example, a fund that had huge contributions just prior to a bull market and/or withdrawals just prior to a bear market would have significantly better performance than a fund that had no cash flows over the period, even though both funds may have been fully invested in the identical securities.

The banking industry in the late 1960s, which was acting as trustee for a big chunk of the pension funds in the country, recognized the need to measure the performance of the investment adviser exclusive of the timing of the cash flows. The Bank Administration Institute (BAI) came up with a solution, which was to calculate the effective discount rate for the portfolio at regular time intervals, then chain the results together for multiperiod return calculations. The formula is an iterative one, that is, it needs to solve for the return using a trial-and-error process:

$$\text{Ending Val.} = \text{Beginning Val.}\ (1 + R) + \text{Net Contributions}\ (1 + R)^t$$

Using this equation involves solving for (R) where (t) represents the fraction of the period that the net contribution was available for investment, usually assumed to be ½ for simplicity.

About a year before the BAI method was published, I adopted another method. Consider that what we are really attempting to find is the dollar amount of profit divided by the average amount of funds that were available for investment over the period. Accordingly, the following formula is logical:

$$R = \frac{\text{Ending Val.} - \text{Beginning Val.} - \text{Net Contributions}}{\text{Beginning Val.} + t\ (\text{Net Contributions})}$$

where (t) is the average fraction of the period that the net contributions were available for investment.

Peter Dietz published a formula that is the algebraic equivalent of mine, but a whole lot simpler. The Dietz algorithm, which became the basis for almost all future enhancements of time-weighted rate-of-return formulas, is as follows:

$$R = \frac{\text{Ending Val.} - .5\ (\text{Net Contributions})}{\text{Beginning Val.} + .5\ (\text{Net Contributions})}$$

Most of the enhancements to the Dietz algorithm involve either more accurate weighting of the cash flows, other than where (t = .5), or manipulations of investment income (including reinvestment), other than simply including it in the ending value of the portfolio.

It is my contention that the *only* way to accurately measure the *real return* of an investment account is the dollar-weighted method of computing an internal rate of return of the cash flows relative to the beginning market value. And, the *only* way to accurately compute the *performance* of the investment adviser is a time-weighted methodology that computes the account return *every time a contribution or withdrawal is made,* then chains those results together for the entire period being measured. This latter method should be required of the investments industry, since we now have the use of high-speed computers and maintain databases. The database should have records of accrued interest and dividends. The transactions date should be made to equal the trade (viz. settlement) date since it is the trade date that, legally, determines ownership of a security. Some prefer using settlement date for performance measurement because that is when the cash flows take place. Although that is a good reason, the problem with settlement-date accounting for performance measurement is the time lag that causes the actual results for the last few days of the period to be pushed into the next period; therefore, index comparisons lose effectiveness, and maybe the vested interests in a fund are unrealistically computed.

Nonetheless, many investment operations still use a simplistic time-weighted rate of return where the timing of the cash flows is merely estimated, and the results are chained together only monthly or quarterly. Table 15–2 shows the different results that can be attained using the simplest versions of the methods discussed in this section.

Table 15–2 shows various return or performance calculations over a period where the market was basically unchanged from start to finish, but where there were significant price changes as well as cash flows in the interim. It is assumed that the investment adviser was fully invested in the equivalent of the market index at all times, and that the cash flows occurred precisely in the middle of the

TABLE 15–2 Various Methods of Computing Performance

Period	Market Index	Percent Change	Contributions (Withdrawals)	Portfolio Value	Cash Flows
Initial	100.00			$1,000	($1,000)
1	110.00	10%	($200)	890	200
2	88.00	−20	$500	1,162	(500)
3	105.60	20	($200)	1,174	200
4	100.32	−5	$0	1,116	1,116
			$100		

	Unchained	Chained
Dollar-Weighted Return	0.37%	0.56%
Time-Weighted Return	1.49	0.32
BAI Return	1.49	0.52

periods. The unchained results are obtained by making one calculation for the combined periods, as if there were really just one period—that only one $100 contribution came in right at the end of Period 2.

The chained numbers involve the compounding of four separate calculations where the cash flows were treated as though they came in exactly in the middle of each of the four periods. Under the time-weighted method in Period 1, for example, it is assumed that an average of only $900 was available for investment, which grew by 10% to $990 before the other $100 unaccounted for was withdrawn. Under the other two methods, it is assumed that the contributions were made in the middle of the period and would, therefore, earn a return for half the period.

Periodic results are chained together according to the following formula:

$$R = [(1 + r)\ (1 + r)\ (1 + r)\ (1 + r)] - 1$$

where (R) is the total return for all the periods combined and (r) represents each of the returns for the individual periods.

Notice that there is a difference of over 1% between the highest and lowest calculations, even though it always was assumed that the account received contributions and paid out withdrawals in the middle of the period and that the amount of funds the manager had available always earned a market rate of return. Now a difference in return of 1% might not sound like much, but over an extended period of time, it might make the difference between the adviser's performance being in the top quartile relative to other advisers or being in the bottom of the second quartile.

The best solution to the problem of accuracy (regardless of the particular formula used) is to compute and chain the performance as often as possible. Mutual-fund performance numbers are extremely accurate because they involve unit values that are computed every day.

WHEN TO BEGIN THE MEASUREMENT PROCESS

If a client changes investment advisers, what should be the base period for the new manager? Definitely not the day he or she is given the account to manage. One or two quarters (preferably one) should be allowed to slip under the table, even though the actuaries for an employee-benefit fund still will need to make the *return* calculations to determine the vested and nonvested employee interests in the fund. But, for *relative performance* purposes, a time-weighted rate of return for the first few months would not be a fair computation for the following reasons:

1. Most likely, the new manager "inherited" a bunch of securities that he or she would rather not own. But the plan sponsor does not want to incur extremely heavy transactions costs all at once; that might hurt particular employees. Plus, the sponsor usually is not convinced that the new manager's security picks will outperform the existing securities over the next few months, anyway.
2. Most likely, the new manager does not agree with the prior asset allocation of the fund. If the intended asset allocation is substantially different than the "inherited" allocation, the new adviser may be (understandably) reluctant to make a major shift all at once. He or she may come up with egg on his

or her face at the first review meeting if the markets move in the "wrong" direction in the short term. There is also the issue of excessive transactions costs being concentrated into a short period of time.

3. Frequently, there is a change in the custodian(s) of the funds. If securities need to be physically delivered (even under a book-entry system), it never goes smoothly, which means that certain securities may, temporarily, get lost in the shuffle and can't be traded.
4. Sometimes an account owns mutual funds that involve a back-end sales charge. The new manager doesn't want to own the funds; but if they are sold, a deferred load of several percentage points could kill the performance of the first period.
5. The previous manager may not have structured the portfolio to adequately meet the risk parameters or income needs of the client. For no other reason than this, securities may have to be bought and sold, which will create transactions costs. The new manager should not be penalized for the negligence of the prior adviser.

Despite all these reasons, the client should not wait more than six months before holding the new manager accountable for the performance of the portfolio. After all, new advisers usually are given complete discretion over the securities, and at some point in the not too distant future, they need to be held accountable for the performance of the individual securities as well as the effects of asset allocation.

THE VARIOUS YARDSTICKS: NEW CONCEPTS

Traditionally, the return of a portfolio was compared to the target return over various periods of time. Then it became customary to compare portfolio results to the appropriate market index or some blend of market indices such as 60% S&P 500 and 40% Shearson-Lehman Government/Corporate Bond Index, or 33.3% S&P, 33.3%

Shearson-Lehman, and 33.3% money-market or T-bill indices. Then, with the proliferation of consultants, a client could compare the performance of his or her fund to that of a universe of other similar funds. All of these approaches still seem to make sense, but they don't seem to be good enough for the academics.

Many believe that a portfolio's return should be risk-adjusted. That means that the minimum acceptable return should exceed the risk-free (T-bill) rate by an amount that is in direct proportion to the systematic (market) risk, or even total risk, taken. If the return did not adequately reflect the amount of risk taken, then it is assumed that the portfolio manager underperformed. But, what if the portfolio beta or standard deviation was not prescribed by the client? What if the manager intentionally increased portfolio volatility because his or her asset-allocation model called for more equities. The individual securities might not have done as well as they should have, compared to their individual volatilities, but the manager should have been given credit for the asset-allocation shift if, in fact, equities did outperform the other usable investment vehicles.

Whether standard deviation or beta is used as a means to measure portfolio risk, the adviser should not be penalized for taking additional risk, if he or she is free to do so and it turns out to be the correct thing to have done. Risk-adjusted returns overweight the importance of individual securities selection, when it is a fact that the manager's choice of asset allocation is much more important than the securities selection. Why downplay the effects of asset allocation when that is the most important factor affecting the return of the portfolio? Accordingly, risk-adjusted returns only seem appropriate when the investment adviser is not responsible for the asset allocation.

There is another equally important drawback to risk-adjusted rates of return: The entire concept assumes that there is a direct and linear relationship between risk and return. This has never been proven. What if, for example, T-bill rates are out of whack with the returns of other classes of securities. Does that mean that a manager who has been hired as a strictly equities manager and who is required to be fully invested should be penalized by the fact that the risk-free rate might be inordinately high?

Whole families of new performance criteria recently have evolved where the intention is to compare the manager to a universe of securities that is specifically equivalent to what the manager invests in. Again, this overweights the importance of securities selection. It is my prediction that, sometime in the next decade or two, the trend will be to simplify what is now being made complex. It wouldn't be at all surprising if the most common method of measuring relative performance simply becomes the comparison of the portfolio return to that which would have been earned by investing in T-bills. This way, the manager (not the client or the consultant) becomes fully responsible for the asset allocation of the account.

Of course, this can happen only after the clients and consultants become comfortable with allowing the manager to determine the asset allocation. But even when the management firm is not allowed to set the overall asset allocation, it often is authorized to utilize cash as a substitute for securities. With the increasing awareness of the importance of asset allocation, there should be a dramatic increase in the number of viable asset-allocation techniques as well as the number of investment advisers employing them. This book is intended to make a meaningful contribution in that direction.

HOW MANY TIERS OF FEES SHOULD THE CLIENT INCUR?

One of the things that may help to bring about the proliferation of more asset-allocation technology and firms that provide asset allocation as an integral part of the portfolio-management service is the awareness of the amount of the total fees now being paid and their effect on performance.

Today, it is possible for an account to pay, either in hard or soft dollars, four sets of fees: one to the consultant for assisting in the manager search and asset-allocation process, one to the investment advisers for asset allocation and/or securities selection, one to the mutual funds the adviser may have purchased (including money-market funds), and one to the broker (commissions) for execution of trades. How can a portfolio afford all these charges on top of the transactions costs (market effect of the trades), if clients, as a whole, only can expect to earn a return that is equal to a market rate in the first place? It is little wonder that index funds and financial futures have been created.

The investment firm of the future might well determine and update the asset allocation, pick the individual investments, and execute the trades—all for a single fee. Such a "wrap fee" could certainly be in the range of .75% to 1.00%, which is half as much as investment clients are effectively paying today. Hiding the consultants' fees and the execution costs under the commissions umbrella will not last forever; otherwise, employees and plan sponsors will come to believe that investing in stocks and bonds will produce uncompetitive net rates of return.

16

Choosing An Investments Adviser

If you want to succeed, you should strike out on new paths rather than travel on the worn paths of accepted success.

—*John D. Rockefeller*

HOW TO PUT A BLACK BOX TO GOOD USE

Aside from outdoor sports, my main hobbies are electronics, music, and shopwork. One evening, I decided to make use of all three by designing and building a computerized "black box" that would make an interesting conversation piece for my desk at the office. I designed a circuit whose main components were four ICs (integrated circuits or "chips"): one to convert alternating current (AC) to low-voltage direct current (DC), one to act as a timer or clock, one to produce "random" amounts of current from two of the output pins, and one to generate musical sounds (for additional effect). The machine is nothing more than a random number generator with a lot of lights and sounds. The black metal box, measuring about eight inches in each direction, has several knobs, switches, and meters (all of them functional) that give it the appearance of a sophisticated mechanism. When the colored lamps (LEDs) light up, they are "supposed to" signify whether to buy, sell, straddle, go long, or go short a synthetic future or take a position in a spread. The underlying security is supposed to be the stock market index, so the device looks as though it is intended to make a prediction as to the future direction and volatility of the market.

As it turns out, the principal use I have had for the black box is to create a series of random changes (exactly what it was electronically designed to do) so a client can visualize them. Nonetheless, it is surprising to see how often the machine can make correct predictions for the daily stock market results for days on end.

I also use the black box to prove a point to prospective clients: A "system" that has all the appearance of sophistication might be nothing more than a virtually empty shell. Conversely, I also use the black box to show that a philosophy that goes no deeper than relying on a phony machine often can work as well as one that sounds great on the surface.

IS THE ADVISER'S PHILOSOPHY A SOUND ONE?

The investor *must feel comfortable* with the way the funds are being managed. The adviser is being paid to alleviate worry, not add to it. The choice of a money manager should not be made as a result of the fancy rhetoric or "buzzwords" used by the investment firm.

One way to avoid this pitfall is to insist on meeting the principals of the firm. Have them explain their philosophy in detail and prove that it works. The philosophy should not just work for that particular adviser, but for anyone who abides by it. This is important. Otherwise, an adviser could "prove" that the philosophy works merely by showing the firm's own performance numbers, which may be indicative of nothing other than either an ability to use creative accounting or luck.

IS THE ADVISER HONEST AND REPUTABLE?

The investor, plan sponsor, or consultant needs to be certain that the manager will be reporting his or her performance and transaction details properly. The best way to get an indication is to ask a lot of questions about the historic performance numbers that have already been shown to you. First and foremost, did the performance figures include the results of *all* similar accounts under management? If not, why not? Whatever the reason, you want to see them anyway.

Next, you want to be sure that the manager will manage *strictly* according to the ground rules laid down for him or her. One way to get an idea of this is to see for yourself whether the firm has been managing other people's money in exact accordance with the firm's expounded philosophy. Ask the manager to show you a number of representative portfolios currently being managed. Tell the adviser it is okay to white out the names of the clients, but don't tell him or her why you want to examine the portfolios. He or she might think you'll be impressed if you see a lot of unrealized gains in the portfolios; so accounts with many big winners might be selected for your review. That is alright, because what you really will be looking for is proof that the types of investments made are as conservative as the firm claims they are. Are the securities the adviser has been placing in his or her clients' accounts of the quality that the firm has led you to believe will be put into your account?

Honesty also involves the issue of self-dealing. Before you casually sign any trading authorizations or powers-of-attorney, make sure that you know whether the brokers who will be performing the executions have any financial arrangement with the adviser. It may be alright if there is such a relationship; it might save you money. On the other hand, it might result in excessive trading or commission rates. The law protects employee funds from self-dealing, but individuals must specifically authorize it.

Naturally, the best way to deal with the honesty issue is by hiring an investment adviser who is well known and has a good reputation. But, that would exclude many of the "little guys" and all the up-and-comers. I am a great believer in the small money manager, because at these firms, the people tend to have a higher level of motivation and spend a lot less time in meetings or goofing off. Chances are their livelihood is more dependent on their performance and maintaining a high level of quality service. The biggest disadvantage to employing a large consulting firm that, in turn, hires other large money managers is the remoteness of the people or the lack of a close relationship between the investor and the adviser. The most important thing an adviser must understand about the client is the investor's risk profile. Since that usually turns out to be more psychological than scientifically derived, the longevity of a client-adviser relationship is directly proportional to how well they know each other—personally.

WHAT KIND OF TURNOVER SHOULD YOU EXPECT?

Portfolio turnover is *not,* in and of itself, necessarily a bad thing. Very simply, if it makes you money, it can be a good thing. For example, managers who are charged with the responsibility of asset allocation might have an above-average number of trades if they don't use market derivatives. This is okay if the asset-allocation changes are justified. If they're not, you'll need a different manager, anyway.

Don't just ask an adviser what his or her turnover is: ask for some documentation. Investment advisers are required to maintain a trade log. From that log, the adviser should be able to produce whatever statistics you wish to see.

But remember that turnover normally helps or hurts the adviser as much as it does the client. That is because most management fees are based on the market value of the account. If transactions costs amount to 2% per year, then the adviser's income also will be penalized by 2%. It is important to keep that in mind.

An easy and unobnoxious way to get an idea of an adviser's transactions activity is by asking for the historic performance numbers, both before and after commissions. That question usually can be answered easily with the help of all the computers the advisers have. It is surprising how many people don't make this simple request. Pension consultants usually ask investment advisers whether the numbers they report are before or after commissions; they do the same thing regarding management fees. If the answer is "before" in either case, the adviser gets a "black mark" instead of a "star."

In conclusion, the turnover issue should not be overly emphasized. After all, it is the bottom line that really matters. Just make sure you are seeing the real bottom line. Even when the client knows exactly what the turnover rate has been, or will be, what can be concluded from this information? There is no way of knowing, without much analysis—and you should not presume anything—as to whether a portfolio would have performed better or worse had the turnover been different. In that regard, don't forget that low portfolio turnover can be just as much of a warning signal as high turnover. Low turnover might mean that the adviser is asleep at the switch.

ARE YOU COMFORTABLE WITH THE ADVISER'S STYLE?

There is a difference between "philosophy" and "style," even though these words sometimes have been used interchangeably in this book. In reality, an adviser's philosophy is his or her beliefs concerning what makes the markets behave the way they do and what constitutes an appropriate investment. Style, on the other hand, is the way in which the manager operates and implements the philosophy.

Don't hire people who rub you the wrong way, if for no other reason than they rub you the wrong way. Hire a manager the way you would an employee. If you are not the type to hire obnoxious, vague, arrogant, or willy-nilly people, then don't hire investment advisers who exhibit those characteristics. You are the one that will be dealing with them. Why make life miserable when you're the one in charge of the purse strings?

The portfolio managers, analysts, traders, principals, and salespeople within the advisory firm all should exhibit an all extraordinary affinity toward the investment business. It's an easy business to fall in love with and be excited about. But a surprising number of investment people think it is the most high pressure, difficult business in the world. That's their own lack of confidence in themselves. You will be much better off doing business with someone who seems to be on an ego trip than someone who strikes you as a "wimp." You want a decision maker, because the investments business involves decisions nearly every hour of the day. Even when a good investment manager does nothing, it is usually because the decision has been made to do nothing—at least until the next tick of the ticker tape.

Good managers will show a genuine concern for your account and its beneficiaries. A concerned manager will want to meet as many of the people (whose money will be in the account) as possible—not just the people who are in charge of the hiring and firing of the advisers. A good question to ask a prospective investment manager is: How much time is devoted to portfolio management and client service versus client prospecting? In a number of firms, all the principals and most of the other employees spend the bulk of their time making "cold calls." Who stays home to mind the shop?

HOW MUCH SERVICE SHOULD A CLIENT EXPECT?

Service goes a lot further than producing acceptable performance numbers. The manager must be willing and able to meet with the investors or their sponsors as often as needed, by telephone and in person.

Reports should be timely and accurate. There is nothing more irritating to a client than to receive, month-after-month, an account appraisal which differs from that of the custodian bank or broker. Why should the investor have to spend time doing reconciliations?

The adviser should be interested in initiating meetings if there hasn't been one for several months. How else will the adviser be kept appraised of the client's ever-changing needs? The risk-tolerance level of an investor, particularly an investment committee, changes with surprising frequency. That is because risk tolerance is a scientific, mathematical thing only on paper. In the real world, it is every bit as emotional. In that regard, one function of the investment adviser should be to help curb that emotion. How can a manager do that if there is no client communication?

IS THE INVESTMENT ADVISER STABLE?

The irony concerning stability, in the sense of continuity, is that the larger the advisory firm, the greater the probability for a change in the management of an individual portfolio. There is one investor, in Hartford, who has used the same investment manager for half a century—not because it wants to, but because the manager is a bank whose line of credit this investor is very dependent upon. The fact of the matter is that the portfolio in question has had about every conceivable pattern of performance. That is because, on average, the portfolio has been assigned to a different portfolio manager about every two years. People at the big outfits, whether it be the banks, insurance companies, or large investment subsidiaries, come and go. If your account is a relatively small one, chances are it will be assigned to a younger portfolio manager who has an above-average chance of changing jobs. If not, he or she will be promoted to a new position and your account will become a football.

With a smaller advisory firm, the players don't change much. Their lives are tied into their business because they own a piece of it. They're not going anywhere. The biggest risk with a small money manager is that someday it might not be small anymore.

Many giant corporate employee-benefit plans (in the $billions) are managed by small boutiques. Those corporations' monies will be treated with utmost care. These corporations know that *some* of the smaller firms have just as good a chance at producing good results as *most* of the big firms.

Many people incorrectly judge the monetary stability of an investment firm by the amount of money it has under management. That is no different than assuming a large manufacturer is more stable than a medium-sized one, strictly because of the size of its assets. That doesn't necessarily follow. An experienced investment analyst will admit that one of the best ways to judge the stability of a company is by the stability of its cash flow and the number of market cycles it has survived.

Similarly, with a money manager, what is important is the level of free cash flow that is accruing to the owners and how many years the principals have been in the business. If the take-home pay is high and the firm is not overly dependent on just one or two accounts, chances are they will be around for a long time.

Investments is a people business. It is wiser to place your money with a small group of very wise, wealthy people than with the investment subsidiary of some large institution that has been around for a hundred years but can't afford to pay its professionals. Entrepreneurs are, by definition, imaginative businesspeople—the type you want to have analyzing the businesses they are investing your money in.

WHEN TO FIRE (OR NOT FIRE) AN INVESTMENT ADVISER

One of the most disgraceful phenomena that occurs in the money-management business is the frequent hiring and firing of investment advisers. There is absolutely no logic involved when an investor spends a lot of time and money searching for and deciding on an investment adviser then turns around within a year or two and fires the manager solely on the basis of short-term performance. This makes no sense whatsoever; yet, it happens time after time. If investment advisers weren't as greedy as everyone else they shouldn't even both courting an investor who has had a history of this sort of thing.

When you hire an adviser, it should be done with a great deal of thought. As a result, there should be very few reasons—and performance should *never* be one of them—to fire that adviser after only a few calendar quarters. The only reason an adviser should be fired because of short-term performance is when he or she was hired with the understanding that short-term performance was the prime objective of the account!

Normally, a manager should be given one full business cycle or market cycle to be ultimately evaluated. But here are some true-to-life examples of what can happen as a result of a client's emotion (greed or fear) getting the best of him or her:

1. An adviser is hired mainly because of his or her relatively good performance record in bear markets. The client claims to be conservative and is more afraid of loss than anxious to get rich quick. The next four quarters after the adviser is brought aboard, the market goes up and the adviser underperforms (as in the past, during raging bull markets). The adviser is fired because he or she "couldn't even beat the Dow Jones Average."

2. An adviser is hired because he or she has beaten the market in 80% of the calendar quarters over the past 10 years. During the two quarters after being hired, the adviser underperforms the S&P 500 and is let go.

3. An advisor is hired because his or her investment philosophy appealed to the investment committee of a large employee-benefit plan. The committee was afraid of equities, in general, so the adviser kept the equity allocation low; part of the adviser's philosophy was to listen carefully to the client's hopes and fears. The stock market went to the moon and the committee "changed its spots"—they turned around and hired an adviser who *had* fully participated in the bull market.

4. An adviser is hired because of his or her talents in areas of portfolio insurance, financial futures, option-overwriting, and all the other modern techniques. The adviser loses money with the strategies during the first year, so the investor decides to go back to basics and forget about all the latest strategies for beating the market.

5. An adviser is hired because the firm's philosophy is a growth-stock-oriented one. It buys securities that have a much higher level of profitability than the average company and doesn't rely on P/E ratio expansion as a source of profits. But, right after they are hired, a couple of giant corporate takeovers occur. All of a sudden the market has an insatiable appetite for takeover candidates, and the adviser gets left in the dust. The manager is fired for not coming close to the market averages, which were heavily weighted with these takeover companies.

6. An adviser is hired because the firm believes in a value approach to investing. It buys stocks where the intrinsic value is substantially greater than the market price. After being employed, interest rates unexpectedly come down and the growth stocks appreciate significantly. The adviser doesn't own any now and never did; yet, the client calls for a termination.

The examples could go on and on. The basic cause for early firing of advisers is the occasional manifestation of the client's fear and greed. When the client is making the decision on which manager to hire, to begin with, he or she is very logical and broad-minded and makes an all-out effort to hire the adviser who is most appropriate for the long-term objective of the portfolio. But, when the market moves sharply higher or lower, the client forgets all about the long term and suddenly wants either performance or to run for the hills. Emotion takes over and the adviser has had it.

But there are legitimate reasons for firing an investment adviser; some of them even apply to the near term. Personnel is an important reason, particularly if the people at the top change, because that probably signals an upcoming transformation in style or philosophy. You want your account to be managed in the fashion that was presented to you and by the person who you expected to be assigned to your account. When top management changes, or the particular individual who manages your portfolio moves elsewhere, so should you—right away. Do not wait around to find out if the new manager will be as good as the last. Better yet, find out where the original players went, because you might want to stick with them. A money-management firm is not an institution; it is a small group of people who perform in their own unique fashion. When the people change, the performance changes.

Another reason to terminate a manager is when you don't get the service you were promised. Maybe the adviser was so successful that the client base grew too fast, or maybe his or her firm is having financial difficulties or maybe it is more interested in new clients than in existing clients. Whatever the reason, express your concern—don't fire the manager without warning because of poor service. Hopefully, the people will get the message. But if they don't, it's aufwiederseh'n.

A good rule of thumb is that as long as the key person or people don't leave the firm, the chances are that whatever the short-term problem is, it can and will be corrected.

WHY BEING UNIQUE IS IMPORTANT

Because the investments marketplace is dominated by the professionals, it will not be possible to earn a rate of return in excess of the market averages if your investment adviser is a "me-too" company or individual. This is true almost by definition.

Virtually every professional investor reads the same newspapers and annual reports, goes to the same company presentations, hears the same research that comes out of Wall Street, has access to the same financial databases, and is capable of buying whatever investments software is currently in vogue.

The differences in performance, then, are the result of the way all of this tremendous amount of information is interpreted. First, the expert investor has a good understanding of the way business, in general, functions. This is something a lot of people think they have, but they don't. An uncanny number of hours are expended by investment professionals in trying to analyze a business about which they really know very little. It would be expecting too much for an investment analyst to understand everything about a company to make a good securities evaluation. But, the collective marketplace *is* capable of doing just that. That is why it is very difficult for one individual to outsmart the market with a whole portfolio of securities, over a long period of time. There are exceptions, of course. But these are the members of the unique subset of the investments community who have a special talent for recognizing the unrecognized or for understanding all the ramifications of securities market behavior.

The commonplace investment adviser is not going to make a lot of money for the clients over the long term. That is a well-documented reality. It is a difficult task for the non-investments person to figure out who will beat the market in the future. Be assured that, except for the sporadic burst of good fortune that blesses almost every professional from time to time, the average investment adviser will do no better at picking the best investments than a chimpanzee throwing darts at the quotation page from the evening newspaper. The average investor cannot beat the average (investor) when they are one in the same.

The bad news for anyone who expects success from the process of securities selection is that the flow of information is currently so efficient that securities prices themselves have become mostly efficient. "Mostly" does not mean "completely." There still will be, probably for a long time to come, securities that have been overlooked. As long as short-term performance is so all-important, that will always be the case. Only the brave investment adviser, who is not afraid of getting the axe from his or her clients, will seek out those overlooked situations that may not be performing well today, but could be the gems of tomorrow.

A successful investment adviser sees and hears things the others don't. For that reason, he or she is unique. All the computers, databases, and financial statements cannot peer into the innermost thought processes of the individuals to whom the destiny of their companies' securities prices has been entrusted.

Successful money managers, as individuals, know a great deal about a lot of things. They are lifelong students, otherwise they couldn't begin to understand all the dynamics of the marketplace. A prosperous money manager couldn't have achieved what has been achieved by working only an 8-hour day and 40-hour week. He or she must be ever aware of what is going on in the socioeconomic scene; not necessarily the events of the day—the marketplace has already discounted all of that—but rather the underlying changes that are taking place. An uncommon sense of history is a prerequisite for long-term profit making.

The successful investment professional is a pioneer who is as much involved in the state of the art and the progress of the science as his or her academic counterpart. There is no honest way to get rich quick in the investments business, except through luck. That is an inescapable fact. An investments person without an imagination and an inclination and ability to innovate will not stand out from the crowd over the long haul.

The first question some professional consultants (those who will be nothing but overpaid paper shufflers in a few years) ask of investment advisers is: Will you send me your performance record? The first question the consultants, who will be worth their weight in gold in the future, ask is: What are you doing that is different?

One thing investment advisers should be doing more of, which would be different from the past, is to learn much more about asset allocation. Asset allocation usually accounts for 80 to 100% of the differences in performance between the various investment managers. Yet, these same managers spend 80 to 100% of their time, when they're not marketing, trying to pick the next winning stock or bond.

Asset allocation came into its own following the Crash of 1987. Then it took a major step backwards in the minds of investors as many so-called asset allocators fell flat on their faces in 1989. They stumbled because most didn't know what they were doing. But that shouldn't taint the *concept* of asset allocation. It is a good, sound concept. Most investment people just need to broaden their understanding of the asset-allocation concept and sharpen their skills before trying to take the bull by the horns. Although it may be difficult to predict the short-term movements of the securities markets, estimating the relative long-term rates of return for those markets is a straight forward task. The intent of this book is to provide the tools to perform that task. Properly performed, the asset allocation function makes a major contribution to portfolio return over any time-horizon and within the parameters of any risk-profile.

Index